A History of Transportation in the Eastern Cotton Belt to 1860

SOUTHERN CLASSICS SERIES

Mark M. Smith and Peggy G. Hargis, Series Editors

A HISTORY OF TRANSPORTATION

in the Eastern Cotton Belt to 1860

ULRICH BONNELL PHILLIPS

New Introduction by Aaron W. Marrs

The University of South Carolina Press

Published in Cooperation with the Institute for Southern Studies of the University of South Carolina

Cloth edition published by the Columbia University Press, 1908
This paperback edition published by the University of South Carolina Press,
Columbia, South Carolina 29208

www.sc.edu/uscpress

Manufactured in the United States of America

20 19 18 17 16 15 14 13 12 11
10 9 8 7 6 5 4 3 2 1

Library of Congress Cataloging-in-Publication Data

Phillips, Ulrich Bonnell, 1877–1934.
A history of transportation in the eastern Cotton Belt to 1860 /
Ulrich Bonnell Phillips ; new introduction by Aaron W. Marrs.
p. cm. — (Southern classics series)
Reprint. Originally published in 1908 by Columbia University Press.
"Published in Cooperation with the Institute for Southern Studies of
the University of South Carolina."
Includes bibliographical references and index.
ISBN 978-1-57003-965-2 (pbk : alk. paper)
1. Transportation—Southern States—History. 2. Railroads—Southern
States—History. I. Title.
HE208.P5 2011
385.0975—dc22

2010035276

This book was printed on Glatfelter Natures, a recycled paper with 30 percent
postconsumer waste content.

Publication of the Southern Classics series is made possible in part by the generous
support of the Watson-Brown Foundation.

CONTENTS

CHAPTER II

CHAPTER III

CHAPTER IV

CHAPTER V

CHAPTER VI

CHAPTER VII

ILLUSTRATIONS

MAPS

PLATE

TABLES

SERIES EDITORS' PREFACE

Ulrich Bonnell Phillips's *A History of Transportation in the Eastern Cotton Belt to 1860,* reprinted here with an insightful, new introduction by Aaron W. Marrs, is an enduring book. Written by one of the twentieth century's most important historians of the Old South, *A History of Transportation* offers us a wealth of detailed information about one of the most salient, if understudied, aspects of the region's economy. Phillips's treatment is compelling in its central argument, faithful in its excavation of evidence, and, as Marrs helpfully points out, relevant to a new generation of historians. While these historians might not always agree with Phillips, they are indebted to this classic book for helping frame our understanding of transportation in the Old South and for gesturing toward areas for further study.

Southern Classics returns to general circulation books of importance dealing with the history and culture of the American South. Sponsored by the Institute for Southern Studies, the series is advised by a board of distinguished scholars who suggest titles and editors of individual volumes to the series editors and help establish priorities in publication.

Chronological age alone does not determine a title's designation as a Southern Classic. The criteria also include significance in contributing to a broad understanding of the region, timeliness in relation to events and moments of peculiar interest to the American South, usefulness in the classroom, and suitability for inclusion in personal and institutional collections on the region.

MARK M. SMITH
PEGGY G. HARGIS
Series Editors

NEW INTRODUCTION

Few historical monographs stand as a preeminent work in their field for decades, let alone a century. Yet Ulrich Bonnell Phillips's *A History of Transportation in the Eastern Cotton Belt to 1860,* first published in 1908, is still routinely cited by contemporary scholars on the topics of steamboats and railroads in pre–Civil War South Carolina and Georgia. To be sure, there have been some important monographs on southern railroads after Phillips's work, and there have been a host of shorter studies on individual lines or railroads in a single state.[1] But southern railroads have not generated much wider interest, and while Phillips certainly laid significant groundwork for future scholars, he also left a number of questions open for further investigation. Phillips raised a number of issues, such as the use of slaves and the profitability of the South's economic system, that remain of historiographical interest today. A closer examination of Phillips's work can reveal what he still has to teach us about these important topics and where historians can build on his work to address new topics.

Phillips published this book early in his career, while teaching at the University of Wisconsin. His major works, *American Negro Slavery* and *Life and Labor in the Old South,* still lay in the future.[2] Columbia University Press agreed to publish the book on terms that required Phillips to "pay the entire cost of manufacture."[3] These terms were beyond Phillips's means and required him to have the publication underwritten by a friend, Alfred Stone.[4] Phillips's effort to get the book published paid off: *History of Transportation* would be an important building block in his career, even if it has since been overshadowed by his larger interpretive works on slavery.[5]

The bulk of *History of Transportation* consists of Phillips's detailed examination of railroad companies in South Carolina and Georgia. This central portion of the work demonstrates Phillips's skill as a researcher. He doggedly tracked down numerous details about these early corporations.[6] Phillips thus provided a great service to readers by placing detailed information in front of a broader audience that would not have had access to the source material. But Phillips's work was not simply an antiquarian accounting of bygone firms. Rather Phillips used this material to advance arguments in his introduction and conclusion.

In the introduction Phillips laid out a number of the large, unifying ideas that would govern the remainder of the work. For Phillips the railroads of the Old South reflected the section's character: that of a staple-producing region. "The South," he declared on the opening page, "was chiefly concerned in developing a system of internal transportation and commerce, by providing communication between the several staple areas and their gateways."[7] Unlike northern states, which needed railroads for passengers or to sustain commerce among cities, the South was primarily concerned with transporting large volumes of staple crops, principally cotton, to the coastal cities. Southerners left to others the development of transportation beyond their borders (that is, from southern ports to northern cities). Likewise the large plantations through the South stifled consumer demand, meaning that there was no need for robust internal transportation networks. The South's main concern was transporting staple crops to the coast.

Phillips recognized that the development of railroads generally, and in the South especially, was constrained by a number of factors. An obvious constraint was geography. Different regions presented their own topographic challenges to civil engineers. Such topics seeped into political considerations, as when communities argued for the "natural" advantages of a route (which conveniently favored their town). The eastern cotton belt possessed its share of geographic features that affected railroads, and Phillips began his study with an examination of these features. Notable among them were the pine barrens that needed to be crossed to connect the coast with some cotton-producing regions and the mountain ranges that prevented easy access to the markets of the Old Northwest.[8] The opening passage on geographical limitations allowed Phillips to place railroad construction in its fullest physical context.

Phillips then outlined the economic barriers to constructing railroads. They were substantial. Railroads required tremendous sources of capital to finance their construction, a large and mobile workforce to build them, and a population with a healthy demand for both travel and the goods that railroads would carry. For Phillips none of these were characteristics of the antebellum southern economy. Rather the population was "scattered," the uniform southern economy meant that there would be little "interchange of products between neighboring districts," and the reliance on cotton meant that trade would be unbalanced during the year (with a "great rush of business in the marketing season").[9] All of these economic barriers were related in part to a fundamental barrier: slavery.

Phillips argued that slavery presented a range of challenges to the successful construction of a comprehensive and viable railroad network. Slavery made funding railroads difficult: railroads required large amounts of up-front investment, but most southerners of means plowed their capital back into slavery and staple agriculture. Trapped in the bodies of slaves, southern capital could not break free to fund the expansion of transportation. The slave system was damaging in another respect: widespread slavery meant that the South had no large class of free laborers available to build the railroads. Without such a labor pool to draw upon, southern companies could not quickly add capacity or expand their operations. Slavery had a damaging effect on the market for educated labor. In the South, Phillips argued, all "men of capacity" were drawn to agriculture—the clear path to social, political, and economic success in the antebellum South—and not to areas such as civil engineering, which would be critical for the development of a transportation system. Finally the South's conservative nature led to a strong brand of individualism, which "operated against joint undertakings and new enterprises."[10] In sum, the South had a range of economic barriers, according to Phillips, that militated against railroad construction, and the most significant of these was slavery. The result was that, by the end of the antebellum period, the South had "at least the skeleton of a well-planned railway system," but one that only accomplished "the extension and the intensifying of the plantation system and the increase of staple output."[11] Southern railroads may have aided and expanded the southern economy by making it easier for cotton to get to market, but they did little to transform the southern economy or carry it beyond its staple-agricultural base.

The bulk of *History of Transportation* consists of Phillips's detailed exploration of antebellum transportation in South Carolina and Georgia.[12] Phillips accomplished a number of important tasks in this section and demonstrated his thoroughgoing research. As befits the title, he considered the primary predecessors to railroads: roads and canals. Although both continued to play an important role in the transportation mix in the South throughout the antebellum era, railroads quickly overtook both as the primary means of transportation. Thus railroads form the primary subject of the remainder of the book.

Phillips then surveyed all the major and minor railroad companies in South Carolina and Georgia. He accounted for each company's financing, chartering, traffic, earnings, and other information culled from the voluminous annual reports of these companies. The South Carolina Railroad, as a critical railroad in the history of U.S. railroad development, warrants two chapters.[13] Three major Georgia railroads—the Georgia Railroad, the Central of Georgia, and the Western and Atlantic—receive one chapter apiece. The last substantive chapter includes the numerous smaller roads that traversed these two states and makes a brief excursion into Florida. Some of these corporations have yet to receive fuller exploration by historians, making Phillips's work all the more valuable.

In addition to his analysis and detailed description of these railroad companies, Phillips provided an additional service to readers by reproducing charts compiled from railroad company annual reports, printing a large fold-out map of the region with railroads' routes illustrated, and reprinting several primary documents that shed light on the operation of early railroads. Particularly useful in this regard was his decision to reprint the passenger and freight regulations from 1835 of the Charleston and Hamburg Railroad (the predecessor company of the South Carolina Railroad), thus providing some of the earliest extant operating rules from a southern railroad company.[14]

In his conclusion Phillips reiterated the interpretive analysis laid out in the introduction. The southern economy was unable to expand beyond its agricultural base and into industry because of its reliance on African American labor. Phillips argued that the practice of slavery rendered African American labor expensive because of the initial purchase price of the slave, and moreover, this labor was "inefficient for any tasks but those of crude routine." Slavery "locked up" capital, which could not then be released for other types of economic development.[15] Railroads in the South (unlike those in the North) did not "vastly increase the volume of commerce" or transform the types of commerce in the South. Rather than being "trade makers," they were simply "trade-catching agencies," scooping up what trade already existed but doing little to change the basis of the southern economy. For Phillips additional proof of the damaging effect of slavery on the southern economy came from the changes after the Civil War. He argued that, following a period of "chaotic transition" (by which he meant Reconstruction), railroads in the postbellum South, contemporaneous to the publication of his volume, "furnish a large part of the equipment by which, as a result of the freeing of capital from its bondage to the slavery system, the cotton belt is developing widely diversified industry and is beginning to enjoy a prosperity unexampled in its past."[16] While the Civil War freed the slaves from their bondage, Phillips argued that capital too needed to be released from bondage for the South to succeed economically.

The interpretive chapters that frame this work illustrate Phillips's view that economics was the "prime force in the historical process," a view he shared with other Progressive historians such as Frederick Jackson Turner, Charles A. Beard, and Carl L. Becker.[17] In Phillips's view the economic conditions of the South placed large barriers in the way of southerners wanting to develop railroads and limited the value that railroads would provide to the region once constructed.

While Phillips blamed slavery for economically stunting the South, he did not condemn those who benefited from the slave system. Indeed Phillips dedicated the book "to the dominant class of the South who in the piping ante-bellum time schooled multitudes white and black to the acceptance of higher standards." Phillips must have felt strongly about the appropriateness of this dedication, because it was printed over the objections of Columbia University Press. On October 16, 1907, William Carpenter of the press informed Phillips that the press's Committee on Publication and the president of the university disapproved of the language. While reassuring Phillips that "I myself believe that what you say of the 'Hell that is called reconstruction' is perfectly true to the facts of the case," Carpenter argued that the dedication represented "an appeal to sectional feeling which the University and the Press which represents it can not stand for, since in the eyes of the community it must occupy broadly a judicial position without prejudice in any direction." Carpenter urged Phillips to write another dedication or "omit it altogether."[18] Phillips prevailed, and the dedication appeared in the book as he desired.

Phillips respected and admired the white masters who created the system of slavery that ruled in antebellum times, but he did not regret slavery's downfall, insofar as it allowed the South to overcome the economic barriers he detailed in this work. In *History of Transportation,* Phillips certainly demonstrated that the South did have a history of achievement in the area of transportation, by outlining the pioneering efforts of companies such as the South Carolina Railroad. But he also outlined the reasons that the South could never reach its full potential. In 1907, with slavery stripped away and capital "liberated," Phillips could hope that southerners would grasp more fully their potential and pursue greater accomplishment in transportation and industry.[19]

Phillips's book was well received upon publication. The vast amount of information on these companies that Phillips included clearly caught the eye of readers. Writing in the *Journal of Political Economy,* Emory Johnson praised the book as "rich in detail."[20] G. G. Huebner, in the *Annals of the American Academy of Political and Social Science,* called it a "detailed and excellent work."[21] The *American Historical Review* was less enthusiastic: the reviewer criticized the book for not having a wider geographic scope but otherwise found that the subject received "adequate treatment," with the chapters on Charleston particularly of "absorbing interest."[22] As previously noted, the work helped cement Phillips's reputation. While more major works would follow, *History of Transportation* established Phillips as an emerging voice in the historiography of the antebellum South.

More than one hundred years after its composition, what value does Phillips's work have for historians? The study of transportation invites historians to consider broader insights about social and economic relations generally. "Transportation is not an end in itself," Phillips wrote, "but, when rightly used, is a means to the end of increasing wealth, developing resources, and strengthening society."[23] For the historian as well, railroads can unlock larger stories. Historians following in Phillips's footsteps will necessarily return to some of his themes, since Phillips's work is so wide ranging. Yet there are important ways in which historians have begun to move beyond or complicate Phillips's analysis.

Race is the most obvious and significant subject that modern historians treat differently than Phillips. Phillips's racial blinders are well known to historians of the antebellum South; it is impossible to read this volume (and his other works) without noticing them. The presence of this handicap, however, should not prevent historians from taking Phillips seriously. Eugene Genovese was primarily responsible for rehabilitating Phillips's reputation among historians, encouraging them to not let their distaste for his undoubtedly racist views overshadow the value of some of his more penetrating historical insights. Unfortunately there are areas in which Phillips's racism affected his historical judgment, and present-day historians cannot pass over them lightly. One passage in *History of Transportation* illustrates this well. Although Phillips castigated African American labor as being "as a rule inefficient for any tasks but those of crude routine," the sources he used demonstrate this not to be the case.[24] Phillips quoted a railroad superintendent who in 1846 stated that slaves rented from masters year after year "have acquired the knowledge and skill necessary to make them valuable," thus leaving the company vulnerable to higher wage demands from the slaves' owners. Phillips noted, rightfully, that this "raised the question" for the companies as to whether slaves should be owned or hired, but he is silent on the larger point: that railroad companies came to value the skilled labor of enslaved African American workers.[25] Antebellum whites valued these workers in a way that Phillips's racism prevented him from doing.

Historians seeking to move beyond Phillips's work could thus undertake a reassessment of the role of slave labor on southern railroads; indeed such a movement is already underway.[26] While the purchasing of slave labor was not widespread due to the high initial cost, many railroads acknowledged the advantages that slave labor had over white labor in their efforts. Thousands of slaves labored to build the railroad lines of the South. Some companies even argued that corporations were capable of carrying out the individual and personal paternalistic obligations that slavery imposed on individual owners.[27] Historians, moreover, should dig deeper into evidence that shows how railroad corporations came to value slaves in their employ, whether hired or owned. One civil engineer in South Carolina, John McRae, wrote numerous letters to slave owners assuring them that their slaves were being well cared for, and he also requested the labor of specific slaves by name.[28] Over time slaves could develop valuable skills that made it economically sound for companies to retain their labor and to go to the lengths that McRae did to ensure that the same slaves could be brought to work on specific projects. Therefore historians should continue to explore the extent to which railroads relied on enslaved labor.

Phillips argued that railroads made slaves "more easily mobilizable by their masters, but otherwise affected them very little in slavery times."[29] Newer research, including research using material not available to Phillips (such as the Works Progress Administration collection of slave narratives), demonstrates that this statement is inaccurate and needs serious reassessment. Some slaves certainly noticed the impact that railroads had on their lives. Traveling near Weldon, North Carolina, in the mid-1850s, abolitionist James Redpath was told by a slave that railroads made it "much easier to carry off the produce and sell it now," thus the "slaves are druv more and more to raise it."[30] The railroad had a clear impact on the life of this slave—railroads allowed planters to respond rapidly to changes in prices, and the slave felt the increase in work as a result. A glance at the WPA interviews with former slaves also shows that slaves recalled railroads: either they heard stories about them or remembered their first train ride.[31] Phillips was certainly correct that railroads had an impact on the ease with which slaves could be transported to other parts of the South, but he was incorrect in assuming that there was no greater impact upon the slaves, or that the slaves themselves took no notice of the iron horse. Historians seeking to understand the impact of railroads on the Old South should take the African American experience more seriously.

Another area that Phillips left underexplored is the work of the railroad. This may seem counterintuitive given the space he devoted to earnings and income. Historians, however, may want to reexamine the sources of that income. Phillips characterized railroads in the South as chiefly concerned with the carrying of staples. To be sure, the desire to take cotton to the coastal cities drove railroad expansion. But there are two aspects of Phillips's argument that warrant reconsideration. First, railroads were built in regions that lacked a strong commercial crop.[32] A fuller explanation of railroads in the entire South (not just the eastern cotton belt) needs to account for this. Second, the evidence left behind by railroad companies demonstrates that they relied on more than just commercial crops for their income. While railroads did not report their incomes in any systematic way, some companies reported annual receipts in a manner that allows historians to understand how much income was derived from traffic flowing back to the cotton regions. The South Carolina Railroad, for example, obtained at least half of its income from "upfreight" (that is, freight from Charleston to the interior) every year except six from 1834 to 1857.[33] While the centrality of cotton and other staple crops to the economic health of southern railroads is undeniable, clearly historians need to dig deeper where they can and determine what these railroads were carrying.

Accomplishing this task will help historians bring the Old South in line with another growing area of contemporary historiography: the history of consumerism. The history of consumerism has grown substantially in U.S. historiography in the past several decades.[34] Yet the Old South has remained somewhat removed from this literature. Ironically we know much more about the internal economy of slaves and the transactions slaves executed illicitly with whites than we do about the country stores of the South.[35] Some raw figures should tell us that railroads played a role in changing the types of goods available to southern consumers; in Chester, South Carolina, for example, the value of year-end store inventories increased from $88,950 in 1848 (when no railroad existed) to $137,880 in 1852 (after the completion of the Charlotte and South Carolina Railroad).[36] Digging deeper into the actual account books and ledgers of these country stores should tell us more about the transformation of consumer life that occurred for southerners and the role that railroads played in this movement. While the Old South lacked the more numerous urban spaces of the North, what villages and stores did exist may have been adequate to allow similar transformations to take place. We need more research into the consumer demand that drove these growing inventories and into how railroad development aided that demand.

Phillips's main concern was economics, but he hints at another theme that could use more exploration by historians: the social impact of railroads. Phillips addresses the social effects of railroads in a paragraph at the end of *History of Transportation,* and he does so in a way that limits the social impact to the upper classes: "In the matter of social relations, a characteristic item was the stimulating of the penchant among the well-to-do for making visits to kindred and friends. Not only did everybody who was anybody have scores of cousins scattered throughout their own and neighboring states, but with the aid of railroads thousands of these cousins of one generation after another were able to become personally acquainted with and bound to one another." The end result was "greater social solidarity in a state or section."[37]

There are a number of insights worth unpacking in Phillips's statement. First among them is the idea that railroads were only used by the "well-to-do." Passenger figures are available for some railroads. Ridership on the South Carolina Railroad, for example, increased consistently throughout the antebellum era, serving 15,109 passengers in 1835; 29,279 in 1840; 117,351 in 1850; and 171,554 in 1857.[38] While these figures many not suggest complete democratization, they certainly suggest that more than the wealthy were able to ride the trains. Companies established special fares for slaves and clearly expected them to be potential passengers.[39] Furthermore the open design of American railroad cars made it difficult to maintain rigid social and racial distinctions. There are also numerous accounts in the letters, diaries, and newspapers of antebellum southerners about railroad travel. Exploring these accounts may shed light on the accuracy of Phillips's assertion about the class status of railroad travelers.

Phillips closed the section by arguing that traveling promoted social cohesion. To be sure, some southerners hoped that railroads would accomplish precisely that, and the logic of using iron rails to bind people together was hardly limited to southern thought.[40] Yet railroads could also spark fierce rivalries. In a region where private capital could not sustain railroad development, requests for railroad funding were made to state legislatures, where intrastate rivalries blossomed.[41] States and communities welcomed the railroad, but also feared that the railroad could destroy business. For example, some residents of Fredericksburg, Virginia, worried that the completion of the Richmond, Fredericksburg and Potomac Railroad would leave them less important in the north-south trade, pushed for a westbound railroad to connect to the main line at Fredericksburg. Such a connection would make the town a junction, increasing its importance. But another group of citizens in Louisa County were stronger advocates, and the western connection to the RFPRR joined the main line south of Fredericksburg. Fredericksburg suffered as a result of this loss. Railroads could expand social relations, but the location of tracks inevitably made some areas winners and others losers. Historians should look beyond the boosterish rhetoric of "binding the union" to see how choosing routes actually played out politically in the Old South.[42]

Finally historians should consider Phillips's argument that slavery held back the development of the Old South. At one level this argument is certainly correct. There is no doubt that in terms of earnings, mileage built, or ton-miles, southern railroads trailed behind their northern counterparts.[43] Yet these figures may not tell the entire story. Recently historians have been taking a more nuanced view of the Old South and its economic and technological capacity. More historians have examined the ideology of planters, as well as their actions, and have found them to be open to time management, new technologies, and other putatively "modern" concepts. Genovese has argued that southern elites sought an "alternate route to modernity," one that allowed their society to prosper, but did so without disturbing their social relations or encouraging the development of free wage labor.[44] Other historians have been substantiating this argument, charting how southerners embraced technological developments or adding nuance to our understanding of the southern economy and economic thought.[45] The cumulative effect of such work should help us move beyond judging the South as a failure—as the progressive Ulrich Bonnell Phillips did in part based on his own hopes for a New South—and toward an understanding of southern society and those who created it on their own terms.

The fact that *History of Transportation* has stood for so long as a crucial work in the field and remains worthy of the modern historian's attention is a testament to Phillips's depth of research and interpretive skill. Historians today ask questions on a different range of topics—such as race and consumerism—than Phillips did. Such questions can cause historians to look at the same evidence in a new light and reach different conclusions than their predecessors. This introduction has suggested some ways in which historians can build upon the strong foundation that Phillips laid out in this book. Doing so can only lead us to a more complete understanding not just of railroads, but of the fascinating society through which they ran.

NOTES

I would like to thank Mark M. Smith and Melissa Jane Taylor for their comments on an earlier version of this introduction.

1. See, for example, James A. Ward, "A New Look at Antebellum Southern Railroad Development," *Journal of Southern History* 39 (August 1973): 409–20; Eugene Alvarez, *Travel on Southern Antebellum Railroads, 1828–1860* (University: University of Alabama Press, 1974); and Kenneth W. Noe, *Southwest Virginia's Railroad: Modernization and the Sectional Crisis* (Urbana: University of Illinois Press, 1994).

2. Ulrich Bonnell Phillips, *American Negro Slavery* (New York: D. Appleton and Company, 1918; Baton Rouge: Louisiana State University Press, 1966); Ulrich Bonnell Phillips, *Life and Labor in the Old South* (Boston: Little, Brown, and Company, 1929; Columbia: University of South Carolina Press, 2007).

3. Letter from William Carpenter to Ulrich Bonnell Phillips, March 8, 1907, folder 2, U. B. Phillips Papers (#2832), Southern Historical Collection, Wilson Library, University of North Carolina at Chapel Hill (hereafter Phillips Papers).

4. Contract between Columbia University Press and Ulrich Bonnell Phillips, June 19, 1907, folder 2, Phillips Papers. See also Merton L. Dillon, *Ulrich Bonnell Phillips: Historian of the Old South* (Baton Rouge: Louisiana State University Press, 1985), 63.

5. Dillon, *Ulrich Bonnell Phillips,* 64–65.

6. For a more critical view of Phillips's research technique, see W. K. Wood, "U. B. Phillips, Unscientific Historian," in *Ulrich Bonnell Phillips: A Southern Historian and His Critics,* eds. John David Smith and John C. Inscoe (New York: Greenwood Press, 1990), 169–77.

7. Ulrich Bonnell Phillips, *A History of Transportation in the Eastern Cotton Belt to 1860* (New York: Columbia University Press, 1908; Columbia: University of South Carolina Press, 2011), 1.

8. Ibid., 4.

9. Ibid., 8.

10. Ibid., 9.

11. Ibid., 19–20.

12. Phillips noted that transportation developments in Alabama and North Carolina had already been studied by other authors (ibid., 351n1). The studies are William Elejius Martin, "Internal Improvements in Alabama," *Johns Hopkins University Studies in Historical and Political Science* 20, no. 4 (1902): 127–208, and Charles Clinton Weaver, "Internal Improvements in North Carolina previous to 1860," *Johns Hopkins University Studies in Historical and Political Science* 21, no. 3–4 (1903): 1–95.

13. At the time of its completion in 1833, the railroad from Charleston to Hamburg was the longest in the world at 136 miles—a tremendous achievement. Aaron W. Marrs, *Railroads in the Old South: Pursuing Progress in a Slave Society* (Baltimore: Johns Hopkins University Press, 2009), 12.

14. Phillips, *History of Transportation,* 165–66.

15. Ibid., 388–89.

16. Ibid., 396.

17. Dillon, *Ulrich Bonnell Phillips,* 22–23; W. K. Wood, "Rewriting Southern History: U. B. Phillips, the New South, and the Antebellum Past," in *Ulrich Bonnell Phillips: A Southern Historian and His Critics,* eds. John David Smith and John C. Inscoe (New York: Greenwood Press, 1990), 57–78.

18. Letter from William Carpenter to Ulrich B. Phillips, October 16, 1907, folder 2, Phillips Papers. Phillips's response to Carpenter has not been found.

19. Eugene Genovese, "Race and Class in Southern History: An Appraisal of the Work of Ulrich Bonnell Phillips," in *Ulrich Bonnell Phillips: A Southern Historian and His Critics,* eds. John David Smith and John C. Inscoe (New York: Greenwood Press, 1990), 122.

20. Emory Johnson, review of *A History of Transportation in the Eastern Cotton Belt to 1860,* by Ulrich Bonnell Phillips, *Journal of Political Economy* 16 (October 1908): 539–40.

21. G. G. Huebner, review of *A History of Transportation in the Eastern Cotton Belt to 1860,* by Ulrich Bonnell Phillips, *Annals of the American Academy of Political and Social Science* 33 (March 1909): 252–53.

22. Unsigned review of *A History of Transportation in the Eastern Cotton Belt to 1860,* by Ulrich Bonnell Phillips, *American Historical Review* 14 (January 1909): 371–72.

23. Phillips, *History of Transportation,* 19–20.

24. Ibid., 388.

25. Ibid., 205–6.

26. See, for example, Theodore Kornweibel Jr., "Railroads and Slavery," *Railroad History* 189 (Fall–Winter 2003): 34–59, and Marrs, *Railroads in the Old South,* chap. 3.

27. Marrs, *Railroads in the Old South,* 61.

28. Ibid., 65.

29. Phillips, *History of Transportation,* 395.

30. James Redpath, *The Roving Editor, or, Talks with Slaves in the Southern States,* ed. John R. McKivigan (University Park: Pennsylvania State University Press, 1996), 118.

31. See, for example, Marrs, *Railroads in the Old South,* 138, 195.

32. Donald W. Buckwalter, "Effects of Early Nineteenth Century Transportation Disadvantage on the Agriculture of Eastern Tennessee," *Southeastern Geographer* 27 (May 1987): 34.

33. Marrs, *Railroads in the Old South,* 117. For a more detailed analysis of southern freight income, see 113–21.

34. For an overview, see Lawrence B. Glickman, ed., *Consumer Society in American History: A Reader* (Ithaca, N.Y.: Cornell University Press, 1999).

35. See, for example, Jeff Forret, *Race Relations at the Margins: Slaves and Poor Whites in the Antebellum Southern Countryside* (Baton Rouge: Louisiana State University Press, 2006), chap. 2. For country stores, see Lewis E. Atherton, *The Southern Country Store, 1800–1860* (Baton Rouge: Louisiana State University Press, 1949).

36. Lacy K. Ford Jr., *Origins of Southern Radicalism: The South Carolina Upcountry, 1800–1860* (New York: Oxford University Press, 1988), 237.

37. Phillips, *History of Transportation,* 395.

38. Marrs, *Railroads in the Old South,* 137.

39. Ibid., 151–56.

40. John Lauritz Larson, "'Bind the Republic Together': The National Union and the Struggle for a System of Internal Improvements," *Journal of American History* 74 (September 1987): 363–87. For southern examples, see Marrs, *Railroads in the Old South,* 16.

41. See, for example, William A. Link, *Roots of Secession: Slavery and Politics in Antebellum Virginia* (Chapel Hill: University of North Carolina Press, 2003), 35.

42. Marrs, *Railroads in the Old South,* 23–24.

43. Ibid., 4.

44. Eugene Genovese, *The Slaveholders' Dilemma: Freedom and Progress in Southern Conservative Thought, 1820–1860* (Columbia: University of South Carolina Press, 1992), 13.

45. For literature that charts the "alternate route" to modernity or explores capitalism within the context of the Old South, see Joyce E. Chaplin, *An Anxious Pursuit: Agricultural Innovation and Modernity in the Lower South, 1730–1815* (Chapel Hill: University of North Carolina Press, 1993); Mark M. Smith, *Mastered by the Clock: Time, Slavery, and Freedom in the American South* (Chapel Hill: University of North Carolina Press, 1997); William Kauffman

Scarborough, *Masters of the Big House: Elite Slaveholders of the Mid-Nineteenth-Century South* (Baton Rouge: Louisiana State University Press, 2003); Michael O'Brien, *Conjectures of Order: Intellectual Life and the American South, 1810–1860* (Chapel Hill: University of North Carolina Press, 2004); Jonathan D. Martin, *Divided Mastery: Slave Hiring in the American South* (Cambridge, Mass.: Harvard University Press, 2004); Walter Johnson, "The Pedestal and the Veil: Rethinking the Capitalism/Slavery Question," *Journal of the Early Republic* 24 (Summer 2004): 299–308; Tom Downey, *Planting a Capitalist South: Masters, Merchants, and Manufacturers in the Southern Interior, 1790–1860* (Baton Rouge: Louisiana State University Press, 2006); S. Max Edelson, *Plantation Enterprise in Colonial South Carolina* (Cambridge, Mass.: Harvard University Press, 2006); Bruce W. Eelman, *Entrepreneurs in the Southern Upcountry: Commercial Culture in Spartanburg, South Carolina, 1845–1880* (Athens: University of Georgia Press, 2008); and Marrs, *Railroads in the Old South.*

PREFACE TO THE FIRST EDITION

American history is largely the record of the adjustment of a migrating people to their new environment and the modification of the environment to subserve the greater welfare and comfort of the people. Popular self-government has been a means of facilitating that adjustment; and the work of parties and statesmen has been in large part to readjust the people to the environment and the several groups of the people to one another. Captains of industry and captains of transportation rank in substantial importance near the political leaders of similar merit and service; and the promotive campaigns for "internal improvements" bear as much significance in the general development of the nation as do many of the campaigns of president-making.

Transportation facilities and traffic play a very large part in the life of any modern people, and the study of this theme of development, along with many others, is an essential for thorough historical knowledge and understanding.

To me the *ante-bellum* South is the most interesting theme in the history of this continent. I seek to understand the history of the South, and hope to explain it. The economic and social aspects seem to offer the best line of approach to the general problem, and hence my attention to the present subject along with others parallel, such as the plantation system. Migration, industry, commerce, politics, society, and even race relations are all inter-related with the transportation development. My attempt has been to keep this constantly in mind and to indicate its bearings at the salient points where such generalizations would be in place.

The present book is a treatment of a part of a field, of which the whole is sketched in broad strokes in the Introduction. The Eastern Cotton Belt, falling mainly in South Carolina and Georgia, is perhaps the most important part of the South in its *ante-bellum* transportation development, and is in many regards illustrative of the whole. The other economic provinces, except the Charleston-Savannah coast district which is discussed in chapter one, are left for future treatment, whether by my own or another's pen.

Acknowledgment for material assistance is due to the Carnegie Institution of Washington, and particularly to two scholars in its service, Professors W. Z. Ripley of Harvard and B. H. Meyer of the University of Wisconsin. Professor F. J. Turner of Wisconsin has kindly read and criticized some of the manuscript. Colonel A. R. Lawton of Savannah and Julius L. Brown, Esq., of Atlanta, and numerous librarians, have aided by lending and permitting the use of rare materials.

ULRICH B. PHILLIPS.

Madison, Wisconsin
October 4, 1907.

TRANSPORTATION ROUTES
IN THE ANTE-BELLUM SOUTH.
RAILROADS COMPLETED BY 1861.
CANALS.
RIVER NAVIGATION
CONTOUR LINES DESIGNATING ALTITUDES IN FEET.
100, 500, 1000, 2000, 3000.
MISSOURI
KENTUCKY
VIRGINIA
NORTH CAROLINA
TENNESEE
ARKANSAS
SOUTH CAROLINA
MISSISSIPPI
ALABAMA
GEORGIA
LOUISIANA
FLORIDA

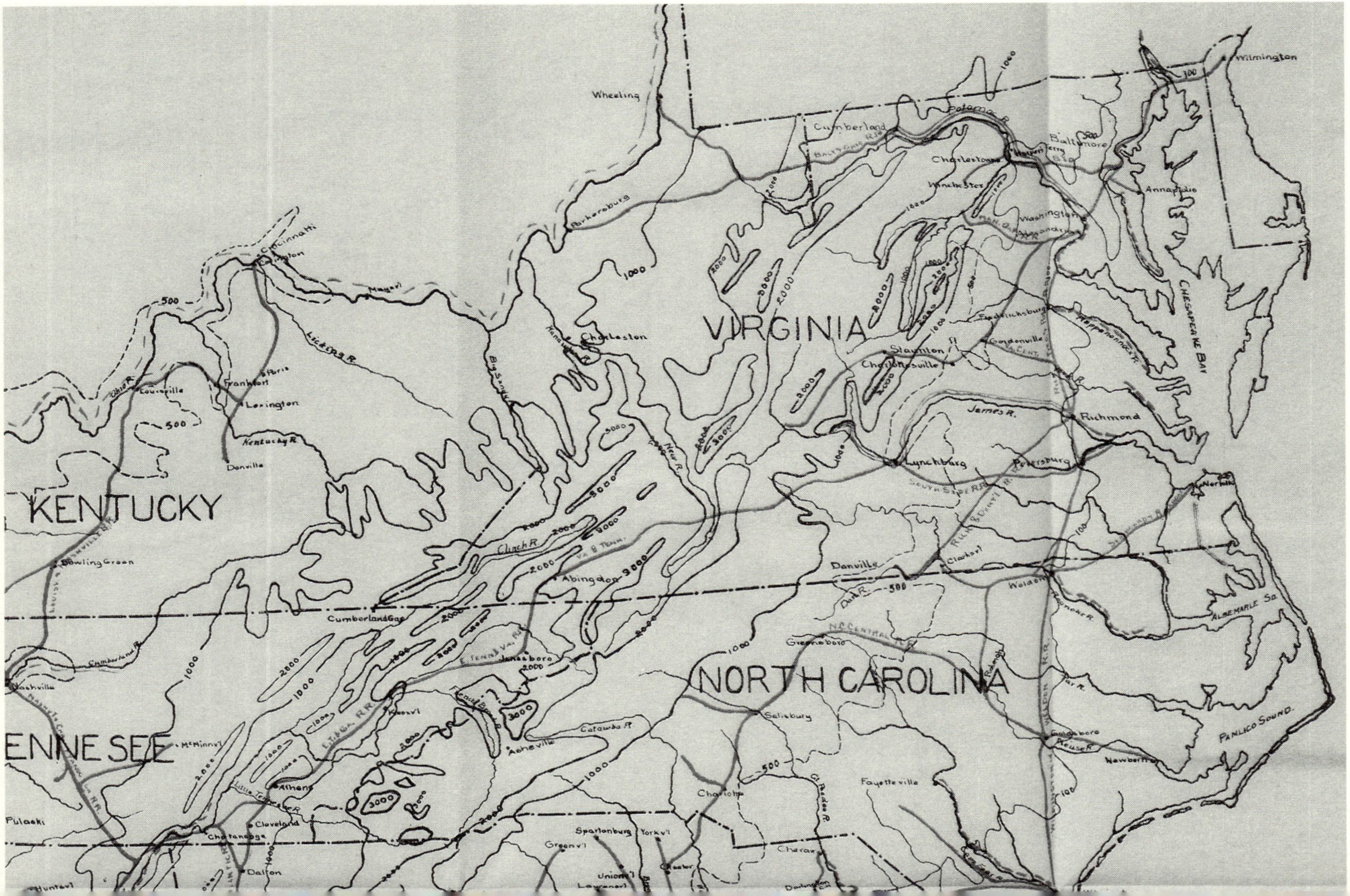

VIRGINIA
NORTH CAROLINA
KENTUCKY
ENNESEE
CHESAPEAKE BAY
PAMLICO SOUND
ALBEMARLE SD.
Wilmington
Baltimore
Annapolis
Washington
Cumberland
Charlestown
Winchester
Wheeling
Parkersburg
Charleston
Cincinnatti
Frankfort
Lexington
Louisville
Danville
Bowling Green
Nashville
Cumberland Gap
Abingdon
Staunton
Charlottesville
Lynchburg
Richmond
Petersburg
Danville
Greensboro
Salisbury
Charlotte
Fayetteville
Goldsboro
Newberne
Asheville
Knoxvl
Athens
Cleveland
Chatanooga
Dalton
Pulaski
Spartanburg
Greenvl
James R.
New R.
Clinch R.
Licking R.
Kentucky R.
Big Sandy
Potomac R.
Neuse R.
Catawba R.

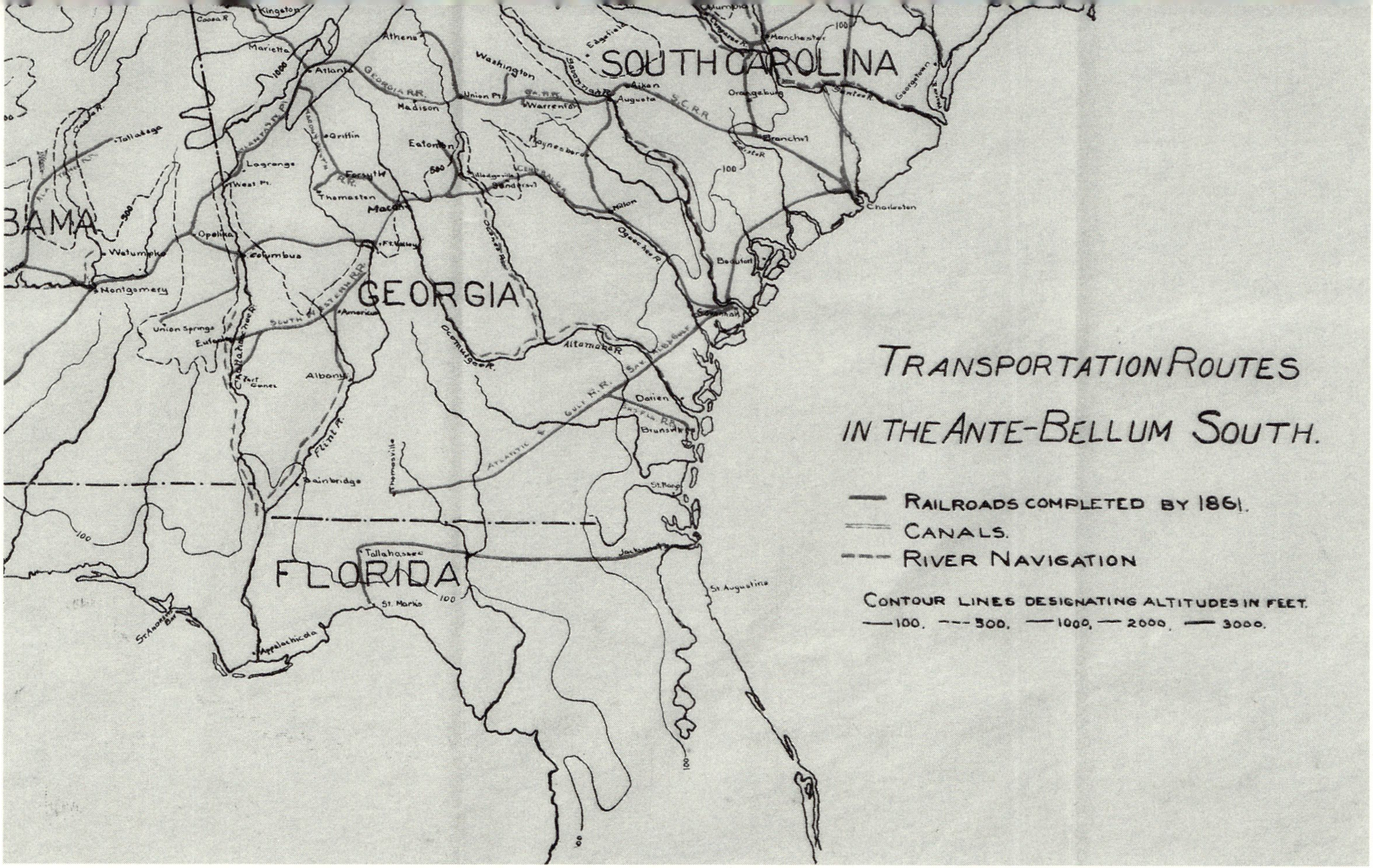

Transportation Routes in the Ante-Bellum *South* (east detail)

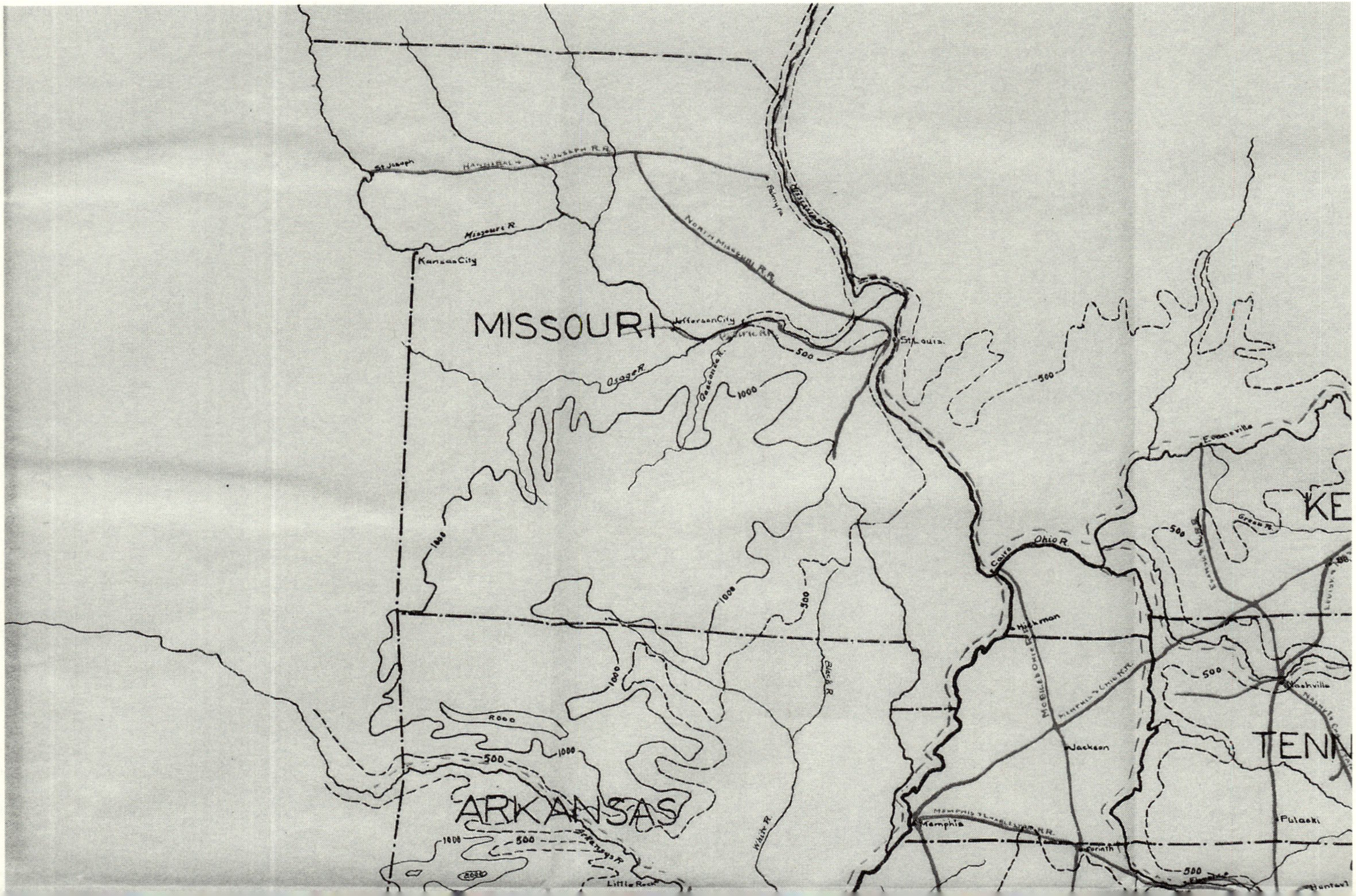
MISSOURI
ARKANSAS
KE
TENN
St. Joseph
Hannibal & St. Joseph R.R.
Palmyra
Missouri R.
Kansas City
North Missouri R.R.
Jefferson City
Pacific R.R.
St. Louis
Osage R.
Gasconade R.
Ohio R.
Cairo
Hickman
Evansville
Green R.
Nashville
Jackson
Memphis
Memphis & Charleston R.R.
Corinth
Pulaski
Mobile & Ohio R.R.
Memphis & Ohio R.R.
Black R.
White R.
Arkansas R.
Little Rock
500
1000
2000

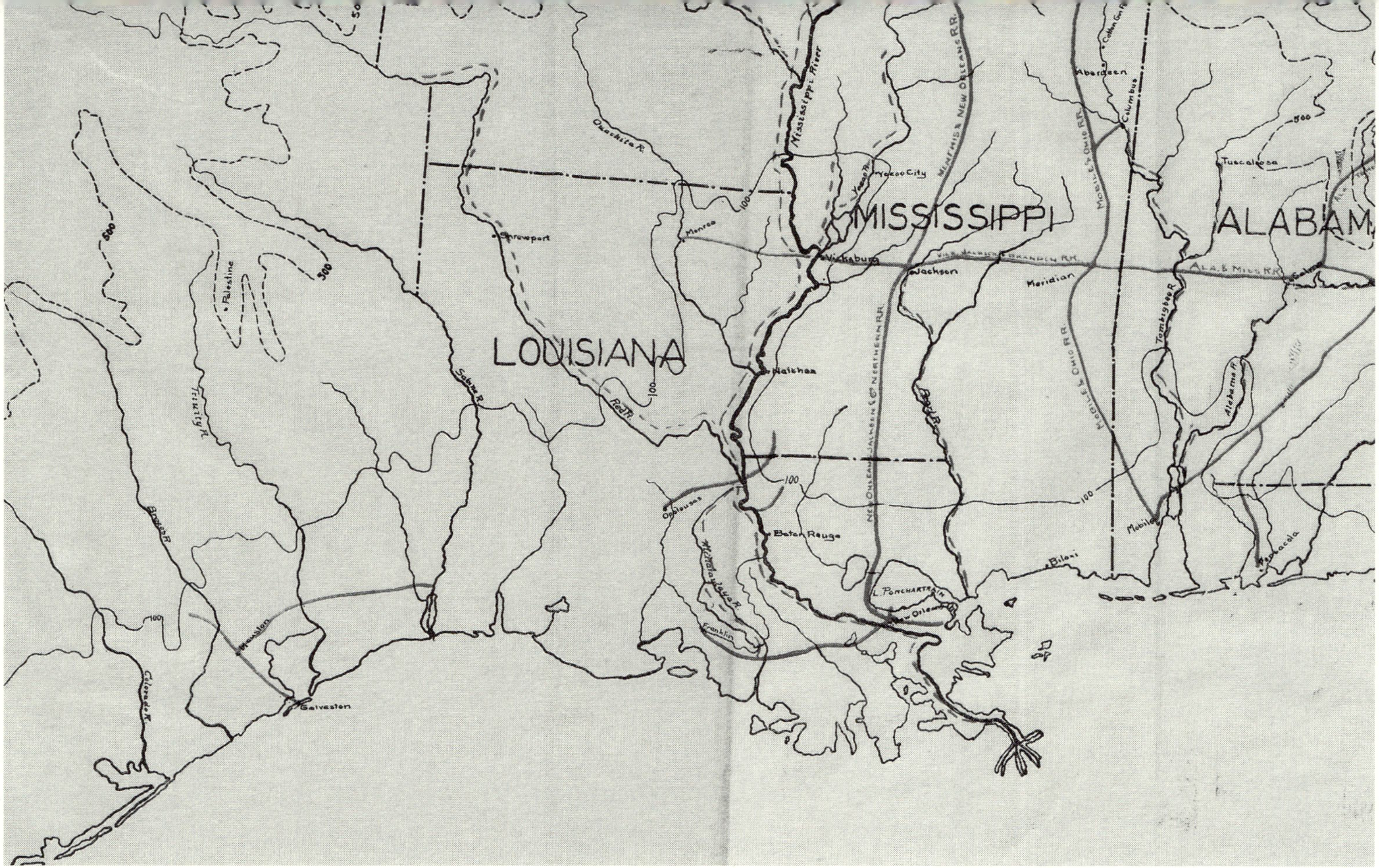

Transportation Routes in the Ante-Bellum *South* (west detail)

TO THE

DOMINANT CLASS OF THE SOUTH

Who in the piping ante-bellum time
schooled multitudes
white and black
to the acceptance of
higher standards
who in the war time
proved staunch
and who in the troublous
upheaval and readjustment
which followed
wrought more sanely
and more wisely
than the world yet knows
of the men's work
in one direction
this book is
part of the record
to the work of the women
no prosing pen can do
justice

INTRODUCTION

TRANSPORTATION IN THE *ANTE-BELLUM* SOUTH: AN ECONOMIC ANALYSIS[1]

EVER since the resort to tobacco culture at Jamestown and to rice in Carolina, the South has been mainly a group of staple-producing areas, requiring means of exporting their products and seeking the greater part of their miscellaneous supplies from beyond their own limits. The principal transportation problem has always been that of sending the staples to markets abroad, and obtaining food supplies and manufactures whencesoever they might best be secured. The specific problems differed somewhat in the various localities and periods, and certain other considerations had at times some degree of importance; but the predominating and fundamental purpose remained ever the same. Feeling little desire to possess a carrying trade, and leaving to outside agents the external commerce between its own ports and the rest of the world, the South was chiefly concerned in developing a system of internal transportation and commerce, by providing communication between the several staple areas and their gateways.

When fully developed in its staple system of the *ante-bellum* period, the South comprised the following great economic provinces, more or less distinguished by their staples and their natural facilities for transportation: —

1. Lowland and Piedmont Virginia: a tobacco region,

[1] Reprinted from the *Quarterly Journal of Economics*, May, 1905.

gradually encroached upon by the cereals. The transportation problem was simply that of getting products to the navigable rivers and the great Chesapeake. Most of Maryland was an annex to this province, and the Albemarle district in North Carolina was a subprovince tributary to it.

2. The Charleston-Savannah coast district, with a multitude of shallow waterways to transport the crops of rice and sea-island cotton to the deep-water harbors at Charleston, Beaufort, Savannah, and Brunswick. This alluvial area was fertile and prosperous from early times; but its people were not content with their narrow bounds, and sought energetically in the later period a means to overthrow the obstacle of the pine barrens which shut them in.

3. The Eastern Cotton Belt, stretching from the southern edge of Virginia to central Alabama. This province was mainly confined to the Piedmont region, a country of many hills and rapid streams. Its outer edge could be reached by navigation upon a few of the larger rivers, but easy natural means of transportation within the belt itself were wholly lacking. The problem was to send cotton to the coast and to get supplies from across the pine-barrens, on the one hand, or the mountains, on the other. The first system was that of using as main stems the rivers which crossed the barrens, and supplementing them with a network of country roads radiating from the heads of navigation. As regards intercourse with the Northwest, the resort was either to caravans across the mountains or to the circuitous water route of the Mississippi, the Gulf, the Atlantic, and the Carolina and Georgia rivers. The eastern cotton belt confronted by far the most difficult transportation problem in the South; and not only the local

planters, but all the world of commerce, were much concerned in its solution.

4. The Western Cotton Belt, reaching from Alabama to Texas and sweeping as far north along the Mississippi bottoms as the southern edge of Kentucky, was quite similar to the eastern belt in its all-important product of short-staple cotton; but it was in contrast in point of transportation advantages, for its great reaches of navigable stream extended to nearly every district where the best cotton lands were located. The planters had only to haul their cotton to the river, tumble it over the cliff, and let it await the coming of a boat bound for Mobile or New Orleans. The building of artificial avenues was a later and less pressing need than in the eastern cotton belt. The sugar district of southern Louisiana was a part of this province.

5. The region of Kentucky and middle Tennessee, with its products of tobacco, live stock, and grain, had a water outlet by way of the Ohio or the Cumberland and the Mississippi to New Orleans; but it needed an equipment of direct routes to the Atlantic seaboard and to the eastern cotton belt, as well as a local system to supplement the rivers.

6. The Tennessee-Shenandoah range of connecting valleys, with their fertile limestone soil, producing much the same commodities as the great basin to the northwest, but deprived of their natural advantage of vicinity to the staple belts by the forbidding Blue Ridge, until at length, after many plans and efforts, the mountains were pierced, and a system of railways brought the great wave of prosperity which had so long been awaited.

7. The peninsula of Florida, afflicted with a barren soil,

and leading nowhither, is negligible as a part of the economic South. It is more to be noted, perhaps, as an obstacle in the coasting trade than as an economic province.

These several provinces in some cases shaded into one another; but, as a rule, they were separated by pronounced obstacles, among which the most important were the belt of pine-barrens, and the Blue Ridge and the Cumberland Mountains. The pine-barrens were a stretch of sandy, infertile, pine-grown country intervening between the coast and the cotton belt throughout most of the latter's extent. The population in the barrens was sparse and self-sufficing, producing no staple for export, and making little effective demand for articles from without. The transportation problem was not that of putting the region itself into communication with the rest of the world, but that of crossing the barrier and connecting the coast with the inland cotton areas. The obvious method in the railway period was to build a single trunk line from each seaport across the barrens, and then to lay out a system of radiating lines in the cotton belt which would gather freight and serve as feeders to the main stem. With the completion of the main stem, remunerative business began, and the extension of the road was then a matter of comparative ease.

The Blue Ridge and Cumberland Mountains, running in great parallel ridges from Pennsylvania to Alabama, sharply divided off the economic provinces in their neighborhood. The flanks of these ranges were turned by the Potomac and Tennessee rivers; but the one was hardly navigable at all in the uplands, and the other was broken in two by the great obstruction at the Muscle Shoals in northern Alabama. And, even if these rivers had been more easily navigable, they would still have been inadequate to meet the needs of the situation, for their courses lay in the wrong directions. What was most needed was direct routes connecting the grain and live stock producing intramontane valleys, and the Ohio basin beyond, with the cotton belt which consumed much of this product of grain and live stock. And no one was content until that direct communication was at length established by the building of southeast and northwest railway systems.

In other regions where there were no such conspicuous barriers the factor of mere distance was of considerable importance in causing and directing a demand for transportation facilities. Social, political, and military needs, as well as economic considerations, required that these facilities, wherever established, should be of the greatest efficiency feasible.

The lie of the land directed the currents of transportation and commerce; for those currents, of course, followed the lines of least resistance. The provinces of the South demanded intercourse with one another, with England, Europe, and the West Indies, with Pennsylvania, New York, and New England, and with the great American Northwest. The particular channels through which the volume of commerce should flow were chosen and developed by the activity of the people under the general conditions of their environment. There was in some instances a choice of routes, but in no case was the range of alternatives a wide one. Physical geography was imperative in dictating the routes; and, even after nature had apparently been conquered by the steam railway, it still continued to play pranks with the fortunes of the cities along the routes. More was needed than a railroad and the survey of town lots before a city would arise. And the land-lookers were frequently at fault in their efforts to found commercial cities.

The strategic points, or centers of trade, as finally developed, had always two features in common: (1) access to the outside world; (2) a tributary area around or behind them. These trade centers in the South were of several classes. First, of course, there was an equipment of seaports. There were Baltimore, Norfolk, Wilmington, Charleston, Savannah, Mobile, and New Orleans, and potentially Galveston, in the first rank, each with an adequate harbor, and each with an important hinterland. Inferior to these were Beaufort, N.C., Beaufort, S.C., Brunswick, Ga., St. Augustine and Pensacola, Fla., Bay St. Louis, Miss., which possessed good harbors, but were cut off from the great hinterland by the unrelieved pine-barrens; and another group, comprising Georgetown, S.C., Darien, Ga., and Appalachicola, Fla., which possessed a river communication with the interior, but lacked harbor facilities.

In the interior the principal group of trade centres, in the older parts of the South at least, were those located at the head of navigation, or "fall line," on the larger rivers. To these points the planters and farmers brought their output for shipment, and there they procured their varied supplies. If the boats which carried the freight down-stream could return against the current, they would fetch cargoes of manufactures, groceries, and salt to the merchants of the fall-line towns. And even if the river craft could not ascend the stream, — and this was generally the case before the days of steamboats, — the goods would be brought by pack train or by wagon to the point whence the staples had been shipped. It was a great convenience to the producer to be able to sell his crop and buy his goods in the same market. Thus the towns at the heads of navigation grew into marked importance as collecting points for produce and distributing points for supplies of all sorts. Some of the great planters, it is true, gave their business to factors at the seaports or even in England; but that practice was customary only among those planters who lived below the fall line. For the upland producers, before the coming of railroads, the transit of produce to the coast had to be broken at the nearest point where the freight could be transferred from wagon to boat; and this was generally at the head of the river navigation. These points where the rivers crossed the fall line were therefore strategic points which had access to the sea, and had each a productive tributary area: the growth of commercial towns there was inevitable. On the Atlantic slope the fall-line towns were Alexandria, Fredericksburg, Richmond, Petersburg, Fayetteville, Columbia, Augusta, Milledgeville, and Macon. On the rivers that flow to the Gulf were Columbus, Montgomery, Shreveport, Nashville, and Knoxville.

In the case of mighty rivers flowing in their navigable course not only from, but through, fertile districts, there was occasion for subsidiary towns along their courses. Where no one spot upon the river bank had any distinct advantage over any other, as, for example, on the Tombigbee, the tendency was hostile to towns. But upon the Mississippi and its branches the physiographic conditions favored Natchez, Vicksburg, Memphis, Louisville, and St. Louis in their commercial growth even more than if they had been at the fall lines of smaller streams.

A fourth group of towns owed their origin to the penetration of the mountain barriers, and owed their growth to the development of the direct trade in food supplies. Thus by the building of railroads Atlanta became the gateway to the eastern cotton belt from the Northwest, Chattanooga sprang up at an important crossing of the routes, and the trade of Nashville and Knoxville and Louisville and Cincinnati was much increased.

Aside from physiography there were certain features of social economics which strongly influenced the development of transportation and commerce. 1. Population in the South was widely scattered, and nowhere in compact masses. Passenger traffic must therefore be relatively light. 2. In each great economic province nearly every locality was issuing the same sort of output, and there was little interchange of products between neighboring districts. No traffic of volume between way stations might therefore be expected. 3. But the demand for transportation of staples outward and supplies inward was urgent, and offered opportunities for profit to common carriers. The principal staples, however, were relatively light and precious, the producers had their teams at leisure in marketing season, and the rivers always kept flowing to the sea. That is to say, the planters could, if need arose, assert their independence of even the railroads, and thus could always keep the freight rates within bounds. 4. Another awkward feature for the common carrier was the great rush of business in the marketing season and the lean months following in spring and summer. On the cotton railroads the whole year's profits had to be gained practically between September and January.

And there were still greater difficulties, affecting the building as well as the operation of canals, railroads, etc. 5. The institution of slavery involved the investment of wealth in slave labor, and tended strongly against the presence of floating capital. The slave-trade, whether domestic or foreign, drained capital out of the districts where it had earned, and tended to make all the people debtors seeking money to borrow instead of capitalists seeking openings for investment. 6. The universal inclination towards agriculture diminished the available supply of native white labor for any other purpose; the presence of negroes and slavery reduced the number of European immigrants; and the plantation form of organization for staple production almost completely monopolized the supply of negro laborers. There was thus a singular dearth of floating labor, — a dearth which discouraged, crippled, or ruined many undertakings. 7. The plantation system, dominating the whole industrial life of the South, attracted nearly all the men of capacity into agricultural management, and caused a shortage of efficient promoters and managers in other industries. Many of the men who were active in plans of river improvement, railway building, and the like, had more enthusiasm than judgment, while men of greater wisdom and poise often contented themselves with merely stating their opinions, and refrained from active part in the battle of ideas. More than one bubble was blown in spite of the moderate remonstrance of the conservative planters and more than one bubble burst as they had said it would burst. 8. Individualism and conservatism prevailed in the South to a marked degree, and operated against joint undertakings and new enterprises. Many a project failed on this account, and those which succeeded had in every case to earn their victory.

As might have been expected, when such were the conditions, the initiative came mostly from the cities, and the cities furnished the greater part of the capital employed.

In methods of transportation there was, of course, greater development in the civilized world during the first half of the nineteenth century than in any other period. Experiments were made in the South with nearly or quite all of the transportation devices which were being discussed and applied in the Northern states and Europe. Some of these methods were wholly unsuccessful when used to meet the Southern conditions; some of them were successful for certain localities, but failed in others. The general system, as it came to be developed in the South at large, was, of course, made up of heterogeneous parts, working together with more or less efficiency for the common end.

There was first, of course, the ocean highway, which needs no discussion here, except perhaps a jotting that the resort to ocean steamships after about 1820 freed the traffic from dependence upon currents of wind and water, and enabled mariners to use the shortest transatlantic route, thereby building up the Northern ports at the expense of those of the South. Closely akin was the navigation of inlets and sounds and such so-called rivers as the Potomac and the James in their lower courses, and the bayous of Louisiana, in which there was no appreciable current. Here the possession merely of primitive boats would make the planter independent of costly mechanism. On the more rapid streams there was usually a long navigable stretch, which accommodated descending freight;

but these rivers had to be supplemented by roads to serve the returning voyagers. Even in the Piedmont country the rivers could be used in flood season to transport small boats with light cargoes, but, of course, could hardly be used at all for the upward journey. The introduction of steamboats provided the means for the upward navigation as far as the fall line, but they affected the river problem within the Piedmont very little.

Across country and away from the streams, recourse was first had to buffalo paths and Indian trails, and then to roads which were cleared to permit the wagon traffic. Then came the need of ferries, causeways, and bridges, and the resort to the toll system or to public ownership.

The rapid increase of settlement in the uplands in the later eighteenth, and especially its rapid growth in importance in the early nineteenth century, brought a demand for something more than local roads with county officials in charge. And yet that demand, so far as the planters and farmers were concerned, was often more apparent than real. Canals were projected in many regions, and in some cases were actually built; but in general they were found to be unsuited to the physical conditions, except for certain concrete cases in special localities. The rivers in the South flow mostly in deep valleys or even gorges, which furnish many obstacles to the building of canals along or across their courses, while the very heavy and irregular rainfall and the frequency of freshets and floods, especially after the extensive clearing away of the Piedmont forests, caused great danger of destruction of works, and exerted a deterring influence when canals were considered. Furthermore, the soil in some places was so porous that the water would seep through and leave a canal bed dry; and in other places there was so much rock that canal digging was too costly. Canals, on the whole, were clearly not the solution of the problem, except for such special localities as, for example, that of the Dismal Swamp.

Efforts were made at systems of turnpike roads, and in Kentucky and Tennessee they were built with considerable success. But in the cotton belt the case was peculiar, and hostile to the prosperity of a toll system. The cotton producers harvested and marketed their cotton in the fall and winter season, when there was little other work demanding attention with men or mules or wagons. The crop was precious enough, though somewhat bulky, to justify its transportation for long distances by wagon, on bad roads. In fact, with the journey once begun, it did not matter particularly — since it was the leisure season on the farm — whether the team returned from market in three days or three weeks. Therefore, paved roads which quickened speed were, in the eyes of the cotton producers, who were their own carriers, a smaller consideration than the tolls which must be charged upon them. It is not surprising, accordingly, that when a system of turnpikes was built in South Carolina, in the twenties, it was permitted by the planters to fall into absolute neglect and decay. Plank roads were the subject of experiment in Alabama in the forties, with the same lack of success as the Carolina turnpikes had had.

Realizing the insufficiency of all these earlier inventions to the needs of their case, those who were looking to the final solution of the general problem were satisfied with nothing short of railroads. Railroads with steam locomotion, when once invented, were speedily recognized as dwarfing in importance all that had gone before; and nowhere was their acceptance more eager than in the staple regions of the South. The press and the people in the later twenties and the thirties were all agog with the new invention, which, it was thought, would carry cotton to the coast for a song, and bring groceries and manufactures and the mail, and perhaps immigrants, with marvelous speed and cheapness. The building of a system of railways was a far more costly and difficult undertaking than the early projectors imagined; yet the building of that system did actually bring the solution of the Southern problem of transportation, and the story of its progress and its work is a most important part of the economic history of the South in the later *ante-bellum* period. But with railroads in contemplation, the pressing question became one of finance.

In early times there had been a general reliance upon individual enterprise for transportation, whether by boat, pack train, wagon, or stage. But private means were not adequate to the later and larger problems. There had been stage lines and canals and turnpikes established by private stock companies, and the device of joint stocks was now relied upon in large part for railway building. But capital was scarce and timid, and though in some cases the hope of profit, together with patriotism for the South in its race with the North for population and wealth, led to the enlistment of considerable sums from private sources, public activity of some sort was generally an essential requirement for success. The federal government had a practice of building federal roads to and through the Territories; and when Gallatin was Secretary of the Treasury he had planned a system of transportation to be built by the federal government throughout the whole country. But in the succeeding decades the hope of federal railroads practically vanished. And the South, being mainly a stronghold of strict construction, furnished little advocacy of such a system. The idea of state ownership was more popular; but there were many individualists who opposed it on principle, and many others opposed particular propositions of that sort because they objected to the levying of taxes upon their own localities for the building of roads which would not reach their own districts. In fact, the agitation for state railroads was not successful except in special instances. In general, the sentiment of individualism was too strong.

For most of the railroads for which the demand was efficient, the resources were these: a number of individuals were willing to invest a portion of their fortunes in the enterprises; the state governments were friendly and anxious to facilitate the projects; the states could do this by granting charters giving permission to build, by subscribing to stock with state funds, and by granting special money-making privileges, such as banking and issuing bank-notes;[1] capitalists at the North or abroad were willing to aid Southern railway projects indirectly by the purchase of state bonds, and later, when some of the roads had proven financially successful, they even subscribed directly for railroad stock; and, last in this enumeration, but not least in practical effect, the city governments in

[1] The issuing of lottery privileges had gone out of fashion. Some of the newer states held in trust a fund from the United States derived from the sale of public lands, to be devoted to the improvement of transportation. In 1837 all of the states received a windfall in the distribution of surplus revenue; and this was used in many instances as an additional resource for internal improvements.

the South were among the parties most keenly interested in the building of transportation lines which would increase and extend the commerce of their own cities.

In the actual progress of road, canal, and railway building these several resources were utilized in varying combinations. In South Carolina, for example, the state subscribed for stock on an equal footing with other shareholders; in Tennessee the state pledged itself to provide funds to pay for rails when enough other subscriptions had been secured to build the road-beds; in Georgia the state made no subscriptions to the stock of the company roads, but pledged a great assistance to them in the building of a railway at state expense to connect their termini with the Tennessee River and the projected railways beyond; some of the shorter lines were built entirely with private capital; and at least one short road in North Carolina, begun in 1847, owed its establishment to the subscription of a Northern syndicate.

Thus, by one means or another or by a combination of several, the Southern transportation system grew. Its broad outlines only can here be indicated.

The first noteworthy enterprises of internal improvement begun in the South were the Chesapeake and Ohio and the James River and Kanawha canals, chartered in 1785, and the Dismal Swamp and the Santee canals, chartered in 1790. The two former were intended to serve, not only the Virginia-Maryland uplands, but ultimately the Ohio valley as well. The economic conditions which led to the beginning of these undertakings continued without material change for a number of years, and work on the canals, beset with financial difficulties, was slowly pushed forward, at times hopefully, at times despondently; but they were finally eclipsed by railroads, and were never completed. The Dismal Swamp Canal, intended to connect Albermarle Sound with Norfolk and the sea, was carried forward haltingly, and not completed, short as it was, until 1822. Thereafter it proved of considerable utility for several decades, until partly replaced by improved avenues. The Santee Canal was undertaken with a vim and quickly completed by the lowland Carolinians under the lead of Charleston. Its purpose was by connecting Charleston with the Santee River to institute a direct trade between the inland food-stuff producers and the staple producers of the coast, thus affording the one a ready market and the other cheaper supplies, and fostering a greater unity in the state. The canal was soon completed; but its great number of locks hampered transit, and the principal need of it in connection with the food supply of the lowlands having disappeared with the invention of the cotton gin and the resort to staple production in the interior, the canal was left in neglect. In the same period a number of river improvements were under way in the Carolina uplands; but the overwhelming impetus to cotton planting engrossed the attention of the people, and projects recently held to be important were completely neglected.

For twenty or thirty years after the invention of the gin, in 1793, the one great economic phenomenon in the lower South was the development of the cotton industry. Cotton prices were high, and profits on the output were phenomenal. There was a rush of people to the cotton belt, and every one was anxious to become a producer on a large scale. The result of this was a tremendous demand for negro slave labor. But the negroes must, of course, be bought and paid for, and this required the expenditure of all the money at command. People were so eager to utilize their resources to this end that they were impatient of all other suggestions. The consequence was that internal improvements were quite neglected.

But after about 1817, when the development of the western part of the cotton belt began to have effect in reducing the price of cotton and diminishing profits in the older fields, the Carolina planters began to cry out for cheaper access to market. Hence the resort to turnpikes; but the turnpikes were a demonstrated failure almost before they were built. The westward progress of the center of cotton production continued remorselessly, and Charleston, with grief, perceived that Savannah, Mobile, and New Orleans were waxing prosperous at her own expense. Then came the authentic news of the successful operation of railroads in England. At once the city, the state, and the people combined their resources, and built their railroad from Charleston to Augusta. The purpose was partly to accommodate the planters in the interior of the state, but it was principally to divert the trade of Augusta from Savannah to Charleston, thus depriving Savannah of the natural advantage which its river had afforded. Towns and citizens in middle Georgia soon after combined in the Georgia Railroad Company to build a railway west from Augusta, which was expected to serve as an extension of the South Carolina Railroad.

Savannah now became alarmed. Enlisting the aid of the town of Macon and of many private citizens, and securing the indirect aid of the state of Georgia, a group of Savannah promoters, with the backing of the city corporation, instituted the Central of Georgia Railroad Company, and built the road to Macon. A continuation of that road to the northward of Macon was undertaken by other companies; and the state government determined to insure the success of both the Georgia and the Central of Georgia lines by building a state-owned road to Chattanooga, expecting connections to be provided in Tennessee by other parties. The building and operation of these lines in Georgia, with others supplementing them, resulted in diminishing the cotton receipts and the commerce of Mobile and New Orleans, and spurred those cities to railroad enterprise.

All of the chief ports of the lower South, as well as several inferior ones, were thus reaching out with railroads for the trade of the cotton belt. And, with still greater ambition, they began to strive further for the trade of the great Northwest. Baltimore, Richmond, and Norfolk, each with its special road, as well as Philadelphia and New York, were also ere this in the race for the West; and eventually all of them reached it, but with differing results. Charleston especially was disappointed in her hopes of Western traffic, for her great scheme in the later thirties for a direct road to Cincinnati fell through; and as regards Western trade, the South Carolina Railroad proved to be merely an annex to the Georgia system. In fact, all of the sea-ports of the lower South had built their hopes of Northwestern traffic much too high; for when the lines were completed, and freight began to flow southward, most of the Western commodities of course found their market in the cotton belt, and never reached the Southern seaboard. Atlanta arose, and throve upon the adversity of the ports.

Contemporaneous with this building of railroads perpendicular to the coast, another system, parallel to the coast, was gradually extending its length from Washington through Richmond, Raleigh, Augusta, Montgomery to Mobile and New Orleans, and also a system connecting the Shenandoah-Tennessee valley with the Northeast, the Virginia coast, the South, and the Southwest. In addition, a moderate number of branch lines were being built from the main stems, and a few short roads were in progress in the West to supplement the rivers.

Not every project was destined to succeed: not every demand was proved to be efficient. The panic of 1837 and the long and severe depression from 1839 to 1845 killed many a flimsy railroad company as well as many a bubble bank. After that trying-out period the projects were brought to a more common-sense basis, and the less urgent and less efficient demands were relegated to the distant future.

After the main lines had been built, in large degree independently of one another, the process began of building connecting links, providing transfer facilities, and integrating the system of roads. And by 1860 every province of the South, east of the Mississippi, had been put in railway communication with every other province and with the outside world.

By the end of the *ante-bellum* period the South had come to be equipped with at least the skeleton of a well-planned railway system, reaching throughout nearly all of its extent and answering all the principal needs of transportation. And yet, in the larger aspect, that system was a source of weakness and a failure. Transportation is not an end in itself, but, when rightly used, is a means to the end of increasing wealth, developing resources, and strengthening society. And in the South these greater purposes were not accomplished. The building of railroads led to little else but the extension and the intensifying of the plantation system and the increase of the staple output. Specialization and commerce were extended, when just the opposite development, towards diversification of products and economic self-sufficiency, was the real need. In their actual effects the Southern railroads increased the competition in staple production, diminished the prices of the exports, and thus inured to a certain extent to the injury of the Southern producers, though to the benefit of the outside world.

CHAPTER I

THE SOUTH CAROLINA-GEORGIA LOWLANDS, TO THE END OF THE EIGHTEENTH CENTURY

IN the coast region in the neighborhood of Charleston and Savannah the influence of physiography upon social, industrial, and commercial history can hardly be overestimated. Coast configuration, soil, and climate have all been shaping factors.[1] Besides being semi-tropical, the economic life of the district may be characterized as somewhat amphibious. While the people dwelt upon the dry land, they tilled their rice upon fields periodically submerged, and they relied for transportation largely upon the abundant waterways.

The location and character of the watercourses was in early times of specially great importance, often controlling the spread of settlement, and determining the commercial economy. A fact of large consequence, for example, was the shallowness of these channels. In contrast with the Virginia lowlands, where the so-called rivers are really arms of the sea, permitting the ocean-going craft of colonial times to sail directly to the individual wharves of a thousand planters, the South Carolina

[1] For topographical descriptions see John Drayton, *View of South Carolina*, Charleston, 1802, pp. 6 ff.; Robert Mills, *Statistics of South Carolina*, Charleston, 1826, pp. 130–133; Harry Hammond, ed., *South Carolina Resources*, Charleston, 1883, pt. i; Edmund Ruffin, *Sketches of Lower North Carolina and the Similar Adjacent Lands*, Raleigh, N.C., 1861.

coast was water-broken in a way which required the loading and unloading of cargoes at a central point and the collecting of produce and distributing of supplies by means of small river craft. In Virginia, little concentration of commerce was required, so long as settlement was confined within the lowlands; and commercial towns, in spite of official efforts to promote them, failed to develop. On the coast of South Carolina and Georgia, on the other hand, commercial towns tended to grow spontaneously at the few points where dry land abutted upon deep harbors, and where the network of interior channels gave access to an industrial area.

The land of this district has had an interesting geological history in comparatively recent times. Only a few thousand years ago the district was raised from below the sea-level as a broad, infertile sand-flat. The rivers from the uplands have since then been carrying down fertile silt and laying it upon the sand in strips along the water-courses. This means, of course, that very much of the fertile area is so little above the ordinary level of the water as to be frequently inundated, as a result either of freshets from the interior or of tides from the ocean. Where the flood on these lands is of sea-water, salt marshes prevail. Further inland, where the rise of the tide has the effect only of raising the level of the river water, and no brine is in the overflow, the conditions favor a forest growth. The inhabitants have always distinguished sharply between the salt marshes, which they have made little attempt to utilize, and the fresh-water swamps, which, in spite of their jungle growth, they eagerly reduced to readiness for rice planting and other tillage. The remaining portion of the fertile tracts, which lay above the reach of high tide, was in many cases also utilized for the production of rice or other crops.

The climate, unusually hot and moist for North America, made the region as friendly to Africans as to Europeans; the swampy character of nearly all the fertile tracts, and the intense prevalence of malaria, from which the negroes were mostly immune, turned the scale decisively in favor of the Africans for agricultural labor.

For twenty odd years after the settlement of South Carolina, in 1670, the chief labor supply was white men, and the chief industries those of the forest — lumbering, naval stores, and the Indian trade. The colony little more than kept alive. Then it was discovered that rice could be grown with negro labor and exported as a staple with excellent profit. Plantation methods were borrowed from the West Indies and adapted to Carolina needs. Large numbers of Africans were imported and set to work by the men of strength and enterprise, who sought out the best lands available and established rice-producing estates on a large scale.

The rice plant requires not only a fat soil and a warm and steady temperature, but also a large regulated supply of water. Periodical inundation of the fields became the established method of success. Every rice field was required to have a level surface, plentiful ditches, adequate banks surrounding it, and a copious supply of fresh water available without the cost of pumping.[1] The easiest way to secure lands which could be flooded and drained at will was to examine the land at the borders of some

[1] Cf. Edmund Ruffin, *Agricultural Survey of South Carolina*, Columbia, 1843, pp. 99 ff.; John Drayton, *View of South Carolina*, Charleston, 1802, pp. 115 ff.

stream whose waters rose and fell with the tide without becoming salt or brackish, and select a tract which was covered with water at the flood, and dry at the ebb. Such a tract, once cleared, ditched, banked against the outside waters, and equipped with flood gates, was established as a rice field for indefinite decades to follow. If a tidal flow could not be had, the reservoir system was an alternative device. The water in this case came from the rainfall on the slopes above the rice fields, caught and held by earthen embankments until needed. Land which did not lie conveniently for flooding by either system could be used for Indian corn, but the ease of getting cereals from abroad and the scantiness of the local yield per acre tended against the spread of that crop. The resort to the additional staples, indigo and sea-island cotton, in later times, led to the use of some of the lands which the rice planters had neglected. The laboring population, however, was not at any time large enough to press all of the available land into use. The lands left out of cultivation were not neglected as a rule because of their distance from Charleston, but because of the quality of the soil and the lie of the land as concerned its availability for producing rice. The settlement as actually developed took the form, chiefly, of plantations in long double lines facing one another across each river, or in groups, where the alluvial tracts were wider than usual.

The plantation system, which had practically a monopoly of agriculture in the region, was dependent upon commerce with the outside world for its prosperity. The primary purpose was not to produce the things needed on the estate, but to produce a staple which could be exchanged for miscellaneous supplies. Plantations in the same district, producing the same staples, had little need, of course, to trade with one another. The great bulk of commerce was with the outside world.

In plantation industry with unfree, unwilling, stupid, and half-barbarous laborers, a premium was of necessity put upon routine. A negro, when once taught to do some simple task to any degree of satisfaction, was encouraged to continue performing the same sort of work to the end of his days. The nature of the labor supply in colonial times prevented the gain of as much profit by any other system as by that of routine. With the planter usually absent from his estate for the sake of his health, during each summer, an abnormally small amount of brains was used in plantation industry in proportion to the supply of muscle. In view of the presence of the great number of negroes, and the fear of disturbance among them, regulation and order were more to be desired than industrial progress. Under the circumstances the planters were fairly content with simple expedients and crude processes. For example, clumsy hoes were almost the sole implement of tillage on the rice and indigo estates throughout the colonial period. The use of the plow was scouted by the great majority of the planters as impracticable with their stupid and careless labor.

The transportation régime was in keeping. Ox carts by land and pole-boats or clumsy sailing craft by water were, for a very long period, the most efficient means for the carriage of freight in the lowlands. The chief avenues, whether for passengers or freight, were the waterways, and the most common vehicles were those which went by the name of pettiaugers. The word "pettiauger" seems to have been a generic name for boats which could be propelled in turn both by sails and by oars. Some were dug-out and some were frame-built, some were round bottomed and some were keeled. The coastwise channels were usually broad; and when the channel itself was narrow, there was generally a broad expanse of salt marsh or of cleared land on either side which would give the wind free play upon the sails of the craft. Where such was not the case, the sails would be taken in and the use of oars or poles substituted. Sloops were used instead of pettiaugers in some cases where the course was clear, while in others, where the route to a plantation was too crooked or too much overhung with trees to permit the use of sails, pole-boats and rowboats were the steady resort.

Each well-organized plantation in the lowlands had one of its ablest negroes established as master of the boats, with the title of patroon. Acquaintance with the channels, the shoals, the snags, and the tides was expected of him, as well as ability to handle sails, oars, and poles and to command his assistants. To aid him in navigating the barges, field laborers were often detailed for temporary duty as boat hands. With these plantation crews, heavy-laden boats would carry rice to market and bring back the simple but somewhat bulky supplies which the plantation needed. Sometimes transportation within the estate itself would be done by canoes or pole boats on the canals which ran through the rice fields. If plantations by any chance lay at some distance from a waterway, the crops were usually carried by ox carts to the nearest creek and there transferred to boats for the rest of the distance.[1]

Land traffic was, of course, in come cases necessary.

[1] John Drayton, *View of South Carolina*, Charleston, 1802, p. 141.

A small stock of horses was imported into South Carolina at an early date, and they were used with both saddle and harness by the planters when quick locomotion was needed, and especially by the Indian traders in pack-trains to the homes of the distant tribes.

The South Carolina assembly seems to have made its first provision for road building in 1682. Thereafter it gave considerable attention to providing for the building and repair of roads and bridges as well as to the care of navigable waterways. In view of the danger of attack from Indians or Spaniards and the possibility of slave insurrection, the making and maintenance of roads for swift rallying by the militia was dealt with by the government as a military necessity of importance. In times of peace, however, a prevailing sentiment of security made the people very easy-going on this score, and the roads, in consequence, were often in wretched order.

The general provisions of the law were that all male inhabitants above the age of sixteen years were liable for road duty to a specified amount each year in their respective road districts. Local commissioners were authorized to call the road-workers into service and superintend their labors on the public highways. Private roads were in many cases built by planters, singly or in coöperation, to supplement the highroads for their own convenience. In general there was large prevalence of individualism and little dependence upon public authority. The planters were disposed to decide upon their personal and local needs and to do the needed work informally with their own plantation gangs at times when the crops gave a respite from tillage. The chief concern with the law usually was to secure its permission for citizens to do with their private resources what their interests required. For example, when in 1785 the planters on the Edisto River wished to secure the clearing of its channel, they were content with an enactment by the legislature authorizing commissioners to receive private subscriptions for the promotion of the work.[1] No public expenditure was provided for, it seems, and no tolls to be levied nor dividends to be paid upon subscriptions. The planters whose interests were to be promoted simply combined their resources on a voluntary basis. Another instance was the plan, of which La Rochefoucault[2] tells us, according to which the planters near the Stono River were projecting in 1802 to build a canal by contributions and local assessments to connect their estates more directly with Charleston.

In the sandy districts the making and tending of roads required very little labor. To make a road meant simply to clear away the trees for a width of ten or twelve feet. Little ditching or grading was needed, and certainly, as a rule, none at all was done. The sand formed a hard enough road-bed in wet weather, and was fairly good even in dry seasons unless heavy traffic had "plowed the road." In that case the loose and yielding sand would make it slow and heavy going for both man and beast. Often where the sparseness of the pine trees allowed it, side roads would be made by teamsters of their own motion in order to avoid deep sand-beds which lay in the main track. So long as the pine ridges were followed, it was possible indeed for any driver to "steer by compass" and

[1] *South Carolina Gazette*, June 2, 1785.

[2] *Travels through the United States of North America*, quarto edition, London, 1799, vol. i, p. 596.

make his way through the forest without regard to beaten tracks. The same easy-going, free-for-all régime in travel prevails in some measure to the present day in the pine-barrens country.

Where swamps were encountered the state of things was very different. In wet weather the ground was often of soft mud to an indefinite depth, and impassable for vehicles; in moderate seasons it was soft enough to cause the wheels to sink for several inches; and in dry weather the roads were so filled with deep ruts and rough clods as to furnish wretched opportunities for traffic. The swampy ground was so covered by dense forest growth as a rule that new tracks could not be opened without great labor. In a word, while roads in the sandy country had only to be cleared, in the swamps they had literally to be built. The laying of rough logs across the track for a "corduroy road" was a temporary device; for permanent roads, causeways had to be built and frequently repaired with earth and brush or wooden slabs. Bridges or ferries had also to be provided at the crossing of streams. To meet particular local needs in these cases a number of special legislative acts were passed, appointing special commissioners for particular bridges and causeways, and in some cases granting privileges of establishing ferries and collecting tolls.

For the sake of economy in labor and expense the highways were laid out as far as possible to follow the pine ridges and to cross the swamps and streams only when absolutely necessary. The lie of the land, furnishing pine-ridge peninsulas extending down from the uplands as watersheds between the several parallel rivers, made it easy to establish roads from points in the middle country to corresponding points on the coast. The building of roads parallel to the coast was in the lowlands a much more difficult matter; and when roads were built, their maintenance, because of the problem of causeways, was also troublesome and expensive. The result was that the roads along the coast were usually in bad repair, in spite of the legislative enactments, and they were in large measure avoided by the inhabitants, who had learned by experience to choose the water-routes in preference.

The colony of Georgia was under a more paternal government than South Carolina. James Oglethorpe, in the period of his control, showed remarkable vigor, part of which went to the opening of roads and trails. As an example, a news item from the town of Frederica, on the Georgia coast, published in the *Gentleman's Magazine* for January, 1739, relates that in September, 1738, after the arrival of a regiment of troops from Great Britain for garrison duty, "The Inhabitants of the Town went out on the 25th with the General, and cut a Road thro' the Woods down to the Soldiers Fort in a straight Line, so that there is an open Communication from thence; they perform'd this Work in three Days, tho' it is near 6 Miles thro' thick Woods."

The more important road which Oglethorpe opened, from the Savannah to the Altamaha River, had the effect of revealing the richness of some of the intervening land and promoting the emigration of the Dorchester congregation from South Carolina to establish the Midway settlement and the town of Sunbury.[1] In 1735 the town of Augusta was laid out by order of the Georgia Trustees, and soon replaced Fort Moore on the Carolina side of the

[1] C. C. Jones, *History of Georgia*, vol. i, p. 491.

river as the focus of the Indian trade. The importance of the town led Oglethorpe quickly to have a path marked out through the woods from Savannah to Augusta, to supplement the river communication.[1] The general development and system of transportation in Georgia was on the whole entirely analogous to that of South Carolina.

The only demand for avenues to the distant interior in early times was that made by the requirements of the Indian trade. The need of the traders was met as a rule by the traders themselves without any call upon the government or upon the planters for assistance. In fact, the trading routes supplied avenues to the commonwealths at later times without the trouble of initial location by the authorities. Except where rivers were available, the method of transit used by the Indian traders was by packhorses in trains. Since no wheeled vehicles were used, there was no need of anything more than trails; and there was no demand for bridges and causeways sufficient to secure their construction. The routes of the Indian traders were mere bridle-paths through the wilderness. In view of the boggy character of most of the bottom lands, and the general disadvantages of crossing large watercourses, these paths usually followed the watersheds as far as possible. When routes lay of necessity across river valleys, they were so located as to avoid steep ascents, and to cross the streams at points where the banks were firm. It has frequently been noted that the buffalo trails and the paths of the Indian traders, which often followed the buffalo routes, were laid out with such good judgment that the lines of the modern railways connecting

[1] "A State of the Province of Georgia," 1741, in Georgia Historical Society *Collections*, vol. ii, pp. 72, 73.

the same strategic points have in many cases nearly coincided with them. Intervening between the primitive era and the railroad epoch, the wagon roads leading from the trading points to the interior also tended to follow the routes of the Indian traders.

In colonial times, Charleston exported a very great quantity of furs, which her merchants obtained mostly from the distant hunting grounds of the four great tribes of Southern Indians.[1] The Cherokees dwelt to the northward and northwestward in the foot-hills of the mountains and beyond; the tribes of the Creek confederacy held the land from the middle district of South Carolina westward to the Tombigbee River on the edge of the present state of Mississippi; the Chickasaws and Chocktaws lay beyond the Creeks. The Carolina traders had dealings with all of these by means of their periodical journeys with their packhorse men and laden beasts of burden over the long and immensely tedious trading paths.

The system of trading paths which extended northward and westward from Charleston has been excellently described by J. H. Logan in his *History of Upper South Carolina.*[2] Leaving Charleston for either of the four "nations," the trader would journey up "Charleston Neck" and follow the course of the Ashley River until the site of the settlement of Dorchester was reached. There the path to the eastern Cherokees branched off to the northward, running near the site of the present city of Columbia, and thence, swerving to the northwest, it

[1] Governor Archdale reported, in 1707, that the town of Charleston traded for nearly a thousand miles into the continent. B. R. Carroll, *Historical Collections of South Carolina,* vol. ii, pp. 85 ff.

[2] Charleston, 1859, ch. 12.

passed the old trading house at Ninety-Six and thence followed the watershed east of the Savannah River to the mountains.

From Dorchester, earlier known as Monsieur St. Julien's, and a great camping place for the caravans, the path to the Creeks and the farther tribes continued in a direction a little north of west, following the watershed until the middle country was reached, and then descending to the Savannah River a little below the present site of Augusta. At that point was a trading post for the eastern Creeks, called Savannah Town or Fort Moore, and thence well-beaten paths ran northwestward to the western Cherokees and westward to the western Creeks, the Chickasaws, and the Choctaws.

In 1736 the planting of Augusta, on the Georgia shore, deprived Fort Moore of its business. The new town of Savannah, at the mouth of the river, also had ambitions for Indian trade, but for some length of time was successfully excluded by Charleston. The trading path between Augusta and Charleston, however, was largely abandoned in favor of the navigation route of the Savannah River and the connecting waterways along the South Carolina coast, which gave a very much cheaper transit. The path running northward from Charleston continued somewhat longer in use, because of the greater difficulty of using the rivers in that quarter. The settling of the up-country by the whites destroyed the utility of the trading paths as such in South Carolina, before the end of the eighteenth century. In later times they have been the subject of little more than antiquarian interest.

The chief products of agriculture were much less valuable than furs of corresponding weight and bulk. The planters, in consequence, were deterred in colonial times from all extensive land traffic. It was in fact a source of great annoyance to any of them when the location of their estates made the water carriage to Charleston difficult enough to bring the use of horses and wagons into contemplation as a substitute. The most important instance of this in a plantation district occurred with the planters in the rich swamps along the Santee River.

The Santee River, which drains the whole of the central South Carolina uplands, and whose lower course offered splendid soil to attract the planters, had a most inconvenient lack of harbor facilities at its mouth. The river empties into the ocean through a swampy delta, some fifty miles northeast of Charleston. The mouths of the river are choked by a shallow bar, as is also the entrance to Winyaw Bay just northeastward. The string of sea islands in the direction of Charleston is broken at several places, and the protected waterways are accordingly not in complete series. The Santee boats were obliged by turns to navigate shallow waters and risk the perils of the ocean. A desire to relieve this hardship on transportation prevailed from early times among all those concerned. For many years, however, it remained strictly a local problem, and general conditions were not conducive to its solution. The planters in the other parts of the lowlands were not eager to see the Santee planters relieved of their difficulty; for the facilitation of Santee commerce might lead to expansion of the staple industries on the Santee lands to such a degree that prices for the produce would be driven down. The planters in the other districts would certainly not have favored the devotion of public funds to any Santee projects; and furthermore, so long as South

Carolina remained a British province, the people did not fully control their own government.

Throughout the whole period, from the establishment of the colony until well into the nineteenth century, the public policy of South Carolina was entirely controlled by the city of Charleston. This applied, not only to politics, but to society, commerce, and all large enterprises. Outlying localities might make feeble demands for various things; but to be effective, every important demand must either be the demand of Charleston originally, or secure the full support of the city. It was not until after the achievement of independence and the rise of new economic problems that Charleston became decisively interested in securing closer connection with the Santee River.

The eventual rise of this interest in the part of Charleston and the rest of the lowlands was due, not to a greater desire for trade with the rice and indigo planters of the Santee swamps, but chiefly to the need of getting food-stuffs from the settlers who from 1750 had been entering the South Carolina uplands and establishing themselves as small farmers, producing grain and live stock. The downward navigation of the Santee River system would furnish an economical outlet for the surplus produce of these farmers and encourage them to enlarge their scale of industry, if in any way the Santee could be directly connected with a seaport.

The planters of the low country were accustomed to buy much of their food supply from distant sources, paying high freights and middlemen's profits. An effect of the American Revolution was to ruin the staple of indigo and reduce the coast planters to a severer economy than before.

Cheaper food supplies were more acutely needed. Charleston, of course, felt this depression and was eager to relieve it. She wished to increase the general welfare, and particularly if in so doing she could add the trade of the distant interior to that of the coast which she already so largely controlled.

The ruin of the indigo staple and the depression in rice had sadly diminished the profit from slave labor, and had, of course, reduced very much the rates at which slaves could be purchased or hired. Labor was cheap, and some floating capital was available for new enterprises. Canals had some years before become a demonstrated success in England. The time was ripe for a large canal project in South Carolina.

The winding course of the Santee River approaches within fifty miles of Charleston, due northward from the city, and then turns east and southeast to reach the ocean at a point some fifty miles away from Charleston harbor. In the northward direction, about one-half of the route from Charleston to the Santee is covered by the navigable course of the Cooper River; the remainder lies through a fairly level country except for a ridge near the Santee which reaches a height of some seventy feet above the sea-level. The opportunity was thought to be attractive for a canal with locks to bring the Santee trade directly to Charleston.

In February, 1786, Chancellor Rutledge presented to the legislature of South Carolina a petition for the chartering of a company to open a canal between the Santee and Cooper rivers. It was proposed to have the cost of the enterprise divided into one hundred shares of indefinite par value. The greater number of these shares, the chan-

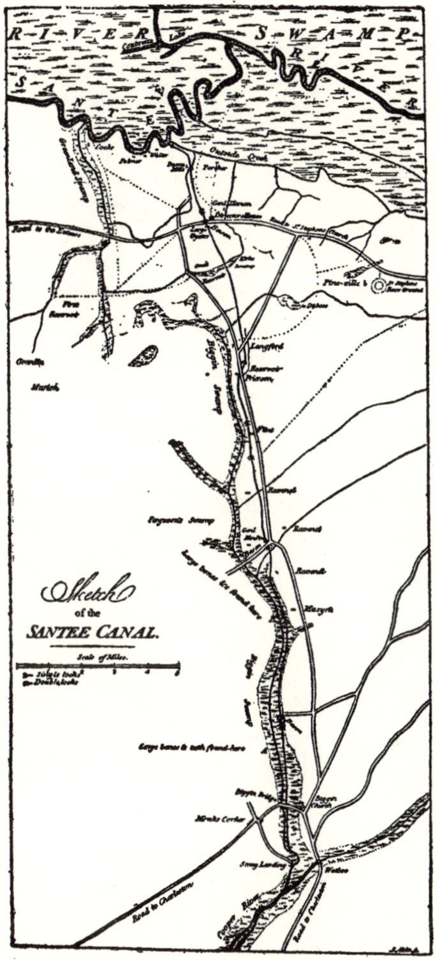

Sketch of the Santee Canal.
Reprinted from John Drayton, *View of South Carolina*, Charleston, 1802, p. 156.

cellor said, had already been subscribed for.[1] The petition was favorably reported by committees of the legislature and an act granting a charter was shortly passed. An incidental feature of the charter was a probition of collecting tolls in any year in excess of twenty-five per cent net profit upon the capital expended in building the canal.

Colonel Charles Senf was appointed chief engineer, or "director," soon after the charter was secured. The preliminary surveys made by him showed a choice of several routes from the head of navigation on Cooper River, near the village of Monck's Corner, to the course of the Santee, twenty-two to twenty-five miles away. The principal engineering problem was to secure a sufficient water supply for the high level at the crossing of the Santee ridge. A minor one was to avoid crossing the rice fields of planters along the route in such a way as to cut off their water supply.[2] A route was finally chosen running west of north and reaching the Santee River some three miles west of Pineville. Water for the summit level was to be secured through ditches from reservoirs on slopes several miles away.

Dissension in the company is indicated by a letter from Senf to General Thomas Sumter, January 3, 1790: "I find my Zeal and few Abilities do not meet with that Incouragement I could, with honest pride, have expected—my too great confidence has exposed me to suffer Indignity—I thank God, that through the Interference of my friends I have been able to pary the Blow on my Reputation till

[1] *Charleston Evening Gazette*, February 7, 1786, proceedings of the South Carolina House of Representatives, February 7.

[2] Tradition in the Ravenel family, preserved in a manuscript genealogy, has it that Daniel Ravenel threatened Senf with pistols and forced him to avoid cutting into the rice field of the Wantoot plantation.

this time."[1] The company, after a partial reorganization and an increase in the number of shares in 1792, began the active work of construction.

The specifications for the canal required a width of thirty-five feet at the surface of the water, and of twenty feet at the bottom; there was to be four feet depth of water, a tow-path on each side, six single locks and two double ones, all of brick or stone and large enough to accommodate boats fifty-four feet long and nine feet wide.[2] At places there were to be excavations of thirty feet or more in depth.

The rules adopted by the company in 1792 provided that shareholders must pay £5 on each share on the third Monday in January, 1793, and £5 on the third Monday in each July and January following until the canal should be completed. Extra assessments not greater nor more frequent than the regular ones might be made by the president and a majority of the directors. A large number of the most prominent citizens of the state subscribed for stock; and the progress of the work was a matter of widespread interest.

Plantation industry about 1792 was at its lowest point of profitableness. Prime gangs of slaves were occasionally sold at less than two hundred dollars per head, and buyers were few. Planters were anxious to find employment for their slaves which would relieve the usual necessity for complete reliance upon plantation profits. They now welcomed the bid of the Santee company for labor, and

[1] Original in Wisconsin Historical Society, Draper Mss., *Sumter Papers*, vol. i, no. 75.

[2] John Drayton, *View of South Carolina*, Charleston, 1802, p. 156, map. The number of locks was afterward increased to thirteen.

supplied it with as many able-bodied men and women as the company could pay the hire of.[1] Digging was begun at both ends of the canal.

The laborers were stupid, the methods were primitive, the control of the negroes was poor; and progress was much slower than had been anticipated. By the beginning of 1797 it was seen that the work would be much heavier and more costly than expected. Meanwhile the rise of the new cotton industry was diminishing the number of hands available and raising the price of labor. A campaign was made to promote the canal as a patriotic enterprise. With the permission of the legislature, a lottery was established for the benefit of the company, and five drawings were held in the course of the years 1795 and 1796. The scheme for each drawing provided for the sale of tickets to the amount of about thirty thousand dollars, of which about eighty-eight per cent was to be distributed in prizes and the remaining twelve per cent to accrue to the Company for expenditure on its work.[2]

At the end of 1795, about five miles of the excavation at each end had been completed and several locks were under construction.[3] The directors of the company now redoubled their efforts to push the work to early completion. They advertised in the hiring season at the end of the year that they wanted additional laborers and masons for the year 1796, and would pay £18 for laborers for the year, and £25 to £30 to negro bricklayers, the company fur-

[1] Samuel Du Bose, "Reminiscences of St. Stephen's Parish," in T. G. Thomas, *History of the Huguenots in South Carolina*, pp. 66–68.

[2] Advertisements of the lottery in the *Charleston City Gazette*, March, 1795, to April, 1796.

[3] *Charleston City Gazette*, March 7, 1796, letter of "A Friend to Inland Navigation," who had recently visited the canal.

nishing, as usual, food, shelter, and supervision. That year six hundred laborers were employed.[1] The resources of the company were strained in meeting the cost of wages and supplies; but the end of the year, in spite of Senf's prophecies, failed to bring into sight the completion of the project.

Within the next year or two there began a failure by a number of stockholders to meet the recurring assessments, which, it seemed, would never end. The rule of the company was that any default in promptly meeting assessments would at once cause a forfeiture of the stock. The annual meeting of the stockholders on February 1, 1798, however, resolved that, whereas the expense of the canal had already exceeded every estimate, the enforcement of the forfeiture rule would be highly inexpedient. They provided that any person in arrears for requisitions prior to 1798 might consolidate his payments into shares paid up to date at £71 each and thereby avoid forfeiture, on condition of paying in each case the £10 assessment for January, 1798, within sixty days after the date of this resolution.[2] An advertisement by one Francis Robertson in the *Charleston City Gazette* of February 5, 1798, offering to buy Santee Canal shares, indicates that disgusted stockholders had a chance to unload, though probably only at a sacrifice.

Assessments were doggedly kept up and work of construction persisted in, until in July, 1800, the canal was completed with all its locks and reservoirs, and a boat laden with salt at Charleston passed through and carried its cargo unbroken to the town of Granby at the foot of

[1] *Ibid.*

[2] *Charleston City Gazette,* February 14, 1798, advertisement of the Santee Canal Co.

the rapids on the Congaree just below Columbia. The building of the canal had consumed eight years of actual work, and about seven hundred and fifty thousand dollars in money. The amount of capital invested was so large that there could be no prospect of a large rate of dividends from tolls. The later requisitions on stock had been paid by the subscribers merely to save the early payments from being a total loss, and to further an enterprise which was expected to prove a public benefaction. The burden on the stockholders was in many cases more apparent than real; for many of the subscribers of stock were also leasers of labor to the company at profitable rates, and received in wages for their negroes more than they were paying as stockholders. Furthermore, the custom then periodically prevalent among the planters, of buying as many fresh negroes as possible, was draining away their capital anyway, and to sink money in the canal was no worse in effect than to sink it in expensive slaves.

The canal was expected to perform large and useful functions in the commerce with the interior. The chief traffic was expected to be in food-stuffs. The friends of the enterprise often fondly estimated the prospective saving of time, labor, and wear of men, horses, and wagons to result from the boats which would ply upon the canal and the rivers which it connected. The estimate generally accepted was that each boat of twenty-two tons burthen with a crew of five men would do the same work on the down trip from Granby on the Congaree or Rocky Mount on the Wateree, and in about the same time, as twenty-two wagons with four to six horses and two men to each wagon. The down-traffic in grain and other produce was expected to be very heavy. The up-traffic could also be accommodated by the water route, though with less ease and speed. Its bulk, however, would of course be much lighter.[1]

The dreams of heavy traffic on the canal and considerable net profits from tolls were never to come true. The rise of the cotton industry in the uplands checked the growth of cereal production and, by giving a local market for the whole output, stopped all shipment of grain to the coast. The yield of cotton shipped in the place of grain was far lighter in weight, and more precious in value. It could bear the cost of transportation by land, while grain could not have done so. The frequent delays from mishaps or the shallowness of streams, the danger of wreck, and the excessive slowness of the upward trip by boat, all lessened the advantage of the water system and promoted the use of wagons. The introduction of steamboats upon the rivers tended, however, to increase the patronage of the canal. No record of the company's earnings is now to be had.

The maximum efficiency of the route by water in the steamboat period is indicated by the following news item from the *Charleston City Gazette* for April 9, 1822: "The Steam Boat Carolina, Capt. Harvey, arrived yesterday morning at 9 o'clock, in the extraordinary short passage of 4 days and a half from Granby, with tow boats carrying nearly 900 bales of cotton." The method of collecting freight for the upward passage is indicated by an advertisement in the same journal for January 15, 1822: "Freight for Granby. The Charleston and Columbia Steam Boat Company's Tow Boat, No. 1, will receive

[1] *Charleston City Gazette,* March 7, 1816.

Freight at Magwood's Wharf, on Monday, the 14th inst., and start for Granby about the middle or last of the week. Apply to Randal Robinson, Agent."

The rate of toll for passing the locks was fifteen dollars per boat in 1821. Previously it had been higher. The cost of operating the locks and keeping up the work was enough to make an appreciable difference between gross and net earnings. The company, it appears, however, for a number of years earned annually several thousand dollars net, which was distributed in dividends. Finding their by-laws to have grown antiquated, the stockholders adopted a new set in January, 1841, dividing each of the existing shares into twelve new ones (issuing 8724 shares in place of 727), providing a sliding scale of votes in the election of officers which gave some advantage to the small stockholders, and ordering that the declaration of dividends be made in February and July of each year.[1]

The patronage of the canal increased moderately in volume, it seems, until the period when railroads began to compete in the traffic of the district drained by the Santee River. The canal receipts then rapidly declined. By 1850 or 1855 the tolls doubtless barely covered the cost of maintenance. About 1858 the canal was finally abandoned, and has never been revived. Pine trees as large as a man's body stand to-day on the tow-path and in the bed of the old canal. The ditch and the masonry of the locks remain a monument to a past régime, a monument to Charleston's aspiring ambition and to her dead hopes.

All other schemes for the improvement of transportation in the South Carolina lowlands were of distinctly minor

[1] *By-laws of the Santee Canal Company, 1841*, pamphlet, Charleston, 1841.

consequence; those on the Georgia coast and in the Cape Fear district, still less important. A few roads and causeways were established, and a little work was done in improving navigation; but the chief reliance was upon the waterways as nature had provided them.

The thickening of settlement on the sea-islands in the neighborhood of Edisto River and southward had the natural result of developing a commercial freighting activity by water, to relieve the planters from the need of sending their own boats and laborers to carry produce and bring back parcels from Charleston. This was agreeable to the planters in saving their time and labor. The work was first done by tramp boats, plying irregularly and going for freight where it was likely to be found. In due time packet lines with regular landing places and more or less regular schedules were established. The state of things in 1796 is indicated by the following notice, published in the *Charleston City Gazette*, March 31, 1796: —

CHARLESTON, January 30, 1796.

The Captains of the Coasting Vessels to the Southward, from South Edisto to May River, this day assembled, have agreed on and do constitute the following prices for freight of the under-mentioned articles, to be observed by each and every one of them, viz.

	£	*s.*	*d.*
Rice, per hundred			9
Pitch, Tar, Turpentine, Beef, Pork, Flour, per bbl.		2	0
Iron, per hundred		1	0
Boards, Staves, per thousand, five dollars	1	3	8
Grain, Salt, per bushel			6
Tobacco, Sugar, Rum, per hogshead		10	0
Wine or Brandy in pipes		10	0
Bricks, per thousand		15	6
Cotton, per hundred		2	4

At the end of the eighteenth century the external commerce of Charleston was remarkably great. The rice crops were abundant, and the price satisfactory; the prices of cotton, of both sea-island and upland varieties, was very high, and the output rapidly increasing. Charleston was in fact for some years in that period the greatest exporting point on the American continent. The south of Europe depended on Carolina rice, the West Indies on Carolina lumber, and England on Carolina cotton. Every maritime people sent ships to share in the Carolina trade, carrying thither rum, sugar, and coffee from the West Indies, foodstuffs from the Middle states, rum and fish from New England, manufactured goods from Great Britain, and negroes from Africa. To carry these goods to Charleston was to put them directly within reach of all the people of the lowlands. The presence of the waterways prevented the need of any complex mechanism of commerce. The district was so remote from all other settled parts of America that no great demand for overland connections had made itself felt.

The relative importance of interests in the general region had long remained fairly constant; it had now, however, begun to shift, as the history of the Santee Canal has already shown us. The lowlands had reached their full economic development, but in the uplands the people had barely begun to work out their destiny. The cotton industry in the Piedmont soon developed such great attractions for planters that a heavy migration thither occurred from all the older staple-producing districts. The growth of the problem of transportation to meet the needs of the immensely important upland cotton belt, in the early nineteenth century, reduced the problem of the coast lands to relative insignificance.

CHAPTER II

THE UPLANDS PRIOR TO THE RAILROAD ERA

WITH the close of the eighteenth century the eastern cotton belt began to come into its own. It soon eclipsed the rice district in earning capacity, and with its upland and interior position brought much larger and more pressing problems of transportation than the Lower South had theretofore known.

By the Piedmont region, with a part of which we are here concerned, we mean that stretch of country which slopes southeastward from the foot of the Blue Ridge to the edge of the pine-barrens. Its upper and lower boundaries may be stated roughly as the altitude lines of twelve hundred and three hundred feet respectively above the sea-level. The portion comprising the eastern cotton belt lay between the watershed north of the Cape Fear river, on the northeast, and the watershed west of the Chattahoochee, on the southwest. It fell chiefly within the states of South Carolina and Georgia.

This upland region just indicated formed a fairly distinct economic province; and for many years its settled portion had a separate history of its own. In its several divisions, it is true, it lay within the same political boundaries as the coast settlements to the southeastward; but the connection was in the early period only nominal. The Piedmont was settled by people coming overland from the northeastward, who for years kept in touch with their former homes in

Pennsylvania and Virginia, and sent in that direction what little commerce they plied. The wilderness of sand and pine-trees intervening between the uplands and the neighboring coast delayed the beginning and long hampered the increase of the commercial intercourse between them, which the people of each became anxious to promote.

The pine-barrens are much a wilderness, even to this day, exploited by turpentiners and lumbermen, but little developed by farmers. The forest, whether of the clean-trunked original timber, or second-growth scrub pines, or tangled deciduous growth in the swamps, is broken as a rule only by ill-kept fields in sparsely scattered clearings. A passenger on even the fastest train from Charleston to the edge of the uplands has a tedious journey through a desolate region of pine-flats. This belt of forbidding country, a hundred miles or more in breadth, was in early times a huge obstacle, to be avoided when possible, and to be crossed only when necessity required. In spite of the distance being shorter, the access to the Carolina Piedmont from Charleston was perhaps more difficult and the route certainly less used, for a number of years, than that over the crude roads which led through the interior from Chesapeake Bay and the Delaware River.

The fact that the principal supply of settlers for the Carolina-Georgia Piedmont came overland from the distant northward entrances to the continent gives illustration of the truth that, other things at all equal, it is easier for a tide of settlement to spread over a very large expanse of country whose nature is homogeneous and familiar, than for it to cross a distinct barrier, where the path is not clear and the country beyond is of uncertain reputation.

The coast settlements of the Lower South did not develop

a pioneer class. The occupations of nearly all the people were of a sort which could not with profit be transferred into the back country. The planters were the chief source of enterprise; and in the eighteenth century there was little inducement for the planters to forsake the lowlands. The reputation acquired by South Carolina and Georgia, of offering prospect of success only to planters and merchants, prevented any great number of people of other classes from entering their ports. The use of negro slaves as a labor supply instead of white servants prevented the rise of a yeoman class through the expiration of indentures, and tended against the presence of an unattached population. Virginia developed a larger yeomanry, which began the migration destined to make the Old Dominion a mother of states. But Philadelphia was preëminently the port of entry for the American frontiersmen, and Pennsylvania the first halting place of the horde which furnished the main population of the Southern Piedmont.

The tide of emigrants from Pennsylvania, mostly Scotch-Irishmen and Germans, began to pour across Maryland into the Shenandoah valley, about 1730. It ascended the valley in a fairly rapid movement, and between 1740 and 1750 began to flow out upon the rolling plateau of middle Carolina. It mingled there with a stream of emigrating Virginians, and with them flowed farther southwestward. Braddock's defeat in 1755, by creating uneasiness on the frontier of the middle colonies, increased the volume of this movement.[1]

By this tide of migration a thin population of pioneer farmers was established in all of the districts to which it

[1] David Ramsay, *History of South Carolina,* Charleston, 1809, vol. i, ch. vi.

spread. The farther extension southwestward was checked in the uplands of eastern Georgia, about 1760, by the resistance of the Indian tribes. The next few decades witnessed a gradual thickening of settlement in the region through reinforcements from the same northward sources, aided now also by straggling Irish, English, and other recruits across the barrens from Charleston and Savannah.

The climate of this upland country was far more invigorating and more friendly to white settlers and laborers than that of the coast. The soil was fertile as a rule, whether on the hillsides or in the valleys. The conditions were favorable for raising cereals, live stock, tobacco, and a number of subsidiary crops. Industry in general agriculture would be repaid with considerable abundance.

The country invited the farming class. The roving huntsmen, whether redskin or white, had their game driven away by the farming invasion, and as a class disappeared from the region. The straggling cattle drovers who for a period in the middle of the century pastured their herds in some parts of the Piedmont[1] were likewise gradually driven out by the entrance of the farmers. As the farmers pushed their conquest nearer to completion, cattle droving was destroyed as a separate calling, and cattle raising became a subsidiary industry on the farms.

The Indian traders saw one of their stations after another deprived of business through the crowding out of the tribes by the encroaching farmers. For the time, the trading paths were lengthened and new stations were substituted at points farther northwestward and westward; then followed a narrowing of the hunting grounds and a decline

[1] Alexander Gregg, *History of the Old Cheraws*, New York, 1867, pp. 109, 110.

of the volume and profits of the great peltry trade. The industries of the forest faded from the competition with those of the field. The precedent types gave place completely to the type of the frontier farmer.

This conquest of the Piedmont was the work of backwoodsmen, in a movement entirely spontaneous. The settlement was made by individual families with the primary intention of producing each the articles which it needed to consume. The people were squatters, without encouragement or even recognition from any government, establishing a self-sufficing economy in isolation from the rest of the world. The conditions were in salient contrast with those of the lowland planters.

The government of South Carolina had not completely ignored the possibilities of inland development. In 1732, as soon as order had been established after the overthrow of the proprietary control, the colonial assembly provided for the erection of eleven townships in the middle country, on the courses of the principal rivers of the province, and gave special inducements for settlers to occupy them. The purpose was both military and economic: to protect the coast district from Indian forays, and to develop a local supply of food-stuffs to meet the demand of the planters and the Charleston people. Eight or more of these townships were actually laid out on the courses of the Pee Dee, Black, Santee, Edisto, and Savannah rivers, not to mention two provided for on the Altamaha River which were soon removed from South Carolina's jurisdiction by the establishment of the new province of Georgia.[1]

Liberal offers of land and privileges were advertised in promoting the inland settlements. Public funds even

[1] Edward McCrady, *South Carolina as a Royal Province*, ch. viii.

were used to some extent for the furtherance of the purpose. Small colonies of Germans, Swiss, Irish, and other needy exiles were planted in several of the townships, and set to planting corn and raising cattle. Most of the enterprises, however, came to a speedy end. The officials and surveyors had had an eye chiefly to transportation facilities. For the sake of easy communication by water with the coast, the townships had been located in the midst of the pine country. They proved to be in most cases barren and miasmatic. Orangeburg alone, on the North Edisto, with its German Palatine settlers, proved to have resources for prosperity and permanence as an organized community. The rest of the so-called townships promoted by the government were practically dead before the squatter inpouring from the northward entered the neighboring Piedmont. One or two of them, however, such as Williamsburg on Black River, though abortive as towns, gave origin to thin groups of permanent farms.

In 1737 an act was passed by the South Carolina assembly, which alluded to the settlements lately made by several families in Orangeburg township, and directed a road to be made to their locality from the "head of the path that leads from Dorchester to Capatin Izard's cow pen." In 1762 another act provided for a ferry for passengers, horses, and cattle across the Santee River and a road to be made in connection with it, "to facilitate the passage of travellers from Charlestown to Williamsburg and other, the northwest [northeast ?] parts of this Province."

These two roads, running respectively west of north and east of north from Charleston, were the first legal extension of the road system beyond the limits of the tide-water country. The failure to mention vehicles in the act for the ferry to Williamsburg indicates that these roads were intended at first only for horsemen and cattle drovers. They were converted, of course, into wagon roads at a later time. The occupation of the Piedmont behind these points by the pioneers from the northward resulted by about 1760 in the informal opening of paths to radiate from Orangeburg, Williamsburg, and other places in the middle country, to the various parts of the uplands. The availability of the greater rivers, the Santee system and the Savannah, had the effect, however, of dwarfing the importance of the points whence the roadways radiated. Orangeburg and Williamsburg had merely a fork-of-the-road position, and did not long remain even on the main roads to the distant interior. The navigable river courses dominated the situation, directing the currents of traffic and promoting the rise of commercial centers at the points where their navigation was broken. The road system of the middle country soon became subsidiary to the rivers, with the chief function of putting Charleston and Savannah into touch with the head-of-navigation points by land as well as by water. In the uplands, the roads were developed mainly in a system radiating from these same strategic points on the rivers. As we have seen above,[1] the river navigation, in all cases concerning the eastern cotton belt, reached only to the edge of the Piedmont country. Water transportation within the uplands was difficult and dangerous down-stream, and up-stream impossible.

The pioneer farmers of the Piedmont country were curiously independent of commercial relations in the early years of their occupation. They had, most of them, brought small supplies of salt, nails, axes, ammunition,

[1] Introduction.

and other indispensables along with them from the northward; and probably the later-coming families brought a small surplus which the earlier settlers could buy from them. A few enterprising settlers, furthermore, it seems, made trips to Philadelphia or Baltimore and brought back a few wagon loads of supplies to their neighborhoods. On the whole, the first settlers in the backwoods were self-sufficing to a remarkable degree. The forest and their half-cleared fields provided them with meat and bread; coarse cloth and rude furniture were the product of their homely skill; luxuries were dispensed with. No money was at hand, and the work of clearing land and building cabins kept down the scale of productive industry. For the time being, no efficient demand for commerce was made. The people were in complete isolation.

Such a régime could not long continue among a civilized, industrious, and ambitious people. With clearings once made, the time soon came when the work of a family would produce larger crops of grain and stocks of cattle than the family needed for its own consumption. A surplus arose and demanded a market. The planters in the lowlands were buying these same commodities from abroad at high prices. Trade relations between the uplands and the coast, if at all feasible, would be distinctly of advantage to both sections. A portion of the upland farmers lived near enough the navigable rivers to ship their surplus produce and sell it on the coast. The arrival of goods from the coast in exchange for upland products relieved the backwoodsmen from the need of making all their supplies, and promoted a specialization of industry. It raised the standard of comfort, and impelled the people who dwelt farther inland to discover some means of sharing in the prosperity.

Grain was too heavy to bear the expense of marketing, except from the close neighborhood of navigable waters. Tobacco, flax, hemp, and other crops were tried as experiments in the search for an export commodity for the remoter districts, and tobacco proved in a measure successful. From the close of the American Revolution to the beginning of the nineteenth century, tobacco ranked among the important exports from both South Carolina and Georgia. Tobacco raising for export seems to have begun just at the close of the Revolution. Six hundred and forty-three hogsheads of it were shipped from Charleston in 1783, and in the next year 2680 hogsheads. The volume increased until it reached 9646 hogsheads from Charleston in the year 1799, after which it rapidly declined.[1] The tobacco export from Savannah was probably at all times considerably smaller than from Charleston.

For tobacco carriage on land, in case of necessity, vehicles could be dispensed with. In many instances in this region, as in the Virginia uplands, the owner fitted an axle and a pair of shafts to the tobacco hogshead, hitched to it his horse or steer, and rolled the hogshead on the ground for scores of miles to where it could be sold or transferred to a boat. Where streams were available they were used in preference, even though the current were too swift and turbulent for regular traffic. One or more hogsheads could be loaded on a small boat or raft and floated downstream from the very heart of the Piedmont to where the regular freight boats could pick them up. The very dangerous rapids could be portaged with the aid of a horse borrowed from some near-by farmer.

[1] David Ramsay, *History of South Carolina*, Charleston, 1809, vol. ii, p. 219.

The production of tobacco reached a sufficient volume in its day to call into existence a definite commercial system for the uplands. Inspection of the staple by public officials was necessary for the welfare of the industry, and public warehouses were found a great convenience. The legislatures of these two states, following the example of Virginia, Maryland, and North Carolina, provided for inspection and warehousing at numerous points convenient to the tobacco-producing districts.[1] Some of the points selected were towns with commerce already established, such as Augusta; others were incipient towns whose trade was considerably stimulated by the tobacco business. Of these, Camden, S.C., is an example.[2] The remainder were points which had thereto possessed no trade. A few of these experienced a mushroom growth in commerce, which depended entirely upon the tobacco traffic, and vanished with its disappearance. An example of the short-lived tobacco towns was that of Petersburg,[3] Ga., located at the junction of the Broad River with the Savannah, some thirty miles above Augusta. George Sibbalds in 1800 described Petersburg in a pamphlet as follows: "In point of situation and commercial consequence it is second only to Augusta. . . . It is a handsome, well built Town, and presents to the view of the astonished traveller, a Town which has risen out of the Woods in a few years as if by enchantment: It has two Warehouses for the Inspection of Tobacco."[4] It contained about that

[1] *E.g.* Marbury and Crawford, *Digest of the Laws of Georgia*, Savannah, 1802, pp. 545–553, act of 1791.

[2] Cf. Alexander Gregg, *History of the Old Cheraws*, p. 430 *et passim*.

[3] C. C. Jones, Jr., *The Dead Towns of Georgia*, pp. 233–238.

[4] *Notes and Observations on the Pine Lands of Georgia*, pp. 62, 63.

time some forty stores and perhaps seven or eight hundred inhabitants. Its merchants exchanged general supplies for the tobacco which the farmers brought in, and they themselves depended on the hazardous boating to Augusta and the seaports for selling the staple and replenishing their stocks of goods. This tobacco of the Lower South was not of fine grade, and the price was never particularly high. The cost of marketing from the Piedmont prevented the rise of any substantial profit for the producer. Tobacco was but a makeshift in the absence of a more suitable staple. The spread of cotton culture into the uplands, beginning shortly before 1800, soon completely destroyed the tobacco industry in that quarter, shifted the basis for the organization of commerce, and led to a great intensifying of the problem of transportation. The rise of the great short-staple cotton industry began to give the world of commerce for the first time a concern in the uplands of the Lower South, and gave the people of that district a paramount interest in securing easy connection with the ocean highway.

The surprising profits made by the few inland cotton producers in the closing years of the eighteenth century led the settlers further up country in rapid succession to resort to the great new staple. F. A. Michaux, in his *Travels,* writing in the upper country of South Carolina in 1802, says: "The low price to which tobacco is fallen in Europe within these few years, has made them give up the culture of it in this part of the country. That of greenseed cotton has resumed its place to the great advantage of the inhabitants, many of whom have since made their fortunes by it.[1]" Cotton prices from 1795 to 1805 ranged

[1] *Early Western Travels,* R. G. Thwaites, ed., vol. vi, p. 298.

in the principal markets between forty and twenty cents per pound. Profits were large, and interest widespread and keen. From the sea to the foot of the mountains, from the Potomac to the Indian boundary in Georgia and Tennessee, the talk of the people soon came to be all of cotton, methods of culture, gins, prices, and lands. As rapidly as seed could be had, experiments were made far and wide to test the suitableness of soil and climate. Where the crop was successful, the people bent all their available energy to cotton production; where conditions for cotton were not good, a large number of people gathered up their movable belongings and migrated to established cotton areas, as to a promised land. Many of these new-comers brought gangs of slaves with them from their former plantations, and many of the older settlers, prosperous from a few cotton crops, hastened to buy and bring in slaves of their own. This concentration of effort caused the output of the staple to increase by leaps and bounds.[1] The cotton crop of the United States in 1795 had been about 35,000 bales of 225 pounds each, mostly of the sea-island variety. In 1800 the crop was 155,000 bales, and in 1806, 348,000, of which by far the larger part was of the upland sort.[2] The first decade of the nineteenth century saw the new régime firmly instituted which was to shape the destinies of the South. The actual volume of the industry, however, was still, of course, very small in

[1] For the development of the cotton industry, see Whitemarsh B. Seabrook, *Memoir on Cotton*, Charleston, 1844; M. B. Hammond, *The Cotton Industry*, New York, 1897, ch. iii; E. von Halle, *Baumwallproduktion und Pflanzungswirtschaft*, Leipsic, 1897.

[2] G. L. Watkins, *Production and Price of Cotton for one Hundred Years*, U. S. Department of Agriculture, Washington, 1895.

comparison with what it became in the following decades. The influence of cotton before 1807 was merely incipient. The restrictions on trade from that time, and then the prevalence of war, gave the industry a backset. With the arrival of peace, in 1815, King Cotton may well be said to have begun his reign.

In the early years of cotton culture, the new staple merely continued, in the large, the influence which tobacco had begun. No inspection was required, however, and hence no public warehouses and concentration of stores around them. The cotton gins drew away attention from the tobacco centers. Later the gins became so numerous that each plantation, or at least each neighborhood, had its own, and there were no points of concentrated activity except at the cross-roads stores and those points where transit of goods was broken in their carriage to and from the seaports.

It was said as late as 1818 by Colonel Abraham Blanding, at that time perhaps the best-informed man in the state, that in South Carolina two-thirds of the market crops were raised within five miles of some river, and the remainder not more than ten miles from water which could be rendered navigable.[1] For the transportation of cotton, as of tobacco, watercourses were used in most cases where possible, and the function of the roads was mainly to supplement the rivers. Whether by land or by water, the avenues of travel and commerce long remained extremely crude. Much complaint was made from time to time of the hardships upon men and beasts, the mishaps to vehicles and boats, and the great expenditure of time and effort which the marketing of produce required.

[1] *Niles Register*, vol. xv, p. 135, quoting the *South Carolina Gazette*.

But conditions did not ripen for resorting to the methods of decisive progress until some years after the peace of 1815.

Before studying the more ambitious projects, it is advisable to take a view of the road and river system as developed prior to the War of 1812. The area of South Carolina and Georgia is, of course, our chief concern.

The road system was first devised for the coast region, where the demands for transportation by land were strictly local. With only minor alterations, the same system was later extended into the middle country and the uplands, where the demand for through traffic was steadily increasing. By 1810 the people of the uplands were concerned in the transit of their cotton to the seaports far more than in any neighborhood relations. Through traffic to the coast was essential for their prosperity; and, other things being equal, the quicker and easier that traffic, the greater would be their welfare. The road system as established had inevitable defects for such a case. The basis of the road laws[1] was that of local autonomy for the handling of local problems. It was presumed that through the care of each locality for the roads and rivers in its area, the through routes in their various portions would be sufficiently attended to. Experience with the traffic of the uplands showed that presumption to be ill founded, but led to no important new measures until after 1815.

[1] Thomas Cooper and D. J. McCord, *South Carolina Statutes at Large*, 10 vols., Charleston, 1837–1840; *Acts passed by the General Assembly of the Colony of Georgia*, Wormsloe, 1881; H. Marbury and W. H. Crawford, *Compilation of the Laws of Georgia, 1755–1800*, Savannah, 1802; A. S. Clayton, *Compilation of the Laws of Georgia, 1800–1810*, Augusta, 1813; O. H. Prince, *Digest of the Laws of Georgia*, Athens, 1837.

In the infancy of the colonies, the assemblies had naturally dealt with minor local matters as well as with general legislation. The laying out of specific roads was considered part of the legislature's business. Commissioners were appointed by name in each act, with duties assigned, and with power to require labor to a certain amount from all male inhabitants of certain ages who dwelt within specified districts. As the colonies grew, and affairs became more complex, the assemblies relieved themselves of part of their burden by authorizing the local courts or commissioners to open new local roads at their discretion, and keep their districts' roads in repair by means of a systematic levy of work from all inhabitants who were subject to road duty — usually all males between the years of sixteen and fifty or sixty, except millers, ferrymen, ministers, and sometimes school-teachers, etc. Fines were provided for failure to meet road-work requirements, and other devices were added in some of the acts to increase the power and resources of the road commissioners. Special acts of the legislature were still resorted to from time to time for opening important new highways, until a skeleton system of main roads had been provided. Special enactments were likewise for a long time the resource for the establishment of ferries, causeways, and bridges, and provision for tolls. Not until about 1825 did general legislation put these matters entirely into the hands of the local authorities.[1]

As to the repair of roads, it was throughout the whole period entirely in charge of the local authorities with the

[1] *E.g.* First general road act for South Carolina, enacted 1825, Cooper and McCord, *South Carolina Statutes at Large*, vol. ix, pp. 558–566.

local road levy as the labor supply and the local needs the main incentive to work. The convenience of the people who lived beyond their district and had to pass through it on their way to market, was of less concern to the local road workers than their own needs. Through routes were likely to suffer for repairs wherever they did not coincide with routes which were important to the locality in which they lay.

The distant wagon traffic had its specific difficulty in each section of the country. In the lowlands and parts of the middle country there were swamps and streams requiring causeways, bridges, and ferries, which were likely to be dangerous from want of repair and carelessness in management; in the pine-barrens, great expanses were unpeopled, and the road levies were totally inadequate to the care of the important highways; in the uplands, the frequent washing of gullies in the hillside roads gave more work than the road-hands usually accomplished; and in general, in all gorges and valleys of any sort, the recurrence of great freshets endangered permanent improvements of all sorts.

The regularly established road system was more or less adequate to the needs of strictly local traffic in fair weather. Through traffic, special needs, and emergencies were not provided for by it. To remedy its shortcomings in part, special devices were applied in a number of instances. The chief of these was for the legislature to give to some citizen or company the privilege of building a causeway or bridge, or, after 1800, a turnpike at a specified place, and collecting tolls for the use of it. For example, by an act of 1803, the Georgia legislature contracted with Ebenezer Jenckes to causeway where necessary, and care for the road from Savannah to a point twenty-one miles distant, in Effingham County, and receive pay from tolls, at rates provided in the act, for the term of thirty years.[1]

General Wade Hampton of South Carolina was conspicuously active in building toll bridges, about 1790. One which he owned, crossing the Congaree River at Granby, and another over the Savannah River at Augusta, were destroyed in a great freshet in 1796.[2] A third bridge of Hampton's, in the ownership of which he was in partnership with the notorious James Gunn of Georgia, crossed the Great Ogeechee River. An act of the Georgia legislature in 1800 recited that this bridge was not kept in good repair, and provided remedies for the dereliction of its owners.[3] The largest of all the bridge enterprises was that of the Charleston Bridge Company, chartered in 1808, with the purpose of bridging the broad expanse of the Ashley River a short distance above the city of Charleston.[4] The bridge as built was a trestlework nearly half a mile long, on piles which were sheathed with metal between the high and low water marks, to prevent the destruction of the timbers by cockles. Causeways above a quarter of a mile long at either end of the bridge were a part of the construction. The company expended about $150,000 on the work. It yielded a satisfactory revenue in tolls for about two years, when a great hurricane, on August 27, 1813, swept away the greater portion of the bridge.[5]

[1] Clayton, *Compilation of Georgia Laws*, pp. 145, 146.

[2] Drayton, *View of South Carolina*, pp. 32, 33.

[3] Marbury and Crawford, *Compilation of Georgia Laws*, p. 409.

[4] Cooper and McCord, *South Carolina Statutes at Large*, vol. ix, p. 434.

[5] R. Mills, *Statistics of South Carolina*, Charleston, 1826, pp. 422–423.

The company had not the money nor the courage to rebuild the bridge. Traffic had again to depend upon the services of a ferry at that place, where, with the motive power then available, the plying of boats across the estuary was exasperatingly uncertain. Some years later the Charleston Bridge Company, with the aid of a loan of $10,000 from the legislature, established a horse-power ferry-boat, which plied across the river near the site of the former bridge once every half hour. Just how this "team-boat" was operated, we shall see later.

One of the chief instances of the authorizing of a private turnpike was that of the road through the Saluda Gap. A wagon road from Tennessee had been opened about 1800.[1] A large traffic in horses, hogs, etc., soon began to cross the "Gap," to supply the cotton belt with the products of east Tennessee. The road on the mountain side was not well graded, and was very hard to keep in repair. An act of the South Carolina legislature in 1809 granted to Gabriel Benson the power to lay out and build at his own expense a turnpike road from the Saluda River to the North Carolina boundary, and collect tolls at rates, prescribed in the act, ranging from seventy-five cents for a loaded four-horse wagon, to one cent per head for hogs, sheep, or goats in droves.[2] No record is at hand of Benson's having established his pike. Another act of 1809 gave permission to a company to build a pike in the South Carolina lowlands; but nothing came of it.

The private toll roads and bridges were distasteful to the people,[3] who, while not usually objecting to payment

[1] Drayton, *View of South Carolina*, p. 158.

[2] Cooper and McCord, *South Carolina Statutes at Large*, vol. ix, p. 438.

[3] Drayton, *View of South Carolina*, p. 159.

for the services of ferrymen, balked at paying tribute to invested capital. The system of private works and tolls was merely an emergency device, to tide over the time until a better general system could be instituted.

As to the care of waterways, the system for opening the channels of rivers, etc., and keeping them free from obstruction by logs and sand-banks was wholly analogous to that for the opening and care of roads. An act of the South Carolina assembly as early as 1734 directed the clearing of certain streams for navigation.[1] Commissioners were appointed for each section of each river and authorized to make assessments of labor or money on all persons who lived within certain distances of the waterway, or who were to be benefited by the improvement. Enactments through most of the following century, whether in South Carolina or the neighboring states, followed the general plan set forth in this act of 1734. In some cases, the persons liable for service in clearing the rivers were exempt from road duty. In a few instances, in the early nineteenth century, where considerable money was needed for the work, the commissioners were allowed to establish lotteries for the purpose.[2] To secure the same general purpose, an act of the Georgia legislature in 1799 chartered a stock company to render the Savannah River navigable from Augusta to Petersburg, and to collect tolls on the traffic.[3] A similar act in North Carolina, 1792, amplified in 1796, gave similar powers on the Cape Fear River to the Cape

[1] Cooper and McCord, *South Carolina Statutes at Large*, vol. vii, pp. 482–486.

[2] *E.g.* Clayton, *Compilation of the Laws of Georgia*, p. 66, act of 1802; C. C. Weaver, *Internal Improvements in North Carolina*, p. 49.

[3] Marbury and Crawford, *Compilation of the Laws of Georgia*, p. 371.

Fear Navigation Company, which was chartered by these acts with an authorized capital of $8000.[1] The Savannah Navigation Company seems to have done no work at all. The Cape Fear Company was practically inactive until after 1815.

A later instance was that of the Oconee Navigation Company, chartered by the Georgia legislature in 1810, to improve the navigation of the Oconee River both below and above the fall line at Milledgeville, by locks, dams, canals, or otherwise, and to collect toll at rates fixed by the act on all traffic on the river after the completion of the improvements. Upon the completion of a survey of the stream, and the making of rough estimates of the cost of the work, the directors provided for by this charter were elected by due process at Greensborough in January, 1812. It was then determined that the capital stock of the company should be $30,000, divided into shares and half shares at $25 and $12.50, and that stockholders must be given "a decided preference" in supplying labor and provisions at "a fair price," as needed for the opening of the river. A prospectus was issued, urging the importance of the work, stating that nearly $10,000 had already been subscribed, and pleading for further subscriptions.[2] The approach of the war with Great Britain probably prevented the beginning of work by the company. Before the end of the war the company had disappeared; and in November, 1816, the legislature authorized the holding of a lottery to raise $10,000 for Oconee improvement.[3] By 1815 this

[1] C. C. Weaver, *Internal Improvements in North Carolina,* pp. 50 ff.

[2] *Georgia Express* (Athens, Ga.,) April 24, 1812.

[3] L. Q. C. Lamar, *Compilation of the Laws of Georgia,* p. 493; *Athens Gazette* (Athens, Ga.), March 23, 1815, advertisement of the lottery drawings to occur at Greensborough in November.

device, too, was abandoned, and the state began to make appropriations of money outright for the improvement of the river.[1]

Prior to the War of 1812, the system of caring for the rivers was in general the same as that for the roads, and it inflicted many of the same hardships upon through traffic. None of the rivers were large enough to keep free from serious obstructions from fallen trees and débris except as a result of frequent attention by caretakers. But, as the wagoner confronting a break in a causeway could stop and mend it for his own crossing, so the crew of a pole-boat could likewise free the channel of its river from an impeding log. Traffic by land and by water was slow-going, and was rough-and-ready. Perfect avenues, if not to be had, could be dispensed with. Traffic was still too light in volume before 1815 to make effective demands for expensive systems of improvements. Cotton prices were very high, and labor scarce. Most of the people of the uplands were in a frenzy of eagerness to exploit their opportunity of raising cotton. Every one who could raise cotton in the Carolinas and Georgia could get it to market in some way or other, and the price of the staple would more than pay any charges incurred. In spite of the difficulties, the fall-line towns waxed very prosperous, and Charleston and Savannah developed a very large trade with the uplands by boats and by wagons. For some years, indeed, Charleston had the largest export trade of all the cities on the continent.[2] The general dis-

[1] Lamar, *Compilation*, pp. 500, 513, appropriations of $10,000 each in 1815 and 1816.

[2] For Charleston's wagon trade, etc., see Charles Fraser, *Reminiscences of Charleston*, Charleston, 1854, pp. 12–16.

position was to leave to the future all problems which threatened, by calling for labor, to trench upon the energy which the farmers and planters might apply to the cultivation of their crops. The competition by the Western producers of cotton, which began just after the peace of 1815, was necessary as a spur to the Eastern cotton states to cheapen the cost of marketing their crops through the improvement of the means of transportation.

In view of the thinness of population, in the first decades of the nineteenth century, the dearth of capital, the length of the transit, and the forbidding character of the intervening country, the effective improvement of avenues leading to and from the Piedmont was a staggering task. Prior to the War of 1812, while the down-traffic in cotton was reaching large dimensions, there was effective demand for upward transit from the coast only in salt, sugar, spices, and other light groceries, liquors, and the lighter sorts of manufactures. The tendency to specialize in a staple product had not yet overwhelmed the pioneer system of diversified industry except in the districts close to navigable water. The flour, meal, and pork supply of each farm and plantation was practically all raised at home. The food supplies which were brought into Charleston and Savannah by sea were consumed by the lowlanders and the people of the fall-line trading towns. The demand of the Piedmont people for them had not yet grown strong enough to overcome the obstacles. The country stores in the region were very thinly distributed, and had exceedingly light stocks of merchandise. The commerce of the towns at the head of navigation, indeed, employed only a few pole-boats for each town, to stem the current with light cargoes, and a few dozen wagons, lightly laden, of necessity, but dragged with great labor and delay over the wretched roads. The pole-boats required at least fourteen days to ascend from Savannah to Augusta, for example, and five to seven days for the down trip. Laden wagons could make the trip between the same points in about a week, barring accidents; and stage-coaches in three or four days. So long as the motive power was the labor of men and horses, the up-bound freight charges were prohibitive on all but precious articles.

Aside from the trade with the seaports, the only traffic with which the Piedmont was concerned was that in live stock and sundries which came in slender volume across the Blue Ridge. The cotton country was poorly off for hay crops and grazing, and inferior in the yield of cereals. East Tennessee excelled in these things. The increased employment of negroes in the Piedmont led to a great increase in the use of mules, valuable for their ability to stand neglect and ill treatment as well as hot weather. The mules being an infertile stock, the supply required frequent replenishment from without. Hence the opportunity of the Tennesseeans and even the Kentuckians to cross the mountains with droves of mules and horses and market them with profit in the cotton country. Droves of cattle and even of hogs were also brought at times, and wagons of cured meat, dried vegetables, and the like. Some of the Tennessee wagons would peddle their wares as far down the country as the river towns, and there take on packages of the precious coffee, cloth, gunpowder, etc., for families or merchants in the mountain-locked region whence they came. Most of this traffic was along the French Broad River and through Saluda Gap. Shortly after 1815 the federal government built a road through the

Cherokee country from Athens, through the northwestern part of Georgia to Tennessee, affording a new and cheaper avenue for this traffic, and giving the Georgians perhaps a slight advantage in it over the Carolinians.

Parallel to the coast, the roads of the interior had little long-distance traffic of a steady character except for the stage-coaches with passengers and the mails. In special periods, however, they were used by throngs of home-seekers removing from the older regions to the booming southwest. The east and west roads where under the care of the local authorities were probably in a worse condition than those leading to the coast, because the people of the locality used them less. Where the Indians were still in possession, the United States government opened a few east-and-west roads as, for example, one in 1811 from Milledgeville, Ga., to Fort Stoddert near Mobile. But the activity of the federal authorities generally ended with clearing the route; it did not extend to systematic repairs. These roads were exceedingly crude, and developed no traffic aside from migration.

The demand for traffic between the uplands and the seaports was by 1810 pressing severely upon the existing facilities. The continued and extending prosperity of the cotton producers caused a great increase, not only in the staple output seeking down transportation, but also in the demand for the comforts of life and the appliances for more efficient industry, which could be had only through the channels of external commerce. Betterments in transportation were about to become a vital issue.

The restrictions on commerce and the War of 1812 checked this development and reacted for the time toward self-sufficing economy. The great reduction in the cotton traffic led to a diversion of labor from cotton raising to the cereals and even to hemp and flax for home use, and quite largely to domestic manufactures. The issue of internal improvements was quiescent.

The arrival of peace in 1815 brought a great rise in cotton prices, and a tremendous zeal again for cotton raising. The merits of diversified industry were forgotten. Every one who could plant cotton did so, devoting only the leisure seasons to the tending of food crops. A heavy tide of immigration set in from the Virginia region, and the cotton output again began to increase by leaps and bounds. The traffic facilities were now quickly found to be entirely inadequate to the needs. Transportation on a large scale became for the first time a paramount problem.

A totally new factor in the situtation was the rise of the southwest in effective competition with the Georgia-Carolina Piedmont in cotton production. The lands there were fresh and fertile, the rivers abundant and deep. With high cotton prices, the Southwest was an eldorado. With great chagrin, the older cotton districts found that the westward movement was now flowing past them and carrying with it many of their most enterprising citizens. To check this unwelcome decline, heroic measures of remedy must be discovered and applied. The chief remedy discussed was that of internal improvements, to lessen the cost of marketing. Public sentiment quickly came to favor the investment of public and private capital and the use of public credit in works which were expected to facilitate commerce in all quarters of these states, and to lessen the burdens under which industry was laboring.

Public interest was keenly concerned with projected improvements in both motive power and avenues of transportation. The water system was thought more promising than that by land. The waterways were already carrying the larger portion of through traffic. Cotton piled on flatboats and keel-boats was floated down-stream, guided clear of snags and sand-banks by poles and sweeps in the hands of the crews. The flatboats on these cotton-carrying rivers were usually made on a special plan, with high sides, to accommodate the fleecy cargo, and were colloquially known as cotton-boxes. None of the flatboats could be carried back up-stream, before the time of steamboats, without excessive cost of labor. At the end of the down trip the cotton-boxes were usually sold for lumber. Such up-bound freight as went by water was carried on the pole-boats, each of which had a keel, for better balancing and steering, pointed or rounded bow and stern, for the sake of reduced resistance in the water, and plank ways along each gunwale for the use of the crew in propulsion. The crew, usually of negro slaves, was divided into gangs for starboard and port, and perhaps into shifts alternating work and rest. Each poleman in the gang would in turn walk to the bow, thrust his pole into the water, plant its point against the bottom of the stream, bear against its upper end with his shoulder, and walk from stern to stern, thus forcing the boat forward at the rate of his walking. The simultaneous work of several men on each side, forming a continuous procession, would cause the boat to advance at a fairly steady rate. The captain at the helm would guide the boat with the rudder, or when turning sharp bends might order one gang or the other to leave off shoving, or to shove laterally, as the case might require.

A crew of fifteen or twenty men could pole a boat with several tons of cargo up-stream at the rate of, say, ten miles a day, by hard labor. Any feasible substitute for this extremely laborious method would be highly welcome.

Robert Fulton had launched a workable steamboat as early as 1807. In the next few years, he and others improved the boilers and machinery to such an extent that steamboats became available for commercial traffic. The citizens of the Lower South were alert to apply such inventions to their own needs. In 1816, Samuel Howard of Savannah memorialized the Georgia legislature, stating his wish to adopt a new method of freight traffic upon the Georgia waterway, by towing laden boats by means of other boats propelled by the aid of steam. To encourage the purpose, the legislature, upon Howard's petition, granted him and his associates a monopoly of traffic by steam towing for the term of twenty years, upon all the Georgia waters upon which Howard should actually ply his boats.[1] Howard soon formed a company, which by an act of 1817 was incorporated as the Steam Boat Company of Georgia, with $200,000 capital stock. This company was granted by the act the exclusive privilege of navigating the waters of the state with steamboats, whether for towing or employed alone, during the term of twenty years from the date of this act. On rivers on which the company should fail to ply its boats for periods of stated length, the monopoly privilege should lapse. On the whole the effect of this act was to give and guarantee to the company the privileges already possessed by Howard, its promoter.[2]

Howard had already begun to ply his steamboats on the Savannah River. The beginning of the service, in April,

[1] L. Q. C. Lamar, *Compilation of the Laws of Georgia*, pp. 490–492.

[2] *Ibid.*, pp. 510–512.

1816, was described by the *Savannah Republican* as follows: —

THE STEAMBOAT, *Enterprise,* with a numerous concourse of citizens on board, started from Howard's wharf yesterday morning at 12 o'clock on a party of pleasure. She moved beautifully through the water, and was certainly an interesting curiosity to those who have not seen steam vessels elsewhere. To behold a large and apparently unwieldy machine, without oars or sails, propelled through the element by an invisible agency at a rate of four miles an hour, is indeed a novel spectacle. We understand from the proprietors that the *Enterprise* fully meets their expectations and behaved very well yesterday. Our enterprising townsmen have our very best wishes for so laudable an undertaking.[1]

That the steamboats introduced upon the Savannah by the company were not entirely adapted to the needs is indicated by the following news item from the *Savannah Museum* in June, 1818, which shows the makeshift to which the managers were obliged to resort: —

The Steam Boat *Carolina* started last evening at 6 o'clock with boats Nos. 10 and 12 in tow, being the commencement of the company's summer arrangement, under which the steamboats will ascend the river as high as circumstances will allow them to act with advantage; the tow-boats will then be delivered to hands provided for the purpose, to pole them the remainder of the distance, and the steamboats will be employed a few days in the neighborhood of the place they select to stop at in clearing and improving the river, and will then return here to meet other boats by the time they are loaded; thus affording a double benefit to the public.[2]

An attempt was made by outsiders to compete with the company's steamboats by the use of horse-power in boat propulsion. The device of horse-power had been applied, it appears, as early as 1816. We have mention in 1818 and

[1] Reprinted in the *Athens Gazette,* April 18, 1816.

[2] Reprinted in the *Augusta Chronicle,* June 24, 1818.

again in 1827 of a team-boat, worked by eight horses, plying as a ferry across the Ashley River at Charleston.[1] Timothy Flint mentions a similar ferry at Cincinnati in 1819.[2] Attempts were made with moderate success to ascend the Mississippi and Ohio by the use of teams of horses on board. The only mention of a team-boat on the Savannah River which has come to light is the following news item from the *Augusta Chronicle* of August 25, 1820:—

> The Team Boat, *Genius of Georgia,* Captain Wm. Bird, with a cargo of sundries, left Savannah on Friday 12th inst., and arrived at this port on the morning of the 24th, at 8 o'clock, after being detained at Ebenezer, Greenwood's Bar, and Sand Bar Ferry three days. She draws 30 inches water, and is calculated for 24 horses, but arrived here with five less than her complement.

The South Carolina board of public works in its report for 1820 expressed some reliance in animal power for river navigation. It related an instance of a boat propelled by the labor of eight mules and navigated by five men, which carried 300 bales of cotton 250 miles in 15 days at a cost of $116.25.[3] The method of using the teams was to drive them, hitched to a beam, in a circle on a platform above the main deck. The power was transmitted from the pivot of the beam through gearings to paddle-wheels like those on the steamboats. The use of horse-power continued for some years in ferry service, where the work was intermittent, stabling could be done on land, and

[1] William Faux, *Memorable Days in America,* London, 1823, p. 50; *Georgia Courier,* October 11, 1827, anonymous letter of a traveler, entitled "A Plague o' this Cotton."

[2] *Letters from America,* in Thwaites, *Early Western Travels,* vol. ix, p. 149.

[3] *North American Review,* vol. xiii, pp. 150, 151.

a food supply need not be carried on board. But for through traffic, team-boats never passed the experimental stage. They are now a long-forgotten expedient whose name occurs in the travelers' accounts only to puzzle the reader. From "team-boats" the steamboat monopoly on the Savannah had nothing to fear. From the original pole-boats and cotton-boxes, however, it suffered injurious competition, heightened by the fact that the company's steamboats were of too great a draft for really efficient service on the river.

In the *Georgia Journal*, a Milledgeville newspaper, there was printed, April 17, 1821, a schedule of the property, debts, credits, etc., of the Steam Boat Company of Georgia, which shows the company to have become insolvent. According to the schedule, the company then owned six steamboats, which had cost from $29,500 to $50,000 each, thirty-one freighting boats and twenty lighters, barges, etc., thirty-five negro slaves, cost $30,410, real estate, a dry dock, a quantity of coal, a dairy, and sundry other property, making a total cost of property of $543,143.31. The receipts, stated apparently for the past seven months, amounted to $83,302.27, and expenditures for the same period to $77,256.93, leaving as profit $6,045.34. The receipts included down freight collected, $48,459.59, and up freights collected, $31,175.38.

Bills payable amounted to $129,331, and bills receivable, to but $29,074.29, and cash on hand to $1,808.66. The company was operating to but a small book profit, while its property was depreciating in value. To meet the cost of its property, for which the company had obligated itself to the amount of $543,143.81, there was paid-in capital amounting only to $417,600, leaving a deficit, after deducting profits, of $119,498.47.

No record is at hand of the sale of the company's property and franchise; but from a later mention of existing conditions it seems that the control of the Georgia company's boats and monopoly passed into the hands of capitalists in Charleston, who shortly began to use the advantage which this gave in directing the trade of the Savannah River to Charleston.[1] The monopoly enjoyed by the company on the Savannah River under the Georgia law of 1817 was precisely similar to that which the New York legislature had granted on the Hudson River and which was brought into question by the celebrated case of Gibbon *v.* Ogden. The decision of the United States Supreme Court in that case, by invalidating the Hudson River monopoly, destroyed also the monopoly steamboat privilege on the Savannah. In this way, much to the gratification of the Georgians, the trade of the Savannah River, by this time a subject of much dispute, was again laid open to free competition.[2]

The purpose of the Charlestonians was, by controlling the Savannah River steamboats in the interests of Charleston trade, to have the boats extend their voyage from that river onward through the coastal waterways to Charleston, thus making the town of Savannah a mere way-station on the through route from Augusta to Charleston and return. So long as Charleston interests controlled the steamboat monopoly, this plan could be carried out with some success by establishing a through rate on a basis lower than that of the rate to Savannah. That success in diverting trade from Savannah was modified in part by the steamboat company's failure to subordinate completely

[1] *Savannah Republican,* March 29, 1824, editorial.
[2] *Ibid.*

its desire for profits to the city's desire for the traffic, and further by the ability of pole-boats, etc., to compete in the local traffic and check any disposition to cut Savannah out of the trade of the area tributary to the river which it naturally commanded. The destruction of the steamboat monopoly in 1824 enabled all who would to launch steamboats on the river. The control of the original "Steam Boat Company of Georgia" seems soon afterward to have been disposed of by the Charlestonians. The boats of that company had proven to be too deep of draft for successful use in the dry months, and whether through boiler explosions, destruction by snags, or sale to other parties, the number of craft on the river owned by that company declined, until in 1833 it had only two steamboats and seventeen towboats. Meanwhile another Charleston company had established a new line of steamers of lighter draft, which plied over the full course from Augusta to Charleston. From certain resolutions adopted by the Georgia legislature in 1820 and 1824, it appears that between those years the state held stock and mortgage bonds of the Steam Boat Company of Georgia to the amount of $100,000 as a part of the invested internal improvement fund, but in 1824 released the stock and bonds apparently at something of a sacrifice.[1]

A conspicuous item in the effort of Charleston to encroach on Savannah's area was the founding of the town of Hamburg. In this project, as in most others, the State of South Carolina made the cause of Charleston its own, and gave all encouragement to her efforts.

The city of Augusta, which handled the whole trade of the upper basin of the Savannah River and much of the

[1] Dawson, *Compilation*, Resolutions, pp. 3, 40.

adjacent territory, happened to lie on the Georgia side of the river. It comported ill with South Carolina's pride and Charleston's ambition to have a large part of the state pay commercial tribute to an outside market.

Henry Shultz, formerly a resident of Augusta, moved to the Carolina side of the river about 1820, and bought a large tract of land with a water frontage, lying opposite Augusta and a mile or two down-stream. Here he surveyed town lots in the early months of 1821, and named the place Hamburg. At the beginning of July he began to erect a cotton warehouse and other buildings, to attract the cotton crop in the fall, and to induce a mercantile and industrial population to develop a permanent market town to rival Augusta. When the South Carolina legislature convened in the autumn, Shultz presented a memorial of his doings and his plans. He pointed out the benefit which might be expected to accrue to the state from the growth of his town, proposed an alliance with the Charleston interests by means of low freight rates and mercantile connections, and in aid of his general scheme asked of the legislature a loan of $50,000 for five years on security, without interest. He was able to show that before the first of December he had built a town of eighty-four houses, in which he had settled forty-four families comprising upwards of two hundred persons; and further that 3600 bags of cotton had been entered at his warehouse.[1] Mr. Shultz, "a manufacturer of cities," was esteemed "a very useful citizen" by public opinion in South Carolina.[2] A joint committee to which the memorial

[1] *Georgia Journal,* December 25, 1821, news letter from Columbia, S.C.

[2] *Ibid.*

was referred reported in favor of granting it; and accordingly the general appropriations act of that year included provision for the loan of $50,000 as requested.[1] The legislature in further encouragement of Hamburg exempted the town from every sort of taxation for five years, and authorized the establishment of a bank.[2]

At the end of 1821 Shultz advertised the attractions of his town in all the South Carolina papers, and in those of Savannah and Augusta.[3] By the middle of 1823 the town had about two hundred houses and six hundred inhabitants. Shultz ran short of money and met many embarrassments; but managed to sustain in some measure the progress of his town.[4] At the end of 1824 he advertised that, beginning on January 18, 1825, and continuing from day to day thereafter, he would sell three hundred improved and unimproved town lots in Hamburg to the highest bidders. Payments could be made in the notes of the Bank of Hamburg or of other banks named, or in Shultz's individual notes. Purchasers of unimproved lots would be required to improve thereon.[5] On the first two days of the sale, fifty lots, some of them with houses, were sold for a total of $38,370. There remained to be sold 563 lots, on which there were 296 houses.[6] These appear to have proved a drug on the market.

By this time a rift had begun between Shultz and his Charleston allies. On the one hand, Hamburg had failed

[1] Cooper and McCord, *South Carolina Statutes at Large*, vol. vi, p. 175.

[2] *Niles' Register*, vol. xxiv, p. 146 (May 10, 1823).

[3] *Charleston City Gazette*, January 1, 1822.

[4] *Niles' Register*, vol. xxviii, p. 322 (July 23, 1825).

[5] *Charleston City Gazette*, January 21, 1825.

[6] *Ibid.*, January 26, 1825.

to cut seriously into Augusta's control of the trade of the district; and on the other, the Charlestonians had failed to provide two forty-thousand-dollar steamboats which had been promised, perhaps informally, to ply exclusively from Hamburg. Shultz's debt of $50,000, secured by a mortgage on the town of Hamburg, together with an additional loan of $25,000 on bond with personal security, was due for payment at the end of 1826. In December of that year Shultz memorialized the legislature, attempting to show that the money loaned him had resulted in more benefit to the state than the much greater sums devoted to the building of canals and turnpikes. The assembly ignored the memorial, and by a resolution of December 11 directed the controller-general to foreclose the mortgage and obtain judgment on the bond.[1] Most of the money was forthcoming from Shultz's friends, however, and proceedings against him were suspended.

Shultz and the Hamburg people felt outraged at their treatment by the South Carolina assembly and resolved to retaliate by carrying the trade of the town to Savannah instead of Charleston. The erratic Shultz held a meeting of the citizens of Hamburg, January 29, 1827, who after discussion resolved unanimously, "That the citizens of Hamburg, S.C., have not given their indentures to the state of South Carolina, nor to the city of Charleston, and that they are at liberty to trade whithersoever it be their interest; whether it be to Savannah, Charleston, New York, or elsewhere."[2]

The remaining history of Shultz's enterprise is fragmentary. We have a letter from Shultz to the editor of

[1] *Georgia Statesman* (Milledgeville, Ga.), February 6, 1827.
[2] *Georgia Statesman*, February 6, 1827.

the *Georgia Courier* (Augusta), written from the Edgefield jail, where he had been imprisoned on some charge, stating that a recent sale of the town of Hamburg for $22,000 to a Charleston company was illegal, and his own company was in legal possession of both the town and the money.[1] The facts in the case are not clear. As a conclusion to the whole matter the South Carolina legislature, December 20, 1832, directed the solicitor-general to convey to Shultz or his assigns all right and title possessed by the state to the town of Hamburg, upon his being satisfied that Shultz shall have paid $16,225 into the state treasury.

As indicating the later attitude of Shultz toward the promotion of Charleston projects, we have a brief advertisement inserted in the Charleston papers in the spring of 1829, while the Charlestonians were using every resource and striving to enlist all possible enthusiasm for carrying through the projected Charleston and Hamburg Railroad to completion. A number of steamboats were advertising for cargoes from Charleston to Augusta. In the same columns, Shultz paid for advertising space and inserted the following:—

> ☞ Here are the boats, where is the freight? Does this look like a railroad is wanting?

Shultz soon disappeared from the scene. Hamburg continued a humdrum existence, gradually losing trade to its more efficient competitor, Augusta. Charleston and Savannah continued their strife for the trade of the debatable territory, as will appear below in the history of the railroad enterprises.

[1] *Georgia Courier*, December 17, 1827.

The use of steamboats on the Savannah River, after the period of greatest activity in the early twenties, declined as a result of frequent droughts and the consequent inability of the boats to reach Augusta in the long seasons of low water. Cotton-boxes and pole-boats swarmed on the river in 1827,[1] for example, and crippled the steamboat traffic. The fault was attributed at the time to the narrowness of beam and consequent deep draft of the steamboats.[2] No thoroughgoing steps were taken to remedy this fault, however, for many years afterward. At length, in 1856, the "Fashion Line" introduced a boat of iron construction on a new model with specially broad beam and shallow draft. This boat was 180 feet long, 65 feet wide, driven by stern wheels. Her draft without cargo was twelve inches;[3] when laden with a thousand bales of cotton, she would draw two feet of water, and with two thousand bales, three feet. By that time, however, the operation of the railroads had reduced the water traffic to distinctly minor consequence. Meanwhile some effort had been expended in improving the river channel, as will appear below.

We must now turn to the projects for the general improvement of the avenues of transportation which characterized the period following the peace of 1815, and more particularly that following the panic of 1819, which brought home to the eastern cotton belt its disadvantages in the competition with the western areas.

[1] *Georgia Courier*, June 25, 1827.

[2] *Ibid.*, June 28, 1827.

[3] *Augusta Constitutionalist*, quoted in the *Atlanta Intelligencer*, July 11, 1856.

SOUTH CAROLINA PUBLIC WORKS, 1815-1830

In the so-called era of good feeling, large projects of general "internal improvement" were the order of the day. In the Southern group of states, South Carolina was a headlong leader in this movement. South Carolina never undertook anything by halves, although she left many things half done, and thereby wasted her efforts.

After considerable discussion in the press and among the people and the politicians, in which it appeared that nearly every part of the state wanted some improvement for its traffic, the legislature enacted, in December, 1818, the following statute: —

> Whereas, it is expedient to appropriate one million dollars for the Internal Improvements of the State.
>
> I. Be it therefore enacted . . . That the faith of the State is hereby pledged to appropriate and set apart one million dollars for the Internal Improvement of the State, and that the sum of two hundred and fifty thousand dollars, annually, be, and the same is hereby appropriated for the term of four years, to be paid out of the annual balances in the treasury, and from the yearly dividend of the Bank of the State of South Carolina.
>
> II. And be it further enacted . . . That the said sum of two hundred and fifty thousand dollars per annum, for the term of four years, shall be laid out and expended in improving the navigation of the rivers and other water courses of the State, in opening and constructing turnpike roads, in cutting canals, and in such other works as will facilitate the transportation of the production of the soil to market, in such manner as may be prescribed by the legislature.[1]

The text of the act indicates its character as an "omnibus bill." Another act of the same session directed the

[1] Cooper and McCord, *South Carolina Statutes at Large*, vol. vi, pp. 91, 92.

civil and military engineer of the state to devise and adópt all means he should deem expedient for opening certain specified rivers.

A year later, the legislature enacted a law establishing a state board of public works, to control the expenditure of the appropriation and to exercise very wide powers in the improvement of transportation avenues.[1] The board was to consist of five members, to be chosen by the legislature. Its duties were to collect facts, and facilitate and effect the improvements which should be authorized by the legislature. It was empowered to appoint officers, receive and expend moneys, make regulations for tolls, etc., and to build works through contractors, or by direct employment of laborers, or by any other method at its discretion. The act directed the board to lay off and make a great road from Charleston and Columbia and thence along the ridge between Broad and Saluda rivers, across Saluda Mountain, to the North Carolina boundary; also to improve the Pee Dee River to the North Carolina line, the Santee, Wateree, Catawba, Broad, and Saluda rivers and their tributaries, and the smaller rivers, so far as expedient; and in conjunction with Georgia commissioners to improve the Savannah and Keowee; also to inquire into the feasibility of canals between the Savannah and the Edisto, the Savannah and the Broad, and the Edisto and Ashley rivers; and, finally, to cause to be made accurate topographical surveys of every part of the state, to report on the condition of the roads and rivers, and to recommend further plans. The board was to comprise two engineers on salary, and three public-spirited citizens serving without pay.

[1] Cooper and McCord, *South Carolina Statutes at Large*, vol. vi., pp. 124 ff., act of December 18, 1819.

A canal was contemplated as a substitute for the proposed turnpike from Charleston to Columbia, and supported with warmth by a few enthusiasts [1]; but was not adopted by the board of public works nor by the legislature.

During the year 1819, when the public works were in charge of the state civil and military engineer, perhaps as many as four hundred men were employed on six or eight

[1] This project received a brief mention in *Niles' Register*, December 15, 1821 (xxi, 244). It is explained and advocated at great length by Robert Mills, an engineer on the Board of Public Works, in a pamphlet of 93 pages entitled *Inland Navigation: Plan for a great Canal between Charleston and Columbia, and for connecting our Waters with those of the Western Country*, Charleston, 1821. Mills here proposes that the canal of a mile or two in length already decided upon at Columbia be extended in a viaduct across the Congaree river, and thence for 110 miles to Charleston. This would provide a splendid highway, and incidentally drain swamps, provide irrigation, supply water power for mills at various points, check the overflow of rivers, and furnish Charleston with pure drinking water. It could also supply water to the Santee canal, at that time deprived of half its usefulness through shortage of water. By this great canal, freight could be brought from Columbia to Charleston in twelve hours. The expense of building he estimated at $8000 per mile for excavation, making $880,000 for the 110 miles; Congaree aqueduct, $60,000; other aqueducts, dams, and culverts, $40,000; locks, $60,000; contingencies, 10 per cent, $90,000; total, $1,130,000. If the canal were built by the state, there need be no tolls charged. The writer discusses the resources of the state; and then branches out, northwestward. He thinks the canal might well be carried on across the Blue Ridge, and on to the Ohio River, and in that case thinks it would compete favorably with the Mississippi River. He then takes still further flights; prophesies that the waters of the Missouri and Columbia rivers will soon be connected, and those of the Ohio with the Great Lakes, the copper district, Lake Nipissing, and James Bay. The Charleston-Columbia canal would then share in the spice trade of Asia and the fur trade of Canada. Maintaining always his fine disregard of details, Mills concludes by saying that the minutiæ must be left to be worked out by the engineers.

rivers, removing logs and other light obstructions, and beginning a projected system of canals and sluices on the Saluda and Broad rivers.[1]

Aside from the turnpike through Saluda Gap, and the general work of clearing out logs, etc., the board of public works, from 1820 to 1822, concerned itself chiefly with building canals, dams, and locks at and above the "fall line" on the Wateree and the Congaree and its branches. The falls of the Wateree, at Rocky Mount above Camden, presented one of the greatest problems. The falls and rapids were eight miles long, with a total descent of seventy-eight feet.[2] At Columbia, the Broad and Saluda rivers joining to form the Congaree, all were full of rapids for a mile or more above and below the town. The fall was not so great as at Rocky Mount, but the problem was complicated by the forking of the stream in the midst of the rapids. The plan adopted was to dam the Saluda at the head of the falls; carry a canal thence across to the Broad River, on which a descent was to be made by locks to the middle of the falls; there to build another dam, and thence a canal of three miles, with locks, descending to the steamboat landing near Granby.[3] In 1820 the board, it was said, had not less than a thousand Northern laborers employed on its various works.[4]

Colonel Blanding and Mr. Poinsett, the leading spirits in the board of public works,[5] presented to the governor a large plan of public works in various quarters, the cost of which, according to their estimates, would be covered

[1] *Augusta Chronicle*, September 8, 1819.

[2] *North American Review*, vol. xiii, pp. 143–154.

[3] *Ibid.*

[4] *Ibid.*

[5] Cf. C. J. Stillé, *Life of Joel R. Poinsett*, Philadelphia, 1888, p. 30.

by the original one-million-dollar appropriation.[1] But at the end of 1822, when the million dollars had been spent, the board was obliged to make a report of far less progress than it had expected, and to ask a further appropriation of a quarter of a million to finish the principal works undertaken, to say nothing of the minor tasks which were incomplete.[2] Public dissatisfaction with the work of the board had already found expression in several quarters and now became quite general. The *Cheraw Gazette*, the chief newspaper of the Pee Dee region, reported on May 18, 1822, that the steamboat *Maid of Orleans*, with 150 tons of freight, mostly for merchants in North Carolina, was aground on a shoal in the river. The editor used the incident to scold the board. Had only three inches of the shoal been removed, he stated, the boat would have passed over clear; the people of the Pee Dee country were being called upon each year to pay taxes to be wasted in part by the board of public works in futile projects on the rivers at Columbia.[3] A writer signing himself "Civis," in the *Charleston City Gazette*, January 29, 1823, protested against the projected further expenditure at Columbia and Rocky Mount. The works which the "canal clique" were urging, he thought, would never pay for themselves, and would fail to lower the freightage appreciably on any very important portion of the cotton output. The policy, he declared, was "extravagant, abominable, useless, and ridiculous."

A committee of the legislature had reported, early in December, that the prevailing dissatisfaction with the

[1] *Charleston City Gazette*, January 29, 1823.

[2] *Ibid.*

[3] Editorial, reprinted in *Charleston City Gazette*, May 25, 1822.

board had arisen largely from misinformation, though there were a few cases of dereliction of duty by contractors and agents, and the work far less advanced than had been expected. To put as good a face as possible upon the matter, the committee explained that the works thus far had been experimental and expectations had been too high. Besides the actual building of some canals and other improvements, it said, the state had been benefited by the incoming of industrious white laborers and mechanics, by the gaining of experience for further work on a sounder basis, and by the stimulation of private enterprise in various directions.[1]

By an act of December 21, 1822, the legislature abolished the board of public works, and provided in its place a superintendent of public works, to be elected annually by the legislature, to have all the powers and duties of the former board, except as limited by this act, and to give bond for $50,000, for the faithful performance of his duty. He was to receive a salary of $3000, to appoint and remove at pleasure an engineer for whose skill and conduct he should be responsible, and to commence no work in future except after full examination by himself or the engineer, report to the legislature with detailed estimates, and orders from the legislature for its undertaking.[2] Thereafter specific appropriations were made by the legislature for specified works; and each undertaking was required to be let by contract to the lowest bidder.

The canals and locks at Columbia were completed in January, 1824,[3] without further appropriations. The

[1] *Charleston City Gazette,* December 11, 1822; text of the report.

[2] Cooper and McCord, *South Carolina Statutes at Large,* vol. vi, p. 189.

[3] *Savannah Republican,* February 17, 1824.

locks and sluices higher up the Saluda River were finished in 1825,[1] and it was then possible for a boat laden with forty bales of cotton to descend from Cambridge, near Abbeville, all the way to Charleston, passing three canals and ten locks on the Saluda, one canal and five locks on the Congaree, and the thirteen locks of the Santee Canal — making a total lock descent of 207 feet.[2] A high freshet in December, 1824, had tested the strength of the dams, and proved them good.[3] The turnpike roads from the Saluda and Green rivers through the mountain "gaps" to the North Carolina boundary were also completed without further appropriations.

By an act of 1828, the legislature fixed the rates of toll on all the state-owned canals, except that at Columbia, as follows: for each empty boat, 12½ cents; for each raft of timber, 25 cents; for boats laden with cotton, 1 cent for each bale for each lock except the guard lock; for boats otherwise laden, 37½ cents; boats laden with less than one ton of cargo or thirteen bales of cotton to pass as empty boats. The rates on the Columbia Canal were somewhat higher.[4] The major appropriations of the first six years under the new régime, after 1822, were devoted to the Wateree River. A total of nearly $95,000 was laid out on the "Wateree Canal," in four years, and nearly $200,000 in six years on the Rocky Mount Canal and sluices on the Wateree above. The river improvements next in importance were on the Great Pee Dee, where some $21,000 was expended in 1823–1825. As indicating the success

[1] *Charleston City Gazette*, November 19, 1825.

[2] *Charleston City Gazette*, March 23, 1825.

[3] *Charleston City Gazette*, January 1, 1825.

[4] Cooper and McCord, *South Carolina Statutes at Large*, vol. vi, pp. 368 ff.

of the work on the Pee Dee, we have a news item from the *Cheraw Spectator* of January 5, 1827, that a company had purchased the steamboat *North Carolina*, which was then plying on the Cape Fear River, and would run it regularly between Cheraw and Charleston. The boat was said to be well adapted for the Pee Dee service, carrying a large cargo with a maximum draft of but three feet nine inches.[1] The Pee Dee had been improved without the use of canals, and therefore could be used by fairly large steamboats. Where canals and locks were resorted to, however, nothing as wide as the usual river steamer could be used. The locks at Columbia were a hundred feet long and sixteen feet wide, with a nine-foot lift.[2] All the others in the state were shorter than these, and some of them narrower. They were adapted, of course, to towboats only.

In addition to these major projects, a number of improvements in minor waterways were provided for from time to time by appropriations ranging from five hundred to several thousand dollars. These were largely of the nature of log-rolling appropriations, it would seem, and resulted in little benefit to navigation.[3]

The work of the board and the superintendent of public works in improvement of transportation by land remains to be treated. The mountain turnpikes from Saluda and Green rivers to the North Carolina line were small affairs, and isolated from the main field of interest. The causeway at Buckhead on the Saltketcher, built in 1825–1826, was useful in shortening the road from Charles-

[1] Reprinted in the *Charleston City Gazette,* January 9, 1827.

[2] R. Mills, *Statistics of South Carolina,* Charleston, 1826, p. 705.

[3] See table, *infra,* p. 91.

APPROPRIATIONS BY THE SOUTH CAROLINA LEGISLATURE FOR INTERNAL IMPROVEMENTS, 1818 TO 1838

(Compiled from the Statutes)

1818–1822, four years, $250,000 per year, to be expended in the state at large, at the discretion of a board of public works. In 1822 that board was replaced by a superintendent, and thereafter appropriations were made specifically to local projects.

	1823	1824	1825	1826	1827	1828	1829
State Road, Charleston to Columbia	19,631	14,200	12,493	10,000 & tolls	21,083	21,532	
Wateree Canal	18,000	30,000	28,978	18,000			
Rocky Mount Canal and river above	12,000	20,000	14,788	40,000	56,000	56,000	
Landford Canal		3,000	6,107				
Catawba Canal		1,780					
Saluda Canal and sluices		3,042	600	652			
Columbia Canal		785	935				
Broad River sluices		500		5,081			
Camden road and Santee causeway					4,000	4,615	4,709
North & South Edisto rivers	2,500		3,000				
Seneca & Keowee rivers	6,000						
Great Pee Dee River	10,000	11,050					
Little Pee Dee River	2,000		1,500				
Black River			3,000				
Waccamaw River	2,000		1,500				
Lynch's Creek	1,000						
Broad & Pacolet Rivers	4,000						
Elliott's Cut				3,500	7,000	6,000	
Buckhead causeway			2,100				
Wando & Winyaw Canal							3,591

In 1830 and 1831 no appropriations were made, and likewise in 1833, 1834, and 1835. In 1832 $1,892.20 was appropriated to Elliott's Cut, and $10,000 to locks at Grave's Shoals. In 1836 $7,000 was appropriated for works on Wateree River, $20,000 for Vance's Swamp, $3,000 for Lynch's Creek, and $2,500 for Socastee Creek. In 1837, $25,000 for Wateree River, $10,000 for Vance's Swamp, $10,000 for the Pee Dee rivers, $35,000 for Saltketcher River, $3,000 for Black Mingo Creek, and $2,000 for Lake Swamp, Horry district. In 1828, $2,600 was given to Lockhart's Canal.

ton to Hamburg by about twenty miles, but it was also of small consequence as a state work.

The focal road-building project of South Carolina through the decade of the twenties was the projected "State Road," from Charleston to Columbia. This road was to be made a turnpike for most of the distance, with numerous causeways, culverts, embankments, etc. Work upon it was begun by the board of public works; but most of the construction was done during the régime of the superintendent. Between 1823 and 1828, nearly $100,000, with tolls added, was appropriated by the legislature for the furtherance of this project. As the several sections of the road were completed, toll-gates were established, with rates of toll fixed, as a rule, by the legislature. The standard rates for these gates, as for most of the other toll-gates on state-owned pikes and causeways in South Carolina, was on the basis of 12½ cents for a man on horseback, 12½ cents for each horse drawing vehicles, 6¼ cents for each pedestrian, 2 cents for horses and mules in droves, and for cattle, and 1 cent each for hogs, sheep, and goats. On the Charleston-Columbia pike, when completed, there were to be eight toll-gates, each with the standard rates, except the one nearest Charleston, which should collect double the standard rate.[1]

The several toll-gates were leased to the highest bidders, with security. Each lessee was required to keep his section of the road in good repair at his own expense, except in case of disaster to the larger bridges and culverts, occurring through no fault of his own. In such cases, the lessee might require labor to the amount of twelve

[1] Cooper and McCord, *South Carolina Statutes at Large*, vol. vi, p. 368.

days in the year from all inhabitants and their slaves living within five miles of the toll-gate and accepting the exemption from tolls which they might claim.[1]

The toll exemptions were as follows: the armies and army teams of the United States, of the state of South Carolina, and of sister states, ministers of the gospel, legislators and jurymen going to and from their duties and other persons traveling on public business, and finally all persons living within five miles of the toll-gate and traveling not above five miles therefrom, with their servants, cattle, etc.[2] An act of 1828 further exempted all persons going to or from divine worship. By the same act, any person using a state toll-road and going round a toll-gate or refusing to pay toll was made liable to a penalty of ten times the toll due from him.

Beginning at the Charleston end, and progressing toward the interior, the work on the state road was continued until 1829, when, presumably, it was completed. Meanwhile a similar state turnpike and causeway was begun in 1827, branching northeastward from the main road and crossing the great Santee swamp in the direction of Camden. Some $13,000 was devoted to this between 1827 and 1830. The only other road-building enterprise of importance, by the state, was a causeway branching from the main state road and crossing Vance's swamp. To this $30,000 was appropriated in 1836–1837.

The main state road was a demonstrated failure almost before it was completed. The road seems never at any time to have been in prime condition throughout its length;

[1] Act of December 17, 1824, Cooper and McCord, *South Carolina Statutes at Large*, vol. ix, pp. 545–549.

[2] *Ibid.*, vol. vi, p. 381.

the tolls, amounting to nine dollars for a four-horse wagon on the round trip from Columbia to Charleston and return, were more than the advantage was ordinarily esteemed to be worth; the continued westward movement of the Piedmont population prevented the increase of the total traffic density; and the competition of the parallel river-and-canal traffic hindered the growth of the turnpike's relative importance. Even by land, most of the traffic followed the old free roads, alternating in sand-beds, mud-holes, and crude corduroy patches, in preference to the ill-repaired toll-road. Nothing more than the news of the successful operation of iron railways with steam locomotive power, in England, was necessary to give the *coup de grâce* to the turnpike enterprise in South Carolina. Appropriations to the state road were discontinued in 1829, and the pike soon fell into complete neglect.

A writer in the *Southern Review* of May, 1831, described the ills which the building of a railroad from Charleston to the uplands might be expected to remedy. The climate, he said, presents an obstacle of no small magnitude to transportation either for goods or persons, for at least three months in the year. The rivers are unhealthy and often too low; the roads are sandy, heavy, and hot; the laborers and the draft animals are reluctant and often sink beneath their tasks; the traveler meets these same difficulties, and is frequently made sick even unto death as he heavily and slowly moves through the pontine marshes of the alluvial country.[1]

In spite of these hardships in crossing the pine-barrens, the route through Columbia and Camden and the port of Charleston to the outside world was used for the whole

[1] *Southern Review,* vol. vii, p. 188.

external traffic of an area extending as far northward as the middle of North Carolina.[1] Some of this freightage was carried in the wagons of the producers to the inland centers, Columbia and Camden, and some by a class of custom wagoners, hauling more or less regularly as common carriers. Part of the wagon trade stopped at the head-of-navigation points, where their produce was sold or exchanged for supplies; part was hauled by the original teams all the way to Charleston, camping by night along the road, and halting at established wagon yards in the city of Charleston. By reason of the press of work on the farms, and the heat, malaria, and depth of sand on the roads, the trip to the coast was rarely made except in fall and winter. In the spring, and particularly in summer, the roads crossing the pine-barrens were devoid of teams, the rivers without boats, the Charleston wagon-yards vacant, and the supply stores there without customers. Tillage required the work of every available man and beast, and trade and transportation must await the leisure season. Neither the building of pikes nor the clearing of river channels could alter the general conditions of industrial life nor essentially change the prevailing system of commercial economy.

In fact, the system of state appropriations to miscellaneous "improvements," the building of a few ill-constructed turnpikes and the removal or circumvention of a few river obstructions, was a tinkering enterprise — an attempt to transform a totally inefficient system into an efficient one by means of patching over the bad places. By water, the rivers were too small in volume, too tortuous, and too often broken by rapids to be made the basis of a sure and

[1] Cf. Mills, *Statistics of South Carolina*, p. 545.

rapid transportation system. By land, the distances to Charleston were too great for traffic ever to reach a cheap and satisfactory basis so long as horses continued to be relied upon for motive power. The whole scheme of road and river improvements was a makeshift, pending the invention and introduction of other more effective methods. The plan must have been recognized at the time as a makeshift in the sober thought of all except the visionaries. The name of the visionaries was legion, however; and with the men of balanced minds, the fact was pressing that the economic situation was critical. Something must be done to give relief, or at least the hope of relief, from the severity of Western competition, and thus to check the exodus from the state and the commercial decline of its metropolis.

There was a good deal of opposition at the time to the use of state funds for rivers and roads, just as there was in the following decades to the large state aid to railroads. Some of the conservatives consistently opposed each project of this character as it arose, and though often defeated, were never conquered. One of these, with the *nom de plume*, "Anti-debt," reviewed the history of the state's activities in this connection in a series of letters to the *Charleston Mercury* in the autumn of 1848, under the heading, "The Railroad Mania."

The good state of South Carolina, said he, seems subject to periodical fits of monomania about internal improvements. The first serious development of the tendency began about 1817, when she created the office of civil and military engineer and authorized surveys and preliminary work. The fever quickly heightened. In 1818 she appropriated a million dollars to be spent in four years, and planned to carry by every man's door a canal, turnpike, or navigable stream, to annihilate the cost of freight and travel. In 1822 many improvements had been begun; and heavy appropriations were continued seven or eight years longer. Then the legislature incontinently backed out, refused to give more money, and ordered all unexpended balances to be returned to the treasury. But during the fever, two million dollars had been spent for public works, and $1,550,000 of it was borrowed money which was not repaid till from 1840 to 1846, when the United States surplus revenue gave timely aid. These public works, he said, have been complete failures: on the canals few boats ever floated, and those few are now rotting from disuse; the obstructions in the rivers have mostly returned again; the turnpikes are largely in disuse; the chief relic of the mania is now the office of engineer, which each year is squabbled for in the legislature. The fevers, he continued, seem periodical; they have always been accompanied with a change in the price of cotton; log-rolling in the legislature causes the combination of projects in various sections of the state in the fever periods. Some, as he recollected, were conservative in 1817 and predicted the failure of the public works, but were unheeded as blind to the "spirit of progress"; the ruinous extravagance was checked only by the sad disappointment of the people and their rising against it. He then proceeds to discuss the successive railway ventures of the state in much the same strain, and concludes by warning the state against projects on foot at the time of his writing.[1]

[1] Appeared first in the *Charleston Mercury*, in 16 numbers, beginning October 21, 1847. Reprinted as a pamphlet of 52 pages, Charleston, 1848.

Afterthought is always surer than forethought. Whether it was sound policy, according to the light of the times, for South Carolina to embark so largely as she did upon improvements, is perhaps not to be settled offhand, and is no problem of ours to determine. The historical facts are, that the traffic on the canals and pikes was never large; the project of railroads soon entirely diverted legislative sentiment and completely stopped appropriations; the pikes, canals, sluices, etc., soon fell into greater or less neglect, partly because of their original ineffectiveness and partly because the railroads, when built, drew away their traffic. The disuse of the various works was gradual, and its steps can hardly be recorded.

After 1829, turnpikes and the more costly bridges were built, like the railroads, by private companies, sometimes with state aid through subscriptions to stock. In fact, in 1838 the legislature so far reconsidered its withdrawal from turnpike enterprises as to promise by enactment that whenever any turnpike company should organize, subscribe three-fifths of the estimated cost of its projected road, and furnish plans and convince the legislature of the expediency of the road, the reasonableness of the estimate, and the *bona fide* character of the subscriptions, the state would subscribe the remaining two-fifths and become a stockholder to that amount.[1]

As an example of successful unaided company projects in the period of state activity, the bridges at Columbia may be cited. A private company, incorporated in 1823, began work in 1824, obtained sufficient subscriptions to its stock, chiefly among the citizens of Columbia, and by

[1] Cooper and McCord, *South Carolina Statistics at Large*, vol. ix, p. 611.

1827 completed a great new bridge over the Congaree, just below the town, costing above $30,000.[1] The same company, finding the prospects of profit from tolls excellent, at once began a bridge of similar cost over the Saluda River, two miles above the thriving town. Another company was then chartered, and the stock subscribed, to build a bridge over the Broad River, to cost $40,000, including $4000 which must be paid to extinguish the two ferry privileges on the river near the town.[2]

That private toll-bridges could become sources of much annoyance as well as of convenience, is illustrated in the case of the bridge across the Savannah River at Augusta. That bridge had been built by a company under charters from the two states, and in 1828 was the property, it seems, of Henry Shultz and a certain Breithaupt. The bridge became a subject of litigation between these men and the Bank of the State of Georgia. At one stage of the proceedings the case was thrown out of court, and each party seized one end of the bridge and levied either half toll or full toll at its pleasure. The persons in possession of each end of the bridge were sustained by the courts of their respective states. The consequence was, as a contemporary editor wrote, "that the bridge is held by the parties litigant under circumstances very unfavorable to the public interest." [3]

Aside from sporadic instances of bridge building, and the like, by private companies, the projecting and construction of railways engrossed practically all the capital and

[1] *Charleston City Gazette*, April 14, 1827; clipping from the *Columbia State Gazette*, April 7.

[2] *Charleston City Gazette*, May 2, 1828.

[3] *Georgia Courier* (Augusta), March 10, 1728.

legislative support available for transportation improvements in South Carolina after 1829. The care of the pikes, causeways, and canals was left to the toll leasers, and was in consequence greatly neglected; the care of common roads and the rivers continued to be in the hands of local commissioners, who were in general no more nor less progressive and efficient than before the period of state enterprises.

GEORGIA PUBLIC WORKS

In Georgia the general conditions and problems were entirely similar to those in South Carolina, except that beginning of settlement was more than a half-century later than the founding of Carolina, and the material development of the younger commonwealth did not overtake that of the older until the second third of the nineteenth century.

The rude character of the early land traffic is indicated by the cost of "road making" in Oglethorpe's time. In a letter of October 19, 1739, Oglethorpe wrote to the Georgia trustees, "That he had given £5 for assistance to the cattle hunters, who with that small assistance, under Capt Cuthbert's conduct cut a path thrō the woods (which were before unpassable) 60 miles on our side of the Savannah River, from Augusta to the Uchee town." [1]

The cotton traffic prior to the era of steam was, of course, handled on the rivers in pole-boats, which were often decked, and large enough to carry five hundred bales or more, or in the flat-bottomed boats called cotton-boxes. The latter, built of heavy timbers in the uplands, measured from sixty to eighty feet in length by twenty or twenty-

[1] Egmont, *Journal*, p. 143.

five broad, and were equipped with a long sweep at each end for service in following the channels of the crooked streams. The pole-boat crews, after discharging their cotton cargo would work their craft back up-stream with a light load of merchandise; but the cotton-box men were accustomed to sell their rude boats as building material, and to walk back home and build another.[1] "Rice-flats" were craft similar to cotton-boxes, but built for permanent service. The size and cost of one of these is shown in a rice planter's memorandum in 1850: "Mr. Cooper says Billy Keefer, a colored man in Savannah, built Mr. Braulay's flat for $250. It is 55 feet, by 15 — decked, roofed, etc., complete. My present flat, built 1845 of cypress is 45 ft long, by 15 wide, carries 50 bbls." [2]

The long-continued lack of roadways of any sort in the extreme southern part of Georgia is shown by the charges of Judge Walton to the grand juries of Glynn and Camden counties in 1799. The judge expressed regret that there was no road connecting this district with the rest of Georgia, nor any sufficient roads for local traffic. Until such could be had, he said, the principal cultivation would be confined to the islands and the coast margin, while the interior would be occupied by the shiftless and dissolute. He thought the population in the district too thin to attempt roads to supply its needs by its own efforts, and advised application to the legislature for aid in the work.[3]

In the upper country, things were in much better state

[1] Virgil Powers, in W. T. Switzler, *Report on the Internal Commerce of the U.S.*, Washington, 1886, p. 333.

[2] Extract from the plantation records of Louis Manigault, owner of Gowrie plantation, ten miles above Savannah. MS. in possession of Mrs. Hawkins Jenkins, Pinopolis, S.C.

[3] *Augusta Chronicle*, November 9, 1799.

of progress. There was a main road from Savannah to Augusta, in tolerable repair; and stages twice a week made the trip of 127 miles in two days, with the use of six relays of horses. The passenger fare was $8; with allowance of fourteen pounds of baggage, and a charge of 6¼ cents for excess.[1] The public roads for three miles round Augusta were in charge of the town council, with discretionary powers of taxation. In the distant interior the roads gradually developed from pioneer trails to public highways, ill-kept always, but passable, at least in the good seasons. Lotteries were resorted to for internal improvements in the later eighteenth century and for a time afterward, but very little of effective character was accomplished.

After the War of 1812, the problem in Georgia was much the same as that in South Carolina, though not quite so intense. The commonwealth was younger, the land in cultivation fresher as a rule, and great tracts of it were still held by the Indian tribes in unbroken forestry. The state was gaining largely in population, obtaining fresh lands by occasional Indian cessions, and feeling no special need of heroic measures to check a decline. Savannah, furthermore, was not so populous, so wealthy, nor so spirited as Charleston, and not so active, for the time, in promoting large plans for the stimulation of commerce. The longer settled parts of the uplands, however, were not far behind the adjacent areas in South Carolina in urging that a part of the wealth which flowed in as the result of high cotton prices after the peace of 1815 be utilized in bettering the avenues of transportation. The pine-barrens were as wide or wider than in South Carolina, the roads as crude and ill-kept, and the rivers no greater in volume nor freer

[1] *Augusta Herald*, October 16, 1799, advertisement.

from snags, rocks, and sand-bars. Much the same discussion of internal improvements was carried on as in South Carolina, and some of the same plans tried, though the experiments in Georgia were as a rule later and on a smaller scale.

The first act for state appropriations to river improvements in a general system was passed in December, 1817. This provided specific amounts to be expended by local commissions on each of the important streams in the occupied portion of the state. It gave $5000 for work on the Savannah River below Augusta, $20,000 to the Savannah above Augusta and its branch, the Tugalo, $5000 to Broad River, $3000 to Briar Creek, $3000 to the Ogechee, $5000 to the Altamaha, $10,000 to the Oconee below the fall line, $5000 to the same river above Milledgeville, and $10,000 to the Ocomulgee. The act, further, set apart the sum of $250,000 as a permanent fund, the principal to be invested in bank stocks or other profitable shares, and the interest to be used for internal improvements as the legislature might direct.[1] The amount of this fund was in 1821 increased to half a million dollars.[2]

The degree of success in these works, so far as concerns the channels above the fall line, is illustrated by an editorial account of the Oconee operations published in the *Georgia Journal*, a Milledgeville newspaper, May 13, 1823. Great expenditures had been laid out, it related, and great exertions made to render the Oconee navigable from Milledgeville up-stream to Barnett's Shoals. As yet no good results were apparent; the editor had learned of

[1] L. Q. C. Lamar, *Compilation of the Laws of Georgia, 1810–1819*, pp. 513–515.

[2] O. H. Prince, *Digest of the Laws of Georgia*, 1837, p. 19.

only two boats which had descended the river, and of no attempts by loaded boats to ascend it. The plan followed had been that called sluice navigation; and that system had failed also on the Potomac and elsewhere.

An act of 1819, reciting in its preamble that the several appropriations for river improvements in former years had produced little benefit, created the office of topographical and civil engineer for the state, with a "competent salary," the incumbent to be chosen for terms of three years by joint ballot of the assembly. This official was to be charged with the exploration and survey of streams and the making of reports thereon, and with the expenditure of all funds appropriated by the state to the betterment of navigation. On this also he was to make full reports.[1] No candidate with the necessary scientific training and qualifications was at hand, and for several years no incumbent was appointed.

Lively discussion was carried on in the state. On December 7, 1820, a committee of the house of representatives presented a report which strongly urged activity. This report mentioned the topographical advantages of the state in its waterways, and emphasized the need of improvement in the means of commerce; it alluded to the existing prosperous tranquillity and the prospect of long-continued peace, and urged that the rivalship of South Carolina and the prevailing interest in improvements throughout the country "ought to arouse the State of Georgia from her lethargy, and induce her to adopt a bold and liberal policy, commensurate with her ample resources and the public expectations." It stated the belief of the committee that a bold beginning by the state

[1] Lamar, *Compilation*, p. 274.

would at once inspire confidence in the completion of an adequate system; "its benefits will be felt in anticipation, in the value of lands, in an increased activity, and a general prosperity." The operation of the system, it continued, would strengthen the bonds of the federal union, facilitate the movement of troops and supplies in time of war, in time of peace give value to every product of land and labor, promote all well-directed industry, diffuse knowledge, elevate morals, and in short bring conditions very nearly millennial. As works to be undertaken, a canal was mentioned to connect the St. Mary's River, *via* the edge of the Okefenokee Swamp, with the Suwanee River and thus with the Gulf of Mexico, and the general policy stated of clearing the watercourses, building locks on the rivers from the uplands, and digging canals where advisable. The building of turnpikes to the principal towns was also advocated, and substantial roads to connect the navigation of the rivers flowing into the Atlantic with those flowing into the Gulf. The committee felt "bound to say, from ocular demonstration and woeful experience, that many of the public roads in our state are in a shameful condition." Turnpikes, with light tolls, were declared to be highly advisable in remedy. But after all these preliminary generalities the committee made no specific recommendation except that a state engineer be appointed and that the legislature in future sessions heartily support and develop internal improvements according to the plans which that official should submit.[1]

A candidate with eminent qualifications for the engineer's office, however, was still lacking; and the reports

[1] W. C. Dawson, *Compilation of the Laws of Georgia*, Resolutions, p. 56.

of grave disappointment from the hastily conceived public works in South Carolina deterred the Georgia administration from appointing any amateur to the post, which could grow to such great responsibility.

Encouragement was meanwhile offered for the forming of private companies to undertake a system of turnpikes. An act of 1821 invited the building of a great pike from Augusta through Warrenton, Sparta, and Milledgeville, across the Ocomulgee near the point where Macon was soon afterward built, to terminate on the Flint River at Fort Hawkins, on the edge of the Indian lands. Branch roads to Washington, Greensborough, and Monticello were authorized on the same footing. In case companies should be formed with adequate capital for these works, the act pledged the state to subscribe a total of some seven hundred thousand dollars to their stock, an amount estimated to be one-sixth of the probable full cost of the works. The companies were empowered to collect tolls on the general basis of not above one cent per mile for each horse or mule drawing vehicles, and half that rate for oxen.[1] An act of 1823 authorized the continuation of the projected Washington branch toward Rabun County in the northeastern corner of the state, so as to intersect a projected turnpike from Lexington, Ky., to Augusta, Ga.[2] The invitations offered by these turnpike enactments were not accepted by capitalists. An act of 1827 authorized Thomas Spalding and his associates to cut a canal or build a wooden railroad from the Ocomulgee to the Flint River;[3] but this likewise was without success.

[1] Dawson, *Compilation*, pp. 370–373.
[2] *Ibid.*, p. 380.
[3] *Ibid.*, p. 393.

The method of operating on the river channels through local commissioners using the fund for public works continued, meanwhile, to show glaring faults. The local boards often either wasted money in ineffective works, paid too much for labor and supplies, failed to report on operations, or proved otherwise unsatisfactory in the discharge of their duties.[1]

In the legislative session of 1821 a bill of multifarious provisions had been introduced, looking to the institution of a board of public works and to the improvement of avenues of all sorts in many sections of the state. The bill was opposed on the ground of its too great comprehensiveness, and opposed particularly by the representatives from the western counties because the projects most likely to be undertaken under it would be for the benefit of the Savannah, Augusta, and Milledgeville districts, while the expense must be shared by all parts of the state.[2] In the following years, Mr. Turner, the representative from Putnam County, kept alive the project for a board of public works, and at the end of 1825 secured the enactment of his bill.[3]

Meanwhile the agitation for public works grew more vigorous, and came to include, not only river and turnpike projects, but also a great canal, which should begin at Savannah, run westward to the Ogechee River, follow the course of that stream to near the fall line, thence cross to the Oconee valley and ascend into the Piedmont as far as should prove convenient.[4] Several long series of letters

[1] Cf. Dawson, *Compilation*, Resolutions, pp. 30, 32, 39, 53, etc.

[2] *Savannah Republican*, June 2, 1824, letter signed "Fulton."

[3] *Georgia Statesman* (Milledgeville), December 12, 1826.

[4] *Savannah Republican*, January 23, 1824.

to the public, one of them embracing a history of canals from the time of Chaldea to the Erie Canal,[1] were written anonymously and printed in the newspapers, appealing for unity and concentration of effort, and scolding the opposition for their recalcitrant local selfishness and short-sightedness. A favorite argument of these writers was that, by putting the distant interior into close touch with markets, the price of the distant lands would be raised to the levels already reached in the districts near the best commercial centers.[2] It of course did not occur to these advocates that the facilitation of traffic might increase cotton production to such an extent that cotton prices and profits would heavily decline, and the price of the lands of choicest location would fall enough to counterbalance any actual rise in the value of the distant tracts. The results in New York from the Erie Canal furnished a favorite illustration for use in the debates, but was partly offset by the argument that the conditions at hand were not analogous to those of New York.

A very effective rejoinder to the general argument for pikes, etc., was made in a public letter signed "Giles Scroggins" and published in the *Georgia Journal,* January 14, 1823. The burden of its contention was that the traffic in Georgia was entirely too small in volume to justify or to yield profit upon any expensive highways. The Scroggins letter was directed specifically against a project for the building of turnpikes westward from Augusta by popular subscriptions to stock. Its arguments were applied with force by other writers against the plan of river, canal, and road improvements in general. The best

[1] *Savannah Republican,* May, 1824.

[2] *E.g. Savannah Republican,* June 10, 1824.

rebuttal brought forward was the contention that by the building of pikes, etc., traffic would be greatly increased, and statistics of present travel were therefore not a legitimate basis of reckoning.[1]

The result of the discussion was on the whole to incline public sentiment favorably toward the general project of public works. In December, 1824, the legislature by resolution requested the governor to employ a state engineer and cause surveys and estimates to be made for the beginning of a system of internal improvements, and it provided $10,000 as expense money.[2] For some reason, however, the governor waited still another year before appointing an incumbent to the office.

At the end of 1825 the attempt to create a board of public works at length won success in the legislature. An act approved December 21 established such a board, to consist of the governor *ex officio* and seven members to be elected annually by joint ballot of the general assembly, one from each congressional district. The board was authorized to employ surveyors and laborers and to cause surveys and estimates to be made for improvements of transportation avenues within the state. Members were to receive four dollars per day while in service, to a maximum of sixty days in the year for ordinary members and one hundred days for the two members of the executive committee. Fifty thousand dollars were appropriated by the act for use in the work of the board.[3]

The members of the board were duly elected, and assembled for their first formal meeting at Milledgeville,

[1] *Savannah Republican*, June 10, 1824.

[2] Dawson, *Compilation*, Resolutions, p. 49.

[3] Dawson, *Compilation*, pp. 91, 92.

March 20 to 23, 1826. Minutes of the sessions on these days were published by the board in the newspapers.[1] Upon the organization of the board, Governor Troup, its chairman, delivered an address upon the responsibilities of the members and the high purpose of their appointment. He expressed confidence that enough competent surveyors could be had without delay, and announced that for the post of chief engineer of the state he had decided to appoint Mr. Hamilton Fulton, recently in the service of North Carolina, whom he deemed the most eligible man in the South. The board resolved to appoint two assistant engineers, at salaries of $2500 and expenses; and to fill these places it at once chose E. H. Burritt and John Couty, the former of whom was himself a member of the board. Burritt was directed to procure levels, compasses, sextants, and other instruments for the board, and the president was by resolution requested to ascertain what supply of and at what price malleable iron might be procured.

To execute its duties in the field the more promptly, the board now divided itself into three committees of two members each, to form part of three surveying parties. The first committee, comprising Wilson Lumpkin and J. G. Pittman, was assigned to inspect the country between the Tennessee River and the head of navigation on the Oconee or the Ocomulgee, and to make preliminary surveys with reference to the building both of a canal and a railroad through that region. The second committee, Messrs. Joel Crawford and John Schley, were to examine the country along the fall line from the Savannah to the Flint River, with a view, similarly, to either a canal or a

[1] *E.g. Georgia Statesman,* April 4, 1826.

railroad across the state in that belt. The third committee was assigned to the lower part of the state, but instructed to postpone its work to a later time. The first two committees and the engineers at once set out upon their explorations.

The reconnaissance along the fall line quickly showed the route to be not well adapted to canals, but to be feasible for horse railways with "inclined planes." [1]

The exploration toward the Tennessee was reported upon by Wilson Lumpkin in an able letter, June 21, to the secretary of state. He stated that the only possible route for a canal connecting the Georgia rivers with the Tennessee must lie through the valley of Chickamauga Creek, which separates Lookout Mountain from the unbroken range of the Blue Ridge to the eastward. He believed a canal on that route to be feasible and to promise great usefulness. For a great central road, also, he thought the country excellently adapted: level ground could be found on the whole route in a very direct line; timber and stone abounded; and the country invited development in both mining and agriculture as soon as the Cherokees could be removed.[2] The use of the surveyors' levels, however, showed the necessary ascents and descents on the route to be greater than Lumpkin's eye had appreciated. The ridge between the sources of the Ocomulgee and the course of the Chatahoochee was found to be 194½ and 299¾ feet above the two streams respectively,[3] and the ridges to be crossed northwest of the Chattahoochee were still more formidable. The inspection of these ridges destroyed

[1] *Georgia Statesman,* May 30 and July 25, 1826.

[2] *Georgia Statesman,* July 4, 1826.

[3] *Ibid.,* August 8, 1826.

all prospect of a canal, and reduced the possibilities for success to turnpikes and the newly devised railways. Lumpkin was thenceforward for years a sturdy advocate of a railroad for the route which he had inspected.[1]

The activity and usefulness of the board of public works was soon interfered with by mishaps and by quarrels among the surveyors. Mr. Fulton was withdrawn from the work at the end of May and directed by the governor to aid in the survey of a parcel of land in dispute with the Creek Indians. Mr. Burritt soon afterward was prostrated with fever.[2] Fulton returned to his work of canal and railway reconnaissance during the summer. In the autumn he discharged Burritt for incompetency.

Before his appointment as assistant engineer, Burritt had been one of the two editors of the *Georgia Statesman*, a Milledgeville newspaper. For the better discharge of his new duties, he withdrew from the editorial connection in June,[3] but apparently retained an influence upon the policy of the paper, and perhaps bought back his proprietorship in it when dismissed from the public service. In September the *Georgia Statesman* began a vehement attack upon Fulton.

Fulton was by no means invulnerable. His work in North Carolina had really been a disappointment to the people there, and his exit from that field not entirely creditable; his expense account in Georgia was drawn up in such ambiguous form as to give rise to a suspicion as to its honesty; his arrogance and pretentiousness had lost

[1] *Incidents connected with the Life of Wilson Lumpkin*, MS. in private possession at Athens, Ga.

[2] *Georgia Statesman*, August 15, 1826.

[3] *Georgia Statesman*, June 13, 1826.

him friends; and finally his report to the legislature in November, 1824, it was discovered, included very long uncredited extracts from Rees's Cyclopædia, which laid its author open to a charge of plagiarism. The attack upon Fulton[1] was strong enough to cause his dismissal from office at the end of 1826.

These occurrences reflected discredit also upon the board of public works. Its friends urged that it be continued as a permanent body with authority to concentrate its efforts upon a few tasks at a time instead of being required to scatter and waste its efforts.[2] But its opponents prevailed and by an act approved December 26, 1826,[3] the act of the previous year was repealed and the board of public works abolished, not to be revived.

An act of the same session, 1826, carried the state back to the policy of river improvements through the agency of local boards. Appropriations were made by this act, of $30,000 to the Ocomulgee River, $20,000 to the Oconee, $20,000 to the Altamaha, $5000 to the Ogeechee, and $10,000 to the Chattahoochee. The last-named was now becoming of importance to the state by reason of the recent cession by the Creek nation of its claim to all remaining lands in Georgia.[4] Operations on the basis of appropriations to local boards were from this time continued for three years, and then ended by a joint resolution adopted by the legislature December 21, 1829, which called for the return by the several river boards of all unexpended balances. Still another experiment was by that time in

[1] *Georgia Statesman*, December 12 and 26, 1826.

[2] *Ibid.*, December 12, 1826.

[3] Dawson, *Compilation*, p. 94.

[4] Cf. U. B. Phillips, *Georgia and State Rights*, chap. 2, in American Historical Association *Report* for 1901, vol. ii.

progress, in the effort to find an effectual and economical system.

For a number of years the idea had received occasional notice that a feasible plan for building public works would be for the state to buy or hire slaves for work in gangs under superintendents in the state's employ. As early as 1816 the commissioners for the Oconee River resolved to purchase slaves for work upon the river channel, with a device of shifting them in seasons of high water to the work of navigating commercial freight boats or rafting staves to market. Thus the slaves would be kept steadily busy, and the proceeds from their services on the boats and rafts would help to meet the cost of their sustenance.[1] For some reason this plan, it appears, was not carried into effect. In 1821 an advocate of the same general scheme brought it forward again in the newspapers. He reckoned that the labor of able-bodied slaves could be had through purchase or hire at $120 per year, and the cost of subsistence at ten cents each per day. Overseers for the gangs of twenty slaves each, he thought, could be had at $500 per year.[2] The labor of these gangs, he contended, would be far cheaper and more effective than work done through contractors. Several of the local river boards began from about that time to hire slaves directly for their operations, and in some cases to buy them directly as public property. The device of using state-owned slaves, or "public hands," as they were called, proved in these cases relatively successful.

The legislature of 1829, by an act of December 18, provided for the institution of the system of "public hands" on the public works in general. It appropriated $50,000

[1] *Georgia Journal*, January 17, 1816.

[2] *Georgia Journal*, December 11, 1821.

for the purchase of enough able-bodied negroes to carry the total number owned by the state to 190. Of these laborers, it assigned 25 to work on the Chattahoochee River, 25 on the Ocomulgee and the roads near Macon, 15 on the Oconee and the roads near Milledgeville, 75 on the Savannah and the roads about Augusta, and the remainder on the works near Savannah. Two general superintendents were provided for, and seven overseers. The work to be done by the several gangs was to be designated by the respective city councils of Columbus, Macon, Milledgeville, Augusta, and Savannah.[1] This act was duly carried out by the purchase of laborers, and the system maintained for several years. At the end of 1833, however, the legislature directed that the public hands be disposed of.[2] The slaves were accordingly sold at auction within the next few months, and that system, too, abandoned.[3] By this time the importance of river and road improvements was becoming entirely overshadowed by the agitation for railroads. The state appears to have made no further noteworthy provision for internal improvements of the old-fashioned sort.

The causes of the relative passiveness of the state government, and its conservatism, in the matter of internal improvements, were well analyzed by that strongly edited newspaper, the *Georgia Journal* of Milledgeville, in an editorial of November 30, 1835. Two chief causes, it explained, had retarded the movement: in the first place, sectional jealousy, resulting in legislative scrambles and

[1] Dawson, *Compilation*, pp. 399, 400.

[2] Resolution adopted December 21, 1833, *Acts of the Georgia General Assembly in 1833*, p. 409.

[3] *Federal Union*, January 29, 1834, advertisement for the sale of the hands. Cf. *American Historical Review*, vol. xi, p. 805.

preventing liberal and harmonious action; secondly, a realization of a constant public danger from hasty and improvident legislation along lines where action could not well be revised. Instances of the inadvertent granting of privileges establishing unjust monopoly and other public disadvantages and burdens had excited distrust of all projects of chartered privileges. Wisdom and prudence, the editor thought, were always necessary for progress, and the state might perhaps deserve congratulation instead of censure for its policy, pursued to that period, of making haste slowly.

The Savannah River requires a brief separate treatment for the period with which we have been dealing. Its location on the boundary line between two jealous states gave rise to diplomatic complications and caused it to suffer some relative neglect. The jurisdiction over the Savannah River, it happened, was vested in the government of Georgia by the terms of its original charter, just as that over the Potomac had been vested in Maryland. From this was derived the power of the Georgia legislature to grant a monopoly of steamboat traffic on that river — a monopoly which held good until, in 1824, the jurisdiction was taken over by the United States government. But if the regulation of traffic was exclusively possessed by Georgia, the improvement of the channel was a matter of joint concern to the people of both halves of the river basin, and, therefore, to the governments of both states. The system contemplated for the river from the beginning of the period of public works was that of joint action, with expenses shared equally by the two states. That system, proving more beautiful in theory than in practice, was abided by or departed from as expediency directed. In

1815 and 1817 the Georgia legislature appropriated $10,000 and $20,000 respectively for use on the Savannah River, on conditions that South Carolina should join in the task on an equal footing. In 1817 and 1818 this proviso was removed from the respective appropriations, and the funds made available without condition. In 1818 the state engineer of South Carolina made a cursory inspection of the Savannah River above Augusta;[1] and in 1820 a proposal came from the South Carolina government for joint operations in the improvement of the Savannah and Tugalo, and for the control of their navigation, tolls, etc., by a joint commission. An agreement to this effect was ratified by Georgia in 1823 and by South Carolina in 1825;[2] but it fell to the ground because the congressmen from the two states disagreed and failed to present it for the ratification by the federal government which its terms required. In 1826 South Carolina again expressed willingness to coöperate; but when in that year Georgia appropriated $40,000 for the Savannah, and again invited coöperation, the other state again failed to take action. A committee reported to the Georgia legislature in 1828, that the governor of South Carolina in a letter to the governor of Georgia had frankly admitted that the launching of the Charleston and Hamburg Railroad project would render his state averse to spending any money upon the Savannah River below Augusta, while the exhaustion of the treasury would prevent early appropriations for any part of the channel. The committee expressed the opinion that the divergence of interests by the two states would

[1] *Augusta Chronicle,* May 30, 1818.

[2] Cooper and McCord, *South Carolina Statutes at Large,* vol. i, p. 422.

prevent any coöperation between them: "It would be a paramount consideration with Georgia to render perfect the navigation of the river below Augusta, while South Carolina, with all the facilities for transportation afforded by her railroad, could feel no interest whatever in its improvement. She would bestow all her care and attention upon the river above Augusta, which to us would be an object of secondary importance." [1]

The prosecution of the Charleston and Hamburg railway project spurred the Georgians for a time to further interest in the possibilities of the Savannah River.[2] But after an interval, the project of recouping the trade losses of Savannah by building a railroad to Macon and beyond overshadowed the consideration of river improvements. The legislature lost interest in the problem of overcoming the rocks and sand-bars for steamboats to Augusta. Meanwhile the federal government, by its harbor appropriations, relieved the state of the task of improving the river between Savannah and the sea.[3]

The planters and farmers in the upper part of the Piedmont, however, continued long their insistence that the river channel above Augusta should be improved. John C. Calhoun, in a letter of July 1, 1847, tells of a meeting of the farmers' society in his district to present the views of the people on the subject.[4] In effect, however, the upper

[1] Dawson, *Compilation*, p. 112 of the Resolutions. O. H. Prince, *Digest, 1837*, pp. 700–701.

[2] *E.g. Georgia Courier* (Augusta), January 24 to February 4, 1828.

[3] As late as 1856, however, the city council of Savannah found it necessary to vote $25,000 of city funds for clearing the channel at Tybee Knoll, at the mouth of the river. *Atlanta Intelligencer*, March 31, 1856.

[4] American Historical Association *Report* for 1899, vol. ii, p. 734.

course of the Savannah, by reason of its rapid descent and its frequent heavy freshets, was not capable of being rendered safely navigable at any reasonable cost. The farmers along its upper course had to wait for the coming of railroads to relieve their disabilities.

Two or three other matters in the Georgia development remain to be noticed. The project of a canal from the city of Savannah to the Ogeechee and Altamaha rivers, to establish direct traffic, free from the annoyances of the voyage through the tortuous and deceptive creeks of the sea-island district, had been in contemplation for some years preceding the War of 1812. In 1818 the legislature chartered a "company for the internal navigation from Ogeechee to Savannah River." The company was empowered to cut a canal to the Ogeechee, condemning the necessary land, and to charge tolls upon the traffic, not to amount in yield to more than 25 per cent per annum upon the capital invested.[1] This company did nothing. Its charter seems to have been surrendered in a few years; and in 1824 the legislature granted its privileges afresh to one Ebenezer Jencks,[2] who had already been of some prominence in the management of toll-roads. An act of the year following extended Jencks's privilege of canal cutting to the Altamaha, and authorized the governor to lend him $50,000 in state funds, in promotion of the enterprise.[3] The tapping of the Altamaha River system would, of course, be of far greater consequence than tapping the petty Ogeechee.

The persons chiefly interested in the project, which it

[1] Lamar, *Compilation*, pp. 128–130.
[2] Dawson, *Compilation*, p. 90.
[3] *Ibid.*, p. 91.

was hoped would render the whole middle district of the state commercially tributary to Savannah, were, of course, the merchants and other citizens of Savannah.[1] In 1826 Jencks opened subscription books in Savannah and disposed of a large number of shares in a proposed stock company.[2] Accordingly in December a charter was granted incorporating the Savannah, Ogeechee, and Altamaha Canal Company, with an authorized capital stock of $700,000 and with suitable powers and rules of procedure.[3] Moderate progress was made in construction during the next year or two; but in 1828 the funds of the company began to run short. The legislature came to the rescue with an act in December directing the governor to subscribe for stock to the amount of $44,000 on behalf of the state.[4] Thus aided, the canal was pushed on to completion as far as the Ogeechee River, by the beginning of 1831.[5] It was then 16 miles long, 3 feet deep, and equipped with 5 locks. It soon became evident that traffic between Savannah and the Ogeechee district was not to be greatly developed by the canal, and that the tolls would not yield more than very small dividends. The canal was never extended farther than the Ogeechee. The receipt of tolls barely sufficed to pay running expenses. In 1836 the company was insolvent, and the canal advertised for sale under the sheriff's hammer.[6] The prospects of the company were

[1] *Georgia Statesman*, March 14, 1826.

[2] *Charleston City Gazette*, March 29, 1826; 95 shares were subscribed for on the first day.

[3] Dawson, *Compilation*, pp. 94–98.

[4] *Ibid.*, p. 100.

[5] *Federal Union*, April 14, 1831.

[6] Governor's message, November 8, 1836. *Federal Union*, same date.

so poor that in January, 1837, the governor sold the state's interest in it to W. W. Gordon of Savannah for $10,000.[1] The operations of the railroads later cut into such small traffic as the canal had enjoyed. The Ogeechee Canal, largely analogous to the earlier constructed Santee Canal in South Carolina, was of even less importance than the latter in operation. To build up her trade successfully Savannah was obliged, like Charleston, to resort to railway building.

Of the turnpike projects, some have already been discussed. The others require but brief mention. In 1816 a charter for the Georgia section of its route was granted to the "Unicoi or Unaca Turnpike Company," elsewhere called the Wincoy Company, which intended to build a road from boatable water on the Tugalo across the corners of Georgia and North Carolina and through the range of Unaka Mountains, to the valley of east Tennessee.[2] There is no evidence available to show how much construction was done. The route surveyed was said to cross the Chattahoochee River 28 times in about 8 miles.[3] In 1834 two other companies were chartered for similar purposes;[4] but they likewise, it seems, failed to carry out their plans.

As a final instance of another sort of turnpike project, an act of 1826 appointed commissioners with power to hold a lottery for the state to raise $250,000 with which to build a pike from Augusta to Athens.[5] Lotteries of such a sort were becoming an anachronism at that time,

[1] Letter of Governor Schley to W. W. Gordon, MS. copy in minutes of the Executive Department, Georgia state archives.

[2] Lamar, *Compilation*, pp. 774–776.

[3] Adiel Sherwood, *Gazetteer of Georgia*, 1827, p. 40.

[4] Prince, *Digest of 1837*, p. 402.

[5] Dawson, *Compilation*, p. 276.

and the act was a dead letter. On the whole, all efforts and devices equally failed in developing turnpikes in Georgia. Under the circumstances, those failures were fortunate for the state, since the pikes had been projected in nearly every instance for long-distance traffic, which could be handled vastly better by the railroads which grew upon the adversity of the turnpikes. While South Carolina squandered her money upon attempted internal improvements of the more primitive sort, Georgia reserved her strength and forged ahead in the railway period.

Mention in passing should be made of the Savannah Steamship Company, which sent its vessel, the *Savannah,* as the pioneer steamship on a transatlantic voyage. This company was chartered in 1818,[1] and sent the steamer on its famous voyage the next year. The use of steam for the intercontinental trade did not then, however, prove commercially economical, and the Savannah was not continued in that traffic. When steam power later became common in the traffic across the ocean, it destroyed all the remaining dependence of mariners upon the trade winds, and in consequence definitely established the northeastward ports in control of European commerce. The enterprise of the Savannah company accordingly resulted in no permanent advantage to its port.

A static view of the system of transportation and commerce in Georgia in the decade from 1825 to 1835 may be derived from various sources. Adiel Sherwood's *Gazetteer of Georgia,* edition of 1827, describes the extent and character of the internal navigation at about the time that book went to print.

The largest ocean-going vessels, Sherwood tells us, could

[1] Lamar, *Compilation,* pp. 523–524.

sail 18 miles up the Savannah River, to Five Fathom Hole, three miles below the city of Savannah; and large brigs could sail to the wharves of the city. Steamboats of 150 tons burden commonly ascended except in seasons of low water to Augusta, a distance by water of above 300 miles. Pole-boats of 10 tons burden could mount the main stream above Augusta for a hundred miles to the junction of the Tugalo and Keowee, and perhaps ascend those branch streams for some score or two of miles. At Augusta there were 16 warehouses, from 300 to 500 feet long, and 40 feet wide; and in the trade with Savannah and Charleston there were plying 10 steamboats, making the trip in 4 and 5 days, carrying passengers and from 800 to 1000 bags of cotton, and pole-boats besides, which could carry 500 to 800 bags each. Stages were running daily from Augusta to Savannah, Charleston, and Columbia, thrice a week to Milledgeville and Athens, and also to Greensborough, Madison, and Carnesville. Augusta supplied all the up-country east of the Oconee, and a good deal west of it, with merchandise, and sent many tons into Tennessee and North and South Carolina.

Briar Creek, a more southerly tributary of the Savannah, offered 100 miles of stream just large enough to invite efforts at making it navigable, and just too small to permit of substantial success. After considerable expenditure boats had ascended as far as Waynesborough; but the navigation had proven so difficult that by 1826 it had given way to land traffic.

The Ogeechee River had been cleared of obstructions by an expenditure of $10,000 over and above state appropriations, raised by private subscriptions, chiefly in the town of Louisville on its upper course. Boats carrying 200 or 300 bags of cotton were now able to descend the river, and return with 25 or 30 tons of merchandise.

The Altamaha, with only 14 feet of water at the bar, was largely deprived of port facilities, though the town of Darien, near its mouth, had a lighterage traffic and could receive schooners. Steamboats of considerable size had ascended the Altamaha and its two branches to Milledgeville and Macon; but owing to the shallows at the confluence of the Ocomulgee, it was customary to transfer cargoes there to pole-boats for carriage upward from that point. The labor of re-loading, it was thought, would soon be obviated by the dredging of the shallows. Cargoes of 70 tons could be carried to Macon; and boats of 20 or 30 tons, it was reported, might ascend fifty miles above that town. The Oconee had not been cleared successfully above Milledgeville.

The Satilla and the St. Mary's were each navigable for 60 miles from the ocean for boats of 30 tons; but there was extremely little demand for traffic upon them. The port of Brunswick is mentioned by Sherwood only in connection with a project mooted for a canal thence to tap the Altamaha. Brunswick was at that time not a town, but an aspiration.

The rapid extension of cotton growing in middle Georgia, after the Indian cession of 1821, added the Ocomulgee trade to that of the Oconee, and severely taxed the facilities at Darien. A news item from that town, March 25, 1826,[1] related that the wharves there were groaning under their burden; thirteen vessels were loading with cotton, probably for Savannah and Charleston, and nine boats with mer-

[1] *Charleston City Gazette*, May 1, 1826.

chandise for the interior. Ten years later, Darien merchants attempted to open a direct trade with Boston,[1] but with little substantial success.

The Chattahoochee River came into prominence upon the cession by the Creek Indians of their remaining lands in western Georgia, 1825–1826. The town of Columbus, at the fall line on the Chattahoochee, was laid out by the state government in 1826, before any settlers had arrived — much as Milledgeville had been laid out in 1803 and Macon in 1821 — and town lots were sold by the state to the highest bidders. As at Macon, the growth of a commercial town at the spot was seen to be inevitable before the Indian title had been extinguished; and the state treasury profited by the foresight of the officials. Columbus also had a splendid water-power, like Augusta, which was later to promote manufacturing there. That too was early appreciated. The Chattahoochee, when officially surveyed in 1828, was found to be, from its straightness and the unresisting character of its obstructions, the best of all the Georgia rivers for navigation below the fall line.[2] There was the same disadvantage as in the case of the Altamaha, however, in the presence of a shallow bar at the river's mouth, and the lack of port opportunities. The petty town of Appalachicola grew up on the lower course of the river, with wharves for lighters and schooners to load from; but no adequate facilities, to the present time, have ever been developed at the Chattahoochee's mouth. The Flint River, branching from the Chattahoochee just at the Florida line, was soon made navigable as far as the

[1] *Federal Union,* September 27, 1836.

[2] *Georgia Courier,* June 30, 1828, civil engineer's report on the Chattahoochee.

town of Albany. Steamboats became in a few years quite numerous on these rivers of the southwest; and Columbus

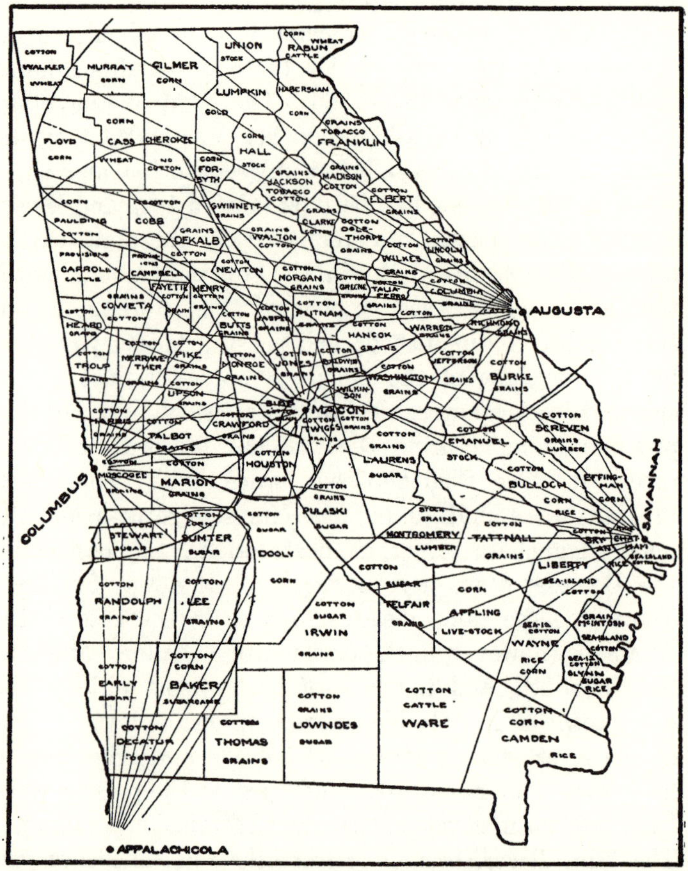

PRINCIPAL PRODUCTS AND TRADE CENTERS FOR THE GEORGIA COUNTIES, 1835

developed a tributary area extending halfway to Macon on one side and Montgomery on the other and reaching well toward the northern border of Georgia.

Wagon roads, of course, radiated in every direction in a network from the head-of-navigation towns as main centers. Their quality may be learned from hundreds of complaints published in the period; or indeed, since these complaints, though still continued, have been largely futile to this day, the quality of the *ante-bellum* dirt roads may be learned to his full exasperation by any traveler through Piedmont Georgia in any winter or spring of the early twentieth century.

The trading areas in Georgia and the towns to which they were tributary just before the building of railroads may be seen charted in the accompanying map, which has been made in accordance with a table of products and markets published in the *Augusta Constitutionalist*, February 3, 1835. In addition to the trading areas indicated in the map, the description in 1835 mentions that the seaboard counties traded with Charleston as well as Savannah; the counties on the Altamaha and the lower Oconee and Ocomulgee traded mostly with Darien; the eastern part of the southern tier of counties with St. Mary's; Houston and Dooly counties traded with Hawkinsville, a way-station on the Ocomulgee; and Paulding, Cass, and Walker counties sent part of their products to Wetumka, Ala. The counties in the group near Cobb and Campbell were just at this time finding a market in the gold-mining district about Lumpkin County for all the food-stuffs they could produce, while of course they drew their supplies of manufactures, salt, etc., from Augusta and Macon. A table a decade later would show the northwestern corner of the state tributary to Chattanooga. Aside from this there would be little change in the marketing map until, in the later forties, Atlanta, the creature of the railroads, began to be a factor most seriously to be reckoned with.

For South Carolina, a satisfactory static view may be gathered by the student from Robert Mills's *Statistics of South Carolina,* 1826, and his elaborate and excellent *Atlas of South Carolina,* of the same date. The states which lay on the edges of the Eastern Cotton Belt need detain us little at this time. Florida is entirely negligible for all present purposes. The development in Alabama is a story in itself, which does not here need the telling.[1]

In North Carolina we are concerned only with the cotton-carrying Cape Fear River and its basin; and this may here be briefly dismissed with a notice of its close analogy to the Savannah, both in natural conditions and the policy of the commonwealth regarding it. With Wilmington corresponding to Savannah, and Fayetteville corresponding to Augusta, the Cape Fear performed the usual service of connecting the seaport with the head-of-navigation town. The early road and river legislation of North Carolina was almost identical in character with that of her southward neighbors. The steps at improving the Cape Fear navigation and promoting the use of steamboats upon it were closely similar to those we have studied for the Savannah, while the degree of success was a little inferior, by reason of the rivers having a somewhat smaller current. The general theme for the State is well treated in Dr. C. C. Weaver's monograph on *Internal Improvements in North Carolina previous to 1860.*[2]

A view of the general system of transportation just prior

[1] Treated by W. E. Martin, *Internal-Improvements in Alabama,* in Johns Hopkins University *Studies,* series 20, no. 4.

[2] Johns Hopkins University *Studies,* series 21, nos. 3–4.

to the railroad era, say in 1830, would show that, except for the introduction of steamboats upon the chief rivers, no great change in the character of either vehicles or avenues had resulted from the long agitation and the many efforts. There was some betterment in the river-beds, and some added bridges and causeways, and a few ill-kept and little-used turnpikes. There were few substantial changes of any sort in the general system, except that by the use of steam, freight could ascend the streams in favorable seasons with greatly increased ease and economy. The rivers crossing the pine-barrens were, as before, the main stems of traffic; the streams above the fall line served for some down freight, but not for much; roads and wagons were there still the chief reliance; teams and wagons also crossed the pine-barrens in the traffic with the coast cities, though in diminishing numbers. Passengers and the mails were carried on the principal routes in stage-coaches running daily, weekly, or at other intervals according to the traffic demand. There were relay stations and taverns of a character not to elicit praise from travelers. The principal line for mail ran parallel to the coast, from Petersburg, whence many news items of the local press were obtained, *via* Fayetteville or Raleigh and Columbia to Augusta, Macon, and beyond, with lines branching to Wilmington, Charleston, Savannah, and to the various small towns of the interior. For the remote districts, particularly those in the mountains and the pine-barrens, there were mails seldom if at all, and stages never.

The centers of traffic were, as we have seen, the seaports and the towns at the head of navigation. In addition a number of interior villages, owing their first rise to their being county-seats, were now developing some commercial activity for the service of the planting population about them, now growing thicker and more prosperous. The towns of high-and-dry location, however, had to wait for the railroad era for their distinctive success. The situation was still in the control of the waterway towns. All towns with commercial prospects had great commercial ambitions for the traffic of the distant interior. Hence a strong rivalry between them, illustrated, for example, in the frequent instances where the merchants would compound for bridge fees and secure the entrance into their town of farm wagons toll free in case a river had to be crossed from a debatable area.

On the whole, the cotton belt was so far removed from the sea and transportation was so costly that the traffic was of necessity slim. Practically nothing but cotton was sent to market, and few things that could be produced at home without great disadvantage were imported. The cotton planters, for example, would have been glad to purchase a large supply of their grain and meat supply, if feasible, at moderate prices; but the immensely long and roundabout transit for such things,—from the northwestern fields to the Ohio, down the Mississippi, transshipped to Savannah or Charleston, there transshiped to the edge of the cotton country, and thence to be hauled by the local merchant or planter,—with freight charges and numerous middlemen's profits, not to speak of tare and delay and risks of loss, made the cost of course too great for the planters to afford except in emergencies. There was some talk of establishing a route for commerce across the mountains; but as yet all men's faces were turned to the river towns and the southeastern coast when looking for actual supplies.

It would have been possible for the residents of the Blue Ridge foot-hills north of the cotton belt to have supplied a part of the planting community with food-stuffs and home-made manufactures, and in small measure they actually did so; but there were no towns so located as to handle this trade, and it long continued on a peddling basis. Not until the founding of Atlanta were the foot-hill people supplied with an organized market for their produce.

The question is interesting as to who did the wagoning business. It is apparent that not every man was his own carrier; but historical data upon the class of professional wagoners is extremely scant. We have enough material to warrant the statement that that class was considerable and important; but beyond that we can say little that is applicable with certainty to the province which we are treating.

A characteristic of the period was the predominance of individual enterprise and self-reliance. Combination of efforts was resorted to only in a few instances of steam-boat, canal, and bridge companies, and the like, while in most instances every man operated in an individual capacity. County officials were depended upon mostly for the care of highways, and were a poor reliance; the system of traffic was mostly informal, irregular, expensive, and inefficient; common carriers were not yet predominant; and under the necessity of every man being in most cases his own carrier, and often his own road mender, the state of affairs was burdensome and exasperating to the community.

CHAPTER III

THE BUILDING OF THE CHARLESTON AND HAMBURG RAILROAD

THROUGHOUT the first half of the nineteenth century, the public intelligence of Charleston was actively awake upon a very wide range of topics in industry, commerce, and politics — alert and active to a much greater degree than is generally known. From the evidences still extant in the newspaper files of the city and in the very numerous pamphlets which have been preserved, largely by chance, in the local collections,[1] it is clear that the city was a forum for the most lively and extensive discussions. Arguments on both sides of nearly every sort of question of public policy were put into print for the swaying of opinion at the time, and to the edification of the latter-day student. Some of the pamphlets and newspaper letters and editorials were conservative, some moderate, some radical; most were sane and well-reasoned, and a few the product of hare-brained scribbling or flighty enthusiasm.

The decline of Charleston commerce was of grave public concern from the time when, about 1821 or 1822, it was observed that the community was not recovering as rapidly as the rest of the country from the panic of 1819. It was found shortly afterward, to the public distress, that the wagon trade of the city was steadily decreasing, and the

[1] The principal ones of these which are open to the public are in the Charleston Library, the Charleston College Library, and the Alabama State Department of History and Archives at Montgomery. Several private libraries in South Carolina also have extensive and valuable collections.

merchants losing business of all sorts; while, on the other hand, Savannah was prospering, and a number of interior towns were springing up to take the upland retail trade entirely away from the seaports. After a good deal of informal discussion among the citizens, which is of course largely unrecorded, a writer with the pseudonym "South Carolina" summed up the issue very tangibly in a letter published in the *Charleston Courier*, October 27, 1827, and printed also as a pamphlet. In describing the situation confronting Charleston, he wrote:—

"The present great depression of commerce and the serious distress pervading almost every portion of the community, are daily becoming matter of deeper concern and higher consideration. . . .

"It is known to us that all the retail trade of Charleston, which was a few years ago the life and spirit of our town, has been cut off and intercepted by a chain of small towns, situated at the foot of our hilly country, and extending across the state from North Carolina to the Georgia boundary line. You will recognize in this chain the towns of Cheraw, Camden, Columbia, and Hamburg. Formerly our back-country people had to look to this city for their supplies even of small articles. Then they were neither wealthy nor numerous, now they have greatly increased in number, wealth, and luxury; and their wants are so general that country stores find encouragement and business, limited, it is true, at first, but now extensive. . . . This was no strained or artificial result; but was the natural progress of natural things. If Charleston yet retained her very great retail trade, it would be a strong evidence of our State being behind her sisters in the solid improvements of life. . . . We must [now] be content to do the retail trade of our immediate neighbors only. If we act wisely, however, we may secure the entire *wholesale* trade of those towns, as well as that of the adjoining states. But to do this we must rouse our sleeping energies, and instead of supinely bewailing our fallen condition, put our shoulders to the wheel. . . ."

The only positive programme this writer had to offer was to intercept the flatboat trade of Hamburg-Augusta by digging a canal parallel to the coast and reaching from the Ashley to the Savannah River shortly above the city of Savannah. "An objection may be raised," admitted he, "that the land through which the canal would pass is not suited to canals. . . . I would reply that the objects are sufficiently great to induce the picketing of its banks with pine timber every inch of the distance."

The status of Charleston's trade with the Piedmont country had been described in 1826 in Robert Mills's *Statistics of South Carolina.*[1] At the time of his writing there were ten steamboats plying between Charleston and the towns of Savannah, Augusta, Hamburg, Columbia, Cheraw, and Georgetown with an average capacity of six hundred cotton bales of the then standard weight of 320 pounds. In addition, flatboats from Columbia or Camden, with capacity of about one hundred bales and crews of a patroon and four or five hands to each, would bring cargoes through the Santee Canal to Charleston, and usually return in tow for the up-stream part of the trip. The tolls on the Santee Canal were at that time $40 on each boat for the round trip. The rate of freight was $1 per bale or $7 per ton. From Augusta and Hamburg, by water, to Charleston the freight

[1] pp. 428 ff. Cf. also W. L. Trenholm in *Resources of South Carolina,* pp. 627–628.

rate was usually about $1.50 per bale, and insurance 25 cents additional. The delays were often great and exasperating.

In his pamphlet of 1821, advocating a great central canal for South Carolina, Mills stated the freight rate by water from Columbia to Charleston at $1.50 per bale of cotton, seven bales making a ton; but this route was so long and hazardous that many shippers preferred to send their cotton by wagon at a cost of $3 per bale, or $21 per ton. The inward transit on salt, liquors, merchandise, etc., he gives as $15 to $30 per ton, the water route being 500 miles in length, and the road 110 miles. On the Pee Dee, the conditions were similar or worse. A team-boat, for example, carrying 300 bales, required 8 mules to propel it, five men to manage it, and took fifteen days to descend the stream from Society Hill to Georgetown.[1] The need for improvements in transportation was crying, and the need for the commercial rehabilitation of Charleston was declared by the leading spirits to be desperate.

Statistics and estimates of Charleston cotton receipts for the year ending September 30, 1827, were published at the time as follows:[2] —

Shipped down the Congaree through the Columbia Canal	45,612 bales.
Shipped down the Congaree from the collecting point at Granby, the old head of navigation, about	10,000 bales.
Shipped down the Wateree from Camden, about	40,000 bales.
Shipped from lower points on the Santee River system, about	15,000 bales.
Shipped from Augusta and Hamburg, about	37,500 bales.
Received from other sources and wagons, about	59,100 bales.
Total cotton receipts at Charleston about	200,000 bales.

[1] W. L. Trenholm, in *South Carolina Resources*, p. 638.

[2] Table taken from W. L. Trenholm, in *South Carolina Resources*, p. 627.

Alexander Black, chairman of a committee of the Charleston city council, reported after investigation in March, 1828: "The trade of Charleston is supported by about 200,000 bales of cotton and 100,000 barrels of clean and rough rice annually. [A bale of cotton averaged about $25 in value, and a barrel of rice, at 3⅛ cents per pound, brought about $20. The whole export trade was only $7,000,000.]" It will be remembered, of course, that in the absence of practically all manufacturing for any outside market, Charleston was entirely dependent upon its commerce for prosperity. The report concludes: "Charleston . . . has for several years past retrograded with a rapidity unprecedented. Her landed estate has, within eight years, depreciated in value one-half. Industry and business talent, driven by necessity, have sought employment elsewhere. Many of her houses are tenantless, and the grass grows uninterrupted in some of her chief business streets "[1]

The Charlestonian business men now had their minds set upon capturing the Augusta trade, as a vital necessity. As early as the beginning of 1822, the device of railways had been under discussion in Charleston;[2] and when in 1827 the problem of the Augusta trade was about to emerge from the academic stage, a railroad was in the public mind as a possibly preferable substitute for the canal which was still receiving the main consideration.

On December 6, 1827, a citizens' meeting was held in Charleston and a petition adopted asking the legislature to cause a survey of the country between the Ashley and Savannah rivers, with a view to a canal which would

[1] W. L. Trenholm, in *South Carolina Resources*, p. 630.

[2] *Charleston City Gazette*, January 1, 1822, advertisement of a patent railway on exhibition in the city.

unite them, and a survey of the country between Charleston and Augusta, with a view to a railroad.[1] The legislature was then in session at Columbia. Mr. Alexander Black, a representative from Charleston, had already introduced a bill, on December 4, to incorporate a company to establish a railway or railways between the city of Charleston and the towns of Hamburg, Columbia, and Camden.[2] The bill was speedily enacted. On January 8, 1828, a second meeting of citizens was held in Charleston, to hear the report of the committee charged by the previous meeting with the presentation of its petition. This committee reported through James L. Pettigru, its chairman, that the citizens' petition had not been granted; but that an act had been passed authorizing the establishment of a company to build canals and railroads to Camden, Columbia, and Hamburg, and a general law enacted providing general rules and powers for chartered companies in the state. The restrictions imposed by this general law, which was devised more for turnpike and bridge companies, the committee thought would be burdensome upon a great railway project like the one now to be launched. The committee advised a petition for amendments designed to encourage citizens to subscribe to stock in the projected company. The meeting adopted the report.[3] To meet the needs as thus presented, the legislature now enacted a new law, chartering the South Carolina Canal and Railroad Company and giving it all desired powers.[4]

[1] *Georgia Courier* (Augusta), December 10, 1827.

[2] *Ibid.*, December 17, 1827.

[3] *Charleston City Gazette,* January 8, 1828.

[4] Charter granted January 30, 1828. The substance of the two chartering acts, 1827 and 1828, is given in the appendix to this chapter.

The Charleston chamber of commerce now appointed a committee, consisting of Messrs. Timothy Ford, Thomas Bennett, Thomas Napier, William Aiken, and Alexander Black, to inquire into the probable cost, revenues, and advantages of the proposed railroad.[1] Meanwhile the city council appropriated five hundred dollars for constructing a model of a railroad in some public place in the city for the edification of the people and the promotion of the great project.[2] The committee of the board of trade reported early in March, in order to prepare the public favorably for the opening of the subscription books, which was scheduled for March 17. This committee reported in a pamphlet, giving liberal extracts from writers upon railroads, etc., expressed itself in favor of a railway as against a canal, and prophesied great success for the project. They expected it to benefit Charleston, build up towns along the route, open up new markets, afford a speedy and safe retreat during the sickly season, provide quick transportation for troops and supplies to the city in time of war, and most of all, to enhance the value of city property. The cost of the railroad to Hamburg was estimated at $3600 per mile for grading and track, or $504,000 for the estimated 140 miles, including turnouts; for bridges, houses, engines, etc., $96,000; total $600,000, at the outside estimates. As to traffic, 100,000 bales of cotton per year were expected, at fifty cents each, yielding $50,000; an equal amount of revenue from up freights, $50,000; ten passengers per day, at one-half the present stage and steamboat fare, $22,500; mail at the present contract price, $7000; and tolls at the

[1] *Charleston City Gazette*, February 19, 1828.

[2] *Charleston Observer*, February 16, 1828; J. N. Cardozo, *Reminiscences of Charleston*, Charleston, 1866, pp. 56, 57.

bridges from travelers, $2000; total, $131,500 per year. Deducting $10,000 per year for repairs, and $10,000 as a fund for reconstruction, $111,500 per year would be left as gross earnings, or about 19 per cent upon the total investment.[1] Curiously enough, this calculation omits all mention of running expenses. It had not been decided definitely at this time whether horse-power or steam locomotion would be used upon the road.[2]

All these proceedings were watched with keen interest by the people of the neighboring towns as well as by the citizens of Charleston. Augusta was particularly excited. Her editors and citizens were full of questions as to whether the railroad would end at Hamburg or be continued across the river, whether it would build up Hamburg at Augusta's expense or whether both towns would have a boom from it, and whether the railroad to Charleston would ruin the trade of Savannah or be offset by some countervailing enterprise by the Georgia port.[3] Their loyalty to their state caused Georgians in general to have mixed feelings in regard to the Charleston project. The men of Savannah were perturbed by the prospect. They were not sure that the railroad could compete successfully with their river; but resolved that, if it should do so, they would strain every resource, if need were, to save their commerce from any decadence. As to the South Carolina towns, Hamburg was too feeble and too uncertain of its own future for its few citizens to play any but a waiting part; and Columbia and Camden, lying away from the initial route of the con-

[1] *Charleston City Gazette*, March 13 and 14, 1828.

[2] *Ibid.*, March 17, letter from Colonel Blanding.

[3] *Georgia Courier*, December 10 and 17, 1827, February 7, March 10, etc., 1828.

templated railway system, whose later branches might reach their gates, bided their time until their own proper turn should come for activity. The Charlestonians alone were devoted enough and had free enough energy and capital to give substantial backing to the Charleston and Hamburg railroad project.

When the day came for opening the subscription books, there were no shares taken at all at the agencies in the inland towns; but at Charleston, mainly by reason of large subscriptions on the part of a few capitalists, stock was taken to the amount of $350,100, which was quite equal to expectations for that agency. Afterward a few small subscriptions were made in the interior as well as additional ones at Charleston.[1] The subscriptions secured in the first few days at Charleston satisfied the charter requirements and justified the formal launching of the project.

The company was organized at the City Hall, Charleston, May 12, 1828; William Aiken was elected president, and twelve directors chosen. The direction began its work at once; correspondences were formed in England and at the North, civil engineers appointed, and the work of instrumental survey actively instituted. Alexander Black, the moving spirit of the enterprise from the first, was soon afterward made the general factotum of the company, with the title of "commissioner"; and he it was who pushed the project through to rapid completion.

The city council had in March, 1828, petitioned Congress to remit the duties on the iron which it might be neces-

[1] *Georgia Courier*, March 24, 1828; Elias Horry (president of the company), *Address at Charleston, October 2, 1833*, pamphlet, Charleston, 1833.

sary to import for the railroad. A bill to that effect was promptly introduced into the United States Senate and was adopted by that body; but in spite of the efforts of Mr. Barney, the congressman in charge of the bill in the lower house, it was there refused consideration.[1] An application by the directorate to the United States war department, asking for a detail of engineers to make the survey, met with better success. The war department had no engineers unengaged at the time of the application, but expected to be able to send a detachment in November, to work through the healthy winter season in the location of the road, and promised to send them at that time.[2]

Prompted by a fear that the funds available through subscriptions would not prove adequate to the task at hand, the company, early in 1829, sent Messrs. Aiken and Black to Washington to ask a subscription from Congress to the stock of the company. These men returned at the end of February, reporting that from the lateness of the season nothing could be effected at the current session, but that an appropriation, they thought, might be confidently expected at the next session.[3] Upon learning of this effort by the company to get a congressional subvention, the state rights newspapers of the South cried it down as a case of truckling to the federal government and an invitation for it to extend its scope of action into unwarranted fields. The *Athenian* (published at Athens, Georgia), for example, remonstrated in an editorial, of March 17, 1829: —

[1] *Charleston Observer,* March 29 and May 31, quoting the *National Intelligencer* of May 24, 1828.

[2] *Georgia Courier,* August 25, 1828.

[3] *Charleston City Gazette,* March 3, 1829.

The South have thus far kept aloof from all participation in the pecuniary gifts and loans of the General Government — Our hands remain untainted with these indirect bribes — we have always opposed them when extended to others, upon principle — and we are sorry to see agents from South Carolina — men of standing — members of the legislature — knocking at the doors of Congress and with cap in hand begging a portion of the treasury scraps. Still more should we regret to see them succeed. We know the language held by pliant politicians on such occasions — that while these good things are going we might as well take our share. This is bad reasoning and will produce bad consequences. It is admitting by our acts what we deny by our words — the power of Congress to make such grants. And it will be a most pernicious example to our younger sisters of the South. If we hope ever to bring Congress to a rigid adherence to the letter of the Constitution, and prevent them from assuming every power by construction, we should abstain from all participation in the unholy thing; and instead thereof steadily assert our principles, and show by our example that we really believe, and wish to establish, what we are contending for.

In the existing status of political sentiment, it was clearly a *faux pas* for the directors of a South Carolina company to ask subvention from Congress. The application by the directors seems not to have been renewed after the public scolding which they received in the spring of 1829.

The survey and location of the route was proceeding to the general satisfaction. The committee of the chamber of commerce appointed early in 1828 had reported that the country toward Hamburg, offering as it did a long, straight, dry, gently sloping ridge for most of the distance, and plenty of excellent timber, was exceptionally inviting for railway building. The extreme western end of the route, it is true, offered a grave problem by reason of the steep slope of the land from the summit of the ridge to the Savannah River bottoms; but the difficulty there could probably be met by an "inclined plane" with a stationary engine and cables. As to motive power, the committee reckoned that a horse could draw upon an iron track eight times as heavy a load as upon a turnpike, and fourteen times as much as upon common roads, and that horse-power, if it alone were available, could be used with profit; but for the sake of both economy and efficiency the committee declared itself in favor of steam locomotion. It had made a study of relative cost from all the available books. Including fuel at $5 per day, and the services of a man and a boy and allowing for wear and tear on the engine, it reckoned that the running of a six horse-power locomotive would cost $2400 per year, while the equivalent force if derived from the use of horses would require seven relays of six horses each, with the services of one man to every pair of horses, and was estimated to cost $8736. Steam was therefore reckoned to be cheaper at the rate of $6336 per unit of six horse-power per year in running expenses. The road-bed advised by the committee was to be made of piles well driven into the earth, in parallel lines, secured by transverse timbers. On these piles heavy wooden rails, eight by twelve inches, were to be fastened, and upon the upper edge of each of these was to be nailed an iron bar, two and a quarter inches broad by three-eighths of an inch thick, upon which the wheels of the carriages were to move.[1]

The first official survey of the route with maps and profiles was reported upon, August 27, 1829, by William

[1] *Report of a Special Committee appointed by the Chamber of Commerce to inquire into the advantages of a Rail Road communication between the city of Charleston and the towns of Hamburg and Augusta,* Charleston, 1828, 32 pages.

Howard, the head of the engineering corps detailed by the United States war department. Howard described the country as of light sandy soil, no rocks, timbered with live-oak and abundant pine, which latter was of excellent quality except for the thirty or forty miles at the Charleston end of the route, where the pine was soft and perishable. The remarkable ridge of land which extends from near Givhan's ferry on the Edisto River, eighteen miles from Charleston, in a line a few miles southwest of the Edisto River and parallel to it, for a distance of eighty miles to the highlands above Hamburg, he described as extremely favorable to the proposed work. This one route was so clearly the most superior possible that he had surveyed no other except for short distances and small departures.

The route which Howard presented ran from Charleston up the neck between the Cooper and Ashley rivers, crossed the Ashley near its source, ran in an experimental line across the Edisto River at Givhan's ferry, then ascended and followed the long ridge with a very gentle incline for 96 miles to the "Horse Pen Pond" at the summit. The grade throughout this 96 miles of ascent was generally 8 to 12 feet per mile, with a maximum of sixteen feet for one two-mile stretch. After crossing a level space, the route must then enter a much more rapid descent to Hamburg. From an altitude of 499 feet above the sea at Horse Pen Pond, the road must descend 383 feet in 17½ miles to the Augusta bridge in Hamburg; and unless a wide detour should be resorted to, 215 feet of this drop must be accomplished in the space of 1⅝ miles beginning near the point then marked by the house of one Williams and in more recent times marked by the well-known town of Aiken. Howard advised a delay in grading this difficult portion of the route until the advantage of experience could be had from the work on the easier stretches. For road-bed and track he advised iron strap rails on wooden timbers not less than 6 by 9 inches, and 4½ feet apart. These wooden rails were to be of the best heart pine, squared on the inner edge for receiving the iron plate, and beveled on the outer edge to shed water. These were to be supported upon sills of live-oak or lightwood, laid transverse at distances of 8 feet and sunk 4 or 5 inches in the ground, with the rail and sill let into each other and made fast with keys or wedges of hard wood. At the middle of each space between the sills, a lightwood post should be placed under each rail. Where the level of the road was to be above the natural surface of the ground, "it is proposed," Howard said, "in certain situations, instead of embankment, to raise the rails on posts or piles, properly tied and braced together, as it is practised on the Delaware and Hudson road." In this case, if horse-power were to be used, the horse path could be built upon one side of the track, and a small friction wheel set to run against the inner edge of the rail to obviate the obliqueness of the pull. Another expedient would be to have paths on both sides of the track and use two horses, as on the Mauch Chunk railroad; but in that case there would be a loss of power in the instance of convoys not requiring the strength of but one horse. The iron plate, if preferred, might be laid upon the outer edge of the rails, if it should be decided, as on the Baltimore and Ohio Railroad, to place the flanges on the outside of the wheels. "In using the road," Howard finally advises, "I would recommend that the maximum weight allowed to any carriage with its load, be fixed at much less than is the usual practice; and that if the locomotive engine be adopted, that its weight should be diminished as much as possible."[1] In the inexperience of all concerned, these crude plans of road construction were acted upon in large measure; and in consequence, within a few years the road had to be almost entirely remade.

In September, 1829, the company employed Horatio Allen as chief engineer. Allen[2] had been a resident engineer upon the Delaware and Hudson Canal, from 1825, and had been active in changing the plan of that company from canal to railroad construction. He was an enthusiastic student of steam locomotion, and upon taking charge in South Carolina put an end to the consideration of horses for motive power. At his advice the gauge was changed to five feet; but the piling construction for the road-bed was retained. The system of piles was dealt with by a writer in the *Southern Review*, May, 1831. It was conceded to be not only economical, but efficient in securing the rail from sinking, if the piling were properly driven and the superstructure well executed. The liability of the rails to cant and spread from the strain of traffic, he thought, might be prevented by the device of slanting the piles. The chief objection to the whole plan, he said, lay in the liability of the wood to decay; and this could not be wholly obviated.[3] As a matter of fact, it was the

[1] William Howard, *Report on the Charleston and Hamburg Rail Road*, Charleston, 1829, 18 pp.

[2] M. N. Forney, *Memoir of Horatio Allen*, n. d. Reprinted from the *Engineering Journal*.

[3] The same writer observed that when the weight of traffic preponderates in one direction, it is best for the road to slope slightly in that direction, and notes that such will be the case in the present instance. *Southern Review*, vol. vii, pp. 159–191 (published at Charleston).

rapid decay of timbers at the surface of the ground which, after a few years' trial, caused the complete abandonment of the piling system in favor of embankments and trestles.

Allen now proceeded to a new survey for the road. Deciding that Howard in his choice of a route had sacrificed too much in distance for the sake of paltry savings in grades, he laid out almost an air-line from Charleston to the site of Aiken. His route, lying through Summerville and Blackville, lay far enough northward to avoid crossing the Ashley River, and crossed the Edisto some thirty miles above the point proposed by Howard. This survey cut off fourteen miles from the previous estimate.[1]

The promoters of the road were much encouraged by Allen's show of zeal and ability. In August, 1830, the stock subscription had increased to $581,340, made up wholly of private takings, except for $20,000 subscribed by the city corporation of Charleston. The directors were authorized by resolution of the stockholders, August 19, to proceed at once to the definite location of the road and the letting of contracts. Allen and his assistants began the location, November 15, 1830, and completed it by June 4, 1831. The first contracts were let in December, 1830, and most of the rest during the course of the following spring.[2]

The work of moving dirt and driving piles was begun early in 1831, and pushed forward as rapidly as circumstances made possible.

[1] *State Rights and Free Trade Almanac*, 1832, Charleston, 1832.

[2] Report of Alexander Black, commissioner, May 1, 1833, printed in the *Annual Report* of the Board of Directors of the South Carolina Canal and R.R. Co., May 6, 1833, Charleston, 1833.

Meanwhile, in March, 1830, Mr. E. L. Miller, a director of the company, who had been present at the opening of the Liverpool and Manchester railroad and had seen Stephenson's engine operated, offered to build a locomotive of his own designing at the foundry at West Point, N.Y. His offer was accepted, the engine was built accordingly, and received in the city at the end of October, 1830.[1] A few miles of track were laid on the route from Charleston for the purpose, and on it the engine was tested, December 9, with unexpectedly good results.[2] In lively anticipation of its future services, the engine was given the name, "The Best Friend of Charleston." It ran at intervals to haul pleasure parties or road materials with entire success until one day in the next summer, "when the negro who acted as fireman, being incommoded by the unpleasant noise of the steam escaping through the safety valve, ventured on the expedient of confining it by pressing the weight of the body on the lever gauge of the safety valve, which experiment resulted in the explosion of the boiler."[3] The engine was made over and rendered good service under the name of "The Phœnix." What became of the negro is not related. Another small engine, the "West Point," was put upon the road before or just after the wrecking of the "Best Friend." The character of

[1] A. S. Salley, in the *Charleston News and Courier*, December 22, 1901.

[2] For experiments with horse power, crank cars, and sailing, see the *State Rights and Free Trade Almanac*, 1832, Charleston, 1832. The "Best Friend" when first received had wheels made of spokes. These were quickly found to be not strong enough for the strain, and others of a more solid and serviceable pattern had to be substituted before the engine could become ready for service. W. L. Trenholm, in *South Carolina Resources*, p. 632.

[3] Report of Alexander Black, commissioner, May 1, 1833.

its operations is indicated in a notice published by the company in the *Charleston Mercury*, July 25, 1831: —

> The Locomotive Engine runs every day for passengers at half past 4 P.M. Parties wishing it at any other hour can be accommodated by applying to the Engineer.[1]

These first engines, in spite of their primitive construction and small power, could run at 16 to 21 miles an hour, carrying 5 or 6 of its little cars and 40 to 50 passengers. With the empty cars they could run from 35 to 40 miles per hour.[2]

The effect of the engine in motion upon the native rustics is indicated by an anecdote published in the *Augusta Constitutionalist*, March 20 1832. A farmer from the up-country who had never heard of steam engines happened to be driving his team near the track when the train came along on full steam. The mules ran away and destroyed the wagon and contents. When picked up the wagoner was asked why he hadn't held on to his team.—"'Hold on,' said Hodge, 'How the d—l could you expect me to hold on, when I saw H—ll in harness coming down on me!'"

In the work of constructing the road-bed and track, progress was delayed and the expense increased above the estimates by a prevailing shortage of labor. When a number of contractors all along the line advertised for laborers at the same time, the floating supply proved entirely inadequate to the demand. Most of the slaves were employed as usual in the routine work of the planta-

[1] Reprinted by A. S. Salley in the *Columbia* (S.C.) *State*, June 4, 1899.

[2] A. S. Salley, in the *Charleston News and Courier*, December 22, 1901.

tions; the free negroes were few and not inclined to hard work; and the native whites of the laboring class not much attracted by the opportunity. The competition of the contractors carried the rate of wages to 50 and 75 per cent above the rates formerly prevailing,[1] and the supply was still short of the demand. Some of the smaller contractors, in fact, were obliged from dearth of labor to forfeit their contracts.[2] The principal firm of contractors, Messrs. Gray & Co., resorted to the expedient of importing a large number of white laborers from the North or from Europe, as their chief reliance. In November, 1831, there were 132½ miles of the road under contract and 637 persons employed in forwarding it.[3] In the spring of 1832 it was reported that two thousand or more laborers were at work on the route. After the stockholders' meeting in May, 1832, the directors made still greater exertion to hasten the work, and kept as many hands constantly busy as they could find for employ. The number of men at work was continually so small as to keep the impatient members of the company in a state of exasperation.[4] The recurrence of the malarial seasons deprived the work regularly of a large part of its force in the spring and summer, and dispersed the laborers beyond easy recall for the succeeding cool season. The labor troubles of the contractors and the company are illustrated in the following extract from the directors' report of 1833: —

> Beyond Edisto River, the white force brought out by the Messrs.

[1] Alexander Black, *Report* of May 1, 1833.

[2] *Charleston Courier*, May 3, 1831, quoted in the *Federal Union*, May 12, 1831.

[3] *Niles' Register*, November 19, 1831.

[4] *Annual Report of the Directors*, May 6, 1833.

Gray was reduced in number on the approach of summer, although as many as possible were employed in healthy situations at the excavations for the Inclined-plane, and on the Road in the vicinity of the Levels. These men, taking advantage of the diminution of their number, and the absolute necessity for having the work forwarded, required a large advance in wages and allowances, all other workmen being engaged in raising a crop. The Engineer was compelled to submit. This compliance was immediately followed by a demand from the owners of the black hands, for an advance also in their pay, which fell heavily on the contractors as well as the company along the whole line of the road.

The same report relates that the building of the inclined plane had from various causes proved much more difficult, tedious, and expensive than had been estimated by the engineer — "chiefly by its double line in the whole slope of nearly a mile, and by the novelty of construction by men unacquainted with the business. Indeed the whole work has been done by apprentices, who only begun to be expert when the work is done."

A financial difficulty and its temporary solution are also explained in the report: "The Direction having been in want of money to defray their heavy expenditures, and unwilling to embarrass the future proceedings of the company by calling for more than $100 on each share, agreed to pledge the 1187 shares remaining on hand from the original stock, with the income from the road when completed, for loans at the rate of 7 per cent annum. Hitherto no difficulty has been experienced in obtaining the necessary funds in this way." A loan from the state government, amounting to $100,000, had already been secured and utilized.

At an adjourned meeting of the stockholders, June 10, 1833, a financial statement was presented, as follows: —

Stock subscribed, 5813½ shares		$581,340
State loan		100,000
Individual loans		75,420
Discounts from banks		53,040
Receipts from the road		18,982.92
Receipts from sales of land		2,717
Expenditures to date	$831,365.81	$831,499.92
Expenditures necessary to complete contracts on the road, for iron, locomotives, cars, etc.	73,044.20	
Amount still to be provided		$72,910.15

The company succeeded in raising the additional sum required, and the railroad was completed to Hamburg at the end of September, 1833, at a total cost of $904,499, or $5,625.92 per mile,[1] including 7 locomotives, 46 cars of several sorts, some horses, a few negro slaves, amounting in value to $6,146, and several parcels of real estate, valued at $15,388.25.

The large excess of cost over the estimates was due to the heightened cost of labor, the partial substitution of trestles for piling in the ravines, the embarrassments from quicksand in some excavations and "hard-pan" in others, and the great expense of the inclined plane.

Difficulties had been met and conquered, one by one. The directors in their report of May 6, 1833, described some of their problems and delays in getting rails and locomotives made and delivered, in altering engines designed for burning coke or hard wood and adapting them to the use of the local fat pine, in remedying and trying to prevent the disasters of broken axles, and in equipping all the cars and engines with springs, so as to reduce the pounding and strain. "Most of the troubles hitherto encountered," they said, "have arisen from the want of care and the want

[1] *American Railroad Journal,* August 2, 1834.

of experience in the management of the engines, in a greater degree than from the defects in the Engines themselves. . . . In fact the whole business of Rail-Roads is new to all the world, and to this company in common with all others. The Direction have availed themselves of the experience dearly bought by others, and have profited by it, and where their circumstances were peculiar, have been obliged to purchase experience, as all others had done before them." Not a life had been lost, they were happy to say, from accident nor from the diseases of the climate: this the more cause for gratitude in view of the distressing mortality among the laborers on the public works in Pennsylvania and New Jersey. No litigious lawsuits had arisen with contractors, agents, landowners, or other claimants. Another cause for congratulation was the immunity of the track from damage by freshets. The system of piling and trestles, nicknamed the "inland bridge," whatever its shortcomings, had at least proven advantageous in times of flood, when embankments might have choked the flow of water and caused disaster.

The road had been put into operation with a regular schedule as far as Branchville, 62 miles, on November 7, 1832; to Midway, 10 miles farther, on February 7, 1833,[1] and to Hamburg, 136 miles as the road actually measured, at the beginning of the following October. The road when completed was the longest railway in the world; and its operation was considered marvelous at the time.

Through the use of a truck devised by the chief engineer of the road, Horatio Allen, who had gone north in 1831 to contract for locomotives, the company in 1832 had added several eight-wheeled engines to its equipment;

[1] Alexander Black, commissioner, *Report,* May 6, 1833.

but by reason of their bad adjustment to the character of the fuel supply, they were not available for service until the summer of 1833. Meanwhile the two diminutive four-wheeled engines, the "West Point" and the "Phœnix," were the whole motive power of the road. With these the company handled all the passenger traffic that offered, but confined their handling of freight to cotton downward and light merchandise upward. Live stock, lumber, and other articles which could pay only low rates, were necessarily declined by the road for the time.[1]

Meanwhile a system of inspection and repairs for the road, and safeguarding against accidents was effectively developed. Sections of four to eight miles in length were laid off, and a watchman and one or two negro hands assigned to each. The watchman was required to walk daily up one side of his section and down the other, minutely examining the road, and with the aid of the negroes correcting every defect, especially securing the wedges and remedying all depression caused by the sinking of piles or sleepers, securing the iron where the spikes were drawn or broken, clearing the road of weeds and shrubbery, to prevent injury to the road by shade and moisture or by fire, and keeping up the supply of fuel and water for the engines. There was also a general supervisor for each of the two general divisions of the road, each with a staff of four colored mechanics and three laborers, to be employed where most needed. Each watchman was required to submit a monthly report of work and expenses.[2] The road was equipped with some twelve turnouts and fifteen watering places with pumps.

[1] Alexander Black, *Report.*

[2] *Ibid.*

As to rates of transportation, the directors said in their report of May, 1833, that the legislature, when fixing the maximum charges in the provisions of the charter granted the company, had taken good care of the people's interest. In view of the absence of competition, they said, they saw no reason in general to put rates on a scale lower than the legal maximum for the railroad, which was only half as high as the rates formerly maintained by stages, wagons, etc. At the rate established, they reported, "it is cheaper to owners of negroes to pay their passage on the Rail Road than to make them walk on the common road free of expense"; and the raftsmen on the Edisto were finding it economical to send their paddling boats back by rail after having carried rafts to Charleston.[1] In the suburbs of Charleston, however, an exception had been made, and rates so reduced "that a poor man cannot afford to walk." On the whole the public seemed "more than satisfied."

For the first three months after the opening of the first division on November 7, 1832, the accommodations offered were very poor, and the receipts averaged only $58 per day. At the time of the report in May, 1833, the receipts amounted, from freight and passage, to $120 per day, in spite of the fact that road materials had the preference over all other freight. The prospect was described as very bright for a great increase in earnings as soon as Hamburg should be reached; for not only would Augusta yield passenger and freight traffic on a large scale, but there was promise of considerable trade from areas as distant as Tennessee, even in the absence of railways

[1] Specific rates and regulations were published, among other places, in the *State Rights and Free Trade Almanacs* of the respective years. Extract reprinted in the appendix to this chapter.

through Georgia. On the other hand, the line of steam packets about to be established between Charleston and New York, would also stimulate traffic by furnishing better connections from the East.[1] The earnings to the end of 1833 amounted to $44,070.73. From the beginning of 1834, detailed statistics are available, as will appear below.

A celebration was held in Charleston, October 2, 1833, in honor of the opening of the road for its full length to Hamburg. Elias Horry, who had succeeded William Aiken as president upon the death of the latter in 1831, delivered an address upon the occasion, congratulating the company and the city upon the completion of the great pioneer task, and at once inviting public attention to the demands and prospects of railroad building to the north and west of the Hamburg line, in order to tap the Piedmont more effectually, and penetrating farther, to pierce the mountains and make the trade of the great West tributary to the Southeastern seaboard.[2] The growth of this idea will be treated later.

A traveler from New England with journalistic talent has left us a record of a trip over the railroad to Hamburg made by him in the first month of its full operation, October, 1833:[3] —

> The road consists of a single track, with turnouts at various places. The rails of the track are built of the timber of the country,

[1] *Annual Report of the Board of Directors of the South Carolina Canal and Railroad Company . . .*, Charleston, 1833.

[2] Elias Horry, *Address*, Charleston, 1833.

[3] *Augusta Constitutionalist*, January 3, 1834, reprinted from the St. Augustine *Herald*, with an editorial note describing the document as a letter dated Columbia, S.C., November 10, from a personal acquaintance of the St. Augustine editor, and one whose accuracy might be implicitly relied upon.

hard pine full of pitch. In the wet and boggy places first are driven piles, ten feet, more or less, into the soil. Over these connecting timbers are placed: then cross timbers keep the connecting timbers at an equal distance from each other. On the ends of the cross timbers the rail timbers are placed: on the inner side of the upper surface the irons are nailed, all of them throughout being of the same width. On the few excavated places that occur, the same construction exists except that there are no piles, the connecting timbers in the former case lying hard upon the ground. The city of Charleston being one dead level, as well as the surrounding country for miles, there are excellent routes for railroads. The expense of them is of course far less than at the North, where bridges are to be built, hills to be cut through, and the like. Indeed the expense of the whole of this road is said to be less than any one of the Northern railroads.

Before we started, the engine was sent off for some distance to be tried. After the passengers had been detained some quarter-hours beyond the appointed hour, they started at the rate of ten or twelve knots. The country, as far as the eye could see, was shaded with here and there a solitary live-oak, and woods of pitch-pine. In a little while the speed of the engine began insensibly to diminish, and soon after came to an end. The cause of this stoppage I was told was "want of steam." So after Sambo had been sent to pick up some brush and other procurable fuel, the engine began to go again — like the Dutchman who while advancing in the march, stopped to light his pipe, that he might attack the enemy under cover of the smoke. . . .

[At Woodstock] the road seemed to vary in construction in no respect from the part at Charleston. The management of the engine was indeed wonderful. Now it went as if Satan were at its heels; now it scarcely dragged its freight. Several times it came to a dead stand, for "want of steam." . . .

After continuing in the afternoon in the above manner — stopping, then going fast, then slow again — we arrived at two or three log houses, and one half built "tavern" amid a half burnt forest of pitch-pine. Here was Blackville. A few fires glimmered on the ground: a square roughboarded fabric stood by the roadside, which was the "store house." Here was to be our tarrying place for the night. We had accomplished the wonderful distance of 90 miles from 8 A.M. to 6½ P.M. on a rail road, through a country with a hard soil, and not a hill rising twelve feet the whole journey. The whole country for 100 miles from the seacoast is as level as your frog pond.

After warming ourselves, we were shown into a room furnished with a few old chairs and a table. The food upon it was good; the cooking probably that of slaves — miserable. After supper I went out and stood by the fire in the open air. . . . At last tired and fatigued I applied for a couch to the landlord. There were, I believe, but five rooms, and twenty-five or thirty passengers were to share them. The landlord led me to a room containing three beds. . . . The room was occupied by four — a New Yorker and a Georgian in one bed, a raal tar in a second and myself in a third. The Georgians have naturally some of the best of hearts. Hence why a Yankee should be thought worthy of one's society. A South Carolinian would have shunned the New Yorker as if a wild beast.

There being no appeal from this mode of sleeping, a submission seemed best. Five rooms were built, opening into one entry separate from each other by a boarded partition, of which the cracks were one inch only in width. Besides, the partitions did not extend to the top. The rooms very much resembled a row of stalls in a stable, open above. Anything said at one end could be heard at the other. In one of them were several ladies.

After having slept soundly, the bell rang, and "get up" was the watch word. Having dressed, the door to breakfast soon opened. Of the latter I make no complaint except of its cooking. The fee of $4.00 was paid, and we started again.

The road continued as before. The land grew uneven. Long and undulating hillocks appeared. Where those were cut through the ground exactly resembled [red] brick dust. Here commenced the upland. Nearly 100 miles had been one vast flat plain.

The country grew more hilly until we reached Aiken, 120 miles from Charleston, where the car stopped, and our baggage was taken out and put into another car, to go down the "inclined plane." The old car immediately returned to Charleston. The new one was let down the inclined plane by negroes. Its perpendicular descent might have been 200 feet, in a horizontal distance of 1200. On either side was a stand with railings. Two negroes on each stand turned a crank in its center. We soon began to go about five or six miles an hour. The country became more hilly in our cruise. At 4 P.M. the car stopped at Hamburgh, 136 miles from Charleston. Having been apprised of the fare — seventy-five cents each — demanded by the stage for carrying passengers across Augusta bridge, I slipped a quarter into a negro's hands and walked on foot while he lugged my baggage to the U. S. Hotel in the city. The stage driver seemed chagrined.

The U. S. Hotel is a large airy building. The fare is $1.50 per day. The building, its furniture, the table, and the attendance are exactly of the same quality as those of the Commercial at Boston, with this difference, that the servants are slaves, and the food much crisped in cooking. . . . Augusta is the finest city I have yet seen at the South. The streets are very broad and fringed like those of Charleston with rows of China trees. Broad Street is about half a mile long.

A more precise description of the inclined plane, after its equipment had been completed, is given in the *American Railroad Journal,* August 2, 1834. The Charleston and Hamburg Railroad, it says, is

the longest railroad ever constructed. It rises 510 feet from Charleston, and then from this point, 16 miles from Hamburgh, descends 360 feet to Augusta bridge. There is an inclined plane of 3800 feet in length, and a descent of 180 feet. It has three grades of descent, the steepest of which is one in thirteen. From the foot of the plane the remainder of the descent is overcome in ten miles with an average inclination of 18 feet per mile. The road is a single track with necessary turnouts, except at the inclined plane, where there is one mile of double track. At the inclined plane there is a stationary power of two twenty-five horse-power engines working on one crank. Locomotive power is used on the road. It has cost, including motive power, cars, and everything complete, ready for use, $904,499, or $6,625.92 per mile. This road will be continued, or rather the Georgia road will connect with it and pass through

Athens, and thence westward, and connect with the Tuscumbia and Decatur, and the Tennessee Railroad, to the Mississippi, thus forming one of the most important works in the Union. The route from Charleston to Hamburgh, 135 miles, is performed in less than twelve hours with great ease, and will be done in eight hours.

By the beginning of 1834, operations had reached the routine stage. The character of the time-tables, rates, and regulations for passengers and freight may be learned from the company's announcements in the almanacs, reprinted examples of which are appended to this chapter.

The scale of operations and earnings is shown by the following table, which covers the first six years after the beginning of regular accounting and the publishing of annual summaries:[1] —

CHARLESTON AND HAMBURG RAILROAD, TRAFFIC AND EARNINGS, 1834 TO 1839

Ye'r	Miles of Road	Miles Run	Passengers Carried	Bales of Cotton Carried	Passenger Earnings	Freight Earnings		Mails, Storage, &c.	Total Receipts
						Up	Down		
1834	136	154,000	26,649	24,567	$79,050	$55,009	$28,205	$4,294	$166,559
1835	136	160,072	34,283	34,760	109,576	89,237	42,546	8,394	249,754
1836	136	161,160	39,216	28,497	129,982	101,335	38,699	1,595	271,614
1837	136	153,000	41,554	34,395	131,282	84,958	53,311	10,663	280,215
1838	136	190,264	44,487	35,346		111,027	52,395		323,381
1839	136	232,832	37,283	52,585		129,776	74,547		422,842

Statistics of running expenses and reckonings of net earnings are not given in the accessible documents for this period. All net earnings, in fact, during the early years of operation were at once devoted to the liquidation of the company's debt, the improvement of the road-bed and track, and the increase of equipment. The original struc-

[1] The statistics here given are gathered from the report of the Louisville, Charleston, and Cincinnati R.R. Co., for 1838, p. 18, and Dawson and De Saussure's *Census of Charleston for 1848*, p. 170.

ture on piles and trestling over the low places was quickly found inadequate to the needs of traffic, and had to be replaced rapidly with earthen embankments; and, further, a still more serious shortcoming was found in the rails of which the original track had been made. These rails were merely flat bars of wrought iron, weighing 15 pounds to the yard, spiked upon wooden stringers. Before the end of 1834 the company had begun to replace these "strap rails" with "flange rails," which were somewhat thicker bars of iron wrought in the shape of the letter L, and spiked to stringers with the lip or flange turned down against the inner side of the wooden stringer[1] — thus protecting the wood from contact with the flanges of the wheels, furnishing a somewhat stiffer bar, and somewhat reducing the unevenness of the track. Injury to trackage and accidents to railway stock would have been much more serious than actually occurred, had it not been that the road was almost devoid of curves and perceptible grades except in the one section at the western end.

The volume of traffic at times in the season of cotton marketing, and the widely extended interest in the success of the road, are indicated by the following item from the *Charleston Courier*, reprinted in the *American Railroad Journal*, December 13, 1834: —

> A most unprecedented and pleasing circumstance was witnessed on Sunday last, at the Railroad Depository, being the arrival of three locomotives at one time, having at their train sixty freight cars laden with nine hundred and eighty bales of cotton.

The small income of the company from the mails in the year 1836 is explained by the following item from

[1] Report of the president of the Louisville, Cincinnati, and Charleston R.R. Co., 1838.

the *Southern Banner*, a newspaper at Athens, Ga., December 3, 1835, which also gives a hint at the unfriendly spirit which many Georgians at times showed toward the South Carolina road: —

> The South Carolina Railroad Company having refused to carry the mail between Charleston and Augusta unless they were exempted from furnishing bond (as required from all contractors) for the faithful performance of their contract and allowed to make as many failures as they choosed without being fined, it is now transported by way of Savannah until other arrangements can be made. The public will doubtless appreciate the wonderful regard manifested by the company for its own interest, and reciprocate it as occasion offers.

The road in the first few years of its operation did fairly well in a small way, and gave promise of yielding, after a time, a moderate return upon the investment. Such a prospect, however, was far from satisfying its promoters and stockholders and the Charleston interests with which they were identified. The mission of the road from the first had been to divert a large traffic from Savannah to Charleston and to develop a much more intense traffic demand than had existed. The line to Hamburg was only one link in a contemplated chain. The Charlestonians accordingly began to promote further enterprises even before the line to Hamburg was completed. Extensions both westward and northward from the initial line were wanted as feeders. The citizens of Augusta and the towns lying westward were eagerly constructing the Georgia Railroad, and thus saving effort for the Charlestonians; and the only vexatious problem in that direction was that of more effectively connecting the roads of the two companies. The city of Augusta, in the interest of its draymen and tavern keepers, forbade the two tracks to approach within a mile of each other. This necessitated a breaking of cargo, and put the Savannah boats on a footing of equal or superior competition with the Charleston railroad in bidding for the cotton brought to Augusta by the Georgia Railroad. This tantalizing problem, however, was not one of construction, but of negotiation.

The chief extension task of the Charlestonians lay toward the north, by means of branch railroads to Columbia and Camden, and prolongations thence indefinitely toward, and perhaps across, the mountains. The first great project to meet this demand was that of the Louisville, Cincinnati, and Charleston Railroad Company, a product of the inflationist sentiment which generally prevailed in the United States in the middle of the eighteen-thirties.

APPENDIX I

Summary of the acts of December 19, 1827, and January 30, 1828, chartering the South Carolina Canal and Railroad Company

The act of December 19, 1827, authorized the formation of a company, with a capital stock of $700,000 empowered to build canals or railroads from Charleston to Columbia, Camden, and Hamburg, and entitled to all rights and protection granted by an existing general law to ferry, bridge, and turnpike companies. The act vested the company with the exclusive right of transportation upon the railroads which it should construct, but limited its charges to the rate of thirty-five cents per hundred weight on heavy articles and ten cents per cubic foot on articles by measurement, for every one hundred miles, and five cents per mile for every passenger. The company was granted a monopoly of railroad and canal building and operation between Charleston and the towns named, for a period of thirty-six years; and was empowered to farm out its privilege of operation, or to open its railroads and canals to public use for toll, if it so desired, provided that the company's annual net income from such tolls should not exceed twenty-five per cent upon its investment. To secure and hold its charter, the company was required to commence its work of construction within two years and finish it within six years from the date of this act, and to keep its routes in operation.

The act of January 30, 1828, repeated much of the substance of the preceding act, in more effective phrasing, vested the company with powers independent of the law governing ferry, bridge, and turnpike companies, and provided definite machinery for the company's organization. Subscription books were to be opened in Charleston, Columbia, Camden, and Hamburg on March 17, 1828, by commissioners named in the act, and were to be kept open for four days; instalments of ten dollars per share must be paid in at the time of subscription; the commissioners at the inland towns were then to report to those at Charleston, and if the total stock had been subscribed in amount exceeding one-half of the authorized capital of $700,000, the company should be considered as having been formed. If above $700,000 had been subscribed, the subscriptions were to be scaled down by the commissioners according to a rule prescribed in the act. The Charleston commissioners were then to call a meeting of the subscribers, with proxies allowed, at which officers of the company should be elected. The owners of not more than eight shares each were entitled under the act to one vote for every two shares which they held; those owning shares in larger number should have votes in a scale decreasing until it reached the basis of ten votes for forty shares and one vote additional for every ten shares above that number. Elections thereafter should be made annually according to the same system of balloting. The company was vested with all the general powers enjoyed by corporations in the state, was empowered to make its own by-laws, and was exempted from the operations of the act controlling ferry, bridge, and turnpike companies. It was empowered to purchase and hold real property and rights of way; and in cases of dispute as to the price of lands or rights of way where required for the purposes of the company, the same might be taken at a valuation fixed by commissioners appointed by courts of the locality and serving under oath. The company was empowered to build its canals or railways across roads and streams, provided it were done in such a way as not to obstruct traffic thereon. The freight and passenger rates were limited as in the preceding act, and the company was declared to be subject to the duties and requirements of common carriers. The company was vested with the sole right for the period of thirty-six years of building a railroad from Charleston to the Savannah River at or near Hamburg, and for that period of thirty-six years the stock of the company and the real estate owned by it and connected with its works as a common carrier were exempted by the charter from taxation. In conclusion, regulations were laid down regarding the collection by the company of instalments on its stock, and the increase of its stock, and regarding the powers of the president and board of directors. *Acts and Resolutions of the General Assembly of the State of South Carolina, passed in December, 1827, and January, 1828*, Columbia, 1828, pp. 73, 87; Thos. Cooper and D. J. McCord, *Statutes at Large of South Carolina*, vol. viii, pp. 354, 355.

APPENDIX II

Passenger and Freight Regulations of the Charleston and Hamburg Railroad, 1835

Reprinted from *Miller's Almanac*, Charleston, 1835

Regulations for Passenger Carriage

1st. All baggage at owner's risk, 75 lbs. allowed. 2d. Servants not admitted, unless having the care of Children, without the consent of all the Passengers. 3d. Passengers not allowed to stand on the outside platform. 4th. Smoking prohibited. 5th. No Gun or Fowling Piece shall be permitted to enter the car unless examined by the Conductor. 6th. The feet not to be put on the Cushions, nor the Cars soiled, defaced or injured in any way. 7th. Dogs not admitted into the Passenger Cars. 8th. At the ringing of the Bell, Passengers will be allowed one minute to take their places. 9th. Seats must be engaged and paid for fifteen minutes previous to the hour of departure. As a general direction the Conductors of the Carriages are instructed not to permit any conduct that is inconsistent with good order, or the comfort and safety of the Passengers: for which especial ends these Rules have been established, and are required to be enforced with civility but strictly.

Rates of Freight

	Per Ft.	Per 100 Lbs.		Per Ft.	Per 100 Lbs.
To Branchville	7 cts	25 cts	To Aiken	23 cts	45 cts
" Midway	8 cts	28 cts	" Hamburg	24 cts	50 cts
" Blackville	10 cts	35 cts			

The above embraces all charges (including Insurance from Fire while travelling) and one week's Storage.

Charges for labour and storage (not exceeding one week) 3½ cents per hundred pounds, or 1 cent per cubic foot. After which storage to be charged at Charleston rates.

N. B. Hollow ware not taken loose. Demijons, Jugs, and every description of Glass or Earthenware, not securely packed, to be at the owner's risk.

Regulations

1st. Freight will be forwarded agreeably to the order of time it is received. That intended for the morning trip must be at the Depository by two o'clock the day previous, in good order, and marked with the name of the station on the line it is to be left at, or it will not be received. 2d. Freight for Jerico and the other stations up to, and including Reeves', is payable at the Charleston Depository, and to be left at the place directed, at the risk of the owner. 3d. All freight must be paid for at the respective Depositories on its delivery. 4th. No packages of any description, for any of the stations, entered on the freight list for less than 12½ cents, and no receipt given for a less amount of freight than 50 cents. 5th. GUNPOWDER prohibited.

SOUTH-CAROLINA RAIL-ROAD,

Between Charleston and Hamburg, S. C. opposite Augusta, (Geo.)

DEPARTS DAILY—The following is the Winter Arrangement.

PASSAGE TO HAMBURG.

LEAVES	ARRIVES	Dist. Miles	Fare $ cts
Charleston at 7 A M	at Woodstock at ¼ past 8 A M Breakfast	15	50
Woodstock at 8¾ A M	at Branchville at ½ past 12 A M	62	3 00
Branchville at 12½ A M	at Blackville at ¾ past 2 P M Dinner	90	4 50
Blackville at 3¼ P M	at Aiken, at ½ past 5 P M } remains all nig't	120	6 00
Aiken at 7 A M	at Hamburg at ¼ past 8 A M	136	6 75

PASSAGE TO CHARLESTON.

LEAVES	ARRIVES	Dist. Miles	Fare $ cts
Hamburg at 3½ P M	at Aiken at 5 P M } remains all nig't	16	75
Aiken at 7½ A M	at Blackville at ¾ past 9 A M Breakfast	46	2 25
Blackville at 10 A M	at Branchville at 12 M	74	3 75
Branchville at 12½ A M	at Summerville at ¾ past 3 P M Dinner	115	6 00
Summerville at 3¾ P M	at Charleston at ¾ past 5 P M	136	6 78

Midway is 72 miles from Charleston—Fare $3 50, and 64 from Hamburg—Fare $3 75. Inabnets is 32½ miles from Charleston—Fare $1 62½, and 133⅝ from Hamburg—Fare $5 12½.

And from one intermediate Station to *another*, FIVE CENTS per MILE. *Children under 12 years and Coloured Persons, half-price.*

At Branchville, passengers for Orangeburgh and Columbia, leave the Road.

All baggage at owner's risk—75 lbs. allowed. For other regulations, see Company's Office, East-Bay, corner of Dewees' Wharf.

OFFICERS.—*President*, John Ravenel. *Directors*—Wm Aiken, W Bell, Ker Boyce, Alex. Black, Wm Davidson, Dr. S. H Dickson, George Gibbon, John Haslett. B. J Howland, Dr. Jos. Johnson, T Street, T Tupper. *Sec'ry & Treas.* Henry Ravenel. *Assist. Sec'ry.* W H Inglesby. *Agent of Transportation*, W. Robertson, jr. *Master of Work-Shops*, —— Ross. *Chief Clerk*, John King, jr. *Agent up.* G. A. King. *Receiver of up Freight*, P. B. Lane. Receiver *of down Freight*, James Smith

Agent at Hamburg, —— Haig.

The Summer Arrangement differs from the above by one hour, as the Cars leave at 6 o'clock, and arrive at their destination at half-past 6 o'clock, each way.

Santee Canal Company.

President, Joshua W. Toomer, *Directors.* John S Richardson, John White, Isaac Lewis, Dr. Wm. Read, Chs. M'Beth. Wm. Clarkson, Thos. Gates, James Lamb, James L Petigru, George Buist, William Birnie, Harris Simons. John Duffus *Secretary and Treasurer.*

S. C. R.R. TIME AND RATE TABLE
From *Miller's Planters' and Merchants' Almanac for the year 1837.*
Charleston, S.C. [1836].

CHAPTER IV

THE CHARLESTON AND CINCINNATI PROJECT; AND THE REORGANIZED SOUTH CAROLINA RAILROAD COMPANY

IN the first half of this chapter we must follow two threads. The Charlestonians, or at least the leading spirits among them, with some support from the interior, were planning and promoting a great railway to the distant Northwest. At the same time they were concerned with the operation of their existing line and its extension for local traffic by branches to sundry points within the state. These two matters were so closely allied that for a time the original small company was absorbed by the new large one. But shortly the great project proved abortive, before any large work had been done; and a reorganization necessarily followed. This had a sobering effect. Thereafter the chief interest of stockholders and officials lay for a time in routine operation, the betterment of their road and equipment, and the offering of moderate encouragement for other companies to build feeding lines. Another inflationist movement occurred in South Carolina in the late fifties; but it did not greatly affect this company, and its treatment will fall in another chapter.

The launching of the Charleston and Hamburg Railroad had of course stimulated the desire already existing for a connection of the southern Atlantic seaports and Piedmont with the grain-growing regions beyond the mountains. Remote communities, impressed by the daring spirit of

Charleston and her show of financial resource, began to inquire into ways and means of getting into touch with her projected railway system. For example, as early as 1828, E. S. Thomas, formerly of Charleston and then a citizen of Cincinnati, proposed in Cincinnati a railroad to connect with the Charleston line.[1] Men of Louisville, Knoxville, and other communities also showed considerable interest. The officials and agents of the South Carolina Railroad Company, meanwhile, were actively promoting and encouraging many plans of connecting lines, whether of pike, canal, or railroad.

At the time of the South Carolina Railroad's completion to Hamburg in the fall of 1833, Elias Horry in his address of celebration [2] dealt chiefly with the prospects of extension. The people of Columbia, he said, were becoming actively interested in the project of the branch railroad suggested in the company's charter, and the citizens of Edgefield and Greenville, in upper South Carolina, were exerting themselves to secure a railway from their towns to the main line at Aiken.

A more important matter, he went on to relate, was the movement for a railroad connecting the West with the Atlantic, initiated by a resolution adopted by a meeting of citizens in Buncombe County, North Carolina, July 4,

[1] *Address of Colonel A. Blanding to the Citizens of Charleston*, 1836, p. 10; E. S. Thomas, *Reminiscences*, Hartford, 1840, vol. ii, pp. 108–111.

[2] Elias Horry, president of the South Carolina Canal and Railroad Company, *An Address respecting the Charleston and Hamburg Railroad and on the Railroad System as regards a large portion of the Southern and Western States of the American Union. Delivered in Charleston, at the Medical College. . . . October 2, 1833, on the completion of the Road.* Charleston, 1833.

1832, inviting their fellow-citizens of Tennessee and North and South Carolina who felt an interest in an interstate railroad along the route of the French Broad River, to assemble in convention. In response, a convention met at Asheville, N.C., on September 4 and 5, 1832. Twenty-eight delegates attended, — 8 from 4 counties in Tennessee, and 20 from 8 counties in North Carolina. One of the delegates appointed by Buncombe County was Mitchell King, of Charleston, who was made president of the meeting. Resolutions were adopted by the convention, one of which was that the president should appoint a committee for each of the states, Tennessee, North Carolina, and South Carolina, who should be charged with all matters of interest in regard to the proposed railway to connect the Western waters with the Atlantic. These committees were to correspond with each other, and act in unison in furtherance of the interests with which they were intrusted. As the committee for South Carolina, there were appointed Elias Horry, William Drayton, C. J. Colcock, Joel R. Poinsett, Joseph Johnson, and Mitchell King. The convention instructed these committees to work for public support for the project and to unite their best efforts to secure such legislation in their respective states as would promote it. The president of the convention was directed to request the President of the United States to detail a competent engineer to make a survey for a railroad from Columbia, S.C., to the mouth of the Nolichucky in Tennessee, and a survey of the French Broad and Holston rivers to Knoxville, and report the result to the committees. At the request of Mr. King, the President of the United States detailed Colonel Long for the desired survey. Of the $3000 estimated as the cost of the reconnaissance the

South Carolina legislature promptly voted $1000 on condition of a like appropriation from the other two states concerned. The North Carolina committee reported that the route within that state was without doubt feasible, and advised application for legislative charters. The committee for Tennessee reported that the efforts of the people and government of that state were for the time concentrated with all energy upon the canal and railroad works at the Muscle Shoals, and there was not much surplus energy for devotion to the transmontane project toward Charleston. This was as far as developments had gone at the time of Horry's address in the fall of 1833. The governments of North Carolina and Tennessee failed to vote any moneys for the proposed survey, and the mass of their people showed a considerable apathy when an outlay of money was wanted from them. In fact, a suspicion arises that if the Buncombe County and Asheville movements could be thoroughly examined, Charlestonians would be found working the wires. Whatever the source of initiative, the project did not find sufficient support for the time, and the Carolinians allowed it to rest for two years, until the fall of 1835. In this interval, however, an apparently independent movement in Cincinnati led to the appointment of a citizens' committee there in the spring of 1835, to inquire into the feasibility of a railroad to the Southern Atlantic states. The committee reported, August 15, that while it had not actually examined the route, it was sure that the Southern mountains were lower than those in Pennsylvania and Virginia, and a railroad connection with the region in question was feasible and highly desirable.[1]

[1] Report published in the *Journal of the Franklin Institute*, xxi, 101-106.

In South Carolina, meanwhile, the proposed local branch road to Columbia was the more active concern of the people. A survey of the route for that road was made in the summer of 1834 by A. A. Dexter and C. E. Detmold, who, like most others of the profession in that period, did extremely crude work in railway engineering. They advised the building of the track in a nearly straight line from Branchville, the junction point, to Columbia. The direction was slightly west of north, and the distance some 55 miles. The route for some 30 miles from Branchville lay almost level upon a watershed, and offered no problems. The upper part of the line, however, crossed several creek valleys, and finally crossed the Congaree River just at the town of Columbia. Inclined planes were proposed by the surveyors for crossing one or two of the creek valleys; and they were quite sure that an inclined plane with a stationary engine would be necessary in the descent to the Congaree River. In their report they explained that inclined planes were in use on nearly all of the English railways and on several of those in America, and had not proved a serious obstacle. The one which they proposed south of the Congaree was to overcome an elevation of 190 feet in a distance of 3237 feet. An engine working there constantly, they estimated, could draw up 522 tons of cotton per day at a cost of $15.96. In crossing the Congaree, the surveyors proposed to save expense in bridging by merely adding a second story to the existing wagon bridge, and having horses draw the cars across the bridge and over the remaining quarter-mile of track leading to the station in Columbia. The track advised by them was to consist of an iron strap rail three-quarters of an inch thick, with a half-inch downward flange, spiked upon wooden stringers which were to be dovetailed into "transverse caps," or cross-ties, five feet apart, and the cross-ties were to rest upon longitudinal sleepers lying in the earthen road-bed. Ballast was then of course unknown. With this substantial track, the surveyors said, a speed of 18 miles per hour might be allowed with perfect safety. The report concluded with an estimate of revenue and expense from operation which indicated net earnings of 11.3 per cent upon the estimated $547,000 of capital to be invested.[1]

Upon the basis of this report, the South Carolina Canal and Railroad Company resolved to undertake the work. The subscription books were opened in the spring of 1835 for three thousand additional shares of stock. The response was so eager that 5757 shares, nearly twice the number authorized, were applied for.[2] At about the same time subscriptions for a new bank with a capital of two million dollars, were opened in Charleston, and the desired amount was subscribed many times over.[3] This indicates that the abundance of credit and the mania for speculation which at that time prevailed all over the country was at least as rife at Charleston as elsewhere. In November, 1835, the stockholders determined to commence the branch to Columbia forthwith.[4] There was dissatisfaction with the survey, however, and probably some debate as to whether the road should run directly from Branchville to Columbia or make a wide bend to the eastward and serve as part of a branch to Camden as well as to Columbia. The ultimate decision was in favor of the eastward de-

[1] Report printed in the *American Railroad Journal,* iii, 690–692, 706–707.

[2] *Southern Banner* (Athens, Ga.), May 7, 1835.

[3] *Ibid.,* June 11, 1835.

[4] *Federal Union* (Milledgeville, Ga.), December 4, 1835.

flection; for that route gave the further advantage of a gradual slope down to the Congaree, and removed all need of inclined planes. As actually constructed, the line ran from Branchville northward 17 miles to Orangeburg, thence 23 miles northeast to the eastern bank of the Congaree, thence 28 miles northwest to Columbia. Afterward the branch to Camden was built, 37 miles north from Kingville, which lay just north of the Congaree crossing on the Columbia road. But all of this local work proceeded haltingly. In its earlier years it was overshadowed and perhaps delayed by the revival of the much more striking project of throwing a railroad across the mountains; and then, like all other such work, it was crippled by the crises of 1837 and 1839 and the severe depression in the early forties. The Columbia branch was opened for 17 miles only in 1840, and for its full length in 1842; the Camden branch was opened in 1848. It appears that such work as was accomplished in branch-road building before 1838, and very small in amount it was, was done by the original South Carolina Canal and Railroad Company with funds secured by the sale of additional shares of its regular stock. The work was continued and the road to Columbia completed by the Louisville, Cincinnati, and Charleston Railroad Company, which bought out the original corporation near the end of 1837. The branch to Camden was built by a new South Carolina Railroad Company, which resulted from a reorganization carried through between 1840 and 1842.

The renewal of activity at Charleston in the project for a transmontane railroad was stimulated in some measure by the activity of the city of Cincinnati, above noted. In October, 1835, the city council of Charleston, at the instance of the chamber of commerce, called a meeting of the citizens for October 22, to consider the situation and take any steps which might seem advisable. The intendant of the city, Edward W. North, presided. Colonel Robert Y. Hayne, formerly United States senator and governor of South Carolina, opened the meeting by presenting the proceedings of the citizens of Cincinnati on the subject of building a railroad from Ohio to Charleston. Hayne advocated the hearty entrance of the citizens of South Carolina and especially of Charleston into the scheme. He offered resolutions of cordial interest and desire to coöperate, and proposed the appointment of a committee of fifteen to report at an adjourned meeting upon the measures proper to take. The motion prevailing unanimously, the committee was duly appointed, with Hayne as chairman. At the adjourned meeting, November 4, Hayne's committee presented an address and resolutions. The address expressed pleasure at the Ohio proceedings, reviewed the discussion which the subject had already received in South Carolina, and declared, "the period has now arrived when the work can no longer be neglected without a criminal supineness and fatal disregard of our own best interests, as well as the duties which we owe to ourselves, and to posterity." The report of the Cincinnati committee and letters of prominent citizens were adduced in the address to show: (1) that it was essential to the prosperity of the Southern and Western states that they be connected by a railroad from the Ohio to the Atlantic; (2) that such a highway would open an inconceivably great traffic; (3) that such a work was practicable and could probably be built within a few years and within the means of the states through which it must pass; and

(4) that the most practicable, cheapest, and shortest route would be one connecting with the South Carolina Railroad, and therefore terminating at Charleston. The mighty power of steam was spoken of, and the opinion expressed that it would be easier to scale the southern Alleghanies than to turn them. The prospect of a resulting political union of South and West was also alluded to. The resolutions appended to the address stated the wish of the citizens of Charleston to coöperate heartily, they provided for the appointment of a committee of correspondence, with power to have explorations made, recommended that such committee's expenses be paid from the city treasury, requested the legislature to make liberal appropriations for surveys, etc., and promised that Charleston would send delegates to any convention which might be called in furtherance of the project. The address and resolutions were unanimously adopted. As the committee of correspondence, there were appointed R. Y. Hayne, James Hamilton, Charles Edmonston, Charles J. Colcock, Thomas Bennett, Ker Boyce, and Alexander Black.[1]

The legislature promptly complied with the request from Charleston, provided for a survey, appointed R. Y. Hayne, Abraham Blanding, and others as commissioners, and appropriated $10,000 to cover survey expenses. The other states concerned were invited to appoint commissioners, and general provisions were made for coöperation in the preliminary work for the proposed interstate railroad.[2] The other states failed to coöperate in the survey,

[1] *The Southern and Western Railroad, Proceedings in Charleston* (Caption), 27 pp.

[2] Act approved December 18, 1835, Cooper and McCord, *South Carolina Statutes at Large,* viii, 406.

and the South Carolina commissioners were able with the funds at hand to make an instrumental survey only in the mountain sections of the route and a general reconnaissance of the remaining easier portions. They reported in July, 1836,[1] that they had found and surveyed two practicable routes crossing the Blue Ridge, and had found the Cumberland range feasible to cross at Cumberland Gap, where the boundaries of Virginia, Kentucky, and Tennessee meet.

The Blue Ridge, they reported, was gradual in its slope downward along the French Broad River flowing toward the northwest; but the eastern face of the range was so abrupt as to afford a possible railroad crossing from the Saluda valley, in which the proposed road must lie, only in two places; and in these instances inclined planes and stationary power would very probably have to be used. One of the two available passes lay just east of Butt Mountain, a short distance east of the turnpike from Greensville, S.C., to Asheville; the other was at the head of Reedy Patch Creek, a tributary of Broad River. The summit of each of these passes lay nearly on a level with the table-land of Buncombe County, gently drained by the French Broad. The route to either of these passes must needs overcome rather steep ascents; in the one case 1344 feet in 11 miles; in the other 1102 feet in 18½ miles. The former, the Reedy Patch Creek route, would probably require the institution of three or four inclined planes; the latter, it might possibly be found, could be overcome without such resort.

[1] *Report of the Commissioners appointed by the Legislature of South Carolina to cause Examinations, Surveys, and Estimates to be made for a Railroad between Charleston and Cincinnati*, Columbia, South Carolina, 1836, 34 pp. The report was presented at the Knoxville Convention, July 4, and ordered printed.

N

Beyond the crest of the Blue Ridge, they said, the route descends along the French Broad from near Asheville to the Tennessee boundary, with an average descent of 13 feet, and a maximum of 45 feet to the mile. The river is often winding, with steep rocky banks, and contruction will be costly because of the probable necessity of several tunnels and of deep rock cuts and fills in the bed of the river. The route in Tennessee may run *via* Knoxville, or in a straighter line, around the foot of Clinch Mountain, 18 miles north of Knoxville, and reach the Cumberland range at Cumberland Gap, which would afford the most feasible crossing. At this gap, the mountain is compressed within a breadth of not more than 5000 feet, with a rise on the eastern face of 362 feet and on the western face of 504 feet. The crossing must be by means of two inclined planes, or through a tunnel a mile in length.

From Cumberland Gap, the route would best lie near Williamsburg, Mt. Vernon, Crab Orchard, Lancaster, and Nicholasville, to Lexington, and thence either along the ridge to the Ohio at Covington and Cincinnati, or along the valley of the Licking River, to the Ohio near Newport. A branch to Maysville might readily be built in Kentucky, and a branch to Georgia through Rabun Gap, or toward the west, turning the flank of the mountains. There were rich deposits of iron ore and coal on the route, especially at Cumberland Gap, the commissioners further reported, and, since provisions and labor could be had cheap in the region, it might be economical for the company to make its own rails for the middle section of the road. After an estimate of probable cost of the road, the report concludes with conjectures as to traffic and the effects of the railroad upon the country. The estimate of cost of construction is here given: —

Probable Cost of Building the Road

Charleston to Branchville, a second track, 62 miles, @ $4500	$279,000
Branchville to Columbia, 62 miles, @ $11,433	711,946
Thence to the junction of the Thicketty with Broad River, 65 miles @ $12,000	780,000
Thence to the junction of Green and Broad rivers, 52 miles @ $14,300	743,600
Thence to Asheville, 40 miles; first 10 miles through Blue Ridge, @ $40,000; next 30 @ $12,000	760,000
Thence down the French Broad to the mouth of the Nolichucky, 60 miles @ $30,000	1,800,000
Thence to the junction of the Elk with the Clear Fork of the Elk, crossing the streams in East Tennessee, 90 miles @ $30,000	2,700,000
Thence to Cincinnati, 190 miles @ $12,162	2,310,780
The branch to Louisville, at the cost of the road from Charleston to Columbia	990,000
The branch to Maysville, 60 miles @ $12,162	729,720
	$11,804,046
As the South Carolina Railroad and Canal Company will probably unite with us, deduct	990,000

Leaving $10,814,046 to be provided. The estimate is made for a double-tracked road for the whole distance.

The South Carolina legislature had already, at the end of 1835, chartered a company of giant proportions to undertake this tremendous task.[1] This act made provisions in detail for the launching and administration of a company called in the act the Cincinnati and Charleston Railroad Company, and later entitled the Louisville, Cincinnati, and Charleston Railroad Company. Books for subscriptions for six million dollars of stock in the company were to be opened at numerous places from Charleston to

[1] Cooper and McCord, *South Carolina Statutes at Large*, vol. viii, pp. 409–418. Charter granted December 19, 1835.

Cincinnati at the middle of October, 1836. A subscription of four million dollars was made requisite for the organization of the company. State and city subscriptions might be received. There was to be a general board of directors, with 24 members, including citizens of each of the states along the route, and at the company's discretion local boards also, consisting of a president and 8 directors to handle so much of the business within each state as might be prescribed by the general rules of the company. Power was given to construct railroads so as to form a continuous line from Charleston to Cincinnati; and, the other states consenting, the respective states were estopped for 36 years from permitting the construction of any parallel railroad within twenty miles of this company's line. A general power to construct branch railroads was also given. Rates of freight and passenger transportation charges were limited to the scale previously established for the South Carolina Canal and Railroad Company. Payments of $5 per share were required of subscribers at the time of subscription. Assessments might then be called for by the company, at a rate not exceeding $5 per share every 60 days, except in the last 2 instalments to complete the $100 per share; these might be of $10 each, with a 60-day interval. The company was empowered to increase its capital to an unlimited extent. Votes in stockholders' meetings were apportioned upon the basis already established in the South Carolina Canal and Railroad Company. The stock of the company, its dividends, and its property was exempted forever from taxation in any of the states in which the route lay (the other states consenting), unless the rate of dividends should grow to exceed the legal rate of interest in such states. The company was expressly prohibited from carrying on any banking operations, or effecting any insurance except on goods in transport or in the company's custody for transportation. A concluding clause provided that the company should be entitled only to such powers and privileges as should be granted to it by all the legislatures incorporating it, and it should be subject in each state to all restrictions and disabilities which might be imposed upon it by any of the legislatures by their acts of incorporation; so that its powers, privileges, and disabilities might be similar in all the states — Kentucky, Tennessee, North Carolina, and South Carolina. This act, finally, was declared to be void unless acts for a similar purpose should be enacted in the other three states. A subsequent act, December 21, 1836, canceled the requirement of obtaining a charter from Kentucky, and in case of failure to secure a charter in that state, relieved the company of all obligation to build its road into Kentucky.[1] Another act of 1836, as we shall see, bestowed very large banking powers upon the company through a very peculiar provision for an ancillary corporation called the Southwestern Railroad Bank.

The states of North Carolina and Tennessee, in due time and without making any difficulty, granted charters closely corresponding to that by South Carolina. Colonel Abraham Blanding, one of the commissioners named for the survey in the South Carolina act, went in person to Kentucky at the beginning of January, 1836, to present the matter to the consideration of the legislature then sitting at Frankfort. The leading spirits in that body were quite willing to see Kentucky connected by rail with South

[1] Cooper and McCord, viii, 431.

Carolina; but they objected to the proposal of favoring Cincinnati at the expense of Louisville and Maysville through making the Ohio city the terminus of the line. Blanding, on behalf of the company, agreed that that hardship upon Kentucky should be prevented by the insertion of a clause in the charter of the company requiring it to build branches to Louisville and Maysville as well as the line to Cincinnati. The charter in this form was granted by the government of Kentucky, and the name of the company was thereafter the Louisville, Cincinnati, and Charleston Railroad Company. Blanding, in a letter to the Charleston committee, January 3, and afterward in an address to the citizens of Charleston on May 14, 1836, explained that this added requirement upon the company would not be a staggering burden, nor without compensating advantages.[1]

In the spring of 1836 a summons was sent far and wide for all the states and communities interested in this transmontane railroad project and kindred matters to send delegates to a great railroad convention to be held at Knoxville, Tenn., on July 4, and following days. A very general interest was by this time aroused in many parts of the South and West; and, stimulated actively by the newspapers which prophesied great things to result from it, an enthusiastic response was made in many quarters in choosing and sending delegates.

The delegates assembled in the Methodist chapel at Knoxville on July 4, three hundred strong. Within the next day or two the number increased to above four hun-

[1] *Address of Colonel A. Blanding to the Citizens of Charleston convened in Town Meeting, on the Louisville, Cincinnati, and Charleston Railroad*, Columbia, 1836, 39 pp.

dred, representing nine states. Colonel Williams of Tennessee, as temporary chairman, soon gave place to Colonel R. Y. Hayne of South Carolina as permanent chairman. The convention began its business by listening to the report of the South Carolina commissioners upon their survey of the route across the mountains,[1] and ordered it printed. It then adopted a resolution for the chairman to appoint a committee of 45 to report forthwith upon charters, routes, commercial and agricultural advantages, and ways and means.[2] On July 5, the Georgia delegates, 60 in number, held a meeting while the convention was adjourned waiting for the committee of 45 to report, and appointed a committee of 5 from their own number to report to the convention upon the commerce of Georgia, and another committee for a report upon the route available in Georgia for a railroad from the West. These committees presented memorials to the convention, accordingly, on July 6, which were duly referred to the committee of 45. The report by the Georgians upon the volume of trade in their state was a surprise to the Western delegates, who were not aware how much that state was growing to overshadow South Carolina. The South Carolinians, as an offset, at once set to work and shortly presented a report upon the commercial advantages of Charleston.[3] An adjustment was reached, after debate, by which the main line was to run, as before intended, through South Carolina, while the Georgians were to be permitted to build a branch road from Knoxville to some point in Georgia

[1] Report published in part in *Niles' Register*, li, 88–89.

[2] Report of proceedings in *Baltimore Patriot*, July 20, 1836.

[3] The Georgia and South Carolina reports are both printed in *Niles' Register*, li, 47.

at their own discretion and at their own expense. The Georgians made no further effort to deflect the Louisville, Cincinnati, and Charleston Road, but upon returning home held a convention of their own and initiated a movement which resulted in the building of the Western and Atlantic Railroad as an independent work. Their course under the circumstances was adroit, and resulted in success, while the main work of the Knoxville convention resulted in a fiasco.

The committee of 45 reported on July 7, with an enthusiastic indorsement of the Louisville, Cincinnati, and Charleston project,[1] and the business of the convention was rapidly carried to completion. The only important regulation adopted for the company was that the directors in any one state might require the general board to apply the funds subscribed in that state, in the first instance, to the construction of the portion of the road lying within that state. At the end of its sitting, the convention was given a barbecue by the citizens of Knoxville, July 8, at which Colonel Hayne delivered a congratulatory address, concluding with the toast: "The South and West. — We have published the banns — if any one know aught why these two should not be joined together, let him speak now, or forever after hold his peace."[2]

Shortly after the adjournment of the Knoxville convention, Mr. Hayne issued an address explaining the general project and urging popular support for it.[3] This noble

[1] Report of the committee, adopted unanimously by the convention, published in *Niles' Register*, li, 109–111.

[2] *Baltimore Patriot*, July 23, 1836.

[3] *Address in behalf of the Knoxville Convention, to the Citizens of the States interested in the proposed Louisville, Cincinnati, and Charleston Railroad. By Robert Y. Hayne, president of the Knoxville Convention*, Charleston, 1836, 38 pp.

enterprise, he said, has now been in agitation for twelve months, during which very much has been done to enlighten the public mind. The main object is to break down the mountain barrier which separates the Southeast from the Western country. An inspection of the route has shown that the elevation to be overcome is lower than that to the northward, as, for example, in Pennsylvania. The prospect for remunerative earnings is good; shares in the Liverpool and Manchester Railroad Company are selling at £280 for every £100 paid, shares in the Charleston and Hamburg Railroad Company are at 25 per cent advance, and many other railroad stocks at home and abroad are at large premiums in the market. As a basis for an estimate of probable traffic, the following data have been secured from one of the most respectable mercantile houses of Knoxville, showing its actual outlay for freight, insurance, and loss of interest on investment in the freightage of its goods to Knoxville: 22,000 lbs. wagoned from Baltimore at 6 cents per pound, $1320; 340,000 lbs. by water from Philadelphia, New York, etc., at 3 cents per pound, $10,200; original cost of these goods, $70,000, of which $45,000 worth came by water from the Eastern cities under an insurance of 3 per cent, costing $1350; interest on the capital invested, $70,000, for the period of transit, 60 days, at 6 per cent, $700; total cost of getting 362,000 lbs. of merchandise to Knoxville, $13,750. The proposed railroad from Charleston, Hayne went on to say, will have a monopoly for much of its route, and will compete favorably with the Mississippi River in the long-distance traffic in food-stuffs. Any one traveling in the mountains at this time, he said, will see long lines of six-horse teams constantly employed on almost impassable roads, hauling bacon and other heavy articles to the Southern states, and returning with loads of foreign goods. He prophesied that not only this wagon traffic, but much of the driving of horses and cattle on foot over the mountains would be replaced by railroad traffic. In the mountain-locked region, corn was selling at from $18\frac{3}{4}$ to 30 cents per bushel, flour at $4 to $5 per barrel, and pork and beef at 2 to 4 cents per pound, while molasses was bought at $1 per gallon, salt at $1.50 per bushel, and sugar and coffee at 25 cents per pound. The railroad, by facilitating commerce, would increase the value of both land and labor along the route. "The apprehended danger to the drover, tavern-keeper, and small farmer is altogether imaginary. The trade in all its branches will be doubled, and all the productions of industry will be so increased as to give a new face to the whole country, — and he must be unworthy of success who does not avail himself of the general prosperity to improve his own condition." In conclusion, Hayne stated the charter requirement of subscriptions amounting to four million dollars prior to January 1, 1837, and he gave the reckless advice that every man should subscribe for as many shares as he could see his way clear to paying the first instalment of $5 upon. He advised, finally, that every one should urge the state legislatures to subscribe handsomely from public funds.

The Louisville, Cincinnati, and Charleston project apparently received more general attention in the region than any similar enterprise before or since. John C. Calhoun, for example, in the summer of 1836 went to the pains of exploring in person to discover the truth or falsity of an informal report which had reached him that an easier route for the railroad could be had through a little-known pass lying westward of the line followed by the official surveyors. Calhoun reported in a letter to the public, September 22, that his inspection had convinced him that by following the old Cherokee trading path along the watershed between the Savannah and Santee river systems, and crossing the summit of the Blue Ridge from Whitewater Creek, a branch of Keowee River, to the Tuckasiege, a branch of the Little Tennessee, a much more direct and feasible route could be had. The pass which Calhoun proposed lay just eastward of the northeastern corner of Georgia. The route lay in a direction pointing between Nashville and Louisville, and Calhoun thought it would be better for a trunk line than the more northerly one surveyed.[1]

Merchants, bankers, farmers, and politicians were all alive to the project, and especially the men of Charleston. The subscription books were duly opened at numerous towns in October, 1836; and in November the central commissioners convened at Knoxville to ascertain the number of shares subscribed. "While it was yet uncertain whether the charter was secured or not," the *Charleston Courier* reported, "Colonel [Wade] Hampton, already a munificent subscriber to the road, patriotically declared his intention to subscribe for two thousand additional shares, if necessary." The commissioners announced that the required minimum of four million dollars in stock had been subscribed. The *Charleston Courier* concludes its report: "The glory of the enterprise belongs to South Carolina and South Carolinians." [2]

[1] Public letter of Calhoun, September 22, 1836, in *Niles' Register*, li, 88–89.

[2] Quoted in the *Southern Banner* (Athens, Ga.), December 3, 1836.

The self praise of the Charlestonians at this time, however, was premature. The men at the head of the enterprise were fully aware that the subscription of four million dollars, while sufficient to secure the charters and launch the company, would meet only a fraction of the cost of the great work with which the company was charged.

The crucial problem was how to enlist enough additional capital to give the full project a fair chance of success. The situation was peculiar and critical. The Charlestonians were moved by the do-or-die spirit: most of rural South Carolina was warmly in support of Charleston; Tennessee was likewise very anxious for the connection to be made; North Carolina was less eager, since no important part of her territory was vitally concerned; and Kentucky was lukewarm. Georgia, meanwhile, was pushing an independent plan of her own, in rivalry with the South Carolina project. On the one hand, credit was not likely to continue long so easy, and money so plentiful, as they then were; on the other hand, the railroads projected from Pennsylvania, Maryland, Virginia, and Georgia were threatening to cut into the hoped-for Western trade, in case there should be any serious delay in building the Charleston and Cincinnati Road. Colonel Hayne, who had been a leading spirit from the beginning, and who was chosen president at the first stockholders' meeting, was a fitting exponent of the prevailing Charlestonian spirit of speed at all costs.

The company proceeded at once to appeal to the several states and cities for franchises and subscriptions. Some success was had, but not by any means enough to insure the success of the work.

The promoters now brought forward, in the fall of 1836,

a great scheme to float the railroad project by attaching to it a bank of large proportions and wide privileges. The South Carolina legislature furthered the work by chartering the proposed bank, December 21, 1836. The charter in substance provided as follows:[1] The members of the Louisville, Cincinnati, and Charleston Railroad Company might establish a separate corporation for banking purposes, with an authorized capital of twelve million dollars, under the name of the Southwestern Railroad Bank, — provided that two out of the three other states, North Carolina, Tennessee, and Kentucky, should concur in chartering the bank. Every present and future stockholder in the Louisville, Cincinnati, and Charleston Railroad Company might subscribe to stock in the bank to a number of shares equal to his holding of stock in the railroad; and no persons not owning or subscribing for stock in that railroad might subscribe for or purchase stock in the bank. Subscription books for the bank were to be opened, during 1837, two other states concurring; and if at the close of the year the stock subscribed in the railroad company had been increased to eight million dollars, the bank should be regarded as formed. In such event the directors of the railroad company were then to call on the stockholders of the railroad company to pay the first instalment of $12.50 per share toward forming the capital of the bank; and any stockholder in the railroad paying the instalments called for should be regarded as a stockholder in the bank, for the number of shares on which such payment should be made. The machinery of the bank's organization was then to be completed by a stockholders' meeting, the

[1] Charter published in Cooper and McCord, *South Carolina Statutes at Large*, viii, 96–102.

election of directors, etc. The president and directors of the bank might then, at their discretion, call for a second instalment of $12.50 per share. Beyond this, additional instalments might be called for by the bank from time to time, "provided, that no call for any instalments subsequent to the two first shall be made, until an amount equal to such call shall have been previously called in by the Railroad company, and shall have been actually expended in constructing the Railroad, or shall be necessary to meet contracts actually made on account of same."

The directorates of the railroad and the bank were to be separate bodies, and their capital also separate and distinct; the bank was not to be liable for the debts of the railroad company, but the railroad was to be liable for the debts of the bank, in case of its failure. The bank was empowered to issue notes to twice the amount of its capital, and might contract debts to thrice its capital. Its capital, all its funds, and its dividends were to be free from all taxation in the states granting the charter, though its real estate and property held in pledge might be taxed. The principal bank was to be at Charleston, and branches might be established at discretion within the states granting the charter. Each share in the bank was to be inseparably connected with a share in the railroad company, and was never to be transferred without it; and the forfeiture of a railroad share by non-payment of any instalment called for was to induce a forfeiture of the corresponding bank share. The life of the banking corporation was to be thirty-one years, provided the construction of the railroad were pushed with speed prescribed. Otherwise, after an interval specified, the banking charter was to lapse and become void.

In brief, here was a giant bank, with special privileges and exemptions, and unusual opportunities for large operations and profits, authorized and established in such a way as to give all its benefit to the railway company whose work the commonwealth was so anxious to promote. The privileges of the bank were expected to put its shares at a premium at once, and to increase the desirability of the railroad shares with which they were so intimately connected. It was expected that the added stimulus of the banking privilege would cause the railroad stock subscription to be doubled, from four million to eight million within the year, and that bank dividends, beginning early, would reconcile the stockholders to delays in the receipt of dividends on their shares in the railroad company.

A bill for a similar banking charter was promptly introduced into the legislature of North Carolina. Of the debate which ensued, we have a report of one speech, a significant one, by a certain Mr. Reid in the senate, who opposed the passage of the charter.[1] Alluding to the censure which awaited any one who opposed any part of the scheme for internal improvement, he professed himself an advocate of the Louisville, Cincinnati, and Charleston Railroad as a most important work. "But," said he, "a railroad is one thing, and a bank is another; and it cannot follow that because I am friendly to the road I must vote for a bank." The railroad project, he thought, ought to stand or fall on its own merits and without artificial bolstering. The proposed bank, he thought, was of dangerously large proportions, and of needlessly great privileges.

[1] Reported at length in the *Raleigh (N.C.) Standard*, January 18, 1837.

Its bills deluging North Carolina would be likely to drive out those of the existing banks, and demoralize the monetary system. He objected especially to a clause in the bill which made it the duty of the state treasurer to receive the notes of this bank in payment of public dues. "Can the state in the payment of her debts compel any man to take this money? No, sir, the constitution prohibits it. Then does policy or justice say that we shall compel ourselves to receive that which we cannot compel others to take?" He feared also that the wide liberality of the charter and the foreign location of the central bank would estop the state from inspecting and regulating the corporation as sound policy might require. In conclusion he raised the general question whether it were wise for North Carolina, with hopes and plans of her own, for building a central railroad through the state and fostering a North Carolina seaport to handle North Carolina commerce — whether in such case it were wise to contribute from her resources and give privileges at the expense of her own citizens and corporations, to build up the rival port of Charleston and make North Carolina still more largely tributary to commercial centers beyond her limits. "I am entirely opposed to a state granting privileges to the extent proposed in this bill to any institution; but, sir, if we are determined to grant such a bank charter at all, why not grant it to a company to improve our own state; for I think I hazard little in saying that with such a charter as this, offered to our citizens, we could build a railroad from Beaufort to the mountains."

In spite of arguments like this against it, the legislature of North Carolina quickly passed the bill and chartered the bank.

During the spring and summer of 1837 the railroad company, aided by the prospect of banking privileges, secured additional subscriptions carrying its stock at the end of September to about $5,300,000. To make the grant of banking privileges valid, there was required a charter from either Tennessee or Kentucky, and a further subscription of $2,700,000 to the stock of the railroad company. Colonel Hayne journeyed to Nashville in October, and by his talent for persuasion secured the desired charter from the Tennessee legislature, and in addition a subscription by the state of $650,000 in the Louisville, Cincinnati, and Charleston Railroad Company's stock. The application to the Kentucky legislature for a banking charter failed by six votes. That, however, was of little importance. The concurrence of the three states, legally required, had been secured, and the only further requirement for the institution of the bank was the getting of $2,050,000 more in stock subscriptions to the railroad.

There had been under discussion for some time a proposal for the Louisville, Cincinnati, and Charleston Railroad Company to buy from the South Carolina Canal and Railroad Company its franchise and the railroad and equipment which it owned. A device was now hit upon to accomplish this, and by the same transaction to add $2,000,000 to the Louisville, Cincinnati and Charleston stock. With authorization from the Louisville, Cincinnati, and Charleston stockholders, voted at their meeting in October, 1837, the directorate in December bought the Charleston and Hamburg Railroad, with its equipment and franchises at the price of $2,400,000.[1] The price was to be paid one-third in

[1] This was at an advance of 25 per cent over the original cost of that company's stock.

cash and the balance in one and two years, while a condition of the purchase was that a subscription should be made in behalf of the stockholders of the South Carolina Railroad and Canal Company for $2,000,000 in the Louisville, Cincinnati, and Charleston Company, the first instalment for which was to be deducted from the purchase money.

This carried the Louisville, Cincinnati and Charleston subscription to within $50,000 of the $8,000,000 required by law as preliminary to the institution of the Southwestern Railroad Bank. This deficiency was promptly made up by the city council of Charleston, and the bank charter thus secured. Colonel Hayne, who gives the narrative of these transactions in his report for 1838,[1] of course had rosy anticipations of benefits from this achievement. The panic in the fall of 1837 had hampered the progress of all financial projects, and dauntlessness was required for the preservation of optimism; but Hayne was in this equal to the occasion. Furthermore, the money market relaxed in 1838, and the prospect had brightened by the time of his report in September. The bank charter, he said, by its extraordinary liberality, conferred such great privileges that, no doubt, the bank could be made to yield full dividends, say 7 per cent, on the whole investment in both the road and the bank. At the time of the report, two instalments of $5 each had been paid in upon the railroad stock. The stockholders were accordingly entitled to acquire stock in the bank to the amount of $30 for each share held in the railroad. The bank was scheduled to

[1] *Second Annual Report of the President and Directors to the Stockholders of the Louisville, Cincinnati, and Charleston Railroad Company, September, 1838,* Charleston, 1838, 23 pp.

begin operations in November, 1838, and earnings could be expected to begin to accrue at once.

Hayne was obliged to admit that progress in construction of the railroad could only be made slowly. The directors, he said, were aware that it was for the time impracticable to call for further instalments on the railroad stock, and they did not wish to do so until by the establishment of the bank a fixed value should be given to the railroad shares. It was clear, in fact, that in the general depression in finance and in view of the prospect of long delay in completing the railroad, very many of the stockholders would forfeit the $10 per share already paid in, rather than pay further instalments at the time.

The possession of the Charleston and Hamburg Railroad, Hayne went on to say in his report of 1838, was of extreme value to the company. Besides furnishing a road ready built to Augusta, it gave the exclusive right under its charter of building from Charleston to Columbia. The Charleston and Hamburg track, however, had proved unequal to the strain of the traffic. Much progress had been made in embanking the road and laying a heavier track, when the road was taken over by Hayne's company. Since then the work had been pushed vigorously, and would probably be completed early in 1839. This would cost about $300,000. The purchase of the Charleston and Hamburg Road and the building of the Columbia branch, estimated to cost $1,500,000, Hayne thought, would be as much as the company could expect to do in the next year or two. The state of South Carolina, he reported, had indorsed the bonds of the company for $2,000,000; and General Hamilton, who had gone to London with the bonds, had succeeded in selling them. Part of this would be used in specie in launching the bank in November. In addition, the railroad company had $150,000 cash on hand, and Charleston and Hamburg Railroad stock to the par value of a million dollars, then in pledge as security for a loan of $800,000. A third instalment of $5 more per share on the stock of the company, yielding $300,000, he thought to be among the possible resources at the end of the next fiscal year, September, 1839.

The surveyors of the company, Hayne continued, had explored a new pass through the Cumberland Mountains, yielding a better passage than any before discovered; and the recent experience of the Baltimore and Susquehanna Railroad, to which Hayne had just paid a visit, demonstrated that locomotives of a new and improved type could climb ascents of 60 feet per mile with ease, and at low speed could overcome grades of 85 or 90 feet. The project of the Louisville, Cincinnati, and Charleston Company, its president declared, was clearly feasible and destined to success in glorious degree. The policy of the directorate, however, he explained in concluding the report, was to progress step by step from the coast into the interior, and not to attempt simultaneous construction in detached and independent parts of the route. No location for the road had yet been made northward of Columbia. The company had induced the South Carolina planters to enter contracts for grading the road-bed through their respective plantations. The planters were at first much disinclined; but finding the first experiments with their slave labor successful, they and others were now eager for contracts on the second division. While Hayne did not remark upon it, this increasing willingness of the planters to enter contracts for grading was probably due to the decline in the price of cotton, which, as usual, caused the owners of slave labor to look about for more remunerative openings for its employment. Hayne's conclusion was that "in the slaveholding states we can command slave labor to any amount . . . at reasonable prices." The truth of such a statement, if meant at all as a prophecy, would depend, of course, upon the continued depression of cotton prices.

Hayne died in 1839; and with him died the company's dreams. The terrific "cotton crisis" of 1839 ended all prospect of the company ever crossing the mountains with its railroad; and before the end of 1840 the corporation reacted from the former inflationist policy and underwent a reorganization to reach a basis of distinct conservatism.

The Southwestern Railroad Bank had begun operations in November, 1838, as scheduled, with Abraham Blanding as president. The importation of $500,000 in specie from England furnished good auspices for the opening;[1] and for some months the bank appears to have been notably prosperous. Blanding, however, died in 1839; and, far more important, the disastrous fall in cotton prices in the winter of 1839–1840, following as it did a desperate attempt at sustaining the price by bullish manipulation, shared in by many of the Southern banks, brought a tremendous crash throughout the cotton belt. The Southwestern Railroad Bank was among those which escaped outright disaster; but the times were such for years following that credit institutions had little chance for marked prosperity.

The railroad company, for its part, was active in the one

[1] *Niles' Register*, lv, 129 and 178; J. B. O'Neal, *Bench and Bar of South Carolina*, ii, 236.

regard of building the line from Branchville to Columbia. Between October, 1838 and October, 1840, five instalments of $5 each, in addition to the two preceding ones, were called in by the company. The payments, however, came in haltingly, and with increasing complaint of hard times and requests for relief, especially from some of the largest stockholders. At the time of the stockholders' meeting in October, 1840, only 17 miles of the branch to Columbia was in operation; public confidence had largely waned; stockholders on all sides were defaulting in payments and begging that the company go slower in its expenditures. The prospect of transmontane road building within the time specified in the charter, if indeed at any time by this company, had shrunk to the vanishing point. A reorganization and adjustment to the more modest purposes had become imperative.

A writer in the *Knoxville Times* in the fall of 1839 had advised that the Louisville, Charleston, and Cincinnati project be abandoned, so far as concerned a direct railroad from Charleston to Knoxville, basing his argument upon the fact that a system of railroads from Charleston through Georgia to Knoxville was in such excellent state of forwardness that the mission of the Louisville, Cincinnati, and Charleston Railroad would soon be accomplished without the service of that company.[1]

In September, 1840, the private stockholders of the Louisville, Cincinnati, and Charleston Company who were citizens of North Carolina and Tennessee, held a meeting at Asheville and petitioned the company to refund them the amounts paid on their stock, less a deduction to cover the

[1] *Southern Banner* (Athens, Ga.), October 12, 1839, copying a notice of the *Knoxville Times* article from the *Kentucky Gazette*.

outlay which had been made for surveys in those two states. The state government of Tennessee expressed a similar wish to withdraw from participation, and appointed J. G. M. Ramsay as its agent to negotiate with the company.[1]

The South Carolina stockholders of the Louisville, Cincinnati, and Charleston Company, after a preliminary meeting to appoint a general committee of 21 members, met at Charleston on October 19, 1840, to reorganize the company. The committee in its report advised that the number of shares held in South Carolina be reduced one-fifth in number, and that all stockholders outside the state of South Carolina be allowed to withdraw from the company, receiving repayment of their instalments, except for a reduction of $2.50 per share to cover surveying expenses. Private stockholders in South Carolina, it advised, should be allowed to scale down their holdings on the general basis of one-fifth reduction, with special arrangements for the very large stockholders. The state of South Carolina, however, was to be petitioned not to reduce its holding of stock, but to consider the embarrassments of the company and encourage its work by holding to its former liberal support.[2] All shares upon which required instalments should not have been paid by February 15, 1841, it was advised, should be declared absolutely forfeit.

In the same report was presented a statement of the number of shares held in South Carolina, with corresponding bank shares, and a statement of resources and liabilities. The number of such shares was stated to be

[1] Letters of Ramsay, in pursuance of his duties as state agent, are preserved among the state archives at Nashville, MSS.

[2] The state had subscribed to 6,000 shares of stock in the railroad in 1839. Seven citizens held above 350 shares each, and one had subscribed for above 1,000 shares.

51,427. With the reductions specially allowed on the large private holdings, subtracted, it was estimated there would be left 48,000 shares. Reduced by one-fifth, to the basis of reorganization, 9600 shares more must be subtracted, leaving 38,400. The seven instalments already called for on the old basis would amount to ten instalments of $5 each on the new basis, yielding a total of $1,920,000. Of this amount there was still due, and to be reckoned among resources of the company, $663,965. Add to this the remaining $50 per share, still to be called for on the new basis, yielding $1,920,000, and the total of resources of the company on the reduction is reached, at $2,583,965. The liabilities of the company included $201,892 owed to the banks of Charleston; $474,077.37 to the state of South Carolina, and $39,139.53 to the city of Charleston for advances on their subscriptions; and $247,897.25 for scrip issued by the company. The claims between the Louisville, Cincinnati, and Charleston Company and the South Carolina Canal and Railroad Company, by this time closely and inextricably connected, were not stated in the report. The total liabilities, exclusive of the $2,000,000 loan granted by the state, and including an estimated cost of $805,038.54 to finish the branch road to Columbia, amounted to $1,969,660.48. The resources exceeded the liabilities, therefore, according to this estimate, by $614,304.52. Accordingly, the committee thought it would not be necessary for the company to call for more than 7 more instalments of $5 each on the reduced number of shares. No further railroad construction beyond that to Columbia was contemplated in this report, and the $2,000,000 owed to the state, it appears, was regarded as a debt to be carried permanently by the company.

The committee, which had been given a very wide range, and which at this time controlled the whole policy of the company, also reported upon several other matters. It approved the suggestion made by Mr. Gadsden, president of the company, for the purchase of slaves as laborers on the road and advised that the directors be empowered to act in the premises; and it advised the appointment of a committee to inquire into the advisability of taking steps to amalgamate the Louisville, Cincinnati, and Charleston and the South Carolina Railroad companies, for the sake of administrative economy and to strengthen public confidence. This report, with its several resolutions, was duly adopted as the action of the stockholders.[1] At the same time action was taken by the Southwestern Railroad Bank to permit a similar reduction of one-fifth by its stockholders.

As to the project of amalgamating the two railroad companies, the committee of 21 was non-committal. The special committee appointed upon its advice to inquire into the expediency, and provided with full powers of investigation, probably reported in 1841 or 1842 in favor of the amalgamation. At any rate, upon request by the companies, the South Carolina legislature passed an act, approved December 20, 1842, providing for that amalgamation on the following basis: The stockholders of the Louisville, Cincinnati, and Charleston Railroad Company were reincorporated under the name of the South Carolina Railroad Company, and vested with all rights and privileges which had been granted and at that time belonged to both the Louisville, Cincinnati and Charleston Company and the South Carolina Canal and Railroad Company, and liable

[1] Report in full of proceedings published in the *Charleston Courier*, November 20, 1840.

to all debts and contracts obligatory upon either of those companies. The stockholders of the new company were empowered and directed to buy up such shares of the South Carolina Canal and Railroad Company as were outstanding in the hands of individuals: or in case such purchase could not be made at fair rates within a year, then the South Carolina Canal and Railroad Company stockholders might make a fair division of its rights and assets and pay to the stockholders who held shares their respective portions, and surrender up the charter of the company; whereupon all rights and privileges formerly granted to the South Carolina Canal and Railroad Company were to be vested immediately in the South Carolina Railroad Company by this act incorporated.[1] A subsequent act of December 19, 1843, perfected the consolidation of the two companies.

For the remainder of the period within our scope, the annals of this railroad are more brief; but the enterprise could not belong to *ante-bellum* Charleston without having a lively and varied career. In outline the successive transitions were as follows: The embarrassment of the company from the stringency of the times gave place in 1845, upon the return of good cotton prices, to a somewhat easier financial condition. The community had little floating capital, however, and the resolution followed by the company of building a branch road to Camden strained its resources, and led to a passage of the customary dividend at the end of 1848. The discontent of many stockholders, after smoldering for several years, now came to a head at the annual meeting in January, 1849, and its expression prodded the directors to renovate the main line and the equip-

[1] *Acts of the General Assembly of the State of South Carolina passed in December, 1842*, pp. 234–235.

ment. This was thoroughly accomplished by 1853; and the remaining years before the war were a time of large prosperity earned by the efficient and economical handling of heavy traffic furnished by feeding lines from many quarters.

A statement of traffic and earnings prior to 1840 has been given in the preceding chapter. A summary of operations from 1840 to the end of 1860 here follows: —

THE SOUTH CAROLINA RAILROAD, FINANCIAL OPERATIONS, 1840 TO 1860

Year	Miles of Road	Gross Earnings	Running Expenses	Interest on Debt[1]	Net Income	Paid-up Value of Stock	Dividends
1840	153	$ 388,127	?	?	?	$ 50	0
1841	166	336,538	?	?	?	65	0
1842	204	408,705	?	?	?	75	0
1843	204	442,931	$253,367	$118,000	$ 71,523	75	3%
1844	204	532,870	274,672	118,000	140,195	75	5%
1845	204	562,296	279,475	109,672	169,549	75	5⅔%
1846	204	589,082	$418.171		170,910	75	5⅓%
1847	204	655,575	303,480	108,461	243,633	75	5₄%
1848	241	800,073	343,488	108,801	347,774	75	2½%
1849	241	892,103	463,933	108,436	318,734	75	4%
1850	241	912,720	384,040	188,991	339,688	100	6%
1851	241	1,000,718	391,007	154,328	455,383	100	7%
1852	241	1,125,195	453,965	165,958	505,271	100	7%
1853	241	1,215,279	555,537	199,773	463,968	100	8%
1854	241	1,363,008				100	8½%
1855	241	1,585,991				100	9¼%
1856	241	1,546,961	780,692	195,829	570,439	100	10%
1857	241	1,449,803	709,268	194,992	545,542	100	8%
1858	241	1,501,008	680,496	192,432	628,079	100	8¼%
1859	241	1,596,696	792,410	176,647	627,638	100	8½%
1860	241	1,499,636	797,693	173,399	528,544	100	7%[2]

[1] In the interest account, after 1850, is included damage payments on stock killed, etc.

[2] This includes a semiannual dividend at the same rate on the 50 per cent of water added to the stock at the middle of 1860.

The sort of experience gained by the managing officials of this road, which even in the forties still had to work out many of its problems as a pioneer, is shown in the directors' reports. The report of 1845 [1] adduces the experience of the year 1844 as supporting a statement previously made by the directors to the stockholders, but apparently not fully appreciated by the latter — "that an increase of business on a railroad does not necessarily involve a corresponding increase of current expenses, where the company is properly prepared with locomotives and the requisite number of cars to meet the business offered." And again, that a larger outlay, judiciously made in the original construction of the road-bed and track may more than proportionally lessen the cost of maintenance. Changes were rung upon this again in 1846, when it was shown that while economy required the employment of heavier locomotives, the unsubstantial flange rail made it dangerous to use them, and the original piling which at some places still constituted the road-bed increased the expense of repairs. For several years, however, the holders of the majority of the stock, engrossed in the project of building to Camden, were deaf to arguments which called for large outlay upon the original line.

At the beginning of 1845 the rolling stock comprised, "18 passenger and baggage cars and 283 freight cars; 147 of which are of four wheels, with canvas sides, and of inconsiderable burden; the whole of them not more than equal to accommodate the loads of two engines." There were 22 locomotives fit for the road, some of which had

[1] Published in the *Journal of the Franklin Institute,* 3d series, vol. x, pp. 156–164 and 231–236. The reports of the company for 1846, 1847, and 1848 are published in part in subsequent contemporary volumes of this periodical.

been in service since 1832. Of these there was constant employment for some 16 on the road. The proportion in use was therefore reported as dangerously large. In the following years a considerable number of engines and cars were added, of course, and their cost charged to expenses of operation. Some of the new cars and engines were built in the company's own shops. The volume of traffic was increasing with fair steadiness, and the earnings also. This, too, in spite of a lowering of rates, in 1843–1844, some 15 per cent on passengers and 10 to 35 per cent on freight, and other reductions made subsequently in meeting new competition in through traffic. By 1847 the stress of traffic upon the track on the main line was such as to cause the officials to report that the weakness and defects of the rail and road-bed were causing or were about to cause accidents to accumulate, delays of trains to happen oftener, damages and forfeitures to be more often incurred, and injury to locomotives to grow more frequent and costly. The purchase of new rails was by this time imperative, and had already been begun. The procuring of labor to lay them at moderate cost, however, was now another serious problem. Cotton prices were excellent, and labor consequently at a premium; and the owners of slaves were in control of the situation. The superintendent reported at the end of 1846: "After hands, for many years in the company's service, have acquired the knowledge and skill necessary to make them valuable, the company are either compelled to submit to higher rates of wages imposed, or to pass others, at a lower rate of compensation, through the same apprenticeship, with all the hazard of a strike, in their turn, by the owners."[1] This raised the question again

[1] *Journal of the Franklin Institute*, series 3, vol. xiv, p. 5.

whether the company had not best buy a large number of slaves,[1] and reduce its dependence upon hired labor.

The problem of special rates for special traffic was handled in various ways at different times. At one time in the thirties, in order to encourage people along the route to go shopping in Charleston, and to attend barbecues, etc., it was provided that any one buying a one-way ticket might obtain a return ticket good for the same day only, without extra charge. In 1844 the Methodists held two great camp-meetings at points on the road; and, at specially reduced rates, several thousand extra fares were collected by the road in consequence.

A much greater problem, one recurring from time to time before the stockholders, and one whose solution was long postponed by them, was that of liquidating the bonded debt of the company, for which the state was standing security. The state legislature, by a joint resolution of December 12, 1845, expressed the opinion that since the stock of the railroad had now risen nearly to par, the stockholders ought to begin to lay aside some of their profits

[1] The company already possessed a small number of slaves, and from 1850 onward adopted the policy of rapidly increasing its stock of them. It had acquired eleven negroes when it took over the property of the South Carolina Canal and Railroad Company. It afterward bought at least as many as are listed below from the official reports of 1860 and 1864, which give data concerning the slaves owned at the times of these reports. No women, apparently, were included in the purchases. The number of slaves bought, and their prices per head are given as follows: 3 in 1845 at $400 to $646, 1 in 1848 at $750, 9 in 1850 at $900 each, 1 in 1851 at $800, 39 in 1852 at from $512.50 to $1004.50, 2 in 1853 at $1000 and $1050, 7 in 1854 at $850 to $1101, 9 in 1855 at $900 to $1010.50, 3 in 1856 at $700 to $1200, 6 in 1857 at $800 to $1200, 4 in 1858 at $959.60 to $1170, 4 in 1859 at $900 to $1500, 1 in 1863 at $2050 (Confederate money), and 32 in 1864 at $2450 to $5637.

as a sinking fund to meet the liabilities which the state had incurred for the company in its hour of need. The resolution instructed the proxies representing the state in the railroad company to insist upon some provision for the sinking of the debt. A committee to which this resolution of the legislature had been referred reported at the stockholders' meeting of February 11, 1846, that the only means of providing such a sinking fund would be to devote to it part of either the bank or railroad earnings. This, it said, would be "to withhold from the stockholders a part of the income they now derive from their stock, without giving them any immediate equivalent. . . . To this diminution of their income the stockholders can scarcely be expected to consent."[1] The meeting apparently took no action in the premises. The company was enjoying a long-term loan at the very low rate of 5 per cent, with the prospect of being protected by the state government from any serious consequences of the debt; and the drifting policy was evidently the most convenient under the circumstances. There was some consideration of applying the capital of the Southwestern Railroad Bank to the reduction of the two million dollar debt, when the bank charter should expire; but the company continued until 1860 to evade positive action.

Another problem, vexatious and constantly recurring, was that of the Augusta Bridge. Augusta feared, like many other inland towns, that if she should allow the railroads running east and running west to connect within her

[1] *Proceedings of the Stockholders of the South Carolina Railroad Company, and the Southwestern Railroad Bank, at their Annual Meeting . . . on the 10th, 11th, and 12th February, 1846*, Charleston, 1846, 45 pp.

limits, she would lose all advantage of her terminal position and sink to the status of a way station. She therefore followed an obstructionist policy, to the exasperation of the Charlestonians and the railroad stockholders. A South Carolina commission, investigating the situation in 1845, reported that whereas the railroad enjoyed nearly all the traffic of the town of Hamburg, it had secured in the preceding year only 20,000 bales of the cotton marketed in Augusta, as against 120,000 sent down the Savannah River. The absence of a railroad bridge was, of course, the crux of the difficulty. The charter for bridging the river had been acquired from private parties by the corporation of Augusta. The city, thus empowered, forbade any crossing by the railroad, and had forbidden the Georgia Railroad Company from laying its track within a mile of the river. All overtures for buying the privilege of crossing the river or for reducing tolls had been rejected by the city, and no early remedy was in sight.[1]

The bridge charter which Augusta held from the state of Georgia was perpetual; but that from South Carolina was limited. As a means of promoting its purpose of crossing the river, the railroad company secured in 1845 an act of the South Carolina assembly vesting in that company the franchise to a bridge on the Carolina side of the river, upon the expiration of the existing South Carolina charter of the Augusta Bridge. This apparently roused great anger in Augusta, which the South Carolina Railroad directors sought to allay by expression of good-will in their report of 1846. This problem continued to give trouble

[1] *Report of the Commissioners appointed to represent the State in the Meetings of the South Carolina Railroad Company, and the Southwestern Railroad Bank.* (Caption.)

until adjustment was reached at the middle of 1852, as will appear in the sequel.

Another terminal problem was that of extending the tracks in the city of Charleston from the depot to the wharves. Certain interests in the city opposed this. There was much discussion, pro and con, resulting in delay of action.[1] With flimsy buildings and unpaved streets, the facilities meanwhile were wretched.

The problem of the inclined plane, at Aiken, was still more serious. It delayed the transit of passengers and goods, endangered life and property, increased the cost of the company's service, and by limiting the road's traffic capacity threatened to interfere greatly with the increase of business. Consideration was repeatedly given to the problem of replacing it with a track on a grade easy enough to permit locomotives to haul trains without the troublesome inclined-plane appliances. Thanks to an investigation made and reported upon in 1845, we have an engineer's description of the operation of the inclined plane at that period.[2]

The power was now supplied by a locomotive which, for the sake of saving time, had been substituted for the stationary engine. The method was for the locomotive to descend the grade on one of the two parallel tracks, tugging a rope which, passing round a pulley at the top of the plane, pulled up the cars from the bottom of the grade

[1] *E.g. Reports by the President of the South Carolina Railroad Company, and the Committee of Seven appointed by the Stockholders on the Change of Location of the Present Depot, and Workshops on Mary and Line streets . . . also, the Engineer's Report upon the Inclined Plane*, etc., Charleston, 1846, 98 pp.

[2] Report of John M'Rae upon the Inclined Plane, August 7, 1845, published in pamphlet of reports last cited, pp. 87–98.

on the other track. The locomotive would then steam up the grade again, and the rope being again attached to cars at the foot, would repeat its down-grade performance. There was danger of boiler explosion, from the exposure of the tubes while the engine was on the slanting track; and there was danger of the ropes breaking. The heaviest load which the rope then in use could pass over the plane at one time was two eight-wheeled cars, carrying about 120 bales of cotton. Twenty or more such cars were required as a load for one of the large engines on the level road to Charleston. With fifteen minutes, the usual time, for each double trip of the inclined-plane locomotive, two and a half hours or more were required to lift an ordinary freight train over the one mile of the grade. The operating crew at the plane were usually kept at work until midnight in the busy season in handling the day's traffic; and there was frequently either a glut or a famine of cars resulting from the plane's obstruction. Passengers had to be transferred to and from a special car on the plane, to their frequent inconvenience. The complaint from them would greatly increase, should the road run trains at night. Passengers expressed great uneasiness at having to trust their limbs and lives to the strength of the rope on the grade; and were continually voicing disesteem for a company maintaining such a makeshift.

This engineer, M'Rae, like most others with which the South Carolina Railroad had been cursed, was amateurish and faint-hearted. He reported that although the modern engines could carry loads up grades of 80 feet to the mile, and although a track available by such engines without assistance could be built, in a detour of five miles, at a cost not above $325,000, the substitution was not then advisable, because, for one thing, all the cars would have to be equipped with brakes for safety on the grades, and, for another, a new rope to be bought when the one then in use should wear out, might be had of strength enough to handle four cars at a time instead of two. His positive recommendations were the substitution of a wire rope for the hempen one, the building of additional side-tracks at the head of the plane, and the keeping of records for data upon the cost of operating the plane. Other investigators at one time or another estimated the expense of replacing the plane at smaller amounts, some of them ranging as low as $75,000. The company in each instance throughout the forties decided to postpone incurring the expense.

The building of the Camden branch was, of course, responsible for most of the company's procrastination above noted. Its construction, begun in 1844, was finished in 1848 at a cost to the company of about $300,000. To meet this, the directors could sell neither stock nor bonds. They skimped operating expenses for several years and appropriated some of the earnings to this purpose; but at the end of 1848, when heavy bills for the construction fell due, the directors had to pass the regular half-yearly dividend. This caused a slump in the market price of the stock, and brought an outbreak of discontent among the stockholders, and a washing of the company's linen in public.

Some of the stockholders published censures upon the directorate, charging it with the neglect of all repairs for the sake of building its pet branch to Camden. They pointed to the delapidation of the track and rolling stock, the heavy expense regularly incurred in mending injuries which ought to have been prevented, the inefficiency of the forwarding system, the stagnation of business, and the loss of profits.[1]

The crisis of discontent occurred in the stockholders' annual meeting which began on February 8, 1849, and lasted to February 13. In the first day's session, the following resolutions were adopted by a majority vote of those present:[2] —

> *Resolved,* That the ruinous decline in the value of our shares, and embarrassed condition of our affairs, require the adoption of some prompt and energetic measures to save us from further loss and discredit.
>
> *Resolved,* That a total change of administration may, by introducing a different policy, and establishing another system of management, promote our prosperity and restore the value of our stock.
>
> *Resolved,* That a Committee of Seven be appointed to prepare and report to an adjourned meeting . . . a ticket in conformity with these views, for President and Directors for the ensuing year.

The committee thus provided for, of which G. A. Trenholm was chairman, reported, on February 10, a ticket nominating A. H. Bowman for president, in place of James Gadsden, who had held the office for about ten years, and nominating some new and some old men for the directorate.

After an adjournment over Sunday, Mr. Gadsden presented the report of the president and directors for 1848, showing, as compared with the year before, an increase of $145,000 in gross earnings, as against only $40,000 increase in running expenses. He reported the road to be in good order, with ten miles of new track laid near Charleston and enough rails ordered to relay as far as Branch-

[1] *Eg. Charleston Courier,* January 22, 1849. Letter to the Editor, signed "Stockholder."

[2] *Proceedings of the Stockholders,* February 8 to 13, 1849, Charleston, 1849; *Charleston Courier,* February 12, 1849.

ville; more cars, also, had been ordered, to provide for the increase of traffic which was sure to result from the completion of the Western and Atlantic Railroad. The Camden branch was shown from its first two months of operation to be earning good profits. As regards the sinking of the company's debt, the opinion was expressed that the surest means to redeem the bonds at the earliest time with the least burden, was to equip the road to its full earning power.

This report put the revolutionists at a disadvantage. While their discontent was acute, their program for reform was vague. After a long debate of wide range, the ballot was taken, and resulted in the reëlection of Gadsden and the former board of directors.

The adoption of the resolutions of discontent on February 8 was apparently by a majority vote of the persons present, each man having one vote; the election of president and directors, on the other hand, was upon the basis of the shares owned. From this it would appear that the malcontents were the small stockholders, and that they were defeated in the final vote by the large stockholders and the proxies commanded by the officials. The result of the contest was the continuance of the old president and board in office. The objectionable policy of road extension, however, was terminated, and the track and equipment renovated in the following years.

The stimulus to be felt in the next decade from the completion of a westward-stretching system of railroads began to show itself as early as 1847, when the Western and Atlantic was in operation for only half its length and had to be pieced out by an irregular wagoning system. Before 1846, Charleston had received practically no grain or flour at all by rail; in 1847 the Hamburg Road brought down 19,043 barrels of flour, 334,761 bushels of corn, and 4087 bushels of wheat to the city. This was, of course, regarded as an earnest of much greater business. Another item of interest is that in January, 1849, a body of "New England Pioneers," bound from Boston to California in the rush of forty-niners, took passage first to Charleston and thence westward *via* the Hamburg Railroad. This gives curious illustration that the Southeast had a better connection with the West at that time than the Northeast or the Middle states.

In the general period preceding 1850, it was characteristic of the successive Charlestonian companies owning the Hamburg Road and its branches that the body of the private stockholders took very active part in discussing and shaping the policies. This was in keeping with the Charlestonian practice of making all public questions the subject of very searching popular discussion. Instead of serving passively as machinery for validating the directors' measures, the stockholders' meetings were usually the scene of hot debating, whether upon proposals by the directors or upon ideas brought forward by unofficial members. After the climax in the meeting of January, 1849, however, the directors adopted the popular policy and thereby removed the occasion for extreme private alertness in the business of the company. Thereafter, the administration of the road was much more like that in the normal case of a large stock company: the president and directors initiated proposals; the stockholders in meeting either approved or referred them back to the directors with power to act.

A striking instance of this practice occurred in 1850. The policy adopted in 1849, of hastening the improvement of the road and equipment, brought a bunching of expenditures. Much money was needed, and quickly. In 1849 the company's debt was increased by $274,295, through the purchase of rails, cars, and engines; and such credit as the company could secure on reasonable terms was nearly exhausted. The president in his report of February, 1850, accordingly proposed that the remaining $25 per share lacking to make up the par value of $100, be called for from the stockholders. The meeting, after casual debate, referred the question to the directors. This board promptly took action, and in March issued a call for the money. This, coming in instalments during the next year, provided some $900,000 cash, and relieved the company from all its financial difficulties and anxieties. By February, 1852, practically the whole track from Charleston to Hamburg had been laid with heavy T-rail, the road-bed greatly improved, the equipment heavily augmented and bettered, and the inclined plane in process of rapid replacement.

In handling the problem of the heavy grade at Aiken, the company had at length enlisted the service of highly skilled engineers; and the plan adopted was extremely well devised. At the expense of some heavy cutting, filling, and trestling, a road was built upon which the stronger locomotives then introduced could handle trains without assistance, and which at the same time actually shortened the route. Leaving the old route at South Aiken, it ran in nearly a straight line on a grade of about 75 feet to the mile, for $5\frac{2}{3}$ miles, and rejoined the old road with a saving of $\frac{1}{3}$ of a mile in distance. This, ironed with a 70-pound rail, was finished early in 1852. Meanwhile the Charleston terminal had been renovated and enlarged.

Best of all, permission to cross the Savannah River was purchased in July, 1852, and the bridge and terminals in Augusta were completed at the middle of 1853. The concession for bridging the river, building a depot on the western shore within the city, and connecting with the Georgia Railroad by tracks through the city streets to be operated by horse-power, was sold by the city of Augusta for $150,000. Of this price the Georgia, the Nashville, and Chattanooga, and, probably, the Memphis and Charleston, railroad companies contributed between them nearly one-half. The remainder was paid by the South Carolina Company. Of course the franchise was cheap at the price, for it remedied the isolation which had long been a hindrance in the increase of the South Carolina Road's traffic.[1]

This great improvement in its road-bed, track, equipment, and terminals, made between 1849 and 1853, brought the road to a fine degree of efficiency and established the solid prosperity of the company. Gross earnings in 1855 reached $1,596,695, and, in 1856, the dividend rate was 10 per cent. Earnings thereafter were to some extent cut into by the operation of a branch of the Central of Georgia Railroad connecting Augusta with Savannah; but, on the whole, profits and dividends continued on a basis quite satisfactory to the stockholders.

Since 1848, a part of each year's net earnings had been set aside as a reserve fund, part of which was applied to the reduction of debt and part to the encouragement of

[1] A supplementary franchise, obtained in 1857, permitted the company to operate locomotives on the tracks through the city, and by establishing a more effective traffic connection with the Georgia railroads, enlarged the South Carolina Company's ability to attract business. To secure this franchise the company agreed to pay the city an annuity of $7000.

companies building railways which would feed this company's own traffic. In pursuit of this policy subscriptions were made to the stock of every company launched for building a railroad in the South Carolina Piedmont. These stocks were usually not good investments from the point of view of dividends received, but for the purpose intended, the policy was fairly successful. This activity, however, as measured in both outlay and results, was upon a smaller scale than in the case of the Georgia and Central of Georgia companies, to be treated in later chapters.

The prosperity of the eighteen-fifties enabled the company to apply earnings and reduce its debt by 1859, to less than two and three-quarters million dollars, of which two million was the 5 per cent loan guaranteed by the state and due for payment in 1866. The company now determined to double its stock by issuing stock dividend of 50 per cent, and selling another 50 per cent issue at par to existing stockholders, to be paid for in ten annual instalments.[1] Thus, one-half of this increase was added in a way intended to reimburse the shareholders for their deprivation of dividends in the earlier years, and the remainder was an intended replacing of bonds with stock. But plans for the future, with the War of Secession in sight, were merely castles in Spain.

After making a résumé, and before carrying further the record of railways in South Carolina, we will turn to the state of Georgia, to trace the growth of a system begun later, but devised better, and in the long run far more successful.

To summarize: —

[1] Report of the financial committee of the board of directors, printed in the annual report of the president, etc., for 1859, Charleston, 1860.

The original South Carolina Canal and Railroad Co. had, from 1828 to 1833, built a pioneer railway of remarkable length for the period and fully abreast of the times in its degree of efficiency. The work had been done economically, and the profits upon the investment were such that by 1838 the shares had risen to 25 per cent above their original cost. The obstruction at the Savannah River hindered the growth of traffic for the time; but with the extension of railroads through the Piedmont of South Carolina and Georgia and eventually to the Tennessee and Ohio basins, a heavy increase in tonnage and earnings was sure to come.

The impatient Charlestonians could not wait for this. Led by the brilliant but visionary Hayne, they went headlong into an immense project for direct transmontane connection, in disregard both of the natural obstructions and of their own financial limitations. After a preliminary survey which reported the route to be vastly more favorable than it actually was, and after a wide and thorough agitation, they launched in 1836 the Louisville, Cincinnati, and Charleston Company. The initial subscription was barely the $4,000,000 required by the charter as a minimum. Aided then by the project of a great bank whose mission was to lift the railroad shares into popular esteem, the strenuous efforts of the promoters, soliciting from individuals, cities, and states, raised the subscription at the end of 1838 to $6,000,000. By the device of buying the Charleston and Hamburg Road and paying for it partly in stock, $2,000,000 more in subscriptions was added, to meet the minimum requirement for the bank charter. Meanwhile, with the state's indorsement of its bonds, the company had borrowed $2,000,000 at 5 per cent from English bankers. This was the company's greatest cash acquisition at any time. The severe financial depression in the late thirties and early forties caused the forfeiture of many shares subscribed for, and led shortly to the complete suspension of calls for instalments, after little more than half the par value of the shares had been paid in. The work of road building was stopped in 1840, the staff of surveyors reduced, and official salaries lowered. The visionary scheme was perforce relinquished, and the subscribers outside the state allowed to withdraw from the company. The corporation was then reorganized under an appropriate South Carolina title, with a reduction in its nominal capitalization.

The Louisville, Cincinnati, and Charleston bubble was expensive in its blowing, and disastrous in its bursting. The reorganized South Carolina Railroad Company had to shoulder the debt and pay the relentless interest charges. This company, moved partly by a sense of obligation, struggled on with the extension of its branch lines, completing that to Columbia in 1844 and that to Camden in 1848. It labored under a shortage of resources, and delayed repairs and betterments almost to the point of disaster. Hence the crisis within the company in 1849. The road had fallen behind the times. The discontented stockholders, however, could find no malfeasance by Gadsden and his staff, and could propose no quick remedy for the ills of which they complained. The real source of the trouble was the $2,000,000 debt, whose proceeds had in part gone as a bonus to the stockholders in the original South Carolina Canal and Railroad Company, and in part had been squandered between 1836 and 1840 in extravagant salaries and fruitless surveys.

The Southwestern Railroad Bank, meanwhile, much vaunted in its first years as a sure and rapid money gainer, had been crippled by the all-pervading distress of the early forties. The stock instalments called for and paid in were few and small; some money was lost through the bankruptcy of men to whom loans had been made; and after the return of easy times in the late forties the institution was able to earn only sixty to eighty thousand dollars per year for its stockholders. The bank was administered in entire separation from the railroad, and its existence had little influence upon railroad policy.

The railroad company in 1849–1850 resolved to take firm hold and develop its property. The collection of the delayed instalments, the renovation of the track, the removal of the inclined plane, and the bridging into Augusta finally equipped the road by 1853 for handling through traffic upon an economical basis. Heavy through freight was ready at hand, at profitable rates. The earnings and dividends throughout the remaining *ante-bellum* years were such as to give full satisfaction. The company, after many tribulations, had at length reached a basis of substantial prosperity. The public functions expected of the road by its early promoters, however, were never fully realized: the stimulation of Charleston trade, the increase of upland prosperity in South Carolina, and the checking of the westward emigration were hardly accomplished in satisfactory measure.

CHAPTER V

THE GEORGIA RAILROAD AND BANKING COMPANY

THE launching of the Georgia Railroad takes us to the village of Athens, in the upper Piedmont, ninety-five miles west-northwest from Augusta. Athens was not a commonplace town. As the seat of the state university, it had attracted families of culture and fortune, and men with power of leadership. Some of the latter were lawyers, some merchants, some planters, and most were men of several professions and interests at the same time. The town was unusually progressive and capable in material lines as well as in the humanities. A sign of the times was the building of two cotton factories on the outskirts of the town between 1828 and 1833. On the basis which these small enterprises furnished, Athens was spoken of in the grandiloquent oratory of the time as "the Manchester of the South."

The first families of Athens have excellent memories. A tradition current among them relates that the inception of the Georgia Railroad was due to the bogging of a steam boiler in transit by ox-team from Augusta: the cotton-mill to which the boiler was destined had to wait for completion for weeks or months until the roads became dry; the owners of the factory, exasperated and determined on preventing similar mishaps for the future, held a conference at the home of James Camak and launched the project for a railroad to Augusta.

The traditional stalling of the great ox-team occurred probably in the winter of 1832–1833. From the following June we are able to gather a complete account of the promotion of the railroad from the files of the contemporary newspapers. James Camak, a leading spirit, was himself an editor of long experience, and knew how to keep the enterprise before the public, with news items and inspired editorials.

The *Southern Banner* was the newspaper of the period in Athens. In its issue for June 8, 1833, an editorial relates that, stimulated by the success of the South Carolina Canal and Railroad Company, "Some of the most influential men and large capitalists in our own immediate vicinity, we are glad to find, begin to speculate seriously on the subject of continuing the [South Carolina] Railroad from Augusta to this place." The editor concluded by quoting the statement of a gentleman acquainted with the country, that the route from Augusta might be laid out quite directly, without serious grades, and without crossing any considerable watercourses except in the immediate approach to Athens.

In the issue of the next week, the editor gave arguments in support of the project. Savannah, said he, had been for a long time the great mart of Georgia, with a large wagon trade as well as the pole-boat traffic. The introduction of steamboats on the river, however, had brought the rise of Augusta into foremost rank as a distributing point, and reduced Savannah to little more than a transfer station on the route to the Northern states and Europe. A railway between Augusta and Athens, he went on to reason by analogy, would perform the same service as the river, and would make Athens in turn the trade center, instead of Augusta, for much of the Georgia Piedmont, and perhaps for part of Tennessee.

The issue of June 22 continued the theme, and announced that a meeting of the citizens interested in the matter would be held in the college chapel on the following Wednesday. The issue for June 29 contains a report of proceedings at that meeting. With Asbury Hull in the chair, and James Camak as secretary, Judge Augustin S. Clayton, the chief mill owner of the town, presented the plan for a railroad and moved the appointment of a general committee. This prevailing, there were appointed A. S. Clayton, James Camak, William Dearing, Stevens Thomas, John Nesbit, William Williams, Jacob Phinizy, and Asbury Hull.

Next week, July 6, 1833, the following editorial described the prospects: —

> It is truly delightful to witness the enthusiastic feelings which pervade our whole community on the subject of the contemplated railroad to Augusta. The capitalist warmly advocates the scheme because it promises a profitable investment for his surplus funds, the planter because it will add to his agricultural resources and save him the necessity of spending so large a portion of his hard earnings in getting his produce to market, the merchant and mechanic because it will enlarge their sphere of action and extend their business, and the holder of real estate because it will necessarily enhance the value of his possessions — indeed, so general a feeling is manifested in favor of the experiment by all classes of our citizens, and so convinced are they of its practicability and utility, that we hazard nothing in asserting that if books were opened, one-half of the amount of the stock would be taken up in this place alone in a few days.

The Athens railroad project when first broached in Augusta met a cold reception. Editorials in the *Augusta Chronicle*, for example, stressed the idea that the prosperity which the railroad would bring to Athens would be taken away from Augusta, and Augusta would sink into a mere way station.[1] The Athens advocates urged in rebuttal that the enormous prosperity to accrue to the whole region from the railroad would permit the growth of Athens without damage to Augusta. In analogy, it was cited that the prosperity of Buffalo and Rochester had arisen without damage to the older trade center at Albany.[2] The Augustans gradually grew out of their opposition and coldness, but long clung to the policy of preventing any close traffic connection of railroads through the town.

Upon receipt of a request from the Athens committee for coöperation, the citizens of Augusta held a meeting and appointed a committee of correspondence,[3] but did little more. The slight expectation of aid from Augusta on the part of the promoters is illustrated in the fact that in the charter obtained by the company at the end of 1833, only 1500 shares were assigned to the commissioners at Augusta, while 2500 were assigned for subscription in each of the villages, Athens and Eatonton, 2000 to Warrenton, 1500 to Greensboro, and 1000 each to Washington, Lexington, Appling, and Sparta. The Augusta people in fact, it seems, gave little support or promise of it until the success of the project was fairly assured, and the prospect of dividends made the stock attractive for private investment. The city council at a later time subscribed for 2000 shares of the company's stock; but with a locally selfish purpose. As a condition of the subscription it required a pledge from the company that its tracks should

[1] Alluded to in an editorial of the *Southern Banner*, July 27, 1833.
[2] *Ibid.*
[3] *Southern Banner*, July 27, 1833.

never be connected with those of the South Carolina Railroad unless with the city council's express consent. This consent later cost the company a round sum to secure.

The Athens committee also sent requests for coöperation to all the intermediate towns and counties on the proposed route, and to others lying southward which might benefit by the building of branches from the Athens line. From all of these came eager responses promising support.[1]

The district lying south of Athens had, in fact, already been active in railroad projects for several years, though with not much prospect of early success in them. A convention had been held at Eatonton in 1831, which had recommended to the state the adoption of a system of internal improvements including an avenue of transportation, whether railroad, turnpike, or canal, from Augusta to Eatonton, and advised that if the state should be disinclined to undertake such work with public resources, companies should be chartered for the purpose and aided by state subscriptions or loans.[2] In the following December a company was chartered with power to build a railroad or turnpike from Augusta to Eatonton and thence westward to the Chattahoochee, with branches at the company's discretion. In July, 1833, about $350,000 had been subscribed to the stock of this company, in large part by the citizens of Eatonton. This was enough to secure the charter; and, on July 26, a meeting was held in Eatonton to organize the company. A president and directors were

[1] *E.g.* meeting of the citizens of Oglethorpe County, at Lexington, Ga., July 20, with William H. Crawford presiding; reported in *Southern Banner*, July 27, 1833. Notes of action in Newton, Morgan, Greene, and Taliaferro counties, *Ibid.*, September 14.

[2] John C. Butler, *Historical Record of Macon and Middle Georgia*, Macon, 1879, pp. 101–103.

elected, agents to solicit further subscriptions provided for, and the employment of an engineer authorized for the survey of the route. A communication from the Athens committee was read at the meeting, and a committee appointed to confer on the subject of a union of the two proposed roads at some point west of Augusta.[1] The Eatontonians, with their charter of 1831, thus had an earlier start of the Athenians, and at this time were able to approach them on a footing of equality; but within the next year, under a new charter, the Athens group, with its enthusiasm and resources, gained a large degree of ascendency. The *Macon Messenger*, in September, 1833, remarked that all the country northward of Macon had become wide-awake in the railroad movement, and Macon and Savannah alone in the whole state were apathetic.[2]

The *Southern Banner*, strongly edited at Athens, maintained a steady and vigorous campaign, reporting all favorable news and eagerly taking up each new suggestion which promised to add strength to the cause. It gave strong championship to the proposition for uniting all possible interests by providing for a main stem, a "union road" from Augusta to the neighborhood of Greensboro, with a branch thence to Athens, another to Eatonton, others perhaps to Washington, Warrenton, and Sparta, and a possible continuation of the main line to Madison and beyond.[3]

In general accord with this plan, the legislature, by an act of December 21, 1833, repealed the Eatonton Railroad charter of 1831 and chartered a new corporation, with

[1] *Federal Union* (Milledgeville, Ga.), August 1, 1833.
[2] Quoted in *Southern Banner*, September 14, 1833.
[3] Cf. *Southern Banner*, September 14, 1833.

large powers, under the title of the Georgia Railroad Company. Its capital was to be $1,500,000, but subject to indefinite enlargement by the company. It was empowered to build a railroad with a main stem westward from Augusta and branches to Athens, Madison, and Eatonton, respectively, and to prolong the Athens branch at discretion as far as the Tennessee River. It was given extensive privileges, some to last for thirty-six years and some in perpetuity. Freight rates were restricted to 50 cents per hundred weight per hundred miles, and passenger rates to 5 cents per mile. Provision was made for stockholders in the union and branch roads respectively at their discretion to form themselves into separate corporations. Machinery was provided for organizing the company, with the Athens commissioners temporarily in charge.[1]

A reconnaissance had already been begun by A. A. Dexter, in the service of the Eaton Company. Dexter was soon transferred to the Athens route. He reported at the end of January, 1834, in great praise of the country from a railway-engineering point of view, showing the remarkable opportunity of following a watershed with a fairly level ridge for the whole of the 105 miles, except for the ascent from the Savannah River at Augusta and the descent to the Oconee at Athens; and these grades at the termini, he showed, need not be excessive.[2]

The subscription books were opened on the first Monday in February. On the first day above 1250 shares of $100 par value were taken at Athens, and considerable numbers at the other places along the route. On February 15

[1] The charter, abbreviated, may be found in O. H. Prince, *Digest of the Laws of Georgia to 1837*, pp. 304–314.

[2] *Southern Banner*, February 3, 1834.

the Athens commissioners issued notice that upwards of $500,000 had been subscribed, and accordingly called a meeting of the subscribers to assemble at Athens on March 10.[1] At that meeting, with harmony and enthusiasm prevailing, the company was organized, with James Camak elected president, and the following as directors: William Dearing, William Williams, and Wilson Lumpkin, all of Athens, Dr. A. B. Linton, Rev. James Shannon, Col. A. J. Cobb, E. L. Newton, and John Nesbit, with residences not specified, John Cunningham of Greensboro, R. B. Thompson and Absalom Jones of Taliaferro County, and William R. Cunningham of Augusta. From the absence of Madison and Eatonton names in the list of stockholders, it is evident that the stockholders in the earlier company did not promptly transfer their subscriptions to the new one. The reason was probably that their attention and support was now diverted by the newly awakened activity in Savannah and Macon. A railroad to Savannah would clearly be preferable for the Eatonton traders and planters as against the proposed one to Augusta. In fact, the Georgia Railroad branch to Eatonton, authorized in the charter, was never built.

The directorate was active and judicious. It sent a delegation at once into Greene and Morgan counties in May, 1834, and extended the list of subscribers. At the end of May the total subscription was reported to be not far short of $1,500,000. In July, President Camak sent a description of the route and the company's plans to the *American Railroad Journal*, which, when published in its issue for August, 1834, introduced the project to the railroad world at large. The route, he said, with a southward

[1] *Southern Banner*, February 15, 1834.

detour from Augusta, to gain the ridge with a moderate grade, ran along the watershed a little north of Warrenton, directly through Crawfordville, seven miles north of Greensboro, and two miles west of Lexington, to the Oconee at Athens. Beyond Athens an extension was contemplated running just north of Lawrenceville, across the Chattahoochee, between the sources of the Tallapoosa and the Etowah, to the Coosa River and thence to the Tennessee at Decatur, whence a railroad was already reported to be building to the Mississippi at Memphis. The road east of Athens was alone in present active consideration. The cost of this he estimated 114 miles, at $10,000 per mile, and prophesied a heavy rate of profit upon the investment.[1]

After a fruitless attempt in the spring of 1834 to secure an engineer from the United States department of war,[2] the directors employed J. E. Thompson as chief engineer, and pushed forward the work preliminary to road building. Thompson, in a report of his survey, January 5, 1835, described anew the exceptionably favorable character of the country, indorsed the plan of following the watershed, and estimated the cost at from $9000 to $9800 per mile, for grading and laying a superstructure to consist of pine mudsills, lightwood or white-oak cross-ties and stringers, and an iron plate-rail 2¼ by ⅝ inches in breadth and thickness.[3]

The directors now called for an instalment of $15 on each share, in addition to the $5 deposited at the time of subscription. This was met promptly, and convinced all

[1] *American Railroad Journal,* August 2, 1834. Letter of James Camak, Athens, Ga., July 10, 1834.

[2] *Southern Banner,* May 31, 1834.

[3] *Ibid.,* January 8, 1835.

who were still doubters, that the project gave good promise of success.[1] With a mandate from the directors, the chief engineer advertised in April that he would receive bids until June 1, for excavation and embankment on the first thirty miles of the route, beginning at Augusta.[2] The contracts in sections of about one mile each were let for twenty-four miles on June 1, and for twenty-six miles more on November 1, 1835. The contractors, however, met an unexpected dearth of labor, and the work of grading, with the primitive methods then in vogue, was slow in its progress.

A stockholders' meeting, May 9, 1835, authorized a call for the third instalment in the amount of $15 per share, to be paid at the middle of October, and a fourth of similar amount in April, 1836.[3] To increase the demand for its shares and the willingness of the subscribers to pay instalments, the company applied for and secured from the legislature a grant of banking privilege. This act, approved December 18, 1835,[4] recites in its preamble that the banking privilege is given to promote the extension of the road beyond Athens to connect with the railroad then being projected southward from Cincinnati. The act renamed the corporation "The Georgia Railroad and Banking Company," increased its authorized capital to $2,000,000, empowered it to establish a bank with as many as three branches so soon as 50 per cent had been paid in on the stock subscribed, and to carry on a banking business with the use in banking of one-half of the company's capital.

[1] *Southern Banner*, February 26, 1835.

[2] *Ibid.*, April 30.

[3] *Ibid.*, May 13, 1835.

[4] Prince, *Digest of the Laws of Georgia to 1837*, pp. 311–314.

It was empowered to issue notes, with a penalty of a 10 per cent tax for any suspension of specie payments, and to incur debts to three times the amount of its banking capital. A similar privilege was granted to the Central of Georgia Railroad Company at the same session. Each company made use of its privilege, but in different measure. The Central of Georgia Company established its bank mainly for convenience in handling the railroad moneys, and always kept the bank strictly subordinate to the railroad. The Georgia Railroad and Banking Company became almost as prominent in banking as in transportation, and in the long run throve so greatly in its banking that when at length in 1880 the company leased its road to the Central of Georgia Company and retired from railroad operation, it continued its banking business, as it does to-day. It is now one of the strongest banks in the South, and certainly the most luxuriously housed of all.

In January, 1836, the stockholders authorized the opening of the books for a further subscription of 7500 shares. These were taken up by the middle of March.[1] At the middle of April the fourth instalment was paid in, completing the amount of $50 per share on the original issue, and the bank was promptly put into operation. Holders of the stock were then demanding a premium as a condition of any sale.[2] At the middle of January, 1837 a thousand shares of the stock were offered for sale at Athens. It was all taken at once at premiums ranging from $10 to $11.25 per share.[3] From its banking operations the company was able to declare a dividend on its whole paid-in

[1] *Southern Banner*, March 17, 1836.

[2] *Ibid.*, April 21, 1836.

[3] *Ibid.*, January 21, 1837.

stock of 3 per cent in November, 1836 and another of $3\frac{1}{2}$ per cent in February following.

Meanwhile the construction of the railroad was in progress, unhampered by any shortage of funds. As early as May, 1836, when the cashier made his first important report,[1] the company had received payments of $35 each upon 12,837 shares of its original stock, and $15 each on 11,741 shares of a later issue. This, with 676 shares forfeited, and $3242.41 obtained as interest, had yielded $622,117.41 as possibly available for railway construction. At that time there had been expended, for salaries, $13,535.16; for hire of rodmen, chainmen, and axemen, $2,456.45; for right of way, $84.43; for stationery, printing, etc., $460; for attorneys, $100; for graduation, $80,823; and for incidentals enough to carry the total of expenditure to $102,024.05. There were at that time bills receivable and cash on hand amounting to above $526,000. The work of grading was reported to be in fair progress, in spite of the dearth of labor, and the prospect good for increased vigor in the autumn; 2625 tons of rail iron had been ordered, enough to lay the track for the 81 miles to Greensboro. The completion of the first 10 miles of the road, from Augusta, was expected for January, 1837, and of 50 miles in May following. Greensboro was to be reached in the winter of 1837–1838. Orders had been given to Mr. Baldwin of Philadelphia for 7 locomotives, the first two to be delivered in November, 1836. The cars, it was intended, were to be built in the company's own shops.

A year later, at the middle of May, 1837, the affairs of the company are again exhibited in the reports of its

[1] Published in the *Southern Banner,* May 26, 1836.

officers.[1] At this time William Dearing had succeeded to the presidency, and James Camak was cashier only, instead of as formerly being president, cashier, and general manager. In this report the affairs of the bank are mingled with those of the railroad. The total stock paid in was $1,416,655; profits, discount, etc., $36,569.83; deposits, $63,602.63; notes of the bank in circulation, $563,105. These items with others made a total debit in the cashier's statement of $2,213,245.24. Among the credits were: expenditures on the railroad, for grading, timbers, rails, engines, cars, depots, and right of way, $634,322.70; bills receivable, $93,358.65; notes discounted, $448,584.24; bills of exchange and business paper, $547,540.33; cash on hand and due by other banks, $274,259.38.

The president called attention to the fact that the circulation of the company's notes was much below its capital, and remarked that the recent rapid fall in the price of cotton had hurt the company less, and promised to hurt it less, than any other corporation in the cotton region. Because of conservative management, he was able to say, "Our bank bills have had a credit at home and abroad to an extent which no new institution has ever heretofore possessed." The panic then partly threatened and partly experienced, he thought, would do the company no net injury; for its loss in interest and discount would be more than offset by the reduction in the price of labor and the supplies which must be bought for the road.

The chief engineer reported, at the same time, that contracts for grading had been let on October 1, 1836, for the remainder of the "union railroad," 26 miles, to Union Point, and for 7 and 4 miles on the Greensboro and Athens

[1] *Southern Banner*, May 20, 1837.

branches respectively. Work was also in progress on a short spur, authorized by a legislative act of 1835, to the town of Warrenton. Iron for fifty-three miles had been received at Savannah, and was in transit to Augusta. Work on the superstructure was in progress, though the receipt of the stringers would be delayed for some three months by reason of the contractor's sawmill having burned. The grading had been delayed by the extraordinary wetness of the seasons.

A separate report on its banking operations was issued by the company in July, 1837, showing the status on July 1.[1] The assets included: notes of individuals and bills of exchange, $915,415.74; stocks owned by the company, $23,000; cash on hand, $173,471.09; and "the railroad, now beginning to yield an income, $727,354.77," — total assets, $1,919,014.40. The liabilities were: notes in circulation, $365,355; individual deposits, $69,086.09; amount due to other banks, $10,638.92; railroad receipts, $1157. The total amount owed was $450,071.66. This added to the capital stock, $1,425,355, and the sum subtracted from the total assets left as profits between January 19 and July 1, $43,587.74. In October a third dividend of 3½ per cent was paid to the stockholders.

The activity of the directorate in this period is shown by its call in November for bids for constructing the roadbed on so much of both the Madison and Athens branches as the company had acquired the right of way for.[2] Its resolve not to encroach upon the banking capital for roadbuilding purposes is indicated by its offer in January, 1838,

[1] *Southern Banner*, July 15, 1837.
[2] *Ibid.*, November 18, 1837.

of 2500 additional shares of stock for sale.[1] That the whole road was not pushed to rapid completion was due to the severity of the times, to which we have had, and shall have, frequent occasion to allude in other connections.

The state of the railroad at the end of 1837 is shown by a letter of Wilson Lumpkin, written at Augusta, December 6, 1837, after a journey from Athens, partly by wagon road and partly by rail:[2] —

> I traveled forty-two miles upon the railroad yesterday . . . in company with about fifty passengers. The structure and finish of the work very far surpassed my expectations; indeed, its incipient operation and everything connected with it is calculated to encourage and strengthen the hopes and hands of its friends. The continuance of the ability and perseverance heretofore devoted to this enterprise cannot fail to insure ultimate and complete success.

Before the end of 1837, lines of post-coaches had been established to coöperate with the railroad, and arrangements made for the handling of freight as well as passengers at the head of the road. A line of four-horse coaches was running every alternate day from Athens and Gainesville by way of Washington, and another from Athens through Watkinsville and Greensboro. The company assumed the care of the horses and vehicles of persons arriving at the head of the road on horseback or by private conveyance, pending the return of the owners from their trip to Augusta. A good deal of cotton was already being handled by the road.[3]

The locomotives in use were of but twelve or fourteen tons in weight, with power corresponding; and the cars

[1] *Ibid.*
[2] *Ibid.*, December 16, 1837.
[3] *Ibid.*, December 30, 1837.

were of primitive and frail construction. J. S. Buckingham, who made a trip over the road in 1839, compares its equipment unfavorably with that of the Northern roads of the time.[1] The sort of mishaps liable to happen is illustrated by this clipping from the Augusta *Chronicle and Sentinel*, printed in the *Southern Banner*, December 14, 1839: —

RAILROAD ACCIDENT

We regret to learn that an accident occurred on the Georgia Railroad, about forty-five miles from this city, on Friday last, which had well-nigh proven to have been of a serious nature. Two freight trains going up met another coming down; the engineer of the foremost train going up, on perceiving the train coming down, stopped his locomotive and returned toward the last station, running backward, when he met the other train which was proceeding up, and a concussion took place between the locomotive of that train and the hindmost cars of his train. The locomotive was slightly and five cars seriously damaged. Nobody hurt or injured in any way. The cars which were injured were going up empty for the purpose of bringing down cotton.

The stockholders, at their annual meeting in May, 1838, adopted measures intended to hasten the construction of the road in all its branches.[2] The actual extension, however, was slow. The prevailing financial depression rendered stock unsalable; subscribers were slow in paying instalments; and the bank competed with an advantage over the railroad for the use of the company's funds: the bank was already yielding profits; the railroad only promised them after large outlay and after a period of waiting. The charter of 1835 required the completion of the "union railroad" within four years, and the branches

[1] Buckingham, *Slave States of America*, i, 187.
[2] *Southern Banner*, May 10, 1838.

within six, from the date of the charter. The completion was accomplished without much margin of time to spare: the track reached Greensboro near the end of 1838, and reached both Madison and Athens in 1841. Much of the grading in 1839 and 1840 was paid for in stock, which the contractors consented to receive in part payment.[1] The

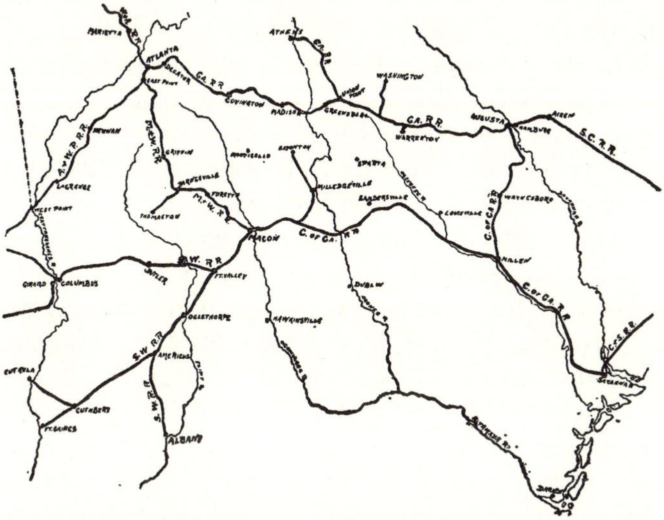

THE GEORGIA AND CENTRAL OF GEORGIA RAILWAY SYSTEMS AND CONNECTIONS

stock was then selling at a little below par, although dividends were being kept up at the rate of about 7 per cent per year. Much of the track from Greensboro to Madison was laid with T-rail; that from Union Point to Athens was of the lightest sort of plate-rail.

The idea of continuing the Athens branch through to Tennessee was given over as early as 1836, when the project

[1] *Niles' Register*, February 8, 1840 (lvii, 377).

of the Western and Atlantic Railroad was launched.[1] The location of the projected southern terminus of the Western and Atlantic in the county of Dekalb at once shifted the prospect of through traffic on the Georgia Railroad from the Athens branch to the line through Madison, which the company was authorized by an act of 1837 to extend to the Western and Atlantic terminus. A crude plate-rail was deemed sufficient for merely local traffic on the Athens branch; and, indeed, until 1847 horses were employed as the chief motive power on that branch. In 1847 a locomotive was obtained light enough not to endanger the thin plate-rail of the track. This pygmy of $3\frac{1}{3}$ tons was, of course, not much more efficient than horse teams.

John P. King of Augusta succeeded William Dearing of Athens as president in 1841, and in 1842 the headquarters of the company were transferred to Augusta, which by this time had wrested the control of the corporation from Athens. Thereafter the combination of votes from Augusta, Charleston, and the towns along the main line to Atlanta continually defeated any local policy of the Athenian stockholders. Thenceforward Athens had grievances to nurse, with little chance of redressing them. The following editorial from the *Southern Banner*, August 3, 1854, is illustrative:—

> If this community were not the most meek, long suffering, and patient on earth, they would before now have been driven past endurance, by the manner in which we are treated by the railroad company.
>
> Our mail now arrives here at dark, and as the season progresses, it will become worse, so that we cannot get our mails until the next morning, just 24 hours later than we might get them. The people

[1] See below, Chapter VII.

in Montgomery get their mails before we do; the people in Nashville get their mails before we can get ours a month hence.

In addition to this, if we go anywhere, we are forced to start before our regular breakfast time, and then lie over at Union Point five hours, if going down the road. If going beyond Augusta or Atlanta, we must, moreover, stay all night in one of these places —neither of them a very agreeable place to stay at.

We say nothing of our freights; how they deprive us of the privilege of having ice in the summer or oysters and fish in the winter, simply because our freight is left so long at Union Point that such things generally spoil before they arrive. How long will these things be submitted to? Is it to be so always? If so, Athens may as well give up all hope of improvement in population or commerce; for no community that has so little energy as to bear such outrages can possibly flourish.

. The Railroad Lords tell us that the Athens branch does not pay. If it were so, it would prove nothing; for it has been so managed that it has never had a chance to show what it could do. But we fear not to assert that in spite of all this, the branch has paid, and if the company will exhibit their books, they will prove it. If proper facilities were offered on the branch, if their track was put in good order, decent depots erected, and trains run at proper intervals, we believe it would pay as well as any other part of the road.

We had hoped something from the accession of Mr. Yonge to the road, knowing him by reputation as an efficient and accommodating man; but things have got no better, partly owing to the fact that Mr. Yonge has never been on the branch since his appointment, and more owing perhaps to that inveterate hostility to Athens on the part of others high in authority, which has often led them to sacrifice the interest of the road for the sake of injuring this community.

As to the remedy for the travel and freight annoyances, we know of none, unless the Savannah people could be induced to extend their Eatonton Road to this place, when we could bid farewell with hearty good-will to Augusta and the Georgia Railroad together. But of this we have little hope; so that we must even submit to our fate; but as to the mails, we can help ourselves, and we deserve to be kicked if we don't do it. Our enterprising fellow-citizens, Salter & Ivey, or Browning & Durham, will, we doubt not, for the same or even less pay than the railroad receives, deliver the mails in a hack from Union Point or Madison, so that we can get our mail twenty-four hours sooner than we now do. A proper representation at Washington could effect this; we will not move in the matter. We call on our town council to take it in hand; the people will back them.

In the period when the Georgia Railroad ended at Madison and Athens, the freight patronage was, of course, almost entirely local. Some little traffic came to it from western Georgia; but barely a trickle from Tennessee and Alabama. The main Southwestern mail was handled by the road, however, and a good deal of through passenger traffic. It is curious that the greatest number of passengers carried in any year of the first decade of operation was in 1838–1839, when the road reached little beyond Greensboro. That year there were more than 28,000 persons carried. The next year the chief engineer reported, that an attempt was being made by the principal line of coaches to divert the Southwestern passenger traffic to a more Southern route, *via* Brunswick and Tallahassee to Mobile. That year the traffic on the road declined to 22,632 passengers. A year later the coach line returned to its connection with the railroad; but at that time and for some years following, the prevalence of hard times kept down the number of travelers. The growth of freight receipts was also, of course, retarded by the general depression. The earnings between 1842 and 1846 were apparently applied to improving and extending the road.

The company's bank, like all the other banks in the cotton belt, found its operations seriously hampered by the great cotton crisis which began in 1839 and lasted till 1844.

Like nearly all the rest, it had to suspend specie payments for a time; and when, on February 1, 1841, it attempted to resume them, according to legislative requirement, so strong a westward drain of specie ensued, that at the end of two weeks suspension was again resorted to. The directors reported that it was impossible, for the time, to collect debts due the bank by individual borrowers without causing immense distress, and highly inexpedient to resume specie payments without having collected such debts. They therefore appealed to the public for relief for the bank from the hardships of the law.[1]

This report from the bank shows sufficiently the financial limitations of the company during the long-continued depression. Meanwhile the Western and Atlantic Road had been checked in its progress northwestward, and offered no early prospect of heavy traffic for connecting roads. The completion of the Georgia Railroad to Atlanta was, accordingly, not for the time an imperative need of the company. The extension of the road was now, in fact, as great a concern or greater with the citizens of Augusta and Charleston than with the company itself. The railroads to the neighboring towns had been thought of doubtful benefit to Augusta; but the tapping of distant territory could not fail to bring advantage. As for Charleston, her citizens had looked with jealousy upon the Georgia Railroad so long as the Louisville, Cincinnati, and Charleston project offered a hope of direct northwestward connection; but now the Charleston and Cincinnati dream was dead, and the completion of the Georgia system necessary if trade was at all to be fostered between the West and the Southeast. Furthermore, Savannah was now reaching out

[1] *Southern Recorder* (Milledgeville, Ga.), March 9, 1841.

with the Central of Georgia Road to catch the Western and Atlantic traffic, and the hope of Charleston for a share in it depended upon the completion and full equipment of the Georgia Railroad.[1] New subscriptions from Charleston and Augusta to the stock of the company, and the prodding of the company by the shareholders in these cities, it seems, were largely responsible for the hastening of the road to completion in 1843–1845.

The state of the company's affairs just before it undertook the extension to Atlanta is shown by a report of the company to the governor of Georgia, dated April 3, 1842.[2] The following are selected items. Resources: the road and its outfit, $2,314,768; real estate for the road, $47,128; banking house and lot, $32,184; negroes, $48,925; stocks in other institutions, $21,981; bonds of the city of Augusta, $20,000; discounted notes, $262,391; bills receivable, $133,157; coin, $37,759. Liabilities: total, $2,311,628; profit and loss, $110,709; deposits on interest, $221,632; individual deposits, $28,585; deposits on long time, $209,000; bank-notes and railroad receipts in circulation, $120,031. The list of stockholders included very numerous individuals, and a considerable number of corporations, some of which are worthy of note in passing: the Bank of Augusta held $2282\frac{1}{2}$ shares, the city council of Augusta 1144, the inferior court of Morgan County $52\frac{4}{5}$, the trustees of Mercer University $63\frac{4}{5}$, and the trustees of Emory College $57\frac{2}{5}$ and $42\frac{3}{5}$ more for the endowment of a chair. Several business partnerships also held shares. The stock had, thus, clearly come to be esteemed a secure investment.

[1] *Federal Union* (Milledgeville, Ga.), August 1, 1843, quoting an editorial from the *Charleston Mercury.*

[2] *Federal Union,* April 25, 1842.

The dividend policy from 1840 to 1846 was irregular. In 1841 no dividends were declared; in April, 1842, one of 10 per cent was paid; but the following years until after the end of 1845 were entirely without dividends. Early in 1846 the policy was resumed of regular semiannual dividends, though for several years they were at the rate of only from 4 to 6 per cent per annum.

The passing of the dividends in 1843–1844–1845 was a feature of the extension policy. Very few shares were salable during the hard times. The earnings of the road, together with the proceeds of nearly $700,000 in 7 per cent bonds, were all devoted to building the road to Atlanta. The route thither, especially in the neighborhood of Stone Mountain, was more rugged than that in the eastern district, and yet was not on the whole unfavorable. The cost of the extension, with a T-rail of about forty pounds to the yard, was estimated at $11,366 per mile, and the actual cost did not greatly exceed the estimate. The Western and Atlantic terminus, by that time called Atlanta, was reached by the rail-laying gang in September, 1845. The first train from Augusta, bearing a festive party of officials, entered Atlanta amid great rejoicings on September 15.[1] A month later the line from Savannah, after vicissitudes, also reached Atlanta. At this time the Georgia Railroad, with 170 miles in its main line, had a total mileage of 213. To that was added a spur of eighteen miles to the town of Washington in 1853. No other branches were ever built by the company, except a line from Warrenton through Sparta and Milledgeville to Macon, whose construction was begun just before the War of Secession and delayed

[1] Thomas H. Martin, *Atlanta and its Builders*, N.Y., 1902, i, p. 32.

by the war. The Georgia Railroad of the *ante-bellum* period, therefore, comprised a main line from Augusta to Atlanta, and three branches of varying length, to Warrenton, Washington, and Athens respectively.

The road had been built, as in all other cases in that

STATISTICS OF THE GEORGIA RAILROAD AND BANKING COMPANY

(Fiscal Years ending May 1, prior to 1840; April 1 thereafter.)

Year	Capital Stock paid in	Miles of Road	No. of Locomotives	Number of Cars		Earnings			
				Fr't	Pass. and Baggage	Freight	Passeng'r	Mail, &c.	Total
1834–35									
1835–36	$ 622,117								
1836–37	1,170,715								
1837–38	1,910,215	40	5	?	?	$ 12,589	$ 23,164	Included in statement of freight receipts	$ 35,753
1838–39	2,116,810	75	10	?	?	68,789	66,140		134,929
1839–40	2,193,952	88	12	?	?	121,098	63,505		184,603
1840–41	?	105	12	?	?	85,963	66,262		152,225
1841–42	2,201,612	147	12	?	?	152,195	71,460		224,255
1842–43	?	148	12	?	?	186,091	61,985		248,026
1843–44	?	148	12	?	?	178,765	69,331		248,096
1844–45	?	155	14	?	?	194,115	77,635		271,750
1845–46	2,288,450	195	18	?	?	221,700	93,642		315,342
1846–47	2,289,200	213	22	214	16	232,891	136,559	$40,484	409,935
1847–48	2,293,120	213	23	?	?	280,486	157,694	38,871	477,053
1848–49	2,262,500	213	25	225	17	376,957	166,484	38,573	582,015
1849–50	4,000,000	213	29	258	19	398,006	189,650	39,149	526,807
1850–51	4,000,000	213	35	304	21	446,499	244,028	38,394	728,923
1851–52	4,000,000	213	41	502	25	486,498	265,201	44,111	795,811
1852–53	4,000,000	213	42	544	21	591,907	297,909	44,306	934,124
1853–54	4,000,000	231	?	?	?	591,671	340,005	(with	931,767
1854–55	4,156,000	231	?	?	?	563,486	343,207	freight)	906,694
1855–56	4,156,000	231	48	683	21	701,150	322,548	44,503	1,068,202
1856–57	4,156,000	231	52	692	24	687,239	377,938	44,503	1,109,681
1857–58	4,156,000	231	?	?	?	625,791	366,278	44,503	1,036,572
1858–59	4,156,000	231	55	635	?	755,554	354,562	44,503	1,154,624
1859–60	4,156,000	231	56	634	?	702,376	412,307	44,503	1,159,188

GEORGIA RAILROAD AND BANKING COMPANY—*Continued*

Year	Running Expenses (Gross)	Net Earnings	Bank Earnings (Gross)	Divi-dends	Bales Cotton Carried	Bushels Grain Carried	Bonded Debt of Company	Stocks and Bonds owned in other Co's	Reserve Fund
36–7			$ 36,570	6½%				$ 23,000	
–8	$ 19,367	$ 16,386	?	7%	8,267			?	
–9	63,362	71,567	?	8%	25,513			?	
–40	70,246	114,357	?	8%	47,235			?	
–1	67,283	90,942	?	none	20,878			?	
–2	97,518	126,737	?	10%	49,611			21,981	
–3	109,819	138,207	?	none	63,276			?	
–4	100,573	147,532	?	none	70,754		?	?	
–5	117,212	154,538	?	none	77,948		?	?	
–6	136,204	179,138	?	2%	56,821	18,223	?	?	
–7	157,902	252,033	25,271	4½%	94,897	149,993	$696,500	42,558	
–8	175,553	301,499	?	6%	86,734	278,651	?	?	
–9	195,785	386,231	26,115	6½%	157,502	176,278	720,900	89,354	
–50	228,282	398,525	50,159	7%	138,810	65,847	679,015	57,093	
–1	302,437	426,486	55,485	7%	132,800	42,768	797,270	137,643	
–2	355,508	440,303	63,661	7%	139,769	70,706	913,798	752,655	
–3	477,655	456,468	95,887	7½%	194,742	310,696	759,548	850,143	
–4	588,552	343,214	?	8%	154,727	429,486	?	?	
–5	600,289	306,395	?	3½%	165,895	219,899	?	?	$ 232,454
–6	750,713	357,689	108,441	7½%	205,503	1,172,331	560,223	805,750	317,411
–7	720,217	389,464	204,881	8%	177,427	633,706	476,895	922,750	514,306
–8	710,401	326,175	?	6%	122,707	1,058,490	?	?	619,350
–9	610,258	544,363	134,324	7½%	219,218	916,291	373,060	889,050	923,848
–60	631,144	528,044	251,530	8%	219,744	353,241	312,500	1,003,650	1,131,384

The income from securities owned by the company were included in the statement of gross bank earnings. Likewise, in the company's accounting, the payment of interest on the bonds issued by the company were charged as a part of the bank's expenses.

period, with so cheap and light and crude a structure and equipment that a short experience in the handling of traffic showed the necessity of relaying with heavier iron, broadening the cuts and fills, strengthening the bridges and trestles, ballasting with gravel or broken rock, and adding more powerful engines and stronger cars. The specially rapid increase of freight traffic rendered some of these needs acute from time to time; and unexpected further increases in business, as new regions were opened, brought gluts of freight again, and necessitated rush orders for still more rolling stock, as well as the more rapid improvement of the road-bed and terminal facilities. Iron was low in 1849, and the directorate took advantage of the opportunity to buy a large quantity of rails for relaying. The price of labor began to rise very rapidly, however, before the relaying was completed; and the iron soon proved to be of very poor quality. A second relaying of the track was therefore necessary in a few years. The president reported in 1852 that the road was in good order and its outfit for the first time complete. "The road is now all laid with heavy iron," he said, "and all its machinery and appliances are in excellent condition." Accordingly the directorate ordered the construction account to be closed. But within three years afterward the operation of the westward feeding lines furnished such very great increases of freight for the road, that the stockholders had to forego portions of their dividends for the sake of the newly demanded betterments and additional rolling stock.[1]

On the whole, the Georgia Railroad was so well managed that its annals may be brief. Most of the facts as to its business may be gathered from the statistical table. The history of the road, furthermore, for the period after 1845 has already been well treated by Mr. Salem Dutcher.[2] A

[1] *President's Reports* for 1856 and 1857.

[2] In C. C. Jones and Salem Dutcher, *History of Augusta, Georgia*, Syracuse, N.Y., 1890, pp. 481–501. The file of annual reports of the president and directors which Mr. Dutcher used has since been acquired by the Wisconsin Historical Society.

detailed narrative may here be dispensed with, and general considerations alone receive our attention.

In its early years the company was fortunate in being able to pay as it went. To secure the Atlanta extension, it assumed a bonded debt of $700,000, it is true, which in the following years it increased to above $900,000 for the sake of equipment and road betterments. This burden, however, was not oppressive, upon a railroad of such heavy traffic and high earning capacity; and from 1852 the debt was steadily reduced by moderate appropriations from earnings.

In 1850 the capital stock was suddenly increased to $4,000,000, for the special purpose of enabling the company to promote the building of feeding lines to the West. The roads chiefly fostered by the company were the Nashville and Chattanooga, whose stock it subscribed for to the amount of $250,000, and the Atlanta and La Grange Road, to the amount of $310,000. The former of these was expected to bring food-stuffs from the West, *via* the Western and Atlantic, and the latter to bring cotton from western Georgia and the Alabama region. Each of them soon began to perform the desired function, and the stocks, particularly of the La Grange Road, soon became handsomely remunerative. Other subscriptions by the Georgia Railroad Company were to the East Tennessee and Georgia Railroad stock, $10,000, and the same company's bonds to twice that amount; to the Rome Railroad Company's stock, $100,000; and to that of the Augusta and Waynesboro Company, $109,000. None of these subscriptions were made as investments, but all for the purpose of developing feeders to the Georgia Road. Part of the capital thus invested remained unproductive for some years, but the rest brought good dividends, and all of it tended to the benefit of the company through the increase of its remunerative traffic.

The Georgia Railroad Company's own branch lines, to Warrenton, Washington, and Athens, were not notably remunerative of themselves, but were profitable chiefly as feeders to the main line. The branch to Athens, of which so much had been expected in the early years, was especially disappointing. The town of Athens was located near the northern edge of the cotton belt of that period, and had not much cotton to ship. It sent some grain and meat down the road, but the traffic would not bear charges heavy enough to yield much profit. The Athens people contended that the lightness of traffic was due to the wretched quality of the service, and the absence of profit to the poor equipment[1] and consequent high operating expense. The company long continued deaf to the Athens complaints.

In its traffic on the whole, the Georgia Railroad showed a remarkably low ratio of operating expense to gross earnings. A comparison made by the chief engineer in 1847 shows the expenses for 1846–1847 to have been only 38 per cent of the gross receipts of the year. The percentages on other roads mentioned by him were 51 on the South Carolina Railroad, 56 on the Central of Georgia, 48 on the Baltimore and Ohio, and 51 on the Boston and Maine. The cost per mile run by trains was given as 61 cents on the Georgia; on the South Carolina, 87; on the Central of Georgia, 67; on the Baltimore and Ohio, 64; on the Boston and Maine, 65; and on the Boston and Lowell, $1.05. In the next decade the percentage of expense on the Georgia

[1] *E.g. Southern Banner*, December 14, 1854, editorial.

Road rose to 50 and 60, and in some years to 75 per cent. This was unavoidable. The cost of labor and supplies was steadily rising, while at the same time railroad rates were declining. Passenger fares were reduced to three cents per mile in 1850, and freight rates were lowered again and again to promote the growth especially of through traffic. As early as 1847 the rates on produce for the 171 miles of the main line were but from 16 to 25 cents per hundredweight. In 1856 the president reported that the cotton received from Alabama and Tennessee, and the grain and railroad iron carried by the road, at the rates then charged, hardly paid the actual cost of transportation. The expenses for repairs and betterments were often heavy, and were charged to maintenance of way, etc. A distinct disadvantage of the road, furthermore, was the dearth of fuel. Its route lay through the oldest and most densely settled portion of the state. The forests had there been more fully cleared away than in any other district in the South penetrated by a railroad. Most of the wood for the engines had to be hauled twenty miles or more to the railroad, and then distributed by rail to the stations where needed.[1] The cost of cross-ties was likewise enhanced by the dearth of forestry along the line. These items, however, were far more than offset by the unusual demand for local traffic, which it was the good fortune of the company to meet. The busy cotton producers all along the line offered heavy traffic in their eastward-bound staple and in manufactured goods from the coast and food-stuffs from the West, as well as in passenger traffic. Unusual in a line of such length in the South, the Georgia Road crossed no district devoid of traffic demand. Local rates were not materially affected by the competition of

[1] Report of the Superintendent, 1859.

other railways; and the local freighting, relatively heavy for a Southern road of the time, was a very important part of the profit-earning business.

For the *ante-bellum* period, tonnage reports, as such, are not available. But for the purpose of comparison, freight earnings may be used. For 1859–1860 these were reported as follows: upward (*i.e.* westward bound) through freight, $123,918; up local, $141,309; down through, $384,243; down local, $41,336. In the westward bound traffic, the local yielded more revenue than the through traffic; but by far the largest item of business was the downward through freight, yielding thrice the gross receipts from the westward through, and nearly ten times the amount from the eastward way freight. The rates on the down through traffic, furthermore, were much the lowest in the road's traffic. The excess of tonnage in the down through traffic is thus seen to be very great. There was little to counterbalance the volume of cotton, grain, and meat carried from West to East. The Superintendent reported in 1859 that his engines annually hauled into Atlanta over three thousand empty cars, whose return journey from Augusta was a dead loss to the company. The freight traffic, furthermore, as on all the cotton-carrying roads, was concentrated in the fall, winter, and early spring; and in summer the equipment of the company was partly in disuse. Another disadvantage, of minor importance, was that the laws of Georgia forbade the moving of freight on Sunday. This at times added to the congestion.

The panic of 1857 did not seriously affect the Georgia Railroad Company, chiefly because it did not long depress the price of cotton. Every year from 1855 to 1860 the road earned above a million dollars gross; and in the last two years of the period, above half of this was net profits. The company had come into the ripe enjoyment of profits from its early good judgment and long-continued conservatism. Its road and equipment were in excellent condition, for that period, and nearly all the side ventures of the company had proved successful. Its traffic and earnings were fairly steady, and bade fair to yield 8 per cent or more in dividends so long as peace and moderate general prosperity should last. The officials anticipated some loss of Western traffic from the completion of other lines then building, in East Tennessee, Alabama, and south Georgia, but thought it probable that the development of the country would offset that loss. Meanwhile they continued to seek new openings for the company's resources to promote its traffic and general interests. About 1858 it succeeded in arranging a better connection of its tracks with those of the South Carolina Road, and began to operate a through sleeping car from Charleston to Atlanta. It also began to take steps, in 1860, to increase the ocean shipping facilities between New York and Charleston, with the hope of making the southeastern route more attractive for both passengers and freight, and thus promoting the increased use of the Georgia Railroad by the Nashville and Memphis merchants, etc. The management thus continued into the war time to live up to its reputation of conservatism, far-sightedness, and efficiency. Common report along the route has it at this day that the Georgia Railroad has always been so careful and capable in its operation that no passenger has ever lost his life on one of its trains.

CHAPTER VI

THE CENTRAL OF GEORGIA RAILROAD SYSTEM

THE Central of Georgia Railroad, as originally built by the company of that name, extended only from Savannah to Macon. The road from Macon to Atlanta, that from Macon to southwest Georgia, with its branch to Columbus, and the local spurs to Milledgeville and Thomaston were built by separate companies. Most of these companies, however, were either heavily subsidized by the Central of Georgia subscriptions or controlled in sympathy with it to such a degree as to make them practically a part of its system from an early time. In the *post-bellum* period they, with still other connecting lines, have all been actually acquired by the Central of Georgia. One of the Central of Georgia circulars of the present day has a chart of the human hand laid upon the map of its system, with wrist and fingers of the hand corresponding to the main stem and branches of the company's present railway system. The cartographical simile is excellent; and it applies almost as well to the relations of the main stem and the branches when the roads were legally separate as to those of to-day when one company operates the whole. The intimacy and mutual dependence has been continuous. The history of the group of roads calls for treatment as a system. Hence the plan of the present chapter.

A distinctive beginning of the Central of Georgia project would be hard to discover. It was in the air from the early twenties, as an alternative for the waterway and turnpike plans, and it gradually reached concrete form as the feasibility of railroads received demonstration in other parts of the world. At the beginning, Savannah was much less eager than Macon and the cotton district northward in discussing a possible railroad to cross the Georgia pine-barrens. In distinct contrast to the corresponding development in South Carolina, the seaport rather followed than led in the early stages of the movement.

This was not strange; Savannah already enjoyed the advantage of a river connection with the Piedmont, which Charleston did not; and as for the external trade of central and western Georgia, she had a certain prospect of a large share in it so long as the natural channels of commerce should not be effectively superseded by artificial ones. Until railway operation should show cause to fear this, Savannah had no strong incentive to begin the great exertion which large-scale railway financing and building would require. By 1833, however, the encroachments of Charleston upon her accustomed tributary province began to rouse Savannah. As the *Macon Telegraph* said, Old Yamacraw was waking up. She then began deliberately and with business-like methods, but at the same time zealously, to make efforts, large in proportion to her size and resources, well directed, and successful.

From 1827 for a few years Savannah was concerned in a small and plodding way with the digging of the canal projected to tap the Altamaha, but never completed beyond the Ogeechee. In contrast, the town of Darien, near the mouth of the Altamaha, a village in size, but a metropolis in aspiration, was clamorously urging the construction of a railroad from the Ocomulgee to the western quarter of the state.[1] Lacking money, Darien was fertile in plans and prodigal in eloquence. Her projects came to naught at the time; but they furnished ideas which Savannah was later able to act upon.

From the launching of the Charleston and Hamburg project, the Georgians were generally in a waiting mood, until the news was spread that the railroad was a success and Charleston was about to capture Augusta's patronage from Savannah. Then came the impulse. State pride was extremely strong in Georgia; and many persons both in the uplands and at Savannah began to consider ways and means of offsetting the Charleston encroachment. Railways from Augusta to Savannah, from Macon to Savannah, and from various points in the Piedmont to Augusta and Macon, were simultaneously discussed in the newspapers,[2] and companies for several of these purposes were simultaneously chartered by the legislature in December, 1833.

After some preliminary agitation in the newspapers, Savannah began officially to stir in the fall of 1833. In October a citizens' mass meeting requested the city council to assist in establishing direct communication with Macon and Columbus by rail or canal.[3] A citizens' committee, with John M. Berrien as chairman, urged that the council should subscribe in the work to the extent of a half-million dollars. Upon inquiry, the council found that the city

[1] *Georgia Statesman,* April 18, 1826, memorial of a Darien town meeting to the Georgia legislature.

[2] *Georgia Courier,* February 7, and September 8, 1828; *Federal Union,* April 14, and June 2, 1831, October 25, 1832, and August 22, 1833.

[3] The narrative of city council transactions is taken largely from Thomas Gamble Jr., *History of the City Government of Savannah,* Savannah, 1900, pp. 170–176.

corporation owned real estate and other property to the value of $412,748, and the value was rapidly rising. Accordingly, on October 31, the council declared that it felt warranted in proceeding to raise $500,000 to aid in the railroad or canal project. Steps were taken to secure concert of action with the city authorities of Macon and Columbus, and to obtain the necessary legislative action in the premises. The charter of the Central of Georgia Railroad and Canal Company was promptly granted by the legislature,[1] authorizing it to construct and operate a canal or railway from Savannah to Macon, and vesting promotive power in the city corporations of Savannah and Macon. In January, 1834, the Savannah council requested Mr. Berrien to employ an engineer to survey the route, and pledged the city to meet a large part of the survey expenses. Delay ensuing in negotiations with an engineer at Washington, the council in the summer of 1834 employed Alfred Cruger, formerly employed on the Ogeechee Canal, to make an experimental survey. Cruger was already on the spot, and began work at once.

Cruger reported on the preliminary survey, November 8, 1834.[2] He recommended a route westward from Savannah, twelve miles, to the Ogeechee River; thence northwest along or near the banks of the Ogeechee for some eighty miles, to Jefferson County; thence up the valley of a tributary creek to the latitude of Sandersville; thence south of west, across Washington County to the Oconee River, and across that and the next watershed, in a westward line, to the Ocomulgee at Macon. The advantages of this

[1] Act approved December 20, 1833. O. H. Prince, *Digest of the Laws of Georgia to 1837*, pp. 300–304.

[2] Text printed in the *Federal Union*, November 26, 1834.

route were that the grade was easy on all but the last ten miles, that the pine-barrens were crossed in the shortest possible line and the traffic-yielding cotton belt reached at the nearest point, and that the road would cross the channels of three freight-bearing rivers at strategic points, and would invite the construction of feeding lines from the upper parts of these valleys. The disadvantages which might have been mentioned were the circuitousness of the route and the danger of injury from floods on the Ogeechee.

For the first hundred miles the maximum grade required was 10 feet. The rest of the route climbed watersheds and descended into river valleys; but the grades need not exceed 25 feet to the mile, except in the case of the final descent to Macon; and for that descent no resort to an inclined plane was demanded. The radii of curves on the route were nowhere short enough to constitute any difficulty. The engineering in that gently sloping country was, in fact, extremely simple, and the expense of grading correspondingly light. For the superstructure and track, Cruger advised a strap rail of iron 1½ by ⅝ inches, weighing 27 tons to the mile, resting upon a smooth scantling of oak and spiked with it to heavy stringers of yellow pine. These stringers, in turn, were to be pinned to wooden cross-ties lying embedded in the earthern roadbed.[1] He estimated the total cost at $10,000 per mile, bridges, side-tracks, and water-stations included. For equipment he estimated 4 locomotives of 4½ tons for passenger trains and 12 "heavy freight engines," of 6½ tons

[1] Descriptions in detail of the track and superstructure of the Central of Georgia Railroad at various periods, and of other roads in the state, may be found in Virgil Powers' essay on Georgia, in William F. Switzler's *Report on the Internal Commerce of the United States*, pp. 341–342. U.S. Government Printing Office, Washington, 1886.

each, the two sorts costing respectively $5000 and $6000 per engine; also, 20 passenger cars at $600 each, 4 for baggage, at $300, and 180 freight cars at $350. The wooden rails he expected to last 15 years, the bridge timbers, being under cover, to have a life twice as long, and the iron rails to last 50 years. The wheels of freight cars would need renewal, he thought, one and a half times, and those of the locomotive 5 times, each year. The road, some 200 miles in length, was to cost, with equipment, about $2,200,000. The earnings to be expected from cotton, groceries, manufactures, etc., might well yield annually, he thought, from 10 to 17 per cent upon the investment.

The charter of 1833 authorized a capital stock of $1,500,000 in shares of $100 each, and permitted the organization of the company when half of that amount had been subscribed. The Savannah council, in the spring of 1835, duly empowered the mayor to subscribe 5000 shares, and took steps to secure money on loan for the instalments when they should fall due. The town of Macon, only twelve years old at the time, and hampered with local problems, did not then see its way clear to make a subscription. The books were opened to the public in June, 1835. Individuals in Savannah took 1849 shares at the time, and persons in Macon, Milledgeville, and Sandersville took about 700 more. This carried the total above the 7500 shares required for the organization of the company; but of course it did not furnish nearly enough to build the road. Other resources had to be found: the stock must be made more attractive to investors.

In December, 1835, after a stiff contest in the legislature, an amended charter was secured which gave the company banking privileges and incidentally doubled the authorized stock. Some additional private subscriptions were then secured, and the city of Macon at length took 2500 shares. The company was organized in January, 1836, under the new charter, with the name Central of Georgia Railroad and Banking Company, and with William W. Gordon, formerly mayor of Savannah, as its president; one or two small assessments on the stock were collected in 1836; and at the close of that year a beginning was made in the task of construction. A further vigorous impulse to the pushing of the project was contributed by the legislature in its act of December 21, 1836, which authorized the building of the Western and Atlantic Railroad at state expense.[1] This act, for whose passage the combined influence of the Georgia and Central of Georgia Railroad companies was largely responsible, promising as it did to all the existing railroad companies in Georgia an opportunity to share in the trade of the great West, spurred each of those companies to more vigorous effort.

From this point the history of the Central of Georgia enterprise is plainly set forth in the annual reports of its officers, which began in May, 1838. These reports numbering 1 to 19 were reprinted by the company in 1854, and another series was reprinted at a later time. The reprints, however, are now scarce.

In the fall of 1836 a question had been raised whether a more southerly and direct route to Macon would not be preferable to the one surveyed by Cruger. A new chief engineer, John Randal, was employed to investigate the question, and, meanwhile, the company began work in grading the first nine miles from Savannah, which would

[1] For the history of this movement, see below, ch. vii.

be common to either route. A force of perhaps a thousand men was set to work there, in the company's direct employ.[1] In the spring of 1837 Randal reported in favor of the southern route for the road; but the company was displeased by his report and replaced him with L. O. Reynolds, who proved a most efficient officer. Reynolds reversed Randal's two chief policies: he determined upon the system of grading by contract as cheaper and more efficient; and decided upon the northern route for the road as promising profitable traffic at an earlier time and heavier traffic on the whole, and as offering a larger opportunity of getting a supply of negro labor from its owners along the route.

The company's operations were hampered somewhat by the crisis of 1837; but by May, 1838, it had completed the grading for sixty-seven miles from Savannah, and engines were running upon a track completed for twenty-six miles of that distance. Most of the landholders on the route had given the right of way gratis, and many had donated also the timber for the superstructure. The city of Savannah, also, had given a five-acre plot within the city as a site for the depot. The cost of the work was running well within the estimates. Nevertheless the stock was reported as considerably below par in the market. This is easily understood. The road had not and would not yet for many months reach paying territory. The prospect of dividends was accordingly distant. Furthermore, the financial stringency of 1837–1838 put cash at a premium, and tended to lower the value of all securities.

In a report of October 31, 1838, the president relates

[1] Report of the Chief Engineer for 1838. The following material, where not otherwise indicated, is from the reports of the president and chief engineer for the appropriate years.

that the road had begun to operate a passenger train, and had even brought down some cotton. The earnings, of course, were infinitesimal. The chief engineer reported that the definite location was nearly completed; that the request of the citizens of Milledgeville for the route to be made to lie through that town could not be granted without too great a detour through broken country. The total length of the route then recommended was 196 miles. A later survey, and location, however, reduced the length of the road as actually built to 190½ miles. Five hundred laborers were at work on the road in November, 1838, and the contractors hoped shortly to treble that force. In the report of May, 1839, it is stated that the grading contracts had reached the vicinity of Sandersville, 133 miles, and the track was laid 76 miles and progressing a mile per week. The Oconee Bridge contract had been let, and the Savannah depot buildings were in progress. In this report Reynolds commends the decision of the directorate to secure T-rail for the rest of the road. This was to be of wrought iron, of course, weighing thirty-two pounds per yard. It was to be laid upon longitudinal timbers, but the ribbon scantling which the company had been accustomed to lay upon the heavier beams to receive the plate-rail, was now to be dispensed with.

In the spring of 1839 some labor disturbances had occurred on the road, in the shape of friction between the whites and negroes employed. The whites were mostly immigrants from Europe and the North. This friction "had led some of the contractors to resort to the employment of blacks altogether." "That negro labor is perfectly adapted to the construction of works of internal improvement," Reynolds said in this report of May, 1839, "is now a well-established fact; and when this fact comes to be more generally acted upon, the public works of this section of the Union will be placed on a basis that will, in a great degree, exempt them from the effects of the fluctuations and vicissitudes in the financial affairs of the country, so detrimental to such undertakings elsewhere." This anticipation was partly justified during the severe depression which began in the fall of 1839. Money and credit became so scarce that stock instalments could not be had but in very small amounts. The planters along the upper route, however, were glad in leisure periods to exchange the labor of their slaves, then a drug on the market, for stock in the railroad. At the time of the report of November 1, 1839, the contractors employing white labor had nearly all withdrawn from the route. All new contracts were being made on the basis of payment three-fourths in stock and one-fourth in cash. At this time trains were running on nearly a hundred miles of the track, and a good deal of cotton was being handled. Passengers were routed through to Macon on stage-coaches from the head of the road. The earnings in October, 1839, were: from passengers $2,215, from freight $11,845; in November, passengers $3,335, down freight $8,324, up freight $6,746. In the late winter and spring the traffic greatly declined, however, as it came regularly to do at those seasons ever afterward.

In May, 1840, the force at work had shrunk to three hundred men, and progress was much slackened. The cotton crisis was crippling the work. The road was operating but one train for both passengers and freight, and its speed had been reduced from twenty-two to seventeen miles an hour, for the sake of reducing the wear and tear on rolling stock.

In November, 1840, the head of the road was still seventy miles from Macon, and progress in construction had almost stopped. The company was looking abroad for an opportunity to sell bonds and complete the road, but American securities were in no demand. The road, however, was handling considerable traffic. In the marketing season an average of two hundred wagons were plying to and from the head of the road, and the year's gross earnings amounted to nearly $114,000.

In November, 1841, the track had been extended 10 miles farther, to the Sandersville depot, and the grading completed for 170 of the total 190½ miles of the road to Macon. The year had been full of rains; a great freshet in March had swept away miles of the road-bed, costing $56,000 to replace, and had interrupted business for six months; the company's resources were so reduced that it had nothing but its own bonds with which to pay its contractors (they would no longer receive stock), and the contractors worked or suspended work as their personal interests directed. Cotton prices were at starvation levels, and hard times throughout the cotton belt so acute that it mattered little whether the road were soon completed or not. The market price of the company's stock had heavily declined; and before the end of the hard times fell as low, it is said, as $20 on the hundred.

Matters dragged on. During the year 1840–1841 the company bought enough rails to complete the road, and ordered rolling stock to increase its equipment; but the contractors were no more assiduous than before. The railway situation was changing, however, in a way to promote activity. Upon the death of W. W. Gordon, Mr. R. R. Cuyler became president of the company, and brought fresh energy into the administration. Furthermore, the state legislature had now directed the early completion of a portion of the Western and Atlantic Railroad, and the Monroe Railroad Company, operating northward from Macon, gave promise of completing its track to the Western and Atlantic terminus within the next year. Cuyler now made special agreements with two of his contractors to hasten their own work to completion, and also to finish the work of all the other contractors on the route. For this they were to receive, in the company's bonds, an advance of 20 per cent upon the former contract rates. By this means the company extended its track into Macon on October 13, 1843, whereupon the officials were duly fêted by the town.

The road was thus completed after seven years of labor and anxious waiting, at a cost, excluding equipment, of approximately $2,500,000, or about $13,000 per mile for its 190 miles. This total cost exceeded Reynolds' original estimate by $200,000. Of this excess, $75,000 was attributed to the flood of 1841, $40,000 to the purchase of motive power not included in the estimate, $50,000 to the disadvantage of having to use credit instead of cash in part payment of contracts, and $20,000 to the cost of right of way above the estimate. The earnings of the company's bank had already yielded dividends to the company's stockholders to the amount of $272,498. The cost of the road per mile was only about half of the average cost in the railroads of the United States. Its cheapness was due to the level character of the country, the lightness of the rail, and to the excellence and economy of administration. The capital stock outstanding at the time of the road's completion was about $2,000,000, out of the $3,000,000 authorized; and much of the amount issued had been issued in payment to contractors. The company at this time also had a bonded and floating debt of nearly $700,000. Cotton prices were still low, and the country depressed; traffic was not heavy, nor earnings large. In 1844–1845 affairs improved, but during most of the next year the Monroe Railroad, becoming bankrupt, suspended operations; and the Central of Georgia's net earnings were

CENTRAL OF GEORGIA RAILROAD COMPANY EARNINGS, 1840–1860

Year	Gross	Net		Gross	Net		Gross	Net
1840	$113,827	$ 79,194	1847	$383,863	$171,395	1854	$1,009,793	$534,526
1841	106,145	?	1848	518,676	247,857	1855	1,428,682	739,654
1842	133,535	62,781	1849	668,383	330,755	1856	1,341,711	694,696
1843	?	?	1850	688,245	325,355	1857	1,122,644	542,310
1844	201,464	?	1851	748,207	406,797	1858	1,353,722	755,614
1845	328,424	180,704	1852	945,508	507,625	1859	1,645,554	851,211
1846	?	90,972	1853	917,082	509,348	1860	1,715,025	764,574

reduced, by the stoppage of its feeding line, from $180,000 to $90,000. In 1846–1847 they rose again to $171,000; and by 1848 the road, with heavy and ever increasing traffic, began to be serenely prosperous. About this time the Central of Georgia Company began a systematic policy of promoting subsidiary lines. We suspend the narrative here, and turn to the situation in the interior districts where these radiating lines were being demanded and built.

Railroads from point to point within the Piedmont were a part of the general railway agitation from the beginning. The sentiment in their favor had in most cases undergone no change at the time when the Central of Georgia was completed. Ranging the Georgia cotton belt from east to west in the late thirties and early forties, a traveler would have found well-nigh unanimous sentiment in favor of railways from the respective localities to connect with the Savannah Road, except in the one instance of Augusta, where the people were of two minds. On the one hand a railroad to Savannah would be a distinct convenience to the people of the city, and was on general grounds desirable. On the other, if built, it would probably take from Augusta and carry to Savannah most of the trade of the towns and plantations along the line, south and southwest of Augusta; and this was for some years the more weighty consideration. The Georgia Railroad Company, furthermore, threw its influence against the project of an Augusta connection with the Central.

The country districts and the towns everywhere else were usually enthusiastic for anything which promised them connection with the Savannah Road. Eatonton, as we have seen, was a leader in the earliest agitation in Georgia; and promptly changed the direction of her attention from Augusta to Savannah as soon as the Central Railway was chartered. Milledgeville, her neighbor to the southward, was of like mind with Eatonton; and the two towns were ready to support the project of a branch road as soon as the main line should reach their neighborhood. The towns and plantation districts northwest, west and southwest of Macon vied in a clamor for railroads to Macon. As in most other cases of rural districts, however, popular enthusiasm did not connote a strong financial backing from a community. The planters and village merchants had little or no surplus capital, especially in these newly settled areas. The reliance for actual financing must be upon the larger commercial towns and cities.

In the general district west of the longitude of Macon, Monroe County, enlisting the support of L. L. Griffin and other Macon capitalists, made the earliest achievement, getting the Monroe Railroad Company chartered in 1833, and the road built to Forsyth, twenty-five miles, before the end of 1840. This road was later extended through Barnesville and Griffin to Atlanta. Thomaston contented herself with promoting a spur from Barnesville to meet her needs. Columbus was anxious for eastward connection, but lost some years in debating as to the preferable route to Macon and in casting about for financial backing. West Point, La Grange, and Newnan, in rich cotton counties, also, of course, wanted railway outlets, and were inclined for a time toward connections with Macon; but the extension of the Georgia Railroad toward Atlanta and the launching of the Western and Atlantic diverted their attention.

The freshly settled country in southwest Georgia felt a hardship in the lack of a seaport at the mouth of the Flint-Chattahoochee river system, and its consequent disadvantage for external trade. All the settlers from Macon and Columbus to the Florida boundary were accordingly anxious for access to the Atlantic Ocean. The best opportunity for this at the time was, of course, to connect with the Savannah Road at Macon. Later, direct roads to Savannah and Brunswick were also projected, as well as outlets through Florida. But in the thirties and forties the city of Macon and the railroad to Savannah were the cynosure of central and western Georgia. We will take up the several concrete projects.

The charter of the Monroe Railroad Company was granted by an act of December 23, 1833, authorizing a corporation to be formed with a capital stock of $200,000, and empowering it to build and operate a railroad from Macon to Forsyth. A proviso in the charter required that one thousand of the hundred-dollar shares be subscribed for within a twelvemonth, and that work be begun in two years from the date of the charter.[1] These conditions were not met; and the charter lapsed. A healing act, however, approved December 26, 1835, reciting that very recently the whole stock of $200,000 had been subscribed, renewed the charter and all the privileges formerly granted. A year later a further act bestowed banking privileges, increased the capital to $600,000 with permission for the company to double it, and empowered the company to extend its road to connect with the Western and Atlantic Railway, then being initially provided for.[2] The act providing for the state road also directed the governor under certain conditions to subscribe on behalf of the state for stock to the amount of $200,000 in each of certain railroads, among which that of the Monroe Company was included.

Grading was begun on the Monroe Railroad early in 1836. The track to Forsyth was completed before the end of 1838.[3] But the goal of the Western and Atlantic terminus was much harder to reach. The cotton crisis, that Charybdis of so many companies, prevented the sale of stock and hampered the collection of instalments on that already sold. The Monroe Company had laid itself especially open to injury from such a crisis by devoting a large sum to the

[1] O. H. Prince, *Digest of the Laws of Georgia to 1837*, pp. 314–318.

[2] *Ibid.*, pp. 345 and 369–374.

[3] *Southern Banner*, December 22, 1838.

construction of a pretentious building for its bank and general headquarters in Macon, and by pushing its banking operations perhaps a little recklessly.

A report of the company in April, 1840, showed outstanding 9400 shares of the regular stock, all paid in, and 1329 shares in the stock of the northward extension, on which $64,990 had been received. Of the regular stock, L. L. Griffin, the prime mover and president of the company, held 1793 shares, and I. G. Hill and Alfred Brooks 1000 shares each. Of the extension stock, the city of Macon held 500 shares, while nearly all the other holdings were of very small size.[1] In October, 1840, of the 77 miles of the route to be covered above Forsyth, 51 miles had been graded. The report on track-laying, however, was not so favorable. Some of the grading contractors had accepted railway shares in payment; but the rolling mills would not do so; and the company was in straits for rails. The track was actually laid for eleven miles in the fall of 1840, with rails of oak instead of iron; and for months the cars brought to the head of the iron track by the locomotives were hauled thence by horses to and from Barnesville on the wooden extension.[2] In the next year iron enough was obtained to replace the wooden rail to Barnesville; whereupon an oaken track was laid to Griffin and operated by horse-power.[3] And for still another year this patchwork, hand-to-mouth policy was continued.

Meanwhile the company memorialized the governor, stating that all the conditions of the law had been met, and asking the subscription of $200,000 by the state, promised

[1] *Southern Recorder*, May 19, 1840.

[2] *Federal Union*, November 29, 1842.

[3] *Southern Recorder*, October 7, 1841.

in the act of 1836. The governor consented to make the subscription; but before paying out the money he sent a memorandum on the subject in a message to the legislature.[1] The legislature proceeded to repeal the clause providing for state aid to railway companies.[2] This repealing act contained a proviso permitting the execution of any contracts already entered into which involved state aid; but the governor did not complete the transaction with the Monroe Railroad Company, and no public money was obtained by it. This disappointment was partially offset by a subscription of $50,000 in November, 1842, by the city corporation of Savannah; but this was not enough to secure the completion of the work. The Central of Georgia Company would have helped; but, as we have seen, was itself in desperate straits at the time. On a very tight loan market the Monroe Company was able to borrow enough on mortgage to extend the track to within twenty miles of Atlanta. Then, in April, 1845, just before the lightening of the long and terrible depression, the company, failing to meet its mortgage obligations, was forced into bankruptcy. The road was sold, under the sheriff's hammer; and the proceeds little more than paid the company's debts. The investment of the stockholders was an almost complete loss.

The road was bought by Jerry Cowles of Macon, who at once proceeded to interest Northern capitalists in it. The running of trains was meanwhile suspended for nearly a year in 1845–1846. Cowles sold the road, it seems, to

[1] Special message of November 10, 1842, *Federal Union*, November 29, 1842.

[2] Act of December 19, 1842, T. R. R. Cobb, *Digest of the Laws of Georgia to 1851*, p. 412.

Daniel Tyler, of Norwich, Conn.; and Tyler joined a number of associates with himself in a new stock company, under the name of the Macon and Western Railroad Company. The operation of trains was resumed; the track was finished to the Western and Atlantic terminus, a new charter was secured in 1847, and the road promptly put upon a good working basis.

The new company was capitalized at $1,500,000, in shares of $100 each. All of the 15,000 shares were disposed of, but only $42 per share was required from the subscribers, the $630,000 thus obtained being sufficient for the present needs of the road. A large proportion of this stock was sold to capitalists in New York City. The bankrupt road was a bargain, and the "high financiers" expected to manipulate it to their advantage. The directors for 1848, the first year under the new charter, were: Nathan C. Munroe, Charles Day, Washington Poe, all of Macon; Charles J. McDonald of Marietta, Ga.; Andrew Low Jr., of Savannah; Ker Boyce of Charleston; Edward Whitehouse, Theodore Dehon, and Adolf Rodewald, of New York City; Rufus H. King of Albany, N.Y.; Azeriah Boody of Springfield, Mass.; and Daniel Tyler of Norwich, Conn. A clause in the by-laws adopted in January, 1848, provided that meetings of the board of directors might be held in New York upon requirement of any three directors.[1]

This inclusion within the membership of the company, and the directorate of persons widely separated in residence

[1] The history of the Macon and Western Railroad Company is written chiefly from a file of the annual reports of the company preserved by Nathan C. Munroe and given by him to the public library of Macon, Ga., where they are now accessible.

and in interests, made friction easily possible. Occasion later arose to produce it.

The road had been completed to Atlanta before the securing of the new charter. Its operations at once became profitable, for prosperous times had returned to the cotton belt, and traffic was growing heavy. In eleven months of 1848 the gross earnings were $141,132, and the net profits $52,258. The price of the stock rose in 1849 to $45 per share,[1] whereas only $42 had been paid in. Dividends of 8 per cent or more per year were begun. The track, however, was of such cheap construction, and so costly in fuel, time, and wear-and-tear, that a renovation was begun in 1849. In that year bonds were issued for $135,000 to buy heavier rails. This was the first and the largest debt incurred by the company. In 1850 the directors decided that all the rest of the route should be laid with heavy iron, in preparation for the stress of traffic which it was foreseen would ensue from the opening of the Western and Atlantic and its feeding lines northward and westward. To meet this expense the directors determined to sell a large issue of new stock. With the approval of the stockholders, they called in the existing stock and issued one share of $84 in place of two shares of $42. They then offered 4625 additional shares for sale at $84 each. At the end of November, 1850, the subscription for the new issue stood as follows: at the Bank of the State of New York, 2020 shares; at the Bank of Charleston, 233; at the office in Macon, 1059 shares, including 300 which the Central of Georgia Railroad Company had agreed to take in payment of freight on iron. The betterment of the road was carried on speedily with the funds thus secured. In 1853 the

[1] *Federal Union*, March 27, 1849.

company decided to make a further increase of its stock to its chartered limit of $1,500,000, and apply the funds to new cars and buildings and to the sinking of the company's debt. Scrip stock was issued *pro rata* among the then stockholders, and in most cases promptly accepted and paid for by them.

By 1853 the Macon and Western Company had a good and thoroughly equipped road, with a small debt, and under a fairly sound administration. The route, 103 miles, was a little devious, partly because the Western and Atlantic terminus had been built farther eastward than the Macon and Western engineer had expected, but the track was good, for the region and period, and the road safe from floods by reason of its watershed location. Gross earnings had by 1853 reached nearly $300,000 per year, and net earnings to above 50 per cent of the gross. Dividends of 8 per cent were easily being earned. The road had become an important part of the route for through traffic between the Northwest and the Southeast; and the remaining problems were mostly those of routine administration.

The Thomaston and Barnesville Railroad, a petty line, 16 miles long, branching from the Macon and Western, was built between 1853 and 1857 by a struggling local company. The road was sold by the sheriff, as bankrupt, in 1860, and bought by a group of local citizens, aided by the Macon and Western Company. The road was later absorbed by the Central of Georgia.

In southwest Georgia there had been some premature activity as an outgrowth of the Darien agitation in 1826–1827, which we have previously noted. In December, 1827, the legislature had granted to Thomas Spalding of Darien the right of building a railroad of wood or digging a canal from the Ocomulgee to the Flint River. Spalding was empowered to do this individually or with associates in a company, as he might see fit. Several years having passed without developments, the charter was renewed by an act of 1834, which authorized a railroad of either wood or iron.[1] The route contemplated lay from the Great Bend of the Ocomulgee, some sixty miles south of Macon, in a line westward to Albany on the Flint. There was little progress until about 1840. At that time a certain General Jones Lee, a resident of the Flint River district, took up the project, promoted a company to utilize the charter, and was himself made its first president. By April, 1841, subscriptions had been secured to the amount of $250,000, and instalments amounting to 15 per cent had been paid in, in the form of notes of hand from the subscribers. No cash had then been received; but the contracts had already been let for grading the eastern half of the route and those for the western half were then advertised.[2] The contractors agreed to take preferred stock, guaranteed to yield 8 per cent, in payment for work. In that level country, the work of grading was, of course, extremely light.

This company is notable chiefly for its irresponsible charter and its experience with a gang of Irish laborers. A. H. Brisbane, its "engineer agent," and later its president and general factotum, was a personage worthy of a place in literature. In some way, whether by service, courtesy, or presumption, he had acquired the title of General. He had a peculiar gift of plausibility, a talent for oratory, and a passion for eulogizing all men and affairs with which he was associated. The climate of Irwin County, oppressively

[1] Prince, *Digest of the Laws of Georgia to 1837*, pp. 324–326.

[2] *Southern Recorder*, April 6, 1841.

hot and malarious in actuality, was bracing and healthful in his description, and sure to attract people over his railroad to summer resorts on the route. The gangs of Irish plug-uglies which by some hook or crook he had enticed into the piney-woods wilderness to grade his moneyless railroad were in his words "several parties of the choicest white laborers." It was doubtless through Brisbane's management that several contractors were found to hire the labor which he imported, and grade the route for the company's paper.

In November, 1841, the grading had been two-thirds completed; but the company was in great need of funds. A meeting of the directors, at Albany, decided that it was useless to call for cash from the stockholders, and sent a call for help to Savannah. To their temporary relief, the city council of Savannah indorsed the company's note for the sum of $5000. Brisbane now hit upon a new idea. He appealed to the Catholic prelates for charity on behalf of the starving Irish laborers whom the company was unable to pay or feed. Aid came in response from Bishop England at Charleston and Bishop Hughes of New York. This, however, was hardly a sound basis for railroad progress. Brisbane reported in February, 1843, a total expenditure to that time of $9000, and an outstanding debt of $15,000 with no visible assets but the naked road-bed, which the contractors really owned. On a subscription of $300,000, the cash payment had been only $3000.[1] Brisbane, with his talent, was still able to describe the situation as hopeful. But a short while afterward the starving Irish mutinied and beat the plausible Brisbane with stones and cudgels. Brisbane fled for his

[1] *Federal Union*, March 7, 1843.

life, and that is the end of the Ocomulgee and Flint River Railroad story. Not a rail was ever laid upon it.

The sober and substantial history of railroads to southwestern Georgia began in the summer of 1845, just when prosperity was returning to the cotton belt. A plan was then set on foot for building a road from Macon southwestward to the Chattahoochee River, to connect there possibly with a road projected northeastward from Pensacola. Branches to Columbus and Albany were contemplated as a part of the road. The promoters drew up a charter with very liberal provisions as to route and privileges, and secured its enactment by the legislature in December, 1845.[1]

When the subscription books were opened, however, no shares were applied for. The commissioners then, with a loan of funds for the purpose from the Central of Georgia Company, assuming unusual functions, employed an experienced engineer, F. P. Holcombe, to make and report on a survey of the route. In a brief time Holcombe's report was prepared and published, and its weight was felt. He described the general district to be crossed as a table-land something less than 600 feet above sea-level, cut mostly into rolling country by watercourses with valleys whose bottoms were from 275 to 350 feet above the sea. The larger valleys and ridges ran across the route, but some of the smaller ones parallel.

His plan was, of course, to make the necessary ascents

[1] The important documents for the history of the Southwestern Railroad Company were reprinted by the company in one volume: *Reports of the Chief Engineers, Presidents, and Superintendents of the Southwestern Railroad Company, of Georgia, from no.* 1–22, *inclusive, with the Charter and Amendments thereto,* Macon, 1869.

and descents along the tributary streams. The first fifty miles would be the most troublesome and expensive, requiring much use of the maximum grade allowed, forty-five feet to the mile, and some heavy cuts and fills. For the remainder of the road, branches included, ridges in the direction desired were luckily available, and grading would be very light and cheap. No rock excavation was anywhere necessary. As to traffic which might be expected, Holcombe made a glowing prophecy. 150,000 bales of cotton were already being shipped from the port of Appalachicola, and the country was as yet but sparsely settled. A large part of this and its increase, and most of the return traffic, would be captured by the proposed railroad. The Chattahoochee, he said, "like most other of the rivers of the country, [is] ultimately destined to yield the palm to the superior speed, certainty, and safety of that great revolutionist, the railroad. [The great Mississippi itself will be deserted, at least by the passenger traffic.]"

As a result of Holcombe's report a few shares were subscribed for; but the prospect was so far from rosy that the company had the legislature reduce the subscription required for organization from $500,000 to $200,000. In December, 1847, the Central of Georgia Company promised a subscription of $250,000 as soon as a like amount should be subscribed in the region in which the road was to lie. The city council of Savannah, too, subscribed $250,000 to be paid in Central of Georgia stock at par, as soon as the completion of the Southwestern Railroad should be placed beyond contingency. The citizens and the corporation of Macon were disappointingly lukewarm, from a fear that the road, if built, would divert a part of the town's trade instead of adding to it. The commissioners sent agents along the proposed route of the road, and, though not brilliantly successful, obtained enough subscriptions to legalize the organization of the company, which was done in February, 1848. The directors, then appointed, soon made contracts for the grading of thirty-five miles of road-bed, beginning at Macon, and the laying of most of this with superstructure and track. All the contractors were large stockholders in the company.

In the course of 1848 the company disposed of enough more of its stock to secure the Central of Georgia subscription; but on the shares taken by individuals, only $5 in cash had been collected, and $28 in notes of hand. Upon the request of the company, the city of Savannah modified the character of its promised aid. It reduced the amount to $150,000, to be paid in 7 per cent bonds of the city and available for the purchase of rails by the company. This, the president said, "gave the company a safe and permanent footing." The construction progressed with fair speed until the middle of 1850; but was then hampered by a general rise in wages and a dearth of labor. A bill introduced in the legislature for a state subscription of $500,000 to the road was defeated. The stockholders in the neighborhood of Albany began to complain that the road gave no early promise of reaching their locality; and many of them forfeited their shares rather than pay further instalments for an enterprise which disappointed the local expectations it had aroused. The company refused for the time to proceed by means of loans; but it used its stock in part payment for grading. In February, 1851, the company had received funds, or their equivalent, as follows: from the Central of Georgia Company, $250,000; from the city of Savannah,

$150,000; from contractors, in work and material, $87,266; and from individual stockholders, $80,087. There was still due in instalments from stockholders, $70,150, excluding the arrears on the forfeited shares, which numbered 1266.

In July, 1852, the road was completed to the west bank of the Flint River, fifty-three miles, at a cost of $13,442 per mile. Meanwhile, E. G. Cabaniss, who owned six hundred acres of land on the Flint where the river reached the west bank, had laid out town lots, distributed a lithographed plan of the proposed town of Oglethorpe, with notice of an auction for January 16, 1850,[1] and had realized a very comfortable return from the sale. The town had a boom of trade, so long as it was the head of the railroad, and then sank into village status.

From 1852 the Southwestern Railroad Company found its prospects in general much brightened. The Muscogee Railroad, promoted by the city of Columbus, was reaching toward Fort Valley as a junction point; and two companies, the Mobile and Girard, and the Columbus and Opelika, were preparing to build railways respectively southwest and northwest from Columbus, and thus offered the hope of through traffic to the roads connecting from the eastward. The people of southwest Georgia furthermore began to show a reviving interest. The directorate resolved to nurse the growth of this interest by letting it be known that the route of the road's further extension and branches would probably be directed toward the locality from which the greatest financial assistance should come.

The capital stock of the company in February, 1852, consisted of 5563 shares, of $100 par and paid-up value,

[1] *Federal Union,* October 30, 1849.

held as follows: by persons outside of Georgia, 81 shares; by corporations and persons in Savannah, 4289; by contractors, 505; and in southwest Georgia, 688 shares. In addition there had been paid in and forfeited, $32,083. For an enterprise largely for their benefit, costing over $700,000, the planters had contributed less than one-seventh. In the further extension and branches, however, the proportions from the localities were larger. In 1852–1853 the citizens of Americus and vicinity subscribed and paid for $75,000 in stock to secure an extension to their town costing about $125,000 in addition to that amount; and soon afterward the people in and about Albany took like measures to bring the rails to their town. The policy of requiring local subscriptions was thus successful, after the company had built its initial stem mostly with resources contributed by Savannah and the Central of Georgia Railroad.

The Southwestern Company in the half-year ending February 1, 1851, earned $76,536 gross, and $49,609 net; in the year following, $129,395 gross, and enough net to

SOUTHWESTERN RAILROAD COMPANY STATISTICS, 1852–1860
(YEARS ENDING AUGUST 1.)

Year	Miles of Road	Capital Stock	Bonds	Gross Receipts	Net Earnings	Dividends
1852	50	$ 556,700	$100,000	$129,395	?	8%
1853				140,008	$ 76,807	4
1854			364,000	220,851	121,605	4
1855	92			256,596	141,168	9
1856				353,092	202,265	8
1857				365,213	199,897	8
1858	192			391,540	208,771	8
1859		2,254,000	631,000	?	?	8
1860	206	3,318,279	396,500	676,895	423,521	13

permit a dividend of 8 per cent. In 1852–1853 the gross earnings were $140,008, and net, $76,807. The company then had a bonded debt of $100,000, and later increased this in extending its road.

The railroad branching from the Southwestern line at Fort Valley and running to Columbus had been fostered and partly built by the Southwestern Company. The story of this, the Muscogee Railroad, is in place before leaving the theme of the Southwestern.

The town of Columbus, founded in 1827 upon the cession of the district by the Indians, was known from the beginning to be at a strategic point for trade. At the fall-line on the Chattahoochee, it soon acquired a thriving commerce, and began to have aspirations also for manufacturing importance through the use of its large water-power. It in fact very quickly became, and has always continued to be, one of the five principal cities in the state.

The Western and Atlantic law of December, 1836, designated Columbus as one of the towns which the state would aid in connecting by railroad with the Western and Atlantic. In 1837 the citizens were busily discussing a project for that connection; and in consequence, on January 29, 1838, the city council passed an ordinance to issue the huge sum of $750,000 in bonds to be loaned upon conditions to the Chattahoochee Railroad and Banking Company, chartered a year earlier for the purpose in hand. In March it was reported that not enough stock had been subscribed to meet the conditions of this ordinance; and the ordinance was thereupon changed to provide for a subscription of $200,000 in the stock of the company. At a meeting of the stockholders in the same month, subscription lists were shown amounting to 10,255 shares. The panic of 1839, however, clouded the prospects of the company, and stopped its progress. By 1841 the company's plan was entirely abandoned. Luckily for the city, the issue of a part of its bonds had been delayed by the raising of a doubt as to the city's chartered powers in the premises; and the city met no serious loss from the failure and death of the company.[1]

Columbus now looked toward the east for railroad connection, and incidentally toward the west also. In 1845 the city sent a committee to Macon to confer with the officials of the Central of Georgia Railroad about building a railroad from Columbus to Barnesville on the Macon and Western. The Central, more interested in the Southwestern Railroad, then projected, advocated a connection with it at Fort Valley, instead. Accordingly, the Muscogee Railroad Company, chartered in 1845, was empowered to build eastward from Columbus in the expectation of connecting with the Southwestern. Little was done, however, until 1847, when the mooting of a project of a rival road from Macon or Barnesville to West Point, spurred the city council of Columbus to subscribe $150,000 to the stock of the Muscogee Company. During the next few years the company pushed its construction, but could not command enough resources to build as far as Fort Valley. To fill the gap, the Southwestern Company took over the eastern half of the Muscogee Company's intended route, and built a track to meet the Muscogee Company's. The connection of Columbus by rail with Macon and the sea was completed early in June, 1853, and celebrated in the usual way.[2] Meanwhile the Columbus city authorities were busily

[1] J. H. Martin, *History of Columbus, Georgia,* pp. 90–115, *passim.*

[2] *Federal Union,* June 7, 1853.

promoting roads reaching into Alabama; and became involved in debt to an uncomfortable degree. Relief was found in 1855 by selling its 1800 shares of Muscogee Railroad stock to private persons for $151,000. The Muscogee Company before long became absorbed by the Southwestern Company, as we shall see when recurring to the theme near the end of the present chapter.

The Milledgeville and Eatonton district was hampered in its getting of a railroad by the peculiarity of status and uncertainty in prospects of the town of Milledgeville. That town was the commercial collecting and distributing point at the fall-line on the Oconee, a stream of minor importance. It was also the capital of the state; and this fact dominated the situation. Its political importance and the possible advantages to accrue therefrom overshadowed the town's commercial and industrial interests, inclined the people in a measure to look for favors instead of for opportunities to labor and invest earnings, and, on the whole, stunted the growth and hampered the progress of the community. Then, too, the occurrence of movements in the state for the removal of the capital to another place, from time to time, added apprehension to apathy, and paralyzed the energies of the town. Such a movement was in agitation during the forties,[1] and together with the cotton depression prevented for years any utilization of the charter granted in 1837 for a railroad branching from the Central of Georgia. The company for this branch road, from Gordon on the Savannah line to Milledgeville, was organized in the late forties, and construction begun in 1850. The Central of Georgia promoted the work by furnishing the new company with the plate-rails from the

[1] *Federal Union,* January 22, 1850.

Central's original track, now being replaced with T-rail. In payment, the Central accepted the Milledgeville Company's stock. The road reached Milledgeville in 1851. Meanwhile Eatonton, securing a similar promise of old rails from the Central, formed a company to connect with and continue the Milledgeville Road. These two little companies were soon merged; and in 1855 the Central of Georgia took over their road, 37 miles in length, on a perpetual lease at a rental of $28,000 per year. The district above Eatonton, particularly the town of Monticello, was restive under its restriction to ox-cart, mule-team, and stagecoach locomotion. The thrifty farmers regretted having to drive their mules all winter with loads of cotton to distant markets, and finding them in consequence worn down and lazy when spring plowing required vigor. They further wished for a chance to market their small crops, which railroads might give. And the merchants, of course, wanted easier and cheaper supplies of the goods in which they dealt.[1] The plan for a further extension of the Eatonton line, however, was opposed by the secret influence of the Georgia Railroad Company, which feared a diversion of its traffic; and was effectively discouraged.

The branch from the Central of Georgia to Augusta had been in contemplation from the middle thirties. A meeting of citizens of Augusta in 1839 resolved: "That a close commercial union between the cities of Augusta and Savannah would promote the prosperity and redound to the honor of both cities and of the state of Georgia"; and advocated for this purpose the building of a railroad from Augusta to the Central's line.[2] The cotton crisis, of course,

[1] *Federal Union*, October 22, 1850, and June 7, 1853.

[2] *Southern Banner*, July 5, 1839.

suspended this movement; and afterward the Georgia Railroad Company and some of the Augusta business men opposed it as probably dangerous to the interests of that company and to the trade of the city. The people along the route, however, especially those in Waynesboro and Burke County, were favorable; and so also the city of Savannah and, most of all, the Central of Georgia Company. The latter took the lead.

The directors of the Central in 1846 proposed to the Georgia Railroad Company that the two corporations should join in offering a guarantee of 7 per cent dividends on the stock of the contemplated railway, popularly called the Waynesboro Road, provided its cost should not exceed $550,000. A stockholders' meeting, December, 1846, indorsed the proposal. But the offer met no favor at Augusta. In 1847 the city of Savannah subscribed $60,000 to the stock of the Waynesboro Company, the Central subscribed $100,000, and individuals in Savannah and along the route, enough more to secure the road's construction. The road, fifty-four miles in length from Millen on the Central to Augusta, was completed in 1854. It was at once taken over by the Central of Georgia Company on lease, at $73,000 per year.

We have thus seen that excepting the case of the road from Macon to Atlanta, which was built before the Central had reached the beginning of the successful and dominant part of its career, all of the feeding lines to that road were greatly assisted by the Central of Georgia Company, were controlled from the outset in close sympathy with it, and were in several cases leased by it immediately upon their completion. In later times all of them, the Macon and Western included, came to be absorbed by the Central of Georgia, either by amalgamation of stocks or by perpetual lease. Most admirably administered, the company steadily extended and more closely integrated its system.

We broke off our narrative of the Central of Georgia Railroad proper at the year 1848, when with general prosperity returning in a flood to the cotton belt, the traffic and earnings of the railroad had been rapidly increasing for several years, the company's stock was approaching par, and its resources for expansion, therefore, about to become very greatly enlarged.

The company had begun the conversion of its debt in 1845, by issuing bonds at 7 per cent. At the same time it resolved that as net profits were applied to sinking the debt, dividends would be issued in stock until the capital should be increased from $2,048,715 to $2,600,000, which was estimated to be within the cost of the road and equipment. In 1847 a new policy was substituted; 8 per cent preferred, non-voting stock was sold to the amount of $500,000, and devoted to retiring the bonds. New bonds were provided for, however, in the same year, to the amount of $250,000, in aid of the Southwestern Railroad Company, then newly organized. Preferred stock continued to be sold from time to time to pay for the new rails used in the rapid relaying of the track. The company was now becoming widely known for its large resources and its extensive policy of feeding-line promotion. In 1848 the Nashville and Chattanooga Company and the Hiwasee Company, both engaged in building lines to connect with the Western and Atlantic, and thus to feed the Central of Georgia, applied severally to the latter company for a subscription in their stock. The directors referred the Nashville and Chattanooga application for $250,000 to be determined by the stockholders. A warm debate occurred in the stockholders' meeting, on the subject; and in view of the strong opposition demonstrated, the question was postponed and never brought to an issue. The road in question was too remote in comparison with the pressing needs for the Central's resources nearer at hand. In the case of the Hiwassee Road, the directorate refused to make a subscription, but granted the company a 20 per cent reduction in the freight charges on the rails to be carried to the road. This reduction was not expensive to the Central, since its up-bound freight was always light, and the expense consequently small. In 1851 the company devoted $95,000 to the purchase of stock in the Waynesboro Road, and $100,000 to the Columbus branch of the Southwestern Road. It had also acquired $20,000 worth of stock in the Milledgeville Road, in payment for the old plate-rails it had furnished. The net earnings in 1851 were above $400,000, and rapidly increasing.

The completion of the Western and Atlantic and the opening of routes in Tennessee now added very heavily to the volume of traffic. Additional rolling stock was in urgent demand, and the need of speedy completion of the track became pressing. A report in March, 1851, showed the capital stock to be $3,000,000, of which $205,790 was appropriated to the use of the bank maintained by the company, and the rest to the railroad. The stockholders, to provide for the betterments demanded, now authorized the issue of $500,000 more stock to be offered first at par, to the present stockholders, on a *pro rata* basis. The stock, rising from $20 in 1844 and $50 at the end of 1845, had now reached quotations above par, in spite of the issue of stock dividends and the sale of preferred stock. Eight per cent dividends were being regularly paid, and the prospect of larger ones was excellent.

The only time of financial discomfort for the administration in the rest of the *ante-bellum* period occurred in the autumn of 1854, and was purely fortuitous. At a time of a brief general reaction in finance, a batch of the company's bonds fell due, a pestilence in Savannah cut down the earnings, and the betterment works demanded funds. The directors, finding it hard to realize upon assets, determined to pass the usual 4 per cent half-yearly dividend and issued instead a dividend of 10 per cent in stock. In 1859 the capital stock stood at $4,000,000. At the end of that year it was increased to $5,000,000: half of the increase was distributed as an extra dividend, and $300,000 used in buying up the stock of the branch to Milledgeville and Eatonton, and thus, with legislative permission, consolidating the companies. The remaining $200,000 was intended for further betterments of track and equipment. The administration was talking of double-tracking the road. In the busy seasons the company was running daily five freight and two passenger trains each way, and a regular lumber train, and frequent extra freight trains from Millen to Savannah. In spite of the disproportion of the down and up traffic, the company earned in 1859, $851,211 net profits, out of gross receipts $1,645,554. The company was the most powerful corporation in the South, and except for the rumblings of war, had prospect of indefinite further prosperity and aggrandizement.

Corporation success apparently tends to produce a characteristic frame of mind and policy in the administration. In an extreme form this is megalomania and hunger for the fullest powers of monopoly. The Central of Georgia administration was always sane and conservative, as well as remarkably capable and successful; but it naturally did not escape all manifestation of the grasping and domineering disposition. Its great rival was, of course, the Georgia Railroad Company, with which it competed for the control of a large debatable land in the Georgia cotton belt, as well as in the sharing of the traffic brought down by the Western and Atlantic. At the beginning these two companies had more occasion to combine strength and influence than to oppose one another; for example, their coalition in the support of the Western and Atlantic project in 1836 and the following years. Later their rivalry grew more salient.

Competition for tributary territory and traffic was unavoidable. The two railroads lay parallel for a hundred miles, at a distance of only forty to fifty miles apart; and the intervening country furnished most of each road's local traffic. Numerous localities in this district were anxious to secure branch roads to their own doors; and they made proposals to one company or the other, or to both, as their local preferences or circumstances might determine. The Waynesboro Road, as we have seen, was the occasion of some antagonism of the two great companies. Another occasion arose from a proposal of the citizens of Washington, Wilkes County, in 1847, to subscribe $300,000 for a railroad to connect with the Central of Georgia, provided $200,000 were raised elsewhere. The Central offered to subscribe $100,000, and Savannah was disposed to take the rest. But the Georgia Railroad Company dragged a herring across the trail. It offered the Wilkes County people, for a $300,000 subscription, to build a branch from the Georgia Road to Washington, and a branch from the same point southward to Sparta, and to aid in building a connection from Augusta to the Central of Georgia line. Not all of these proposals were carried out; but they were successful in breaking the negotiations with the Central.

The issue giving rise to the greatest irritation between the companies was the proposal to extend the Warrenton spur of the Georgia Railroad into a branch from the main line at Camak to Macon, thus establishing a direct line between Macon and Augusta, and introducing a dangerous competition for the traffic of south-central and western Georgia, which the Central considered itself to have preempted. The towns of Sparta and Milledgeville, which lay on the proposed route, of course favored the plan, and so did Macon, Augusta, and Charleston; but the decision to build or not to build lay with the Georgia Railroad Company. Discussion of the plan began in the forties; and for years thereafter the Georgia Company could use the threat of its construction as a warning to the Central to keep within its own territory. A survey of the route was made in 1853, but the Georgia Company procrastinated when memorials on the subject were presented. By 1857 the Milledgeville district had become angered at the high discriminating freight rates of the Central; but Macon had grown lukewarm.[1] The question continued under discussion; and in May, 1860, the Georgia Railroad Company committed itself to the project.

The relations of the two rival companies, and the disposition of the Central toward retaliation, is shown in the report of President Cuyler and the directors in December,

[1] *Federal Union,* June 5 and 19, and August 14, 1849, October 25, 1853, May 16, 1854, January 20, February 24, and March 10, 1857.

1860. Stating the fact of the commencing of a railroad from Warrenton to Macon, they relate that they have offered dissuading concessions without avail, to wit: the foregoing by the Central of all effort to connect its road with the Georgia save so far as respects its engagements with the people of Eatonton and Madison, and a reduction in freight rates by the existing line *via* Millen, provided the Macon and Warrenton Road be stopped at Sparta. The report continues, in a manifesto against the Georgia Company:—

This Board cannot view with indifference the renewed hostility manifested toward the Central Road, and must, ere long, put forth such power as it may possess to counteract the mischief of a road leading from Macon to Warrenton.

A survey has recently been made . . . of a line from the Central Road at Davisboro, Station No. 12, by Sparta to the Georgia Road at Union Point. The distance is found to be 61 miles, and the country is so favorable that a railroad, in every respect equal to the Central, can be constructed for $13,000 per mile, even at the high rate which labor has obtained of late in our State. . . . If the Macon and Warrenton Road is indeed to be built, the policy of this Company will be to expend a large portion of its reserved fund [which then amounted to $1,015,029] towards establishing the road above indicated. This Company earnestly desire to avoid all disturbance of the general railroad system built up by the people of Georgia at so great cost; . . . but if we are to be disturbed by a road so purely mischievous as the direct road from Macon to Warrenton, it will become our duty, in self-defense, to augment our revenues by lines from Eatonton to Madison, and from Davisboro, by Sparta, to Union Point, designed by a system of low rates to draw produce from the whole interior directly to Savannah, and to carry return merchandise directly from Savannah to the interior. An examination of the map of Georgia will prove, clearly, how valuable such connecting links may be to the Central Railroad, and the Port of Savannah, and at the same time, how disastrous they may prove to other existing interests. The fault will not be ours, if any injury shall result from a rivalry of the character referred to. Fortunately for this Company, if a contest is to be had, it will begin when our surplus profit on hand is very large, and when the entire debt of the Company does not exceed $87,000.

The speedy arrival of war times cut short this talk of retaliation. The Macon and Warrenton Railroad, however, was pushed on, and in a fashion completed for most of its length during the war. Slave labor was cheap, and the road from Milledgeville to Warrenton was desirable for military purposes.

Other roads, also, were opposed by the Central, especially those which might tend to build up the port of Brunswick and divert traffic from Savannah. In 1857, 1858, and 1859 several newly formed companies, mainly in south Georgia, were petitioning for state aid. In his reports for each of these years, President Cuyler published his anathema against these efforts, declaring that if built, the roads could only secure traffic by taking it from existing roads, and to do that, must enter a competition which would cut their own throats; they must, therefore, soon go bankrupt, and in the reorganization, the stockholders, including the state, would lose their investment. The legislature, doubtless affected in a measure by the Central's influence, which had become a notoriously strong power in politics, rejected most applications for state aid. President Cuyler went so far as to say in 1857 that upon the completion of the three or four roads then under active construction, Georgia would possess as perfect a system as any state in the Union, and as large a mileage and investment (1300 miles, costing $20,000,000) as the resources and traffic of the state called for.

Freight rates on the Central of Georgia, as on all railroads with complex traffic, were the subject of controversy and occasional readjustment. Passenger fares had been lowered from four to three cents per mile in 1843, and were no longer much discussed. In 1855 passenger rates were raised to four cents for white persons and lowered to two cents for negroes. This led to some complaint, but was a minor matter. In its freight business the Central, from the first day it began to handle traffic from and through Macon, confronted the characteristic problem of railways in the South, the problem of river competition, which in later times has led to the peculiar "basing-point" system of rate-making. Along the route there was no competition; but at Macon was the Ocomulgee. A feature of the problem here encountered was that the river was navigable by steamboats only during high water, and the water was usually low during the autumn marketing season. For several years after the road's completion, the management maintained a sliding scale of rates from Macon — low when the river was boatable, high when the river could not be used. When through traffic from the Western and Atlantic began, however, in 1846, it became necessary to have a constant tariff, ascertainable always by distant shippers. A low basis, also, was necessary, because of the competition by a rival line for Western and Atlantic traffic. The fluctuations of the river flow had to be disregarded, and rates maintained steadily at the low level.

The rates on way traffic were upon a non-competitive basis, and were generally kept very much higher than the Macon tariff. The local business was very light, and the practice of charging what the traffic would bear tended to keep it so. Complaints were frequent that the presence of the road was of little or no advantage to the country along the route. In 1858 the directors awoke to the fact that not a single town had grown up on the whole route from Savannah to Macon, and the stations were still known by their numbers in most cases, and devoid of all houses but the shanty at the roadside to accommodate the small volume of freight. They thereupon determined to reduce the rate upon upward way merchandise, and thus promote the growth of towns at the way stations.

A strikingly new policy was adopted in December, 1858, in the matter of fertilizers. To promote the restoration of exhausted soils in the cotton belt, and thus increase the prosperity and the demand for traffic, the company gave notice that thereafter it would carry guano and all other manures at the rate of two dollars per ton, by the car-load, from Savannah to all points on the road; and the Southwestern Company made a rate of one dollar per ton similarly from Macon to all of its stations. This rate, it said, was below the cost of the service; but the company expected to reap a return from increased traffic in the long run. This policy gave enormous stimulus to the use of commercial fertilizers. Very small quantities of them had formerly been carried by the road; but in 1859 it handled 3,864,850 pounds of fertilizers, and in 1860 a total of 18,540,980 pounds, made up of guano 16,937,430, lime 1,113,120, salt 256,800, and bone dust 233,630 pounds. Of these the guano was distributed very generally along the Central's line and throughout central and western Georgia. The lime was carried mostly to the cities, and the salt to the local stations. In a few years the fertilizer policy would doubtless have brought results to prove its wisdom. The cost of the service was actually very small, since the cars carrying the material would otherwise have had to make the upward trip empty.

A minor item of rate policy was that when, in 1850, the city of Macon gave its consent, till then withheld, for the Central, the Southwestern, and the Macon and Western to make a junction of their tracks, the town exacted not only an annuity of $5000 from the roads collectively, but also an agreement that freight rates from Macon to Savannah should never be more than four-fifths of the Savannah rates from Forsyth and Oglethorpe.

The association of the Central and Southwestern companies became still closer than before when in 1855, upon the death of the president of the Southwestern, L. O. Reynolds, President Cuyler of the Central was made president of the Southwestern, also. This road then comprised a main stem of ninety-two miles to Ft. Valley, a branch to Americus, and a branch to Butler on the route to Columbus. The road stood at a cost of $1,648,806. The company had a bonded debt of $400,000, and was receiving net earnings enough to pay 8 per cent dividends. The road from Butler to Columbus was owned for the time by the Muscogee Railroad Company. In this year a plan was adopted for the consolidation of this company with the Southwestern. The capital stock of the consolidation consisted of: (1) the existing stock of the Southwestern; (2) new stock issued to the Southwestern members to the amount of 7 per cent interest on all instalments for stock from the time of payment to the time of opening the road, and also for such earnings as had been used in building their road; and (3) the existing stock of the Muscogee Company. The new Southwestern Company assumed all debts and took all assets.

In this period the company received several propositions for the further extension of the road to the southwest, but accepted none of them as presented. The directors resolved, however, that the company would undertake the extension of the road to some point near the junction of Dougherty, Lee, Calhoun, and Randolph counties, thirty-five or forty miles below Americus, on condition of a *bona fide* subscription before February, 1856, of $250,000, with 25 per cent cash. The cost of the extension was estimated at $600,000. This proposal was not met. Another company, the Georgia and Florida, had been engaged haltingly in building a railway from Americus southward to Albany. In 1857 the Southwestern absorbed that company, took over its 25 miles of road, at a cost of $266,322 in stock, and set itself to finish the work, estimating a total expense of $400,000 for the road. A branch southwestward from Americus was also provided for in 1857 by the offer of the company to build it on condition of subscriptions to a stated amount for each section of the proposed line. These subscriptions were promptly forthcoming to the amount of $633,300; and the company began to extend its road through Dawson and Cuthbert to the Chattahoochee River near Fort Gaines, and also a branch from Cuthbert to the Chattahoochee opposite the Alabama town of Eufaula. The board paid for grading part in cash and part in stock. Meanwhile it was improving its original road-bed and relaying parts of its old track. In 1859 the force at work on the extension comprised 445 laborers, 115 horse carts, and 19 wagons and teams. "The force is almost entirely black, the only white force on the line being those employed in doing the masonry."

At the middle of 1860 the construction of all the Southwestern Company's lines had been completed except for a bridge which it then projected to cross the Chattahoochee at Eufaula. The company then owned 206 miles of fairly well-built road, with a good equipment. The cost of this had been about $3,375,000, while the stock and bonds outstanding were slightly below that amount. The company issued a regular dividend of 8 per cent in 1860, and an extra one of 5 per cent. The directors contemplated the easy earning of 10 per cent dividends through the coming years. The stock rose in 1860 to considerably above par. With no further plans of extension for the time, the company had reached its goal of large prosperity and routine operation, just on the eve of the great all-ruining war.

Turning again to the Macon and Western Railroad Company, we observe that during the fifties the most notable occurrence was a dispute between its Northern and domestic stockholders over the dividend policy. In this company, which had been formed to take over the bankrupt Monroe Railroad at a bargain, a majority of the stock was held by persons who lived in and about New York City; but a considerable minority was owned locally, and most of the directors, year after year, were citizens of Georgia and South Carolina. The local members and directors were concerned in putting the road upon a substantial and permanent basis, by conservative administration, as well as in earning dividends for themselves; the New York holders were in the company merely for the speculation, and their interests were more temporary than permanent. Their wishes were, accordingly, for the largest practicable dividends.

The facilities for administration from a distant center had not been developed comparably to those of more recent times. The New York stockholders were perhaps afraid to capture the control by electing a majority of the directorate from among themselves. They had no wish to assume the labor and responsibility, but were not backward in making known their preference as to financial policy. In 1856, and again more vigorously at the beginning of 1859, the New York directors and stockholders demanded the increase of dividends. The latter instance, with the proceedings which followed, was related in detail in the report of the president and directors for 1858–1859.

At the meeting of the directors at Macon on February 3, 1859, Dr. Collins, representing the New York interest, presented memorials from the Northern directors and stockholders, to the effect that after making a careful estimate of receipts, the undersigned were convinced that above the funds required for the usual dividends and for redeeming such bonds as would mature, the company would have $90,000 in cash on hand during the year then beginning. This cash, they declared, belonged to the stockholders, and ought to be paid them, even at the risk of having to pass the usual August dividend. They therefore demanded an extra dividend of 5 per cent in addition to the regular 4 per cent February issue. This was signed: A. Iselin & Co., 219 shares; Moran Bros., 344; W. A. and A. M. White, 215; De Rham & Co., 124; S. Livingston, Atty., 275; Hy de Subzer Wart, 29; and others to a total of 112 holders representing 7353 full and 1819 scrip shares. The New York directors supported this memorial in a separate communication. The Board of Directors in meeting resolved to hold to its former policy. The paper before them they recognized, they said, as the work of a few instigators, and not as the deliberate action of all the signers, especially as regards the threat in still another paper, that if the application is not granted, "we shall adopt the means necessary to insure the attainment of our object." The board in its reply continued: "The New York proceedings form an anomaly that has no precedent. Neither director nor stockholder in New York has ever attended a single meeting. They appear generally content to rely on those in Georgia, who furnish them published proceedings, and scrupulously discharge their duty, sparing neither labor nor time. . . . The object in New York is to procure more money for themselves. Our object here, for higher considerations, was to deprive ourselves of it so that all in the result might be made secure." With prosperity dependent upon uncertain crops and uncertain lawsuits, they continued, it is unsafe to anticipate earnings, and depart from the course of prudence: the members and directors in Georgia and South Carolina do not care to be or to pose as expert stock jobbers, to anticipate earnings and run up the price of shares so as to unload them on the public; they hold their shares as permanent investments, preferring for the present a sure and steady dividend of 8 per cent yearly to a variable one, especially if debts of the company remain unpaid. While bonds are falling due, extraordinary dividends are inadmissible; and, in any event, a railroad, like an insurance company or a bank, must have a cash reserve available for emergencies. To stimulate the rise of shares artificially, and then have the purchasers disappointed, would be to discredit the whole company in the financial world; the reserve fund should be some $50,000, which with present indications may be had within the year; when that is secure, the Georgia directors will be as eager as others to put money into their pockets, and will share every dollar earned; until that short time, they see no cause to change their opinions. This reply apparently closed the incident. A large extra dividend was issued in 1860.

The problems of operation were of commonplace but characteristic nature. Yielding to popular demand, the company, in December, 1855, added a second passenger train to its daily service, but found that it didn't pay, and after six months took it off. In November, 1857, however, a revision of time-tables by the connecting roads forced the company to establish its service again of two trains per day in each direction, one of which carried express freight, however, as well as passengers. The president observed in his report for 1856: "From the natural condition of the country, little can be expected from the Passenger-traffic as a source of revenue; for this the company must look to its Freights, and the most than can be expected of the passenger business is that it shall be made self-supporting."

Freights grew heavier year by year, and through the maintenance of fairly high rates, more profitable. The superintendent said in his report of 1854: "The tendency is always to low rates, and in many instances to a point which affords no remuneration. This is especially true of all agricultural products, of which our downward freights chiefly consist. Care should be taken to guard against the pressure of public opinion, the often unwise competition between different lines, as well as against the delusive idea that low rates, by increasing the amount of freight, necessarily make a corresponding increase in the profits. It is believed that many articles are now taken over the road at rates which do not afford an adequate compensation to the company."

Freight over the Western and Atlantic from and to the Tennessee region and beyond, however, could only bear light rates; and the competition of the Georgia Railroad tended in a measure against high tariffs on the Macon and Western, though that strife was carefully kept from reaching a cut-throat character. The indications are that the

MACON AND WESTERN RAILROAD COMPANY STATISTICS
(YEARS ENDING NOVEMBER 1.)

Year	Miles of Road	Capital Stock	Bonds	Gross Receipts	Running Expenses	Net Earnings	Dividends
1848 11 months	101	$ 630,000	none	$141,132	$ 63,247	$ 77,884	$ 30,000
1849	101	630,000	none	198,467	87,698	110,769	75,000
1850	103	684,240	$135,000	208,666	108,228	104,438	67,500
1851	103	1,103,966	135,000	216,621	106,509	110,112	78,532
1852	103	1,214,000	168,000	269,995	119,664	150,331	97,120
1853	103	1,228,370	163,000	280,515	131,453	149,062	97,120
1854	103	1,230,560	129,000	313,178	163,561	149,617	112,822
1855	103	1,353,754	129,000	350,802	157,427	193,375	126,443
1856	103	1,354,500	129,000	349,907	207,791	142,116	135,415
1857	103	1,438,560	96,000	293,260	162,554	130,706	125,278
1858	103	1,438,800	96,000	326,465	162,058	164,407	115,104
1859	103	1,438,800	23,000	375,250	165,465	209,785	158,268
1860	103	1,500,000	none	407,344	192,941	279,492	279,492

Georgia Railroad usually got the larger share of the Western and Atlantic down traffic. For example, there is frequent mention of glut of traffic on the Georgia, and complaint by the administration that the law of 1850 prohibiting the operation of freight trains on Sunday made it very hard to render prompt service in the busy season. The Macon and Western reports do not mention any very great lack of balance between up and down traffic. In 1859, when reporting a defalcation of $6298 by U. L. Wright, the Macon and Western's agent at Atlanta, the president stated that

Wright's activity in solicitation had added largely to the company's business, and that since his removal the cash earnings on Atlanta traffic had decreased $20,000. The business which Wright developed in the interchange of through traffic, the president explained, was of such complex character that Wright had probably not been able to solve the mathematical intricacies, and he had been perhaps more unfortunate than guilty.

The administration complained frequently of the heavy expense from damage suits for accidents on the road. Claims were decided by the juries against the road almost uniformly, they said, no matter what the nature of the accident and the testimony. To diminish the mishaps from cattle on the track, the company considered a plan— the fencing of the line. For the killing of persons crossing the track they could think of no feasible preventive, but lamented the proneness of the juries to penalize the railroad.

It is an item of interest that in the later fifties both the Central of Georgia and the Macon and Western companies replaced their former systems of road repairs on contract with that of leasing slave labor for employment directly by the company. For 1859, reported as a normal year in this regard, repairs on the 103 miles of the road required 40,000 cross-ties, costing thirty cents each and lasting an average of but five years in that climate where decay was not suspended by frosts, and the labor of a hundred negroes with an overseer and supervisor, at an average cost of $200 per hand.

The Macon and Western, like all the other principal roads in Georgia then completed, had reached in 1860 the stage of heavy business and high prosperity for which its supporters and managers had with more or less faithfulness and patience wrought and waited. In this instance alone among the important roads in Georgia, the original projectors and backers lost the profits through failure to survive financially the effects of the great cotton crisis. New capital, local and distant, took up the enterprise, and through the domination of the local directors continued its identification with the general interests of the state. Its president in his report for the concluding year of the *ante-bellum* régime well said: "The present condition of political and financial affairs renders speculation upon the future of [the company's] property useless. Its prosperity has grown with that of the state of Georgia, and with the same it must stand or fall."

CHAPTER VII

THE WESTERN AND ATLANTIC: A STATE-OWNED RAILROAD [1]

THE Western and Atlantic Railroad is of large historical concern in two regards: it was the perfecting member in the well-devised railway system which made Georgia the keystone state of the South, and Atlanta the gate city from the northwest to the eastern cotton belt; and it furnishes the most important example in American history, thus far, of the state ownership and operation of railroads.

The launching of the Western and Atlantic was, as may be gathered from our preceding chapters, a culmination in the early movement for railways to meet the needs of the eastern cotton belt and its coast cities. The idea of a transmontane railroad had been in the popular mind in South Carolina and Georgia for more than a decade. One scheme was to improve the navigation of the Savannah River by locks and sluices and to connect its head waters by a railway portage with the French Broad and thence with the Tennessee River.[2] This scheme contemplated the use of inclined planes with balanced weights in surmounting the steep grades. But inspection showed that the route was not feasible for heavy traffic. In 1826

[1] Reprinted, with alterations, from the *Yale Review*, November, 1906 (xv, 259–282).

[2] *Georgia Courier*, Augusta, April 28, 1828.

Wilson Lumpkin had examined the country through middle Georgia and the Cherokee territory to the northwestward, and reported that an excellent route over the rolling hills and through depressions in the mountain range might there be had for a railroad to the Tennessee at the northwestern corner of Georgia.[1] Upon the death of the Board of Public Works, this project in Georgia slumbered for eight or ten years. Meanwhile South Carolina became strenuously active, as we have seen. The people of the Tennessee river basin, the Nashville neighborhood, and the Memphis district, as well as those of Cincinnati, became interested in the general problem. It seemed probable from the first that the better route would lie through Georgia; but the clamor of Charleston and South Carolina in the interests of a route through that state diverted attention for a time from the opportunity in Georgia. The pendulum of sentiment then swung again to the route through the Cherokee country; and the state of Georgia committed itself to the project by the pivotal act of December 21, 1836.

Some of the preliminaries to this act have already been described. A few others require notice. Outside parties had become interested as early as 1833 in a route crossing Georgia, and this had a stimulating effect within the state. The city of Memphis had a desire for direct trade with the Atlantic ports, and looked mainly toward Charleston. A railroad east and west along the Muscle Shoals in northern Alabama was already under construction, and could be used as a part of the line to the coast. The prime mover in the Memphis and Charleston project was General Edmund P. Gaines, who in the military service had become well ac-

[1] *Infra*, p. 111.

quainted with the whole lower South and its transportation needs. Early in 1834 Gaines wrote to the governor of Georgia and set forth the plan which he was fathering, for a railroad from Memphis eastward *via* Decatur, Ala., to connect with the proposed northern branch of the Georgia Railroad at Athens, and thence give communication with Charleston. The governor, who was now Wilson Lumpkin of earlier experience in the Georgia surveys, replied in great praise of Gaines' general purpose, but urged the adoption of a more southerly route, through central Alabama and Georgia to the port of Savannah. A railroad across northern Georgia, he said, would lie in difficult country, yielding little traffic, and would be of but slight advantage to the state; it would, indeed, in one way be an injury to the state by tending toward its decentralization. Should Gaines and his associates modify their plan as here advised, Lumpkin said he felt he could promise approval and active support from Georgia. But should they adhere to the northern route, Georgia would go ahead regardless, and build a system of her own to meet her own concrete needs.[1] Shortly afterward the citizens of Floyd, Paulding, Cass, and Cherokee counties, Georgia, held a meeting, expressed approval of the Memphis and Charleston project, whose contemplated northern route lay through their district, and appointed a committee to give aid to the surveyors.[2] The existence of the railway ready-built in northern Alabama, available as part of the proposed road to Athens and Charleston, was too strong a consideration to be sacrificed. Gaines' company held to its first plan;

[1] *Federal Union*, May 21, 1834, letter of Lumpkin to Gaines, March 3, 1834, and clipping from the *Memphis Times and Advocate.*

[2] *Southern Banner*, July 19, 1834.

but its resources proved no more than enough to build its track from Memphis to a connection with the road at Muscle Shoals. Georgia's refusal of aid set the limits of success for the Memphis and Charleston project.

John C. Calhoun in 1835 proposed that South Carolina and Georgia should use their portions of the United States surplus revenue in building a railroad from Athens, Ga., to the Tennessee River and beyond, with a branch through Columbus, Ga., to Montgomery and Pensacola, and another *via* the Muscle Shoals Railroad to Memphis.[1] Calhoun's advocacy was an aid in the general movement.

The Georgia and Central of Georgia Railroad companies were vitally concerned in promoting some westward connection; and numerous individuals devoted much enthusiasm to fostering the general purpose and giving it definite shape. An anonymous citizen addressed the legislature in November, 1835, in an open letter in the newspapers.[2] He had recently traveled through northwestern Georgia, and now described the great resources there existing for producing in large amount the flour, pork, horses, mules, etc., for which the cotton belt was then dependent upon the country beyond the mountains. He described the wretched roads and costliness of transportation, and the threatened loss of that region's trade by middle Georgia unless avenues of some sort were built to facilitate it.

All these things kept alive the interest of the Georgia people in the claims and advantages of the northwestern section of their own state when Western railways were mentioned. When the Georgia delegates at the Knoxville

[1] Letter of Calhoun, November 24, 1835, to W. C. Dawson. J. F. Jameson, *Correspondence of John C. Calhoun*, pp. 346–347.

[2] *Federal Union*, November 20, 1835.

convention, July, 1836, found that they could hope for little benefit from the Cincinnati and Charleston project, they returned home and began a movement for an independent and rival system.

Inspired chiefly through the influence, more or less secret, of the Georgia, Central of Georgia, and Monroe Railroad companies, a convention on railroads was assembled at Macon on the first Monday in November, 1836,[1] comprising 107 delegates representing 38 counties and 2 of the railroad companies. Many of the most prominent and able men of the state were present. The convention began work by appointing a committee of 40 to inquire and report upon such a system of internal improvement as would best subserve the great interests of the state. After two days the committee reported, through Absalom H. Chappell, its chairman, a plan for securing harmony and coöperation among the various sections and interests of the state in building a system of railroads connecting the commercial cities of Georgia with the Tennessee River. The preamble presented the desirability of a railroad to the Mississippi valley, and discussed the great benefits to accrue therefrom. It alluded to George Washington's desire, to the Erie Canal, and to the competition of Pennsylvania, Virginia, Maryland, and South Carolina for the Western trade, but asserted that New York and Georgia possessed the two keys to the situation by reason of mountain depressions within their boundaries. A railroad, the report stated, with a single trunk not above 130 miles long, con-

[1] Proceedings reported in the *Macon Messenger,* November 10, and reprinted in the *Federal Union,* November 15, 1836; see also J. C. Butler, *Historical Record of Macon and Central Georgia,* pp. 139–140; and *American Railroad Journal,* December 10, 1836.

tinued in three prongs of lengths from 100 to 160 miles each, would connect the Tennessee River and avenues to all the West with the three main navigable streams of Georgia. The people and government of Georgia, it urged, must not slight the opportunity which Providence had given. Its improvement would change the comparative poverty, discomfort, and desolation in Georgia's extensive domain to wealth, dense population, and high social improvement; the value of lands in the state would at once be increased more than enough to repay the cost of building the road. The strategic point on the Tennessee River was pointed out to be Ross' Landing, at the northern base of Lookout Mountain, the site of the present city of Chattanooga. The route thence to the Chattahoochee River in De Kalb County, Georgia, would be perfectly feasible for an efficient heavy-traffic railroad. At some point near the Chattahoochee in De Kalb County, the committee advised that the road be made to diverge into four branches: one to meet the Georgia Railroad, one to Milledgeville, one to meet the Monroe Railroad at Forsyth, and one to Columbus. "This system of railroads would diffuse over all parts of the state almost a precise equality of advantages. The main trunk would be actually common in its use, and equal in its utility to all parts of the state; and the several different sections of the state would certainly receive equal or nearly equal benefits from their respective branches." The proposed road would have connecting lines built in due time from its northern end reaching all parts of the transmontane country, and would do a huge business in Western products and in goods from the seaports destined for Western consumption: the road would promote Georgia commerce and agriculture alike, and be a safe investment for capital;

it should receive the hearty support of all Georgians. The main trunk, from the Chattahoochee to the Tennessee, the committee recommended, ought to be built entirely at the public expense as a state road; the branches could be built with advantage by joint-stock companies, aided by subscriptions by the state for part of their stock. The convention accepted this report, and with but two dissenting votes, enthusiastically recommended the adoption of its plan by the legislature, and then adjourned *sine die.*

The plan of the committee of 40 in the Macon convention formed the basis for the bill presented to and adopted by the legislature in the following month. The guiding members of the committee, it seems, were A. H. Chappell and O. H. Prince, the delegates respectively of the Monroe and Georgia Railroad companies. The sponsor of the bill in the legislature was W. W. Gordon, president of the Central of Georgia, then sitting as a member from Chatham County. Gordon's right-hand man was H. V. Johnson of Augusta, closely associated with the Georgia Railroad. Independent representatives, however, were not wanting in the support of the bill. A specially strong advocate proved unexpectedly to be Alexander H. Stephens, then a new member from Taliaferro County.[1] The bill was stoutly opposed in both houses, and carried only after a warm struggle. In the original draft the bill had provided the devotion of Georgia's share of the United

[1] For reminiscences relating to the passage of the bill for the Western and Atlantic, see two letters of A. H. Stephens to Williams Rutherford, March 13 and 17, 1857, in H. Cleveland, *Alexander H. Stephens, in Public and Private, with Letters and Speeches.* Philadelphia [1866], pp. 605–621.

States surplus revenue to the construction of the road. The Senate struck out this, and provided that state funds should be used; and the House concurred.

Nearly all the cotton belt, which was making the great demand for food-stuffs, except its southwestern portion, was in favor of the bill. As a rule the districts which expected no local benefit from it were opposed to building a state road. Some of them, however, had projects of their own which they hoped to promote by aiding in the main enterprise. The framers of the bill had in view the practical value of log-rolling, and had proved their adroitness by tacking on the provisions for state aid to branch lines extending to various points in the state. In spite of local and personal opposition, the bill secured a majority, and was speedily enacted into law. It directed the survey and construction of a railroad from a point near Rossville to some eligible point on the southeastern bank of the Chattahoochee River, and provided funds not to exceed $350,000 a year, unless a future legislature should otherwise enact. The road was named the Western and Atlantic. A superintendent and engineer were to be appointed and appropriate powers given them. Additional clauses in the bill provided for state subscriptions, not to exceed $200,000 in any one case, to aid in building branch roads from the Western and Atlantic terminus to the several towns of Athens, Madison, Milledgeville, Forsyth, and Columbus.[1] By an act of December, 1837, the control of the road was given to a commission of three persons to be elected by the legislature; the southern terminus was

[1] Texts of this act, and numerous others relating to the Western and Atlantic, are in Prince, *Digest of the Laws of Georgia to 1837*, pp. 355 ff., *passim;* and Cobb's *Digest*, 1851, pp. 401 ff.

to be located not more than eight miles southeast of the Chattahoochee; and an increased provision of funds was made by authorizing the sale of state bonds in amounts not more than $500,000 in any one year. By an act of 1838 an appropriation of $1,500,000 in state bonds to run for thirty years at 6 per cent supplemented and superseded the earlier provision.[1]

Public finance in that period was in an abnormal condition. Throughout the country prices were high and rising, money was cheap, and credit a universal reliance. The people of the Southern and Western states were full of inflationist spirit, those of Georgia among the rest. In 1828 the legislature had established an institution called the Central Bank, which was really a part of the state government, but was kept nominally separate because of the prohibition in the federal constitution against the issue of currency by any state. The capital of the Central Bank consisted of all moneys, bonds, and stocks owned by the state of Georgia and all debts due it. The directors were authorized to issue bank-notes in amounts left to their discretion, and were required to distribute most of their available funds in loans to citizens throughout the state. All receipts by the state went into the vaults of the Central Bank, and expenditures by the state were made by drafts upon it. The institution was, in effect, the State Treasury, with a somewhat reckless banking system annexed. It could command abundance of funds when times were good

[1] The promotion, construction, and operation of the Western and Atlantic Railroad have been well treated in a series of articles in the *Atlanta Journal,* March 25 to April 29, 1906, by Hon. Hooper Alexander, who wrote them to strengthen his advocacy of extending the state road to the sea. The present chapter has been somewhat modified since reading Mr. Alexander's sketch.

and credit easy; it was likely to be involved in immense difficulties in the event of a general panic. The Central Bank and the Western and Atlantic Railroad for a time went hand in hand as state institutions. The bank furnished money from its receipts and its circulation, and relieved the state from solicitude. This easy state of things lasted, however, only until the panic at the end of the thirties.

Under the act of 1836 the survey for the Western and Atlantic Railway was pushed rapidly forward, and by the end of 1837 specifications for the first 50 miles of the road were ready. The Board of Commissioners organized in January, 1838. In April the contracts for the grading of 50 miles were let, and in October 50 miles more. By February, 1839, the contractors were working about 2000 men on the road, and fair promise was given for the completion of the first hundred miles by the autumn of that year. In some sections, however, cuts and fills were exceedingly heavy, and some cuts which ran through rock formations were necessarily slow and expensive.

In the absence of unforeseen embarrassments, the commissioners expected that the whole route of 138 miles would be ready for the rails in the first half of 1840 and would be completed for the handling of through traffic a year later.[1] But financial troubles now came in a flood. Although its effects were not felt directly by the state railroad commissioners until 1839, the stringency had begun in 1837. The panic of that year gave a shock to the public confidence in the soundness of the general system of credit, and caused a great tightening in the money market. Pri-

[1] Report of the Western and Atlantic Commissioners, *Southern Recorder*, February 5, 1839.

vate loans were extensively called in; debtors were accordingly in straits. This led to an increased demand for the loan of public funds to private citizens. The government of Georgia, instead of calling in the loans of the Central Bank, continued them liberally, and increased their amount by using for the purpose the United States surplus revenue assigned to the state, and, indeed, all the other special resources at the state's command. On the one hand this cut off the Central Bank as a source of funds for the Western and Atlantic Railroad,[1] on the other it added the fuel of false hopes to the raging fire of speculation. Desperate schemes of financial restoration in the cotton belt prepared the way for the tremendous crash of 1839. In that year cotton prices, which had been artificially bolstered, made a heavy slump, and continued at starvation levels throughout the first half of the forties.

The first issue of $500,000 in state bonds for use by the road had proved salable in the market, and of the $1,500,000 authorized in December, 1838, about $300,000 worth were sold at par early in the next year to the Bank of Augusta.

[1] Letter of Governor Gilmer to Joel Crawford, Chairman of the Western and Atlantic Commission, February 21, 1839. Gilmer wrote that Crawford's recent requisition for $200,000 could not be complied with because neither the State Treasury nor the Central Bank had funds to that amount. The president of the bank was of the opinion that it would be impossible for the bank to obtain money upon the loan authorized by law during the existing pressure. — Also, letter of Governor McDonald, July 8, 1840, to Dr. Tomlinson Fort, president of Central Bank. By the law, McDonald wrote, the Western and Atlantic commissioners have the right to call upon the Central Bank for funds, but at the same time no absolute obligation is imposed upon the bank to furnish them, for the law implies a discretionary power on the part of the directors. (MSS. in Executive Minutes, State Capitol, Atlanta, Ga.)

With the rest of the scrip, the chairman of the commission, Joel Crawford, made a journey to New York and thence to London, but found the market so disturbed that no sale could be effected except at disastrous discounts. Crawford returned to Georgia in October, 1839, and reported his failure to enlist foreign capital.

Meanwhile the two commissioners who had remained at home had informed the contractors on the road of the state of finances, and authorized them to suspend work, or carry it on with the prospect of delayed payment as they should see fit. Thomas Hamilton, the commissioner who reported for the board in August, 1839, was faint-hearted. He expressed the belief that the Cumberland Mountains west of Chattanooga would prove an invincible barrier to any possible connection with the West, and accordingly that it would matter little whether the Western and Atlantic Railroad were pushed to an early completion.[1] In the dearth of other opportunities for their labor, in the stagnation of business, most of the contractors were disposed to complete the work on their sections, and even to take additional contracts on the northern end of the line, and proposed to accept payment in the unsalable scrip of the state. The two commissioners on hand were divided in opinion, but Crawford, on returning, cast the deciding vote in favor of the policy of action. The contracts for grading the remainder of the route were let at the end of 1839, with the one important exception of the section which was to include a tunnel of a quarter of a mile in length, — the only tunnel on the route.[2] The continued strain on credit, however, caused such severe decline in the market

[1] *Southern Recorder*, August 27, 1839.

[2] *Southern Banner*, December 21, 1839.

rates for state scrip,[1] that most of the contractors, by the spring of 1842, suspended work.

The delay in the progress of the road, it happened, was not a cause of general regret. The depression of credit, each month more severe, had forced the stoppage of work on all the roads which were expected to connect with either end of the Western and Atlantic. The importance of that road lay in its becoming a connecting link of a general system. It would be of no use to forge the link until the chain was approaching readiness. Furthermore, neither of the railroads from the ocean gateways had reached within sixty miles of the beginning of the Western and Atlantic, and it would be an extravagance to haul rails and rolling stock over the wretched country roads to the isolated state railroad, which, if built, would begin on a vacant hilltop and run through ravines and forests to no terminus of consequence. The completion of the road-bed, without the laying of the superstructure, would entail a loss through the washing of the soil in the cuts and fills. The continued depression of state credit, meanwhile, made it inexpedient to attempt to buy rails.

The commission advised, in February, 1841, that the lower fifty-two miles of the route alone be prepared for the superstructure, and work on the northern part of the route be neglected; that as soon as one of the railways from Macon or Augusta should reach the connecting point, the superstructure should be laid on the fifty-two miles and the road be put in operation for that distance; that meanwhile, the state should give financial aid to the company roads and enable them to make the Western and Atlantic

[1] Georgia bonds are said to have sold in that period for as low as 48 cents on the dollar.

connection.[1] The state government approved such of these items as concerned the state road directly, and an act of December, 1841, dissolved the commission, replacing it with a disbursing agent, ordered the completion of the road for fifty-two miles, when it should become feasible, and the suspension of work on the upper part of the route.[2] The commission, in going out of office, reported an expenditure to the end of 1841 of $2,602,457.26. Much the larger part of this was outstanding in state bonds. The commissioners confessed an inability to make a precise statement of account, blaming the carelessness of their bookkeepers. The laying of the iron for the fifty-two miles was in progress from 1843 to 1845; and thereafter the road was very gradually extended through the application of the net earnings from its operation.[3] Active work was resumed under an act of 1847, and the road was completed to Chattanooga in 1851.

During the whole period from 1839 to 1850 a spirited debate was in progress on the general questions of completing or abandoning the road, and of selling it or retaining it as state property. On the one hand the governor, the majority of the commission, and the sentiment of the commercial towns and of a very large number of cotton producers, favored an early completion of the road throughout its length. A committee of the legislature in 1839 declared itself in favor of the energetic pushing of the whole project. Above $1,600,000, it said, had already been devoted to the

[1] Report of Western and Atlantic Commission, *Southern Banner*, March 2, 1841.

[2] *Southern Recorder*, November 2, 1841. T. R. R. Cobb's *Digest of the Laws of Georgia* (1851), p. 411.

[3] *Federal Union*, October 24 and November 21, 1843.

enterprise, and the state could not afford the dead loss which must result should the work be permanently abandoned.

The argument against completion, on the other hand, was ably set forth in a long article which appeared in the *Southern Banner*, June 25, 1841, over the pseudonym "A Georgian." This writer declared the Western and Atlantic enactment to have been "an impolitic and suicidal measure." The heavy burden and expense in completing the road he passed over as a minor consideration, saying it would be far better to lose what had already been invested than to supply still more funds in a way which would inure to the severe disadvantage of the commonwealth. The burden of his argument was that by tapping the West, Georgia would subject her citizens to ruinous competition and inevitably damage their resources. The people of the state, he continued, had been remarkably happy in their isolation; and to bring in cheap food-stuffs would increase her dependence upon cotton, bring on an overproduction, and ruin the market. The diversification of agriculture in the whole South, he thought, was essential for the maintenance of its prosperity, and the driving of the farmers out of cereal and live stock production would permanently injure the welfare of the community. He concluded by expressing the hope that Georgia would no longer war against nature and the wisdom of experience in building bridges and excavating mountains at huge expense "to unite states together which God had put asunder." Another point of view is shown in an editorial which accompanied the above argument. It contended that governments should not undertake such enterprises, because they could always be accomplished more rapidly and more economically by individuals.

The outcome of the debate for several years hung in the balance. Acts of 1841 and 1843 provided for the road's very gradual extension. The act of 1843 authorized the governor to sell the road, if at any time it would bring a million dollars as it stood. This provision remained in effect for seven years without a buyer appearing. Meanwhile, after 1845, times were growing much better; cotton prices rose again to satisfactory levels, business in general revived, and state scrip could be sold at par. An act of 1847 ordered the completion of the road, providing $375,000 in state bonds as the limit for the work.

The prospect for profitable traffic became much brighter. In 1845 and 1846 lines from Augusta and Savannah had reached the Western and Atlantic terminus. During 1848 the Nashville and Chattanooga Railroad Company was organized, its stock fully taken up, and the construction of the road put under contract. A branch from the main stem of the Western and Atlantic at Kingston, undertaken by a local corporation and aided by a subscription from the Georgia Railroad Co., was soon afterward completed to Rome, and, aided by a steamboat on the river, attracted trade from the valley of the Coosa in Alabama. At the same time the building of the Etowah flouring mills on the line of the state road stimulated the production of wheat to an unprecedented extent.[1]

With the piercing of Tunnel Hill, October 30, 1849, the completion of the road became a matter of relative ease. The last rails were laid in the spring of 1851. In May of that year the first train ran to Chattanooga. The road was 138 miles long and graded through much of its length

[1] Report of the Chief Engineer, Western and Atlantic Railroad, September 30, 1848.

for a double track, though equipped with only a single one, of five-foot gauge. It crossed three river valleys and the dividing watersheds. Its track was a patchwork of strap rails and flange rails laid on wooden stringers, and "bridge rails," of the shape of an inverted U, spiked directly to the cross-ties. Its rolling stock consisted of 13 engines, 4 passenger cars, 2 baggage cars, 4 box cars, and 6 platform cars. The epoch of primary construction was ended; that of operation and its problems had begun.

In June, 1851, a committee of inspection made a tour of the road, and while expressing satisfaction with the work of the officials, reported strong disapproval of the flimsiness of the long stretch of plate-rail and the inadequacy of the rolling stock. It deprecated any further agitation for the sale of the road, and recommended that $500,000 be appropriated for buying T-rail to replace the plate-rail and for properly increasing the rolling stock.[1] The governor made recommendation accordingly, in his message to the legislature in December, and he was supported by a second committee report.[2]

The legislature of December and January, 1851–1852, had to meet the need not only for money, but for a permanent organization. The appropriation of $500,000 was duly made, and by the same act the control of the road was put into the hands of a general superintendent to be appointed by the governor and to act in important matters with the governor's approval. Howell Cobb, then governor, secured as superintendent William Wadley, who had rendered distinguished services in a similar capacity with the Central of Georgia Railroad Company.

[1] *Federal Union,* June 24, 1851.

[2] *Atlanta Intelligencer,* December 18, 1851.

The whole complexion of affairs was at once transformed. The *Atlanta Intelligencer* in an editorial of January 15, 1852, had published a jeremiad on the derelictions of the govern-

WESTERN AND ATLANTIC RAILROAD. FINANCIAL SUMMARY, 1836 TO 1860

(FISCAL YEARS RAN FROM OCTOBER 1 TO SEPTEMBER 30.)

(Dotted lines in the table are equivalent to zeros; question-marks indicate that statistics are unobtainable.)

Year	Legislative Appropriation	Expenditure for Construction	Receipts from Operation	Expenses of Operation	Net Earnings	Payments to the State Treasury
1836–37	$ 350,000.00	....	....	....	....	....
1837–38	500,000.00	....	....	....	....	....
1838–39	1,500,000.00	$ 366,345.55	....	....	....	....
1839–40	....	1,029,941.37	....	....	....	....
1840–41	....	584,163.85	....	....	....	....
1841–42	....	521,051.35	....	....	....	....
1842–43	....	?	....	....	....	....
1843–44	....	?	....	....	....	....
1844–45	....	?	....	....	....	....
1845–46	....	?	$ 38,127.32	....	....	....
1846–47	....	?	89,483.86	$ 51,676.93	$ 37,806.93	....
1847–48	375,000.00	61,258.15	115,585.30	62,022.91	53,562.39	....
1848–49	....	371,434.78	132,105.70	?	?	....
1849–50	....	94,074.98	198,564.34	?	?	....
1850–51	....	255,992.62	285,028.44	?	?	....
1851–52	525,000.00	96,322.05	375,176.62	?	?	....
1852–53	....	450,033.00	478,876.06	251,167.05	227,709.01	....
1853–54	....	324,542.34	591,154.78	253,031.78	338,123.00	....
1854–55	....	239,368.12	688,930.56	259,883.33	429,047.23	$100,000.00
1855–56	....	379,285.65	871,366.53	380,668.85	490,697.68	43,500.00
1856–57	....	383,661.04	900,808.95	435,827.55	464,981.40	100,000.00
1857–58	....	303,405.63	800,001.28	394,227.84	405,773.44	175,000.00
1858–59	....	27,326.40	832,343.03	377,801.50	454,541.53	402,000.00
1859–60	....	....	835,919.55	418,464.95	417,454.60	450,000.00
1860–61	....	....	892,436.96	345,394.63	547,041.73	438,000.00

ment: "While the legislature is wrangling about the matter and coming to no definite arrangements, the road continues with accelerated velocity in its course toward ruin . . .

the lives of travelers are in constant jeopardy in passing over it . . . and the whole commercial community is injured by the confusion of their business affairs consequent upon the irregularity of the state road." News soon afterward arrived that the legislature had acted. The *Intelligencer* of February 5, 1852, expressed delight thereat, and rejoiced particularly in the appointment of Mr. Wadley as superintendent.

An editorial in the same paper for February 26 showed that Wadley's influence was at once felt with benefit. During the spring and summer extensive repairs were made; stations were built, the substitution of T-rail for the plate-rail was begun, and the rolling stock was rapidly increased. The total earnings of the road advanced from less than $200,000 in 1849–1850 and $285,000 in 1850–1851 to $375,176 in 1851–1852 and $478,876 in 1853–1854. Such part of these amounts as exceeded the expenses of operation were applied to betterments and charged to account of construction.

Wadley returned to the service of the Central of Georgia Railroad in January, 1853, and was succeeded as superintendent of the Western and Atlantic by George Yonge, and he in 1854 by Thomas F. Cooper. The position was later held by James M. Spullock from the summer of 1856 until the end of 1857, when the accession of Joseph E. Brown to the governorship and his appointment of John W. Lewis brought a distinctly new régime in Western and Atlantic affairs.[1] Until the businesslike administration of Brown and Lewis began, the commonwealth had continually

[1] The reports of the Superintendent of the Western and Atlantic Railroad for 1853, 1855 to 1864, and 1866 to 1870 are to be found in pamphlet form in the State Library at Atlanta.

felt that it had a white elephant on its hands. The people were anxious lest the road and its money should become the instrument of political tyranny and corruption, but feared, on the other hand, that a still greater power would be established for possible evil if the road were sold or leased to a private corporation.

In the legislative session of 1853–1854 a bill was brought in and vigorously urged to provide for the leasing of the road. The *Federal Union*, the organ of the Democratic administration, expressed strong opposition to this in an editorial of January 31, 1854, which, in its dread of corporation control, has a very modern tone. "The road," it contended, "has never yet had a fair trial; within the last two years large improvements have been made on some parts of it, and great additions to its equipment; several branch roads have also been built which will add greatly to the business of the main trunk; and now, just as the proudest hopes of the friends of the road are about to be realized, it is proposed to turn over this great work with all its splendid prospects to a company of speculators. But the pecuniary loss would not be all that the people would suffer by this transaction. A large corporation, like a mighty Colossus, with one foot at Savannah and the other at Chattanooga, will bestride the state, whilst its iron fingers will be felt in every election and will direct the future legislation of the state. No matter what guards and checks this legislature may throw around such a corporation, when they once get control of such immense resources, they will elect a legislature to suit themselves and will break all these bands like cobwebs. We are willing to intrust the management of the road to the people, whether the Whigs or Democrats are in power, for we believe that the large majority of both parties are honest men, and their agents are always responsible to the people for their conduct, but a gigantic corporation has neither soul nor conscience and owes no responsibility to any tribunal whether in heaven or on earth. The influence of corporations is already felt in every fiber of our legislation; it can be seen in every vote that is taken on this subject, and if ever these corporations get control of the state road, they will govern the state."

The bill for lease in 1854 was defeated. For two years following, there was a lull in the campaign against state operation, although occasional censures were made upon Governor Johnson's conduct of the road's business, which were met with replies by the Democratic press.[1]

At the close of 1855 a joint committee of the legislature was appointed to investigate the finances, equipment, and management of the road, and to report particularly upon the truthfulness of certain charges which had been made of political favoritism and local and personal rate discriminations. The committee reported in March, 1856, describing conditions in detail, exculpating officials, and advising the improvement of the track and equipment.[2]

In 1857 the agitation for a lease or sale of the road again began. General Bethune, of Columbus, editor of the *Corner Stone* and a leading opponent of all forms of paternalism, was the most radical in the discussion. He proposed in January, 1857, that the state should sell the road, pay off the public debt with part of the proceeds, and distribute the balance of the money equally among the voters of the

[1] *E.g. Southern Banner*, September 20, 1855; *Federal Union*, September 25, 1855; *Atlanta Intelligencer*, May 5, 1856.

[2] Report published as a pamphlet, and printed in the *Federal Union*, March 4, 1856.

state. He thought it impossible for the road or any other great moneyed enterprise to be managed by the public to the common interest. He compared the state to a man who had a wolf by the ears—if he held on, he might starve; if he let go, the wolf might eat him. If the state should hold on to the road, the road must be a party engine—if it should put the money into any other shape, it would be worse. The *Southern Watchman*, a Whig print at Athens, while disapproving Bethune's plan, thought it quite possible that the Democratic Party might sooner or later adopt it, and said it would be quite in keeping with the former policy of the state in squandering its magnificent domain through land lotteries, making speculators rich and the people intemperate.[1]

The *Southern Banner* (October 1, 1857) thought the existing system had been maintained at a loss quite long enough to show its ill-advised character. The state, it said, was still paying 6 per cent on most of the $6,000,000 which the road had cost, while the road had never paid to the treasury above 1 per cent on that sum. At the same time the private roads in the state were paying 7 and 8 per cent on their capital. The *Banner*, therefore, favored the plan of a lease.

The Democratic journals replied, however, that the road was just at the point where it would begin to pay, and the state should not forego the full benefit which must accrue. In reply to the argument of the liability of the road, while operated by the state, to be used as a party machine, the *Federal Union* of November 30, 1858, again emphasized the danger from corporations: "The man that has no fear of a company with all the money and patronage of the

[1] *Southern Watchman*, March 26, 1857.

state road at their command, has studied the history of this and other states to but little purpose. We have lately seen, in Georgia, corporations with not one-tenth the power this would have, set the laws of the state, made expressly to bind them, at open defiance with impunity. We have seen them refuse to comply with the express provision of their charter and come to the legislature for relief and get it. It is reasonable to fear companies who are a law unto themselves and care for no other law."

The final quietus was put upon the agitation by Governor Brown. A bill had been presented in the legislature of 1858 to accept the offer of Collins, Dean, Tumblin, and their company to lease the road at an annual rent of $325,000. The proposal contained no offer of security for keeping the road in good order and no provision for betterments. As regards tariffs, the bill proposed merely that the same maximum rates which were allowed to be charged by the Georgia Railroad Company should apply to the Western and Atlantic.

The governor, by way of showing his confidence in the earning power and prospects of the road, stated in a special message that if he believed the legislature and people of Georgia wished him to do so, he, as an individual, would take the road for ten years, paying $25,000 per month for the use of it, with a guarantee of promptness, would give bond with ample security against deterioration, would oblige himself to lay ten miles of track each year with new T-rail, and guarantee that freight rates should at no time be raised above the average actual charges on other roads in Georgia. This is of interest not only as stopping the lease agitation at the time, but also as giving an earnest of Brown's future activity in organizing the Western and

Atlantic Railroad Company in 1870, which did actually lease the state road upon terms not unlike those above set forth.

In fact, the failure of the road until 1858 to pay large sums into the state treasury was not a genuine grievance. The nominal net earnings had risen above $200,000 in 1852–1853, and between 1854 and 1861 did not fall below $400,000. That little of this was available by the state was due to the bad quality of the rails in the original construction and the pressing need of remaking the track with the first available funds. By 1858 the expense of this had nearly all been met, and the state treasury receipts grew to above $400,000 a year. The agitation concerning the road then died away.

With the politicians, the road was an issue of subordinate rank. Charges of maladministration were made at times, but usually disproved. The opposition was continually alert to prevent the rise of any undue opportunity for patronage. Governor Johnson was of the opinion that the political advantage of such little patronage as there might be was more than offset by the burden of administering the road and repelling charges of injustice or inefficiency. The administration press was often disposed to shirk responsibility for any shortcomings in the conduct of the road's affairs, declaring that the governor should not be expected to be a railroad overseer in addition to his regular duties.

From the fact of public ownership arose several peculiar problems of policy. An example of this is shown in a message of Governor Johnson, March 1, 1856, with which he vetoed a bill to empower the Hiwassee Company to build a railroad across north Georgia to connect with the South

Carolina system of roads. A principal reason stated for his veto was that the proposed road, if built, would deprive the Western and Atlantic of a large part of its remunerative traffic.[1] A meeting of citizens at Blairsville, a village on the proposed route, censured the governor for this veto; the *Atlanta Intelligencer*, March 27, 1856, replied in defense, declaring that the interest of the whole people ought not to be subordinated to the welfare of one remote district.

A more vital problem was that of freight rates. Here the crux was in the question of whose interests the state road ought primarily to subserve. Ought rates to be high for the sake of large returns to the treasury, or low to benefit the citizens who were consumers of Western produce? Ought local tariffs to be on the lowest basis, so as to increase the prosperity along the route of the road in Georgia, or ought the through rates to be at the minimum so as to attract business from afar and cheapen the food supply throughout the cotton belt? Ought the rates on goods for transfer to the connecting lines in Georgia to be on a reduced basis for the benefit of the established towns like Macon and Augusta, or ought the tariff to be absolutely uniform, and thus promote the growth of a distributing center of food supplies for the cotton belt at the Western and Atlantic terminus? Personal and sectional attitude on those issues was largely a question of whose ox was gored. It was fortunate for the sake of tranquillity that the fixing of rates was not attempted by the legislature.

The actual policy as to freight rates was based on a few substantial principles: the road ought to yield a reasonable

[1] MS. Minutes of Executive Department, Georgia archives, in state capitol.

return upon the investment; it ought to promote the welfare of the people of the state at large; it ought to subserve the special interests of the people along the route when they did not conflict with those of the state at large, but in case of such conflict the larger interest ought to prevail. These doctrines, of course, were easier to formulate than to apply to the general satisfaction in concrete cases. Indeed, freight rates seem to have been altered with some frequency to allay clamor.

The fact that the road was for a period incomplete and operated for strictly local business, caused the rise of local enterprises which shortly led to vigorous demands on the ground of protection to vested interests. One instance of this was the growing of wheat and corn along the route, which yielded large returns so long as the road was unfinished, but was thereafter embarrassed by the Western competition. Another was the phenomenal growth at the southern end of the road of a town first called Terminus, then Marthasville, and finally Atlanta. The grain raisers, of course, objected to any reduction of rates for Western cereals, while Atlanta protested against any tariff which would encourage shippers to send car-loads past her depot unbroken. These protests were at times of some avail. For example, in November, 1855, Mr. Cooper, the superintendent, put a rule in force that all down traffic on the Western and Atlantic should bear the same charges whether bound for Atlanta or points below.[1] At the same time he fixed the rates on corn on a strictly distance basis; he laid off the road into seven divisions of distance, and fixed the rate for corn in sacks at 5 cents per bushel for 1 unit of distance, 6 cents for 2 units, 7 cents for 3, and so

[1] *Atlanta Intelligencer*, November 8, 1855.

on to 11 cents for the whole length of the road.[1] In modern phrase this would be called a zone tariff; 4 cents per bushel was included in it for terminal charges, and 1 cent for carriage over each unit of distance.

As early as 1854–1855 the receipts from through freights had amounted to $394,457.27, just four times the $98,922.67 earned from local freights.[2] When Dr. Lewis, assuming control in 1857, adopted plans for securing still greater through tonnage by competing as part of a system for much of the trade which had formerly gone to the Eastern roads or to the Western waterways, he cut the through rate on corn to 7 cents, and in general brought the road to apply in large measure the principle of charging what the traffic would bear. Lewis said in his report of October, 1860, that the bulk of freights for the last few months had been from the West, principally from Louisville and Memphis and beyond. "A statement of the amount of Indian corn moved over this Road for the last few months would appear, if stated, almost if not altogether fabulous. We have moved it 138 miles over, I suppose, the crookedest road under the sun, for 7 cents per bushel, and the Nashville, Chattanooga, and Memphis and Charleston roads, with highly commendable liberality, for proportionable amounts. We have all paid expenses [and] cleared a little money on the operation." He explained that the proportion of net earnings would have been much higher but for having to send back the great majority of the cars empty on the northward trip.[3]

The disproportion of down traffic and up traffic was enor-

[1] *Ibid.*, October 19, 1855 (advertisement).
[2] Superintendent's Report for 1854–1855, p. 8.
[3] Report for 1860, p. 4. Report for 1861, p. 4.

mous. No tonnage tables are available for the *ante-bellum* period, but the figures from the report of 1868–1869 are perhaps a fair illustration of this characteristic feature of the road. In that year the through tonnage southward from Chattanooga to Atlanta was 233,022,932 pounds, and the through tonnage northward between the same stations was 6,089,500 pounds. The total freight southward was above 350,000,000 pounds, while the total northward was below 30,000,000. The one was about twelve times as great as the other. This meant that eleven cars out of every twelve had to go back empty, and the profit on the downward load was diminished in all such cases by the cost of hauling back the empty car.

Even with the utmost alertness and economy it proved impossible for the road to earn a percentage on its cost commensurate with the dividends which the neighboring company roads were declaring on their stock. Lewis, among others, said that profits on that basis ought not to be hoped for. The state road, to begin with, had been badly laid out and had been built with unquestionable extravagance; its running in a continuous series of curves made it very expensive to keep up, and the absence of large cotton traffic deprived it of all opportunity for large profits from high tariffs on precious freight.[1] These items, together with the dearth of return freight, describe the limitations of the road for earning net profits. Of these, the extravagance of outlay and the badness of construction alone could possibly be attributed to the feature of state ownership; but a further item in the count might fairly have been the extravagance in salaries and wages which had prevailed in some measure before Lewis assumed control, but which he himself had remedied.

[1] Report of 1859, p. 7.

At the end of 1860 the road was in good repair, with 50 miles of new T-rail and a full equipment of cars and engines; the total earnings were fairly regular at from $800,000 to $900,000 a year, of which a little above 50 per cent was usually recorded as net earnings. With a firm administration in control, the road was scarcely at all involved in politics. It was for the time in normal routine operation and relatively free from controversy. How long this status would have continued in times of peace, it is useless to conjecture.

By way of appendix, a glimpse may here be taken of the brief remaining period, to 1870, in which this road continued under state operation. The decade of the sixties was entirely abnormal. The general confusion between public and private property in that epoch of war and political upheaval reduced the feature of state ownership in the Western and Atlantic to relative insignificance. The problems of the road for most of the decade were mere railroad problems, and very slightly affected ownership.

From 1861 to 1863 there is to be noted the heavy traffic on government account, the large nominal earnings in depreciated currency, and a great deterioration of track and rolling stock. In 1864 Sherman's army destroyed much of the track and equipment, a destruction which was crudely restored in part only by the Confederate government and the state before the end of the war. During April to September of 1865 the road was operated by the United States military authorities, and was restored to the commonwealth on September 25, a rough patchwork of damaged and crooked rails, laid on rotten cross-ties and on rough poles and other makeshifts; eight miles of track at the upper end were entirely missing, while the rolling stock was more nearly fit for the scrap heap than for traffic. In 1866–1867 there followed a period of vigorous rehabilitation and operation under Charles J. Jenkins, the Democratic governor, and Campbell Wallace as superintendent; there was an immense press of traffic to supply the exhausted country, a pressure increased by delay in reopening the seaboard lines. The gross earnings for 1865–1866 were $1,315,756.40, and for 1866–1867, $1,273,191.35; net, $360,655.69 and $585,729.13. Large sums were devoted to rebuilding. During the Republican rule of 1868–1869 under Governor Bullock, E. Hulburt was superintendent of the Western and Atlantic; he was a capable administrator, but failed to improve the road.

Governor Bullock in 1870 supplanted Hulburt by Foster Blodgett; and there ensued a travesty of administration with wholesale mismanagement, extravagance, and plundering, shared in by numerous politicians.[1] Blodgett is said to have stated, with grim humor, that he took charge of the road to manage its "public and political policy." N. P. Hotchkiss, the auditor, when asked how he had managed to save up $20,000 or $30,000 for himself in a year or two out of a $2000 salary, explained that it had been done "by the exercise of the most rigid economy." [2] Blodgett and others were afterward indicted for various crimes, but were pardoned by Conley, the last Republican governor.

By the autumn of 1870 the officials of the connecting lines began to protest against the condition of the Western and Atlantic track as too dangerous to trust their cars upon. Blodgett was robbing the road of all it was earning

[1] I. W. Avery, *History of Georgia*, pp. 449–451.
[2] Avery, p. 451.

and of all he could borrow in its name, and now demanded an appropriation of $500,000 from the state for repairs. As an alternative he proposed that the state should lease the road to some of its citizens.[1] The condition of things had now become intolerable to the people, and a great cry arose for the road to be taken out of politics.

At the meeting of the legislature in October, 1870, several bills were introduced concerning the state road, one of which was to provide for its lease, on adequate security, for twenty years, at not less than $25,000 per month. Capitalists and politicians of various complexions quickly formed two companies, each of which hoped to secure the lease. The promoters of each company supported the bill, and together secured its enactment into law. The governor was directed to assign the lease to the party which with adequate security should make the highest bid. The company headed by M. G. Dobbins bid $34,500 per month, but failed to furnish adequate security; the other, with Ex-governor Joseph E. Brown at its head, and including railroad presidents and politicians, Democrats, and Carpet-Baggers, made a bid of $25,000 per month, furnished acceptable security, and received the award of the lease.[2] At the end of 1870 the Western and Atlantic Railroad accordingly passed out of state operation. As remedying the disturbance in joint rates and through traffic, this transfer was pleasing to the other railroads; as ending the lurid régime in the state road's affairs, it was grateful to the

[1] *Remarks and Statements of the Superintendent [of the Western and Atlantic Railroad] on the Condition of the Road, before the Finance Committee of the House of Representatives, September 23, 1870.* Atlanta, 1870.

[2] *The Lease of the Western and Atlantic Railroad with Correspondence and Other Papers in Relation thereto* (pamphlet, Atlanta, 1871).

people. When the term of the lease expired in 1890, a new lease for thirty years was made of the road to the Nashville, Chattanooga, and St. Louis Railroad Company at $420,012 per year. The state, on the one hand, has declined to sell the road, and on the other has shown no strong desire to resume state operation. As bearing on the general question of state ownership and operation, the history of the Western and Atlantic yields about as many pros as cons. Its operation by the state was, on the whole, fairly successful and profitable; and might have continued indefinitely had not the state government been given over to irresponsible pillagers by the directors of a carnival of radicalism outside the state. Its original construction by the state, however, was without question a master-stroke in railway policy. Had private capital been depended upon, not only would the building of the road have been long delayed, but the whole railway development of Georgia would have been stunted and largely deprived of its success, and the general economic progress of that and neighboring states would have been slackened.

For the *ante-bellum* period, the Western and Atlantic Road was the cap-piece to the railway system which caused Georgia to enjoy well-nigh the whole commerce in Western produce imported by the eastern cotton belt. The addition of this trunk line brought it about that all railroads in adjacent states must hitch themselves to the Georgia system, and thus secure for their patrons the grain and meat which the planters were anxious to leave off raising, in large part, in order to concentrate still more closely upon their great staple of cotton.

CHAPTER VIII

MINOR ROADS AND LATER PROJECTS

THE preceding chapters have treated the railroads which were relatively early, successful, and important; and with these roads their subsidiary lines have been included. There remain a number of independent minor roads and several projects of large dimensions which were begun too late, or otherwise failed to achieve success before the outbreak of the war. The minor roads fall into three groups: (1) upland roads rendering local service and connecting with the trunk lines to the coast; (2) additional lines from the ports across the pine-barrens to the Piedmont; (3) lines parallel to the coast. The unrealized projects would also in most cases fall into one of these groups; the remainder were transmontane aspirations.

In Georgia the interior roads were as a rule associated more or less intimately with one of the two great companies in that state; and most of them have already been discussed as part of the work of the Georgia and Central of Georgia companies. In Piedmont South Carolina, on the other hand, and in the adjacent portion of North Carolina, the railroads were built by independent companies, organized to serve neighborhood needs, relying upon local subscriptions and state aid, and not assisted in any large measure by the city of Charleston or the South Carolina Railroad Company.

The projection and building of the half-dozen railroads in upland South Carolina was done all in a single movement. Prior to the severe hard times which began in 1839 the Piedmont people had been apathetic in regard to railroads; but the distress of the early forties roused them to the need of cheap transit. Every Piedmont locality began to wish for rail connection with the coast. When the passing of the cotton crisis in 1844–1845 made capital to some extent available again, a clamorous demand was begun in a score of towns and "districts" (as the counties were then called in South Carolina), with proffers of stock subscriptions from each of them to any company which would meet the neighborhood need of a railroad outlet. Lines were soon projected from the several prongs of the South Carolina Railroad; and in the Piedmont country a number of adjacent communities began to bid against each other to secure the routing of the respective roads for their local advantage. The outline of the railway network, as actually built, was the result of the victory of the strongest of these competing localities in getting the main lines for themselves, and of the resort by the defeated districts to the building of branches from these main lines for their own service, in consolation.

The three towns at or near the heads of the three prongs of the South Carolina Railroad competed, of course, as prospective termini for the Piedmont lines; and Columbia defeated both Aiken and Camden in each instance of a successful project. The towns and districts in the middle of the Piedmont and at its upper edge contended for the routing of the several lines; and in a measure, it may be said, the resulting railroads were relatively straight or crooked in their routes according as the upper termini were more important or less important strategically and financially than the intervening localities.

The two main lines in this Piedmont group were the twin enterprises, the "Charlotte and South Carolina" and the "Greenville and Columbia" roads, projected in 1845–1846 and advancing almost simultaneously through the various stages of promotion, construction, and operation. Their history includes most of what need be said of the South Carolina feeding lines.[1]

For the service of the area northward of Columbia and Camden, the project was launched in 1846 for a railroad with Charlotte, N.C., as its upper terminus. At once local promoters began in each town and district affected to enlist subscriptions in the proposed company, with a view to fighting for the respective local interests

[1] The material used in the study of these roads, aside from newspaper items, is as follows:—

For the Charlotte and South Carolina: *Proceedings of a Convention of the Stockholders . . ., at Charlotte, N.C., September 9, 1847; Report of the President . . .,* Columbia, 1847; *Proceedings of a Meeting of the Citizens of Charleston,* Charleston, 1847; *Proceedings of the Convention of the Stockholders . . . at Chesterville, January 13 and 14, 1848;* and the proceedings of the Charlotte and South Carolina Railroad Company at its annual meetings, from 1848 to 1858.

For the Greenville and Columbia: *Proceedings of the Railroad Convention at Greenville, S.C., September 21, 1846; A Convention of the Stockholders . . . for the purpose of Organization, held at . . . Columbia, . . . May 11, 12, 1847; An Appeal of the Stockholders . . . to the People of South Carolina,* Columbia, 1847; *Proceedings, . . . May 1 and 2, 1848; Proceedings . . . at the Extra Meeting, December 1, 1848;* and proceedings of the annual meetings of the company, from 1849 to 1857.

The reports of officers, in the case of each of these companies, were printed each year as part of the proceedings.

in the initial meeting of the subscribers. Nearly all the subscriptions proffered, except those from Charlotte, were conditioned upon the decision by the company, when formed, in favor of a route through some particular interested locality. When, after securing the charter, the convention for organizing the company met, at Charlotte, on September 9, 1847, delegates were present from Charlotte and the city of Charleston, and from the following districts of upper South Carolina: Richland, Fairfield, Chester, York, Kershaw, and Lancaster. Of these the two last named were insistent upon Camden as the terminus; the rest either favored Columbia or were neutral. The first issue in the business of the meeting was the choice of the southern terminus. The determining consideration in this was not mileage, grades, and costs, but it was the size of the subscriptions enlisted from the competing localities. The route from Camden was demonstrated to be shorter and cheaper; but it could show only 2776 shares subscribed and committed to its interests as against 6670 cast in Columbia's behalf. A resolution committing the company to the Columbia terminus was promptly adopted, whereupon the delegates from Lancaster and Kershaw gave notice of the withdrawal of all subscriptions offered by citizens of towns in their districts. After this transaction, and the choice of a president and directors, the convention adjourned until more data and more subscriptions could be gathered. It reassembled on January 13, 1848, to decide among the competing localities for the route in the middle distance. Rejecting an overture from the Greenville and Columbia company for combining in a joint track for fifteen or twenty miles of what might be made a common route along the Broad

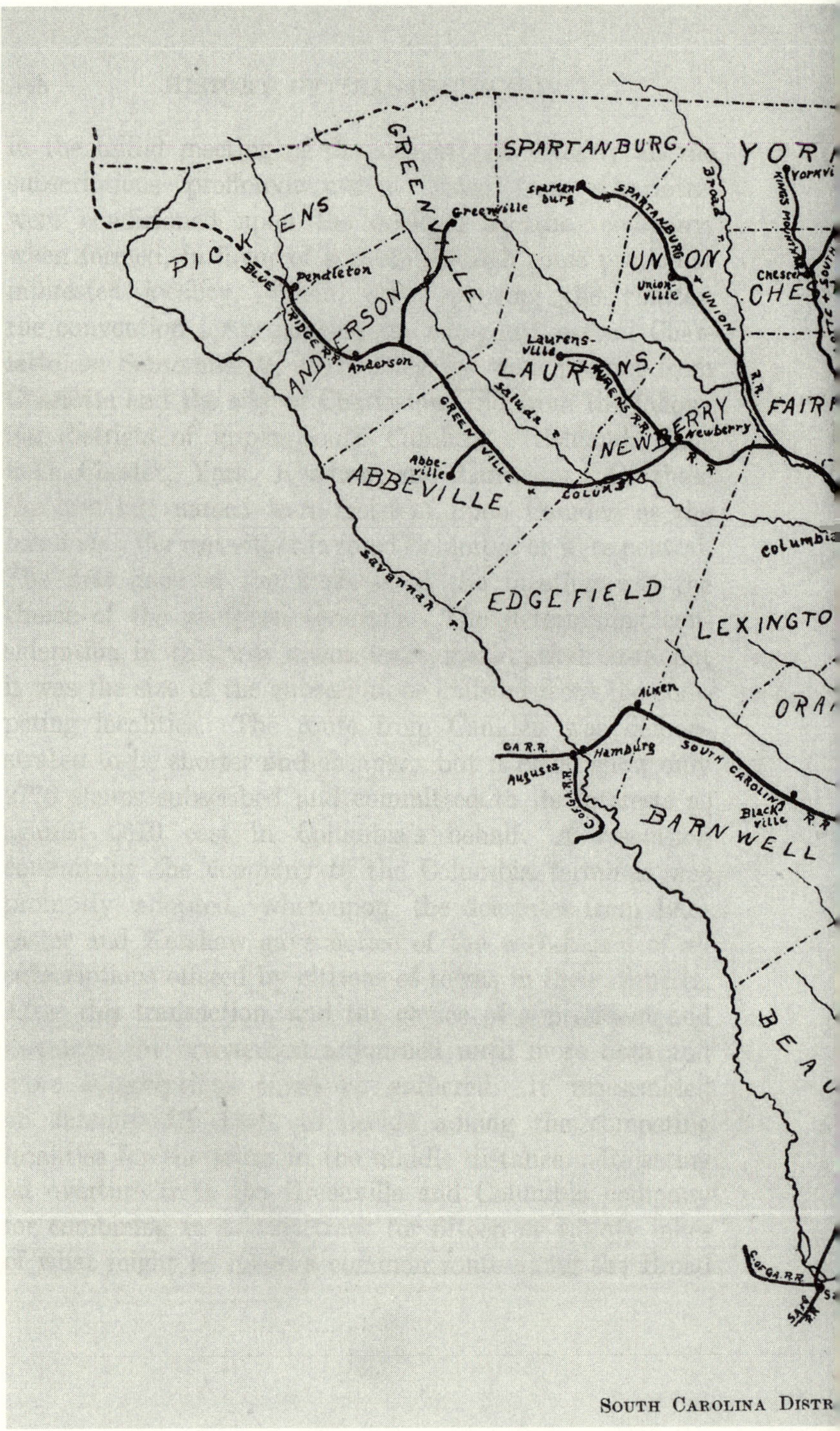

SOUTH CAROLINA DISTR

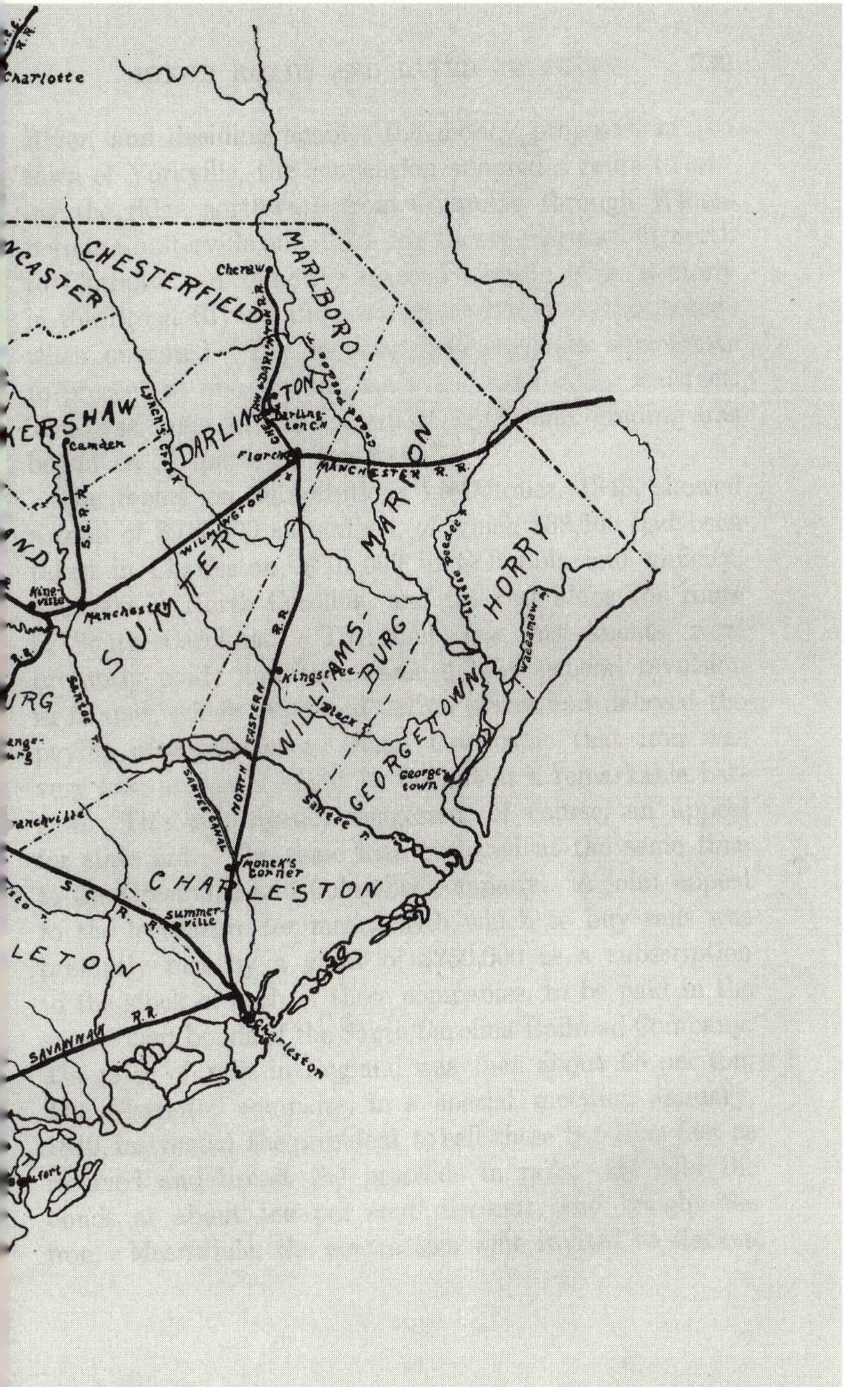

RAILROADS, 1860

River, and deciding against the money proposals of the town of Yorkville, the convention adopted a route following the ridge northward from Columbia through Winnsboro to Chesterville and deflecting thence eastward of north to Charlotte. A minority favored a route lying westerly in the Broad River valley, but its members did not secede when outvoted. The meeting instructed the directorate to proceed at once to put the whole road under contract. This was done in the course of 1848, and grading was begun on all parts of the route.

The report on subscriptions in October, 1848, showed a total of $917,900 subscribed, of which $32,100 had been taken in Charleston, $201,000 in Columbia and vinicity, $200,000 in North Carolina, and the rest along the route in South Carolina. The first few instalments were promptly paid; but then came a brief general revulsion in finance, which depressed cotton prices and delayed the paying of assessments. News now came that iron was very low, and rails might be bought at a remarkable bargain. This contingency suggested, of course, an appeal for state aid. The same idea occurred at the same time to the Greenville and Columbia company. A joint appeal to the legislature for means with which to buy rails was promptly met by a grant of $250,000 as a subscription to the stock of each of these companies, to be paid in the six per cent bonds of the South Carolina Railroad Company. The price of rails in England was then about £6 per ton. The Charlotte company, in a special meeting, January, 1849, instructed the president to sell these bonds as fast as received and invest the proceeds in rails. He sold the bonds at about ten per cent discount, and bought the iron. Meanwhile, the contractors were invited to slacken their speed, in order to give the stockholders more time to meet their assessments. In October, 1850, thirty miles of road were finished. A year later seventy miles of track had been laid, and gross earnings were at the rate of four or five thousand dollars per month. The prospect of future earnings was then brightened, the president reported, by the launching of the Central of North Carolina Railroad, which was to run northeast and east from Charlotte. The final stock instalment in the Charlotte and South Carolina company fell due in November, 1851, with the road still incomplete, and a shortage of funds threatening. By issuing $160,000 in bonds, and devoting to construction $84,312 from earnings, the road was completed to Charlotte in November, 1852, with a floating debt of $108,652. Improvements in road-bed, track, and equipment were already much needed. For three years afterward the net earnings were steadily devoted to construction account and reduction of debt. In 1854 gross earnings were $243,037, and net, $167,167; in 1855, $291,219 and $138,374 respectively. The final cost of construction, as reported in January, 1858, was $1,823,639, of which $390,500 was then still outstanding in bonds. The road and equipment were in fair working order, for the light traffic handled. Earnings in 1856 and 1857 were, gross, $256,041 and $240,722 respectively, and net, $97,936 and $121,554. The road had reached a basis of moderate success by 1854; from 1856 dividends of six per cent annually were issued.

The early history of the Greenville and Columbia Railroad gives a similar example of the jockeying of local interests. The charter was granted by the legislature in the winter of 1845–1846 in response to the demand for an outlet from that portion of the state which lay northwest and west-northwest from Columbia. This demand was most active from the area comprised within the double rank of "districts" or counties which lay along Saluda River: Newberry, Laurens, and Greenville in a row on the northeastern side of the river, and Edgefield, Abbeville, and Anderson balancing them, each "district" having a court-house, town, or village with the same name as the district. Newberry, Laurens, and Greenville villages, respectively forty, seventy, and a hundred miles distant from Columbia, stood upon a single southeast and northwest watershed. A railroad built in a fairly straight line along this ridge would connect Columbia with all of these villages and their districts, without heavy bridging or grading. On the other hand, a road which used any part of this ridge could reach Edgefield, Abbeville, and Anderson districts only after crossing the Saluda by a detour or by branch roads. Greenville seemed at the outset to offer the best objective, and the straight ridge to furnish the most eligible route. In this expectation the company was given the name, the Greenville and Columbia.

After a preliminary meeting at Laurensville, a convention of delegates from the districts interested met at Greenville, September 21, 1846. Not enough subscriptions to validate the charter were reported; and, after adopting an address to the people on behalf of the enterprise, the convention adjourned. By the following May enough stock had been taken to satisfy the charter requirement, and the company then organized in a convention of stockholders at Columbia. Of the 19,813 one-hundred-dollar shares then reported as subscribed, 3025 had been taken in Charleston, 3999 in Columbia and Richland district, including 2500 taken by the Columbia town council, and 1575 by citizens of Henderson County, North Carolina. The report of subscriptions from the South Carolina districts along the route was: from Newberry, 4573; from Laurens, 1187; from Greenville, 5059. The districts west of the Saluda had not joined in the movement.

The total subscription was far too small to finance the contemplated work. The meeting resolved that vigorous effort should be made to raise further subscriptions, and that meanwhile the work should be begun. It elected officers, ordered a preliminary survey, and directed the calling of a stockholders' meeting in due time to take further steps.

The districts beyond the Saluda were now canvassed; and some of their citizens developed the idea of capturing the road for their own local benefit, to the disadvantage of Laurens and possibly of Greenville. In the stockholders' meeting at Newberry, in the fall of 1847, the crucial contest over the route was fought. Such large holdings were there represented from Abbeville and Anderson districts that the meeting was controlled by them, and the company was committed by a definite resolution to a route running around Laurens district instead of across it.

The Laurens stockholders, whose subscriptions, in view of this possible contingency, had been made on a conditional basis, promptly withdrew from the company; and, after the adjournment of the meeting, nearly half of the company's directors resigned. The administration was for a time threatened with paralysis from the lack of a quorum in the directorate. The Greenville subscribers wished also to withdraw, in view of the prospective delay and uncertainty in the company's service to their locality. But their subscriptions had been made unconditionally, and the directorate used legal means to keep them in the corporation. At the meeting in May, 1848, subscriptions stood as follows: from Charleston, $78,300; from Columbia, $85,900; from Fairfield district (lying east of Broad River), $28,450; from Newberry, $130,000; from Abbeville, $189,200; from Anderson, $315,000; from Greenville, $103,650; and from North Carolina, $20,500. In view of the difficulty of recrossing the Saluda amid the high hills of Greenville district, the company adopted Anderson court-house as its terminus, to continue so until considerable further increase should be made in its capital.

This meeting of May, 1848, ordered that the whole route to Anderson be at once put under contract. Shortly afterward, to take advantage of the low price of iron then prevailing, the company applied for state aid, jointly with the Charlotte and South Carolina Railroad Company, and obtained it in securities of $250,000 par value, or some $225,000 market value as actually realized. Other stimuli were the launching of a project for a road by a local company to connect Laurensville and Newberry, and another to build from Spartanburg through Unionville down the Broad River valley. During 1849 both of these enterprises, which would provide feeding lines to the Greenville and Columbia, made good progress. Furthermore, the village of Abbeville subscribed about $75,000 for the building of a branch from that town to the main line; and the state added $75,000 to its former subscription to promote the extension of the main line to Greenville as first intended. The resolution which the company then adopted, to build onward to Greenville, ended the reluctance of the Greenville stockholders and those of the adjacent counties in North Carolina, and even brought new subscriptions from that quarter. In July, 1850, the subscribed capital amounted to about $1,187,000. It had been seen at any early stage that the building of the road would tax the company's resources to the utmost. As a device for saving money the company bought the discarded flange-rail of the South Carolina Railroad instead of substantial new iron.

Track-laying was begun from the Columbia end in September, 1849, but a dearth of labor impeded progress. The town of Newberry was reached in March, 1851, and the village of Greenwood, eighty-five miles, in July, 1852; but in August a huge freshet destroyed bridges, tracks, and embankments in the Broad River valley, checked the extension of the track, and added a heavy unexpected item to the cost of the road. The line was completed to Anderson in June, 1853, and to Greenville in the following December.

But this was accomplished only by the straining of all financial resources. To sell bonds enough to meet the company's needs was found impossible; and in last resort the corporation in January, 1852, assessed its stocks twenty per cent above the original $100 subscribed and paid on each share. The gross amount of capital paid in, including the assessment, was reported July 10, 1854, at $1,293,464.25. Disbursements on construction and outfit, partly paid in stock, then amounted to $1,999,080.41. The deficiency of capital was estimated at $800,000, and bonds to that amount were now authorized, to run ten years at seven per cent. The delay and finally the refusal by the legislature to pay the assessment on the state's stock was a source of annoyance to the company's administration.

The earnings in the year 1853–1854 were $214,865 gross, and expenses ordinary and extraordinary $206,774. For the next year gross earnings were $270,042, and net earnings $77,801. The character of the road is indicated by an allusion in the president's report in 1855. He regretted the prevalence of an opinion among the public "that this is a rickety road, exposed constantly to the danger of being swept away by freshets." To remedy this he insisted successfully that net earnings for several years should be devoted to improving the road-bed, track, and equipment. The whole cost of the road in 1855 was reported at $2,200,000, or $13,414 per mile. At such a cost, with a route through broken country, and with three river crossings, the road was necessarily of the flimsiest.

The earnings in 1855–1856 were $279,102 gross and $97,277 net; and in 1856–1857, $307,808 and $111,838 respectively. In 1857 the accrued interest on the stock assessment of 1852 was paid, and there was some prospect of dividends. The two feeding lines, the Laurens and the Spartanburg and Union, aided more or less by the Greenville and Columbia company, had now been completed.

At this point, 1857, the series of available documents for the Greenville and Columbia company comes to an end. The road at that time was already rendering valuable service to its locality, and had a prospect of considerable traffic; but with its crude, zigzag, hill-and-dale road-bed, its shoddy track, and its cheaply built and insufficient rolling stock, the road was far from an economical basis of operation.

The railroad routes connecting Columbia with Charlotte and Greenville respectively formed an angle within which was a large area demanding other railroads for local accommodation, as we have already noted. This area comprised in particular the four South Carolina districts of Union, Spartanburg, Laurens, and York, each of them having, as usual in that state, a court-house town near its center bearing the same name as the district. After the definitive location of the lines to Charlotte and Greenville, each of these districts promptly began to promote an independent railroad to connect with one of these main lines and render strictly local service. The people of Union and Spartanburg eventually combined in building a single railway for common service to both districts, but in the two cases of Laurens and York entirely separate local lines were built.

Yorkville and its vicinity in 1846–1847 had offered the Charlotte and South Carolina company a handsome cash bonus if it would route its road through that town. Upon that company's refusal, the locality proceeded to use its resources, thus already organized, in building a neighborhood line from Yorkville to Chester, fifteen miles in length. This road, called the King's Mountain Railroad, was finished in 1855, and formed thereafter a prong to the Charlotte and South Carolina road. The capital enlisted, remarkable to record, was more than sufficient for the little company's task, and provided a surplus of $14,000 for investment in the securities of sister companies. The earnings of this road to July 1, 1856, were $27,141, with operating expenses of only $9392. In 1856–1857 the gross earnings and other income amounted to $21,332, and the net income to $10,146, yielding a dividend of five per cent to the stockholders.[1]

The Laurens Railroad Company, undertaking to build from Laurens to Newberry, thirty-two miles, was not strongly enough financed to accomplish its work in comfort. Its total stock subscription was $165,670. To this it added $38,500 in bonds, and was able to contract a floating debt in addition to the amount of about $108,650. With these funds it laid a track and put the road into operation in 1855; but so flimsy was the road that renovation was necessary almost before its completion. In 1855–1856 earnings were $23,766 gross and $11,965 net. Next year practically all net income was devoted to betterments, while in 1857–1858 the gross earnings of $27,568 yielded $8,727. No dividends were declared as yet; but the company, operating a light train on a fifteen-mile-per-hour schedule, was reaching a fairly sound basis as a very small enterprise.

The Spartanburg and Union, the third of these petty roads, was the greatest of them in length and the most beset with vicissitudes. With a plan of branching from the Greenville and Columbia road just below its crossing of Broad River, and running through the district and village of Union to the town of Spartanburg, this company secured a charter at the end of 1847, but for a period of three years thereafter failed to raise enough subscriptions to justify the beginning of work. Then, in December,

[1] The reports used for the narratives of the King's Mountain, the Laurens, and the Spartanburg and Union companies are those made by their respective presidents to the state legislature in the years 1856, 1857, and 1858, printed in broadsides and pamphlets.

1850, the legislature offered a State subscription as a stimulus, and two years later increased the amount of this. The company's authorized stock was $1,000,000, in shares of $25. The acts of 1850 and 1852 offered to exchange stock, at par, which the state held in the South Carolina Railroad Company for stock in the new company, on condition of this company's securing stated amounts of capital from other sources. The first offer was of $125,000, with a requirement of $375,000 in private subscriptions; the act of 1852 raised these amounts to $250,000 and $500,000 respectively. By dint of great effort the company was able to satisfy the half-million requirement and thus to secure the full amount of state aid offered. The total subscription, including that of the state, was reported in August, 1854, at $757,250.[1]

A stubborn competition over the routing of the line delayed the beginning of construction until 1853. A short-sighted policy was then adopted of grading the whole sixty miles of the route at once, and at the end of 1855 the company found itself with funds very low and but a few miles of track laid. In the fall of 1856 forty miles was in operation, but cross-ties and rails were wanting for the rest, and the track had not yet reached paying territory. Bonds were then offered upon the market; but the financial stringency of 1857 made these unsalable unless at a discount of more than twenty per cent. The company then petitioned for a state indorsement of its bonds, and securing this at the end of 1857, was able to raise enough funds to carry its road to completion in 1858–1859. The total cost was about $1,250,000, of which

[1] *Charter and other Documents of the Spartanburg and Union Railroad Company,* Spartanburg, S.C., 1855.

the state contributed nearly one-half in stock subscriptions and bond indorsement. The road began to handle traffic as early as 1856, but no dividends were in sight before the end of the *ante-bellum* period.

The only other railroad of interior South Carolina remaining to be treated is the Cheraw and Darlington, which was built to serve the Pee Dee region. The town of Cheraw had a location upon the great Pee Dee corresponding to Camden's on the Wateree and Columbia's on the Congaree. It enjoyed its navigation for but one-half of each year, and yet for many years it had controlled the trade of most of northeastern South Carolina and much of south-central North Carolina.

Cheraw evidenced as early as the middle thirties a discontent with its vexatious water outlet and a strong desire to replace it with one by rail. The first effort was to launch a railway from Cheraw to deep-water navigation on the Waccamaw River at Conwayboro, about 85 miles away. To promote this plan a convention was held at Marion Court-House in January, 1837, which provided for a survey. A reconnaissance was made at once and reported upon in very favorable terms.[1] The country was described as level, the soil easily handled, the right of way to be secured gratis, and the price of labor estimated at 75 cents per day, provisions included. The total estimated cost, with sixty- to seventy-ton rails, was $607,232. Commissioners reporting with the surveyor estimated annual earnings at $133,000, and expenses at $90,000. The conclusion of their report was: "Assured by the energy and fortitude which has always characterized our State, we

[1] *Reports on the proposed Cheraw and Waccamaw Railroad, by Edward White . . .*, Fayetteville, N.C., 1837.

confidently believe that the present embarrassments, arising from no fault of our own, will only stimulate our fellow-citizens to renewed exertions to accomplish a work which will assist in elevating the prosperity of our beloved State above the control of adventitious circumstances." The panic of 1837, however, and the lean years following, were far from favorable to capitalistic enterprises. Instead of fostering, the hard times killed the Cheraw and Waccamaw plan.

A decade later Cheraw revived its project in a modified form. By this time the Wilmington and Manchester Railroad Company had been launched to build an east-and-west line from the coast at Wilmington, intended to run some forty miles south of Cheraw. This reduced the bulk of the Cheraw people's problem by one-half. During the course of discussion upon the subject, furthermore, the Charlestonians in 1852 launched the North Eastern Railroad Company to build north from Charleston, and the city authorities of Charleston offered to subscribe $100,000 in the Cheraw company if it would so route its road as to strike the Wilmington and Manchester at a common point with the North Eastern. The North Eastern company also subscribed $25,000, to be paid in transportation. Thus encouraged, the Cheraw and Darlington Railroad Company was organized and given enough capital by local subscriptions to enable it to undertake the forty miles of railway wanted. Construction was begun at the beginning of 1854, and the track completed in November, 1855.[1] The grading cost

[1] The narrative is made from the reports of the Cheraw and Darlington company to the South Carolina legislature, 1855, 1856, and 1857, and the report of the president of the North Eastern Railroad Company for 1854.

$77,600, bridges and trestling $22,500, and superstructure with a fifty-pound rail $288,100. Money for rolling stock was wanting, and for several years the company rented its supply from other roads. A freshet in 1856 required heavy repairs, and depot buildings and water stations were imperative. The expenditures for these saddled the company with a mortgage of considerable amount, and by the end of 1857 with a floating debt of $85,000.

Earnings in 1856 were $22,819; and in 1857, from passengers, $11,709, from freights, $7007, and from the mail, $1941. A good deal of cotton was still being carried by the waterway competitors, and even a part of the upward freight. The naval stores industry was now developing in the Pee Dee region, and the North Eastern Railroad, just completed, now provided better facilities for through transit. The Cheraw and Darlington company, however, could have little hope beyond maintaining its status as one of the petty and somewhat precarious corporations of the Carolina interior. Restricted by the competition of Camden, Charlotte, and Fayetteville, each now equipped with a railway outlet, Cheraw, like its railroad, could develop nothing beyond a neighborhood business.

Our second group of the "minor roads" is of those whose route lay from the coast through the pine-barrens.[1] Of these the roads built to serve the border between the

[1] As before mentioned, the railways of *ante-bellum* North Carolina and Alabama have been treated by C. C. Weaver and W. E. Martin respectively in the *Johns Hopkins University Studies*. Accordingly, roads intended entirely for service in those states are left out of the present history.

two Carolinas form one subgroup, those to serve southern Georgia a second, and those in Florida a third.

The Wilmington and Manchester Railroad was one of the projects launched in the middle forties and borne to successful construction on the tide of prosperity which followed the great cotton depression. The interests promoting it were the merchants of Wilmington, the farmers of the east midlands of South Carolina, and a few turpentiners in the middle distance.

A promotive convention at Marion Court-House, S.C., in August, 1846, gave definite form to this project of building a line westward from Wilmington to tap the Camden and Columbia branches of the South Carolina Railroad at the village of Manchester. In the following winter charters were secured from both the states concerned, and a survey was made. The survey report[1] described the route as 158 miles long, of which 151 miles would be straight running; the country level and easy to grade, except for one small district at the High Hills of Santee; the required curves easy, and the grades light. The estimated cost of the road-bed was only $1700 per mile. The superstructure advised was of a sort already antiquated, with longitudinal subsills, cross-ties three feet apart, and wooden stringers wedged into notches in the cross-ties. The rail was to be an iron strap, 1 by 2½ inches. The estimates of costs and earnings were as crude as the building specifications.

Grading was begun in 1850, and half of it completed within that year. In 1851 the subscriptions stood as follows: from individuals, $651,000; from the town of Wilmington, $100,000; and from the state of South Car-

[1] Pamphlet, Wilmington, 1847.

olina, $200,000 for the purchase of rails; total, $951,000. The North Carolina legislature subscribed $200,000 in 1851, but upon terms which caused the company to decline it. Its expectation was to raise the remaining $600,000 needed for its work by the issue of convertible bonds.[1]

The road was pushed on rapidly to completion, and at once began to enjoy a moderate traffic in passengers, cotton, farm supplies, and especially in naval stores. Gross earnings for 1854 were about $300,000, and for the year ending December 1, 1855, $364,204.[2] Of this sum, $213,824 was nominally net profits; but more than two-thirds of the net was expended in repairs and betterments, and most of the remainder went as interest on bonds. For the next year the reports were on a similar scale and basis. For 1856–1857 (year ending September 30) the earnings were $462,516 gross and $240,938 net. Additional outlay was made on the track, and the debt was reduced by about $70,000. Next year, because of the crisis of 1857, receipts fell to $383,192, of which freight made up $128,831; and net earnings were $159,124. The company at this time owned a renovated track and an adequate equipment, and had a good prospect of moderate prosperity in any normal period to follow. It was distinctly a minor road, however, leading from a port of only medium strength, traversing for the most part a barren and vacant country, enjoying no connections of special value at its inland terminus, and of course handling and destined long to handle but a light traffic. It proved a convenience to the

[1] *Exhibit of the Condition and Prospects of the Wilmington and Manchester Railroad Company,* New York, 1851. Signed by W. W. Harlee, president of the company.

[2] Reports of the company to the South Carolina legislature for 1855, 1856, 1857, and 1858.

people in its territory, but led to no new developments except for a moderate stimulus to the naval stores industry. In later decades the road built by the Wilmington and Manchester company has been used by the Atlantic Coast Line in favoring the port of Wilmington, where the ocean terminals of the Atlantic Coast Line system are located. For the time being, and for several decades to follow, Charleston was able to offset the Wilmington and Manchester's damage to her trade through the building of her North Eastern Railroad.

The North Eastern road[1] was as distinctly the result of Charleston's efforts as had been the early line to Hamburg. Under a charter of December, 1851, the company was organized in February, 1852. The survey made in the following spring, from Charleston to the Wilmington and Manchester route at Florence, showed the route to be 103 miles long, almost devoid of either grades or curves, and extremely favorable for railway building, except for the necessity of bridging the troublesome Santee River. The estimated total cost, with a well-planned superstructure and a sixty-pound rail, was $1,240,337,[2] rolling stock included. The city of Charleston subscribed $400,000 to the stock, the Charleston banks $80,000, and the state of South Carolina a block of securities which yielded $220,000. Individual takings carried the total subscription to $668,150 in 1853 and, contractors' takings included, to $889,700 in March, 1854. Meanwhile the price of labor and materials had risen to a point requiring the addition of

[1] Reports of the president and chief engineer to the stockholders, 1852, 1853, and 1854, and reports to the South Carolina legislature, 1855 to 1858.

[2] Of this amount $130,000 was to be expended in crossing the Santee River and swamps.

$250,000 to the estimated cost; and yet another drain was the unexpectedly high cost of the right of way in and near Charleston. The deficit had to be met by the issue of bonds, most of which, although bearing seven per cent interest, proved salable only at ninety cents on the dollar.

Construction was begun early in 1854 and finished in October, 1857, with $700,000 outstanding in bonds and $300,000 in floating debt, and equipment still deficient. The state now came to the rescue by indorsing about $300,000 of the company's second mortgage bonds.

The prevalence of a yellow fever epidemic in Charleston in 1858 prevented the earning of normal profits in the period for which reports are available. The traffic of the road was of necessity light. Only one town, that of Kingstree, lay upon the road, and the traffic supplied by its one small feeding line, the Cheraw and Darlington, was shared in by the competing Wilmington and Manchester. The road ran through a productive plantation district centering at Monck's Corner, and another on the Santee; but both of these had water routes at hand, which served for most of their freight. On the whole, the North Eastern Railroad was built as a forlorn hope to relieve Charleston's decadence. As such it was largely a failure by force of physiographic circumstances. To maintain Charleston's commercial eminence, nothing would suffice, in fact, but to make the wilderness behind her blossom; but railways and all things else have thus far failed to convert the pine-barrens into any semblance of a garden. Charleston succeeded in the concrete task of building herself a second radiating railroad; but again found her labor in large measure unavailing.

The trade of the district west and southwest of Savannah was contended for by the neighboring ports even more vigorously than was that northeastward of Charleston. The center of the theme here is the ambition of the port of Brunswick.

Brunswick harbor lay fifteen miles south of the Altamaha River's mouth, and about halfway (eighty miles in an air line) from Savannah to St. Augustine. The remarkably good roadstead had been known favorably from colonial times. Projects for town building there were periodical; but the barrenness of the soil and the lack of waterways to the interior long kept the site vacant. Brunswick served several times as a promoter's plaything. With its greatly superior harbor it was likely to prove a strong rival to Savannah in case canals or railways should ever give it access to the inland trade. But money in sums greater than available in the *ante-bellum* period was necessary for this large purpose.

In December, 1826, a group of promoters, already controlling the tract on the harbor eligible for wharves and the town, secured incorporation as a canal company, empowered to connect Brunswick with the Altamaha River. Difficulties arising soon discouraged most of the incorporators; but one of them, W. B. Davis, bought out the faint-hearted ones, and agitated for popular support. The newspapers of the state were apparently opposed to the scheme, and Davis had to pay advertising rates for the essays which he published in Brunswick's behalf. This he did, however, for quite a series of articles in 1828, signed "Wm. Brunswick Davis, bona-fide proprietor of the chartered rights and privileges of the Brunswick

Canal."[1] He proclaimed with vigor the faith that was in him, that by reason of its natural advantages Brunswick would prevail in spite of the solid opposition of the Georgia press; but he fought a losing fight, and soon disappeared.

The project was revived in 1834, and a new charter secured, with a promise of state aid under conditions. Backing from Boston capitalists gave the project a promise of success. The route was surveyed and located in 1836 for a canal 12 miles long, 54 feet wide at the surface, and 6 feet depth of water, to tap the Altamaha and bring its trade to Brunswick.[2] Bids for excavation and masonry were advertised for.[3] At the same time there was under way, promoted by the same parties, a project for a railroad from Brunswick to Albany in southwest Georgia, with a branch to the Gulf coast. In furtherance of this a charter was obtained for the Brunswick and Florida Railroad Company, in December, 1835, granting in one of its clauses a guarantee that for a period of twenty-five years no competing company would be permitted by the state to build within twenty miles of the route selected by this company. The financial stringency, beginning in 1837, killed the canal project and postponed all further railroad activity in behalf of Brunswick until the decade of the fifties.

In this interim southwest Georgia grew rapidly in industrial and commercial importance; and the people there began to look to Brunswick with the hope of a rail-

[1] *E.g.* in the *Georgia Courier* (Augusta), in a series beginning April 17, 1828.

[2] *Report of the Brunswick Canal and Railroad Company,* Boston, 1836.

[3] *Federal Union,* September 20, 1836.

road connection.[1] The prospects for traffic on such a road, in the event of its construction, were very good. The project was now revived under the Brunswick and Florida Railroad charter, which had been kept passively in existence; and shortly before 1855 funds were secured with which construction might be undertaken, and preparations were made accordingly.

Meanwhile a Savannah corporation had entered the field with a rival project, — the Savannah and Albany Railroad Company, chartered in 1847, and renamed in 1854 the Savannah, Albany, and Gulf. In 1855 it was ready to begin construction. Thus there were two companies preparing simultaneously to build from the respective rival ports to Albany and the Gulf. Neither company had but a fraction of the capital necessary for its work; but the enmity of their promoting ports obstructed a coalition for the common purpose.

Some one now brought to light the forgotten provision in the Brunswick and Florida company's charter which gave it a monopoly of much of the route which both roads desired to cover. This gave the Brunswick company the advantage strategically; but financially it found itself too weak for its purpose, while its rival was considerably stronger.

The *impasse* was relieved by a compromise proposal, strengthened by an offer of state aid. By an act of February, 1856, a new company, the Atlantic and Gulf, was chartered, to build westward from a junction of the roads from Brunswick and Savannah at a point about 50 miles west of the former town and 90 miles southwest of the latter. On the condition of a surrender by

[1] *Federal Union,* June 14, 1853.

the Brunswick company of its twenty-mile exclusive privilege, the state by the same act offered to subscribe $500,000 to the stock of the new company after $600,000 had been obtained from other sources, and to increase its aid to a million dollars maximum if the private subscriptions were increased proportionably. By November, 1856, the Brunswick company had made the required concession, and subscriptions to the Atlantic and Gulf company had been made of $200,000 respectively by the city of Savannah, the Savannah, Albany, and Gulf Railroad Company, and a group of private individuals. The state subscription of $500,000 was accordingly secured. The rails of the two roads from the coast soon reached the junction, and the state-aided continuation, popularly known as the Main Trunk Railroad, was itself under construction. Statistics of traffic are wanting.

Brunswick had ambitions also for a share in the trade of central Georgia, and in the middle and late fifties promoted a project for a railroad to Macon. The Central of Georgia company's antagonism to this created something of a flurry in the state. The Macon and Brunswick was able to accomplish but little construction before the outbreak of the war. The Brunswick and Altamaha canal project, furthermore, was mooted again in the fifties, but without substantial results.

In Florida, the railroad development was controlled by a policy adopted by the state government of confining Florida trade to Florida ports. Unless it were clear that it would carry no trade from a Florida district to a center outside the state, no railroad was permitted to build across the boundary. In all cases of applications for charters, the burden of proof in these premises was upon the petitioners. As a rule, the only foreign railroad companies permitted to enter the state were those in the territory west of the Chattahoochee, where no trade originated within the state, and the only prospect was for some to be brought from the outside.

Florida was thinly settled, poverty-stricken, unproductive, and devoid of promising seaports or other trade centers. St. Augustine was cut off from the mainland by the St. John's River, Pensacola isolated amid the western barrens, and the other ports were without appreciable trade or resources. But the state was determined to use such resources as it had for the benefit of its own ports and develop something of solidarity within the state in spite of its extremely unfavorable contour. The legislature eagerly granted charters and special privileges to all companies applying for permission to connect Florida localities. For example, to one called the Atlantic and Gulf Railroad Company, chartered in 1849, it granted free range of choice in a route across the peninsula and exclusive construction rights within twenty miles of its road. A year later another company, called the Florida Atlantic and Gulf, was also chartered to cross the peninsula, and was promised large state aid upon moderate conditions. Charters were in some cases offered by enactment to any one who would come and take them; as for example an act of 1849 offering privileges to any persons who will undertake to connect Pensacola with the Atlantic coast.[1]

The stages in the development of actual railways in Florida are hard to ascertain. It appears that in the early fifties a short road was built connecting Tallahassee, the state capital, with the Gulf coast twenty miles south-

[1] Florida statutes for the appropriate years.

ward at St. Marks, and before 1861 a road westward from Jacksonville was extended to or beyond Tallahassee, on the way to Pensacola. A railway to tap the Chattahoochee River and carry the trade of its valley to St. Andrew's Bay, lying west of the obstructed mouth of the river, was partly built, under a charter of 1849; but for some reason the work was discontinued. The abandoned road-bed is traceable at the present day, part of it with moldering remains of cross-ties which probably never bore the weight of a rail.

There were also plans for canalling in Florida, some of them contemplating a route for ships across the peninsula; but none of them were of enough importance to demand place in our narrative.

The roads and projects remaining for discussion are those parallel to the coast and the later transmontane ones.

The northeast-and-southwest lines lay in several tiers: First, the system of roads connecting the seaports, viz. Norfolk, Wilmington, Charleston, and Savannah. Second, the roads through the river towns on the fall-line: Richmond, Weldon, Cheraw, Columbia, Augusta, Macon, and Columbus. Third, a system of projected roads along the upper edge of the Piedmont, through Charlottesville, Lynchburg, Greensboro, Charlotte, Spartanburg, and Atlanta. Fourth, a system lying mostly behind the Blue Ridge, entering the parallel valleys in southwestern Virginia, traversing the Knoxville and Chattanooga localities, and then diverging to Nashville, Memphis, and the more lately risen city of Birmingham. The roads of the system last mentioned, however, were actually built with more view to their transmontane than to their northeast-and-southwest service, and they will be treated in this history among the transmontane enterprises.

The first of these systems listed met the least vital need; for most of its traffic could very well have continued to go by the ocean highway as before. It was, however, the earliest of these systems to be completed, for the reason that in the *ante-bellum* period the seaports were the abiding-places of most of the floating capital within the respective states. The system traversing the fall-line towns was the next to secure completion, because these towns as a group ranked second in wealth, commerce, and banking. The building of the lines through east Tennessee was also accomplished before the War of Secession, for on the one hand the need there for outlets was very acute, and on the other, the merchants and planters of the coast and the Piedmont were glad, for purposes of their own, to lend a hand in the financing. The system of lines along the eastern foot of the Blue Ridge, through Lynchburg, Charlotte, and Atlanta, which now serves the most prosperous towns of the South and is at the present time overwhelmed by the volume of its traffic, had to wait for most of its construction until after the great war; for before the war the upper Piedmont towns were young and small, the cities of the midlands and lowlands jealous, and the great investment value of the direct line for through traffic not fully appreciated.

Of the roads between the seaports, the line from Norfolk to Wilmington falls outside our present scope. The connection of Wilmington and Charleston was made by the two roads, already treated in this chapter, built as rivals, but making a traffic junction at Florence. In the forties there was a company formed to build from Charleston to Georgetown; but, like a multitude of other mooted projects in the field, most of whose number cannot even be mentioned in this history, it died for want of funds.

The railroad from Charleston to Savannah was strictly a port-to-port road, and demands our notice. This was another of Charleston's numerous railroad efforts to increase her trade. Savannah's concern in it was more mild, for she had no prospect of drawing trade from the eastward, and the only great service to her citizens by the proposed road would be an increase in comfort.

After a preliminary meeting at Grahamville, in June, a convention at Charleston in November, 1853, definitely launched the project. Charters were quickly secured, and in the spring of 1854 an experimental survey was made at the expense of the Charleston city corporation. The route was found to be about 110 miles long, through level country; and by means of a detour around Port Royal Sound and the sea-island network of creeks, excessive cost of bridging and trestling could be avoided. The estimate of expense was about $1,750,000.[1]

The people were slow to subscribe for stock. By the fall of 1855 only 103 shares ($100 par value) had been taken by individuals in Charleston, 90 in Savannah, and 315 along the route, a total of $50,800. The city of Charleston, however, subscribed $260,000, and the state $270,000; and in 1857 the state further guaranteed the company's bonds to the amount of $5000 per mile. The remaining deficit was in some way bridged over and the road completed in November, 1860. The road then advertised a rate on cotton of fifteen cents per cwt.

[1] Report of the chief engineer, 1854; reports of the president, 1857, and 1858, pamphlets.

from Savannah to Charleston, and offered free transfer from car to car for that coming from beyond Savannah.[1] It was expected that Charleston's superior harbor and her excellent foreign lines of freighting vessels would attract export cotton over the new Charleston and Savannah Railroad. No statistics of traffic for our period can be had.

The second tier of roads parallel to the coast, so far as built before the war, has been treated in more or less detail under various heads, in our preceding chapters. In 1860 the route as operated was still zigzag, poorly integrated, and not fully complete. One might journey in comfort directly from Alexandria through Richmond to Raleigh, but if determined to go directly at the cost of inconvenience, he would have to take stage thence to the head of the railroad again at Cheraw, proceeding *via* Florence, Manchester, Branchville, and Augusta, to Atlanta direct; or *via* Millen to Macon and thence to Columbus and Montgomery. Or one might, by deflecting eastward or westward in North Carolina, lengthen his route and avoid the resort to the stage-coach; he might take the North Carolina Central to Charlotte and proceed *via* Columbia and Branchville to Augusta, or might go from Weldon to Wilmington, thence to Manchester, Branchville, and Augusta. There were projects to improve the connection by building from Raleigh to the South Carolina system; by building from Columbia directly to Augusta, and from Augusta directly to Macon. The rails were laid on none of these routes before the war; but all of them were built during it or immediately afterward.

The only remaining important northeast-and-southwest

[1] *Charleston Courier*, December 21, 1680, advertisement.

road lying within the Cotton Belt completed before the war is that from Atlanta to Montgomery. This was built by two separate companies, the Montgomery and West Point, and the Altanta and La Grange, later known as the Western of Alabama and the Atlanta and West Point, respectively. The two companies were parts of one plan, and their roads when completed were operated practically as one. For accounting purposes, however, the road was divided at the town of West Point, which lay on the state line, about 90 miles from each terminus. The company for the Alabama portion was aided by a state loan and relieved of financial tribulations. The company for the Georgia portion, chartered in 1845, was unable for several years to raise enough subscriptions to begin its work. This was attributed particularly to the indifference prevailing in the well-to-do and aristocratic town of La Grange. By a campaign in 1849, and with the aid of a heavy subscription by the Georgia Railroad and Banking Company, enough money was raised to authorize the building of the road from Atlanta as far as Newnan.[1] And a year or two later enough to carry it to La Grange and West Point was raised in a stock for the time being listed and handled as separate. The road was completed to West Point in 1853, to connect with the Montgomery road already by that time completed.

The Atlanta and La Grange company did not actually build from Atlanta, but from East Point, a station on the ready-built Macon and Western Railroad six and one-half miles south from Atlanta. An agreement of 1849 between the two companies provided for the use of the Atlanta to East Point trackage by the La Grange company's

[1] *Federal Union*, March 20, 1849.

trains jointly with those of the Macon and Western, at a rental of $3000 per year, with the further provision that, if it should prove desirable, the Macon and Western Company would sell to the Atlanta and La Grange the privilege of building a separate track upon this portion of its right of way for not more than $10,000.[1] At the present time the two companies continue their joint use of the now double-tracked stretch of their common route.

This road traversed much of the best cotton land of Georgia and Alabama, and it began promptly to handle a well-paying traffic. Dividends quickly rose to eight per cent as a steady level. The Atlanta and West Point company, for example, earned in the year 1858–1859 $362,061 gross and $197,259 net. With no bond interest to pay, and with a capitalization of but $945,600, the company distributed eight per cent in dividends and still carried $125,304 to reserve fund. The *Atlanta Intelligencer* said of the road in an editorial, February 16, 1860: "It pursues the even tenor of its way, without any effort at display. The trains run regularly, and [those for both] freight and passengers are usually crowded. The dividends are respectable and comfortable to stockholders, and everything goes on in a manner highly creditable to its managers."

The route projected to skirt the Blue Ridge was called by its promoters the "Air Line" because of its proposed saving of some 200 miles over the shortest route then existing from the Eastern cities to Atlanta and New Orleans. After completion it was for several decades known as the Piedmont Air Line, until taken over by the

[1] Report of the president of the Macon and Western Railroad Company, for 1849.

Southern Railway Company. The several roads needed to fill in the route were projected at the middle of the fifties and promoted with enthusiasm. The enterprise met obstacles and delays, and the rails were not laid west of Charlotte until after the Civil War. Its *ante-bellum* history is that only of a promoting campaign and a wrangle among rival interests and persons. The theme centers in that portion of the route which lay between Atlanta and the South Carolina village of Anderson.

In 1855 the Richmond and Danville Railroad Company was rapidly building its line from the James at Richmond to the upper Piedmont at the Virginia-North Carolina boundary. With a thirty-mile space remaining to be filled between Danville and Greensboro, this road from Richmond, connecting with the North Carolina Central Railroad, ready built, would furnish an "air line" chain of roads as far as Charlotte. It is not surprising that ardent spirits in Atlanta suggested that the route be extended directly to that town, and that the people of the intervening region took up the proposal with zest. The plan adopted was for two companies to be formed, the Georgia Air Line and the South Carolina Air Line, to build the divisions of the proposed road which lay mainly within their respective states, and then to operate them as one road.

Under a charter obtained in February, 1856, the Georgia company opened its subscription books in July, with a flourish in the newspapers and a vigorous personal campaign for subscribers. The managing committee was made to include certain men for the weight of their names, — as, for example, Thomas W. Thomas of Elbert County, then widely known as an aristocrat, full of years and dignity; and others for active work,—among them Logan E. Bleckley, later a chief justice of the state and a venerable patriarch, but then a brisk young attorney.[1]

Meetings were held and subscriptions obtained in the counties along the route; but the burden of the enterprise lay of course upon the citizens of Atlanta, a town at this time of six or seven thousand people, but enjoying a railroad traffic and a volume of commerce several times as great as the normal for a town of such a size, and with ambitions in material things unlimited. But, exceptional to say, in the light of Atlanta's record of many and large tasks accomplished through the strength of united and persistent effort, her leading citizens in this case failed to pull together, and the city's policy vacillated.

The stockholders met for organization in February, 1857. L. P. Grant was offered the presidency, but "had other fish to fry," in Uncle Remus's words; and Jonathan Norcross[2] was elected. During 1857 the Atlanta city council, urged thereto by a citizens' memorial, subscribed $100,000 to the stock, on condition of the company's raising $750,000 from other sources. In 1858 the company applied for an increase of this; and upon the mayor's submitting the question to a popular vote, a second subscription of $100,000 on the part of the city was carried by 458 votes against 98. The Greenville and Columbia Railroad Company subscribed $20,000 to the stock, payable in transportation, and offered to guarantee the Air Line company's bonds for $300,000 upon stipulated conditions.

[1] The *Atlanta Daily Intelligencer* in the summer of 1856 and the summer of 1860 gave numerous detailed reports of Air Line affairs, and in the interim published occasional items upon the subject.

[2] Both Grant and Norcross were New England settlers in Atlanta.

But the Greenville company was itself on so precarious a financial footing that its proffered guarantee was not worth the trouble of meeting its requirements.

In 1858 the amount of $750,000 had been subscribed; but when construction was attempted trouble arose. The funds available were not adequate to build the whole road between Atlanta and the end of the Georgia company's line at Anderson, S.C., and the subscribers at each end insisted upon their portion's being built first. The Atlanta corporation was particularly emphatic in this, incited to dilatory tactics, no doubt, by the discovery that its proposed bonds were salable only at a heavy discount. In 1859 grading was begun at the South Carolina end; but for the Atlanta section things fell into a snarl.

Colonel L. P. Grant, then a member of the Fannin-Grant firm of railway contractors, had transferred his interest from the Georgia Air Line Company to one planned for extending the route farther west — the Georgia Western Company; and he wished the city's subscription to be similarly transferred. He contended in the newspapers in 1859 and 1860 that the line westward would benefit Atlanta much more than that projected northeastward; and to further his purpose he denied the validity of the $750,000 reported as subscribed in the Georgia Air Line,[1] and declared that the company was recklessly proceeding upon an inadequate capital. Grant was replied to by E. M. Seago,[2] who denied his assertions and charged him with glass-house residence while throwing stones. Fannin, Grant, & Company he showed, were at this

[1] E.g. *Atlanta Intelligencer*, July 14, 1860.
[2] E.g. *ibid.*, July 17, 1860.

time operating as contractors on the recklessly under-financed Vicksburg, Shreveport, and Texas Railroad, on a contract basis of payment in stock to an extent which made this firm the majority shareholders in the railroad company. Seago hinted darkly also at the character of Grant's contract with the Southern Pacific Railroad Company to build seventy miles of its road in Texas.

The Atlanta city council first added a third hundred thousand dollars, in April, 1860, to its subscription, and changed the nature of the whole to constitute a fund for the purchase of rails to be laid beginning at Atlanta. Then in August a majority of the council was won over to Grant's view, and carried through a motion to cancel the whole subscription. A group of private subscribers now added to the company's embarrassment by refusing to pay assessments, and filed a bill for injunction against the company's letting contracts or collecting instalments upon stock. The injunction was denied by the court; but the company was in a mood to yield to discouragements. Impressed by the rumblings of the coming war, the directors resolved in October to suspend operations.[1]

The Georgia Western Railroad Company was chartered early in 1856 to build from Atlanta due west to Jacksonville, Alabama, a distance of some eighty miles; but the project did not become conspicuous until the spring of 1860, when Colonel Grant began to wrangle in its favor against the Air Line promoters. On May 18 and 19, 1860, a meeting of citizens was held in Atlanta to consider the Georgia Western plans.[2] Colonel B. C. Yancey

[1] *Atlanta Intelligencer*, October 11, 1860.

[2] *Ibid.*, May 21, 1860.

described the route as penetrating cotton, coal, and iron districts, certain to yield very profitable trade to Atlanta, and spoke of the road's later forming a link in a direct connection with Memphis and Vicksburg. Thomas L. Cooper said that up to that time Atlanta had prospered through adventitious circumstances; but that for further growth she must take a hand in shaping her own destiny — that she was essentially a railroad town, and her future depended upon the increase of her railroad facilities. The meeting adopted resolutions memorializing the city council to subscribe $300,000 to the stock of the Georgia Western company.

The city in the next week made the subscription recommended,[1] and this killed a rival project then under discussion to build from Marietta to Jacksonville instead of from Atlanta. On June 12 the directors of the Georgia Railroad Company subscribed $250,000 to the Georgia Western stock, on condition that $800,000 were secured elsewhere.[1] By July 25 $750,000 had been subscribed, of the $800,000 requirement; but the Georgia Railroad administration now developed the opinion that the Georgia Western company was entering such close alliance with the Air Line Company that the prospect of its feeding the Georgia Railroad's traffic was much less than first thought. That company then withdrew its subscription, pending further developments. The Georgia Western company elected Richard Peters its president in July, and L. P. Grant was shortly appointed chief engineer. Instalments on stock were promptly called for, and in October bids were asked for grading fifty miles of the

[1] *Atlanta Intelligencer*, May 28, 1860.
[2] *Ibid.*, June 26, 1860.

route.[1] And then came — as we may have said some twenty times before — the progress-paralyzing war.

To close our narrative, there are two transmontane enterprises, one built from east Tennessee to Georgia, the other projected, unsuccessfully, from South Carolina to east Tennessee and beyond.

From the beginning of the century, and before, the farmers and merchants of the great valley between the mountains had been willing and anxious to promote economical outlets.[2] They labored for the canalling of the Muscle Shoals, and expended private moneys for clearing the upper course of the river. But the river, even when made viable by steamboats, was too capricious, too circuitous, and too far away in its ending to prove at all adequate to the needs. Railways were the only possible solution.

It will be remembered that the Georgia Railroad Company, chartered in 1833–1835, was launched with a plan for penetrating to the Tennessee region. No sooner did the leading spirits of the Valley learn that this enterprise had been begun with good prospects than they began to work toward building a railroad from Knoxville to meet the Georgia company's road at the state

[1] *Federal Union*, July 31, 1860, quoting the *Atlanta Locomotive* of July 25; *Charleston Courier*, October 23, 1860.

[2] As indicating the volume of outgoing produce from east Tennessee, a committee reported from an inspection of records as follows: "There are 60,000 hogs, 7000 sheep, 6000 horses and mules, 6000 cattle, 800 wagons, and 1500 horsemen passing through Greenville District annually from the West on their way to Augusta, Columbia, Charleston, and the middle districts of South Carolina. These returns are taken from the books of the Buncombe Turnpike Company." Pamphlet report of proceedings of a railroad convention at Laurensville, S.C., 1846, n. t. p.

boundary. The Tennessee legislature readily chartered the proposed company, which was named the Hiwassee Railroad Company, the name borrowed from the Hiwassee River, which, branching from the Tennessee, lay along a part of the course intended for the road.

In 1836 the Hiwassee company completed its organization and prepared for work. In continuance of earlier negotiations, its president, S. D. Jacobs, notified President Dearing of the Georgia Railroad, in a letter of December 7, 1836, that the Hiwassee engineers were ready to survey the route and the company ready to begin construction. He requested Dearing to send the Georgia Railroad surveyors to meet those of the Hiwassee company and agree upon a junction point for the two roads at the state line. A few weeks later the Hiwassee officials were disquieted by the news of the resolutions of the Macon convention which recommended the replacement of the earlier plans in Georgia by one to build a cross-state system terminating near Rossville or the modern Chattanooga. Jacobs wrote Dearing on January 7,[1] asking for reassurance that the Georgia Railroad Company was not abandoning its former pledges to connect with the Hiwassee. Dearing replied, January 24, expressing his company's intention to press on with its line and explaining that the revision of plans in Georgia and the adoption of the plan for the Western and Atlantic by the legislature strengthened the prospect for the Tennessee connection; and saying further that the phrasing of the act appointing "some point on the Tennessee line near Rossville" as the northern terminal of the state road did not at all mean that the

[1] This correspondence was published in the *Southern Banner* (Athens, Ga.), March 25, 1837.

route would, as Jacobs feared, lie too far westward to permit of a convenient Hiwassee connection.

The Hiwassee company, aided by a heavy state subscription, proceeded in the next few years to expend nearly a million dollars in grading the southern portion of its route and bridging the Hiwassee River. The delay of ten or twelve years in completing the Western and Atlantic, however, made it both impossible and useless to lay the Hiwassee's track; and meanwhile the company went bankrupt from a burden of debt, the accruing of interest, and the total absence of earnings.[1]

The enterprise was revived in 1848 under the name of the East Tennessee and Georgia Railroad Company, authorized to scale down the original stock by one-half,[2] and stimulated to exertion by a promise of the State of Tennessee to provide funds for the purchase of rails.

The new company[3] raised new local subscriptions, and disposed of other stock in payment to contractors. It began track-laying from Dalton, Ga., its southern terminus, at the end of 1850, reached Athens, Tenn., fifty-five miles, in December, 1851, and reached the Tennessee River, eighty-two miles, in September, 1852, at an average cost of $17,500. Some volume of remunerative traffic now began, stimulated by the discovery of copper and the development of mining at Ducktown near the route. Earnings in 1852–1853 were $93,935 gross and $51,613 net. Burdened by a heavy floating debt, and by dearth of labor and rising prices of materials, the company conquered obstacles and completed its track to Knoxville

[1] *Federal Union*, March 4, 1845.

[2] Act of the Tennessee legislature, February 4, 1848.

[3] Reports of the president and superintendent of the East Tennessee and Georgia Railroad Company, annually, 1852–1858.

in 1855, and then set to work at once to build a branch from Cleveland to Chattanooga and to renovate the main line. In 1853–1854 gross earnings were $125,028 and net $79,302; in 1855–1856, gross $226,284 and net $124,954. To June 1, 1858, with 140 miles in operation, but with the Chattanooga branch still a year from completion, the cost of the road was $3,795,440, of which $454,381 had been covered by the scale-down of the Hiwassee stock, and $590,726 by net earnings of the road. The balance was made up of stock $1,170,132 and debt $1,579,852. Interest charges were heavy, and no dividends had been declared. From this time onward, however, the road enjoyed a through connection to Virginia at the one end, and soon to Nashville and Memphis at the other, and its earnings were increased in consequence. Meanwhile the operation of the road had provided the people of the district with a cheap outlet for their produce, and had brought unprecedented prosperity to those homespun communities. The monopolistic advantage of east Tennessee produce in the markets of the Georgia cotton belt had only a brief period, till the opening of the Nashville and Chattanooga Railroad in 1854. But the enjoyment of fairly substantial prosperity was lasting, for the east Tennesseeans proved capable of holding their own with fair profit against competition from any and all quarters.

The final transmontane effort of South Carolina, before the war, was a recrudescence of the Louisville, Cincinnati, and Charleston project in a modified form. It was known as the Blue Ridge Railroad.[1] The route was shifted

[1] Reports of the president and chief engineer of the Blue Ridge Railroad Company, annually, 1856–1859, and pamphlet speeches and petitions.

westwardly because of the new importance of Knoxville and Chattanooga as commercial centers, and instead of following the French Broad River was made to lie through Rabun Gap in the northeastern corner of Georgia and thence to follow the course of the Little Tennessee River across the pan-handle of North Carolina, thence deflecting northward to Knoxville, with a connection westward to Chattanooga contemplated. The route, extending from Anderson, S.C., to Knoxville, was about 195 miles long, of which the southern half was through exceedingly rough country; and thirteen tunnels were provided for in the survey, one of them 5800 feet long. A small amount of construction at the southern end of the route was already accomplished by the preceding Pendleton Railroad Company, a petty corporation which the Blue Ridge company absorbed.

Charters were obtained from each of the four states involved, in 1851–1852, and a promise of state aid from two of them — South Carolina and Tennessee. County aid along the route was also given in moderate amounts. The charters were granted by the several states to as many companies for several sections of the route, set off by state boundaries. Each of the other three companies, upon organization, promptly assigned their franchises and resources to the South Carolina Blue Ridge company, and had little more than a nominal existence. The South Carolina company, further, had a chartered control of the route as far northward as the North Carolina boundary, and completely merged the Georgia company's stock and franchises into its own.

In Tennessee the state aid was in the form of a promised loan to a specified amount for the purchase of rails upon the completion of the road-bed. The state aid of South Carolina had a checkered history which requires some detail. The original South Carolina Blue Ridge charter enactment, December, 1852, pledged a conditional guarantee of the company's bonds to the amount of $1,250,000. Next year the company petitioned for an increase in this proposed aid and a change in its form; and after a year's heated popular discussion of the question, the legislature in the session of 1854 replaced its former provision by one granting aid as follows: (1) a state subscription of $500,000 to the stock of the South Carolina Blue Ridge company provided that $1,000,000 should have first been subscribed by responsible persons, companies, or corporations; (2) a further state subscription of $500,000, on condition of an added subscription of $500,000 from other sources, and that at least one-fifth of the subscribed capital of the company should be held by responsible individuals or private corporations; (3) a guarantee of the company's bonds to the amount of $1,000,000 out of a total of $2,500,000 which the company might issue in bonds, to be secured by the whole road and all assets of the several companies in the several states. The city council of Charleston, memoralized thereto by public meetings, had already subscribed $1,049,000 to stock for the route in South Carolina and Georgia; and accordingly the company had met the conditions of the first state subscription beforehand. The directors, in spite of the extremely slight private takings of their stock, expected to meet the conditions for the second $500,000 state subscription through the device of paying its contractors partly in stock.

In the fall of 1853 the company had made with Anson

Bangs & Company of New York a blanket contract for the whole work of building the road and furnishing materials, on the basis of stipulated prices per unit for each sort of work, cutting and filling, tunneling, masonry, bridging, etc. Bangs & Company were to receive payment monthly for work done, one-half in cash, one-fourth in stock, and one-fourth in the company's unguaranteed bonds. In 1855, however, Anson Bangs and his brother sold their interests in the firm to their partners, who reorganized as A. Birdsall & Company. Finding cause to think this firm irresponsible, the Blue Ridge directors canceled the contract and on April 1, 1856, dismissed them from the work. The company, then surveying the route as it stood, found that all the large and heavy tasks, including all the tunnels and bridges, had been neglected; and that the time of the road's completion was as far away as it need have been had no grading been done.

New contracts were let in May, 1856, to a number of men for specific tasks; and work was pushed with all possible haste. But difficulties now began to gather. The grading done by Bangs & Company had cost nearly $700,000, which must for several years be an unproductive investment, depreciating through the washing of the soil, and involving in large part the payment of interest on debt incurred. This and the prospect of delay in completion still further reduced the esteem for the already undesired stock. The new contractors required payment in cash; and the plan for using expenditure in stock to meet the requirements for the second state subscription fell through.

The problem of the directors now centered in the 5800-foot tunnel through the Stump House Mountain on the one hand and in the South Carolina legislature on the other. With the aid of three shafts and the eight working faces which were by that device made accessible, the making of the tunnel must take at least three years, and the track for that period must be confined to a short stretch near Anderson, which would contribute no revenue. To continue the work with any prospect of success, therefore, it was necessary, in the dearth of other possible resources, to secure aid more largely and more freely from the state.

Throughout 1857 and 1858 the chief engineer, Walter Gwynn, bent all his resources upon the tunnels, bridges, and heavy grading; while the president, Edward Frost, labored with the legislature and the public in the endeavor to get more funds. A new survey and estimate was made which placed the probable cost at $7,725,677, exclusive of rolling stock. Frost, aided by C. G. Memminger, B. F. Perry, and several anonymous writers, pleaded by voice and pen that the state could not afford to abandon the work and lose the benefit of the great Western trade, pleaded for additional aid from the state sufficient to guarantee the road's advancement to a point where its prospect of success could be used as an argument in coaxing capital from private sources. The proposal was opposed by a voluminous newspaper contributor signing himself "Nolumus," and by William Gregg and others in public speeches. The bills introduced into the legislature were defeated in 1858 and 1859; and the company had to stop work for lack of funds, with fifteen miles of track laid, and the Stump House Mountain, two-thirds penetrated, still blocking the way.

The private holdings of Blue Ridge stock, aside from the takings by contractors, were so small as to be negligible. The enterprise was the work of the Charleston interests. The state aid secured was the result of Charleston influence, aided by the representatives from along the route. The disappointment was shared by the merchants of Charleston, the planters of the upper Piedmont, and the farmers of east Tennessee.

Railroads have since been built from South Carolina to east Tennessee, but the route is of the French Broad, *via* Asheville. The cuts and fills of the forgotten Blue Ridge Company are studded with well-grown oaks and hickories; and the Stump House tunnel mouths are choked with shrubs. And Charleston still longs in vain for the trade of the golden West.

CHAPTER IX

CONCLUSION

A SOUTHERN railroad association was instituted in 1856 to hold annual meetings and deliberate upon problems of common concern to the companies operating in the territory; and other less formal gatherings of railroad functionaries were held at various times and places to deal with more local problems.

After a preliminary meeting at Augusta in March, the main association held its convention to organize at Ashland, Va., in July, 1856.[1] One or more executive officials were in attendance from each of the principal railroads between the Potomac River and central Alabama. R. R. Cuyler, president of the Central of Georgia, presided. After adopting by-laws for the association, the meeting considered various questions of the day. A standing committee was appointed to inquire at convenience and report in pamphlets upon systems of control for directors and presidents; upon the duties of superintendents and other principal officers; upon methods of appointing subordinate officials; upon freight tariffs on bases of ton-miles; and upon passenger rates with a view to producing the highest revenue. Another committee was charged with the study of rails and track-laying, car ventilation, the exclusion of sparks and dust, and other matters in the field of equipment.

[1] *Atlanta Intelligencer*, July 15, 1856. Report of proceedings.

Special committees reported and their reports were adopted as follows: That the association should not itself build a rolling mill for remaking worn-out rails, but that it should encourage private enterprises of the kind. That a through fast mail-and-passenger schedule from Washington to Montgomery, at a speed of twenty miles per hour, with allowance for brief necessary stops, was feasible, and should at once be put into effect. That the electric telegraph be used in operating these trains. That the price of through tickets from Washington to New Orleans be reduced from $53 to $48. Committee reports and the discussions were inconclusive upon freight classification, express company arrangements, and the need of promoting a railroad to the Pacific Ocean.

In May, 1858, a convention was held at Atlanta which dealt mainly with the question of through freight rates on the several roads connecting with the Western and Atlantic, though little definite was done. Among its incidental transactions, the meeting adopted rules against deadheading except in the case of the chief officials of railroad companies, and it expressed its pleasure at the establishment of a rolling mill at Atlanta.

A convention at Atlanta in May, 1860, revised freight rates, but, like numerous other such meetings not here chronicled, it gave to the press no specific account of its proceedings.

The connecting up and systemizing of the separate roads for through business had been in gradual progress before it was hastened by the institution of these official conferences. In passenger traffic, hardly any trains had run except by day before about 1850; and travelers had had to lay over for a night at such junctions as Atlanta, Macon, Augusta, and Columbia. The enlargement of the railway network in the early fifties increased through travel and enabled each of the main lines to add a second or third daily passenger train to run in the hours when their local patrons were asleep, and led also to the addition of sleeping-cars to railroad equipment. As the years of the decade passed and tracks and rolling stock were improved, the running times were shortened until, in 1860, the speed on the main lines was twenty-five miles or more per hour, excluding stops. Of course a speed greater than this was hindered by the necessary reliance upon wrought-iron rails. The discovery of the Bessemer process did not make steel rails available until some years after the close of the period here treated; and steel rails were not laid generally upon the Southern roads, wrecked and mostly bankrupt from the war and reconstruction, until after 1885.

The facilitation of through freight was an aim with the railroad companies from the beginning. For its furtherance, sharp curves and heavy ascents in the routes were avoided; tracks were generally made of a uniform gauge of five feet;[1] track connections were made as perfect as possible between the linking lines; forwarding clerks were maintained; and tariffs were adjusted and frequently readjusted. In these matters numerous obstacles offered themselves for conquest. The reluctance of cities to the connection of tracks through them has already been mentioned. This was partly removed by the shifting of local interests, partly by purchase of the privilege from the town corporations, and partly by external pressure. In the case

[1] The gauge of all the principal Southern railroads was changed at the beginning of June, 1886, to 4 feet 9 inches, to agree with the gauge of the Northern roads.

of Augusta, for example, the city's obstruction was maintained until in 1852 its people, together with those of Charleston and other neighboring trade centers, became very anxious to promote a through route to the Mississippi which would be secured by the completion of the Memphis and Charleston company's road in northern Alabama. The city of Charleston offered to contribute $500,000 in aid of this work on condition that Augusta permit a connection of the Georgia and the South Carolina Railroad companies' tracks.[1] Augusta, urged also by the offer of a handsome cash price for the franchise, then yielded her obstructive advantage to secure a greater constructive one.

An instance of difficulty in through rate making was the peculiar status of the Western and Atlantic as a state-owned and -operated railroad, not affected by many of the interests which were controlling in the policy of company-owned roads. Another problem, which has proven permanent in the whole South, was that of adjustment of rates so as to keep traffic away from the water routes and yet to avoid undue discrimination among the localities. The "basing-point" system of assigning low through rates to certain selected towns and for all other stations fixing the through rate at the through rate to the nearest basing point plus the local rate from the basing point to the station in question, was adopted as the result of experience; and although it is arbitrary in its nature, and often tyrannical, it continues to be considered the only feasible one for the region. A never-ceasing struggle, of course, has been on the question as to what towns shall be established as

[1] *Proceedings of Public Meetings held at various times in Charleston, calling upon the City Council to make subscriptions to railroads.* . . . 27 pp., Charleston, 1854.

basing points, and at what relative tariff rates. Atlanta, from the high-and-dry location and her complete dependence upon low freight rates for prosperity, has of course been the most chronic and vigorous agitator in the premises.

Telegraph lines under private company ownership, for public patronage, were extended to most of the principal towns of the cotton belt in the early fifties. But there were few, if any, wires installed for operating the railroads. The Western and Atlantic, for example, had no telegraph line before or during the Civil War.

Parcels express service was provided on each railroad from near the time when it began operation. In a few cases this was done by the railroads themselves, but in most cases by independent express companies.

In the matter of subsidiary avenues for local freight service, it was appreciated that many localities desiring railway facilities could not promise enough traffic to justify the building and operation of steam railroads. An extensive agitation was carried on in the fifties over plans for building plank roads for use by teams and country wagons. William Gregg of Charleston, usually a very sound student of things economic, advertised his opinion in 1851 and afterward, that plank roads were destined to be a great factor in human progress, and were for many Southern purposes infinitely superior, even, to railroads.[1] Numerous routes were projected, and several surveyed, during the fifties, particularly in Alabama; but no plank roads of any consequence, it seems, were actually built.

As to the physical qualities of the Southern railroads, a

[1] William Gregg, *Essay on Plank Roads, delivered before the Literary Club of Charleston,* pamphlet, Charleston, 1851.

comparison of them with those of the North was made by F. P. Holcombe, an engineer, in 1847.[1] The great breadth of the coastal plain and the gentleness of the hill slopes gave the South, he observed, a great advantage, and made the average cost of grading only $5000 per mile, as against $15,000 expended on the average in the North, with results not as good. The South also had an advantage in laying superstructure, by reason of the presence of the splendid forests from which even the Northern roads had to draw much of their timber supply. Hence, Holcombe showed, the cheapness of the Southern roads was not, as some inquirers had been inclined to think, necessarily an evidence of bad quality for operation. In the weight of rails he granted to the North a slight superiority, but thought that this was offset by the lightness in general of the grades and curves, and the consequent saving in wear and tear. The cuts and fills he thought to be of adequate width; and as an evidence of the soundness and safety of Southern railroads he cited the fact that in the twelve years of their operation in Georgia no passenger had ever been injured to the extent of losing life or limb. The same general comments would have applied as well in 1860 as at the time they were made.

A general analysis of the motives and interests concerned in the promotion of railroads in the *ante-bellum* South, and of the conditions of their building and operation, has been made in our Introduction. A few observations remain to be added.

There were two conspicuous obsessions which affected perhaps the majority of all the promoters; or at least two

[1] Included in his report on the preliminary survey for the Macon and Western Railroad, November, 1847.

standard arguments with which they tried to obsess the people. One was that the building of any line in question would foster the success of the South in its race with the North to secure the advantage in population, wealth, and strength for any approaching contest. The other was that any road in question, whether long or short, running west or running south, in the highlands or in the lowlands, would shortly become a connecting link in a great chain of roads handling tremendous traffic between the poles of the country.

Most of the promoters were fairly sane, however, and most of the projects were judged on their real merits. It is further to be said that personal probity prevailed almost universally among promoters, officials, and agents. Then, too, there was no stock jobbing in the field, and no countenancing of the attempts made at it in Wall Street. Individual share holdings were usually small in size, particularly so in the case of companies promoted in the remote districts, as for example the East Tennessee and Georgia company. That share takings were rarely speculative is shown by the fewness of the changes in the stockholders' lists as published, year by year, by numerous companies. In very many cases, indeed, the investment feature itself was but secondary in the impulse to subscriptions; for often the controlling motive was that of providing local facilities and promoting a general increase of prosperity in the neighborhoods in which the subscribers lived. This, of course, applied still more strongly to subscriptions made by states, counties, and towns than to those made by private persons.

As to the results brought by the railroads, they were often in detail just what had been expected, — for example, where the routes lay through good producing districts, there was a general boom in the towns through which the railroads ran. In the large, however, the results in the cotton belt were a disappointment. The railroads gave an unneeded stimulus to commerce and competition, and they failed to enlarge very greatly the volume or the scope of industry. Their great facilitation of exchange intensified the popular engrossment in the one great staple which furnished the surest means of buying what the outside world had to offer.

In the earlier period, when freights from the North were high and when a milder prevalence of the cotton mania permitted men to choose other investments than plantations, divers industries, like cotton manufacturing, for the supply of home markets, had prospered. But the plying of the freight trains necessitated a new basis for the factories. They must be refitted with up-to-date machinery, and they must specialize their product in place of catering to general neighborhood needs. At the same time, the engrossment in railroads and raw cotton made it the harder for the mills to command the necessary capital.

One large cause of the South's relatively poor success in manufacturing was, of course, her dearth of skilled and experienced labor. To this was probably due, for example, the inability confessed by the Atlanta rolling mill to remake rails with profit in competition with the Northern mills.[1] But the greatest obstacles to a general diversification were the dependence upon negro labor and the maintenance of slavery as a system for its control.

Negro labor was as a rule inefficient for any tasks but those of crude routine, and under the prevailing "slavery" system it was highly expensive. Through the custom of

[1] *Atlanta Intelligencer*, February 25, 1860.

buying labor in advance for the lifetimes of the laborers, instead of hiring them and paying periodically as work was done, large amounts of capital were "locked up"; and when in any locality slaves were brought in by purchase from other districts, their acquisition involved the exporting of capital in payment. In the period of the most vigorous expansion of the cotton belt, the supply of slave labor was practically cornered by the old tobacco and rice districts. Slave prices mounted to unheard-of levels, while cotton prices did not proportionally rise.[1] The margin of profit in cotton planting became severely reduced; and the cotton communities in many cases had to trench upon any surplus capital which they might have laid aside for employment in diversified industry.

The financial burdensomeness of slaveholding, and particularly the custom of exporting capital in acquiring additional labor, is of course largely responsible for the great difficulty experienced in raising stock subscriptions among the planters, and for the scantiness in the total railroad investment. The Eastern Cotton Belt, with an annual cotton production between 1830 and 1860 of say forty or fifty million dollars value on the average, expended in that period a total of probably less than sixty million dollars; and the Western Cotton Belt in the same period less than half of that amount.

Burdened with their capitalization of labor control, tending constantly between 1815 and 1860 toward a great overcapitalization, the cotton planters were involved in something of a cut-throat competition with one another. The

[1] Cf. U. B. Phillips, "The Economic Cost of Slaveholding in the Cotton Belt," in the *Political Science Quarterly*, vol. 20, pp. 257–275 (June, 1905).

building of railroads, by enlarging the cotton area intensified this, but did not essentially change its character.

The most intense effect of the railroads was upon the cities, injuring some and benefiting others. In contrast with the North, the cotton belt railroads did not greatly increase the local productive resources; nor in our period did they vastly increase the volume of commerce. The cities conspicuously laid out great sums in facilitating a commercial stream which would have flowed just as surely and in no vastly smaller volume had the expenditures never been made. The railroads, in a word, under the existing circumstances, proved less to be trade makers than trade catchers. As trade-catching agencies they were very expensive, and most expensive, of course, to the least efficient competitors. The mere mention of the burdens assumed by the city and the citizens of Charleston without any commensurate benefits accruing, will sufficiently point the discussion.

Pointing the other extreme of the development, the city of Atlanta was born as a railroad terminus, throve as a railroad junction, and has risen to large commercial predominance as a railroad center. The potentialities of the point now known as Atlanta began to be appreciated as soon as the Western and Atlantic Act of 1836 had been enacted. Its commercial prospects became noised abroad, and a few speculators bought up the land.[1] By the time the Western and Altantic railroad began to run trains, the junction had acquired several hundred residents. There was an upper class, of contractors, merchants, and speculators, and a

[1] The principal authorities for the history of Atlanta are: Thos. H. Martin, *Atlanta and its Builders*, n.p., 1902; and Wallace P. Reed, *History of Atlanta*, Syracuse, N.Y., 1889.

lower one of miscellaneous laborers. In the monied and managing class a large proportion was of Northern men, who had come to develop the money-making possibilities, while a minority had been merchants and planters from other places in the cotton belt. The laboring class was mostly of white men, drawn from all quarters, eager to exclude negro competition in their trades, themselves rough and often lawless in conduct, but intelligent and capable as workmen, and many of them thrifty. The laborers usually controlled the city government, and their partial exclusion of slave labor from the crafts doubtless fostered the general progress. The business men of the town kept not their light under a bushel. They were "hustlers," and they early acquired the invaluable habit of pulling together.

The basis of Atlanta's prosperity was, of course, her strategic location; but the degree of her flourishing was largely due to the unusual vigor of her citizens. The town itself originated as an incidental result of the building of roads intended exclusively for the benefit of other cities.[1] The control of the Georgia Railroad continued to be held by Augusta and Charleston interests, and of the Central of Georgia system by Macon and Savannah; and these interests, as also those in Knoxville, Nashville, Montgomery, etc., influencing other roads, used their power to secure freight-rate discrimination against Atlanta.[2] But the opening of the Western and Atlantic quickly made Atlanta the main distributing point for food-stuffs throughout the Eastern Cotton Belt, and the completion of the road to La Grange and Montgomery gave her an important share

[1] So remarked in the *Atlanta Intelligencer*, October 8, 1858.

[2] *Ibid.*, May 10, November 9, and November 11, 1858, and February 21, 1860.

in the east-and-west handling of cotton and manufactures. Her gateway location gave her impregnable intrenchment; the unbounded ambition of the people for their town, and their clamor of self-advertisement hastened her growth;[1] the establishment of a large rolling mill[2] for railroad iron in 1858 strengthened the interdependence of the town and the railroads; and the launching of the Air Line Railroad project gave promise for the near future of immunity from all successful discrimination in rates against her.

In 1860 Atlanta, about fifteen years old as a town, had only some ten thousand inhabitants; but her potentialities were already apparent and her future career was outlined. She had already narrowed the tributary area of every other cotton belt city, she was ready to spring into fame in the time of war as the strategic center of the South for military purposes, and to rise again after Sherman's annihilation to prove her equally vital importance in commercial strategy.

A view of the town in 1860 is given in an editorial in the *Southern Banner* (Athens, Ga.), June 28, 1860:

ATLANTA

We spent two days last week in the new and flourishing city. We had seen the place once before, about twelve years ago. To say that it has improved rapidly within that period, would not convey a correct idea of its progress. It has all been built since we were there in 1848. Then there were one or two hundred shanties. Now there are thousands of fine, substantial, and costly houses. The work of improvement still continues, too, with increasing rapidity. We were told the other day that upwards of two hundred houses are

[1] Cf. *Federal Union*, May 23, 1854.

[2] Employing seventy-five to one hundred and fifty hands. *Atlanta Intelligencer*, November 28, 1860.

under contract at this time. Real estate has reached almost fabulous prices there. . . . The remarkable growth of this place shows what railroads will do towards building up a town. It was called into existence by railroads and is fed and supported by them. Without them it would dry up in a month. We were much pleased with the people of Atlanta. They appear to be intelligent, industrious, and enterprising. We witnessed no loafing there. Everybody, white and black, appeared to have something to do.

In brief, the effect of the railroads was to turn the faces of men from the local seaboard to the Piedmont and the West, and to the eastern centers of trade. For the Eastern Cotton Belt the world of commerce was in effect a triangle with one apex on the near-by coast, at Charleston or Savannah, a second in the Tennessee-Ohio region, say at Knoxville, Nashville, or Cincinnati, and a third in the district of metropolitan commerce, Baltimore or New York. The lines of commerce lay, and do still lie, from each of these apexes to the center of the field at, say, Atlanta, Macon, or Columbia. Before the day of railroads the route from the near-by coast was the only one of these center-to-apex lines in freight operation. All goods, from whatever source or to whatever destination, had to arrive and depart over the coast-to-Piedmont route; and most of the traffic was extremely devious. The railroads when built supplied interior lines from the center to the other two apexes; and at once the local seaports and their patronage began their decline to a minor importance.

Atlanta, we have seen, is the chief example of the urban-promotive effect of the cotton belt railroads. The leading example of their rural promotion is likewise the upper edge of the Piedmont — the territory to which Atlanta is the principal key.

The men of the Georgia and Carolina Blue Ridge and foot-hills had formerly had to depend for their scant money income upon the peddling of their grain, meat, and fruits among the few gold miners and cotton planters who could be reached by a wagon haul of perhaps thirty to one hundred miles. Their market was precarious and their industry far from lucrative. They were upon practically a self-sufficing basis, and in much discomfort. The railroads, however, led to the rise of systematic markets for handling this produce at such towns as Charlotte, Spartanburg, Athens, and Atlanta, on an equal footing with Western supplies. In some of these localities, too, cotton production was spread, and some volume of cotton manufacturing. The yeomen of the foot-hills were getting their first opportunity for industrial and general progress.

To offset this, the railroads caused a retrogression in certain cotton belt communities. The town of Lexington, Ga., is an example. In this case, at the time when the Georgia Railroad was being promoted, the ultra conservatives prevailed with an argument that if the railroad were built through the town it would probably bring in low-caste people, vagrants, and disturbers of the established order. In consequence the road was routed three miles west of the town; and Lexington comprises to-day about the same number of people and enjoys perhaps about the same volume of commerce as it did seventy years ago. There was for many years a positive retrogression, and for the whole period, of course, a relative decline.

In their industrial effects, the railroads brought probably a smaller change to the plantation districts — the black belts — than to any other important part of the country. This for the reason that these districts were already working in an economy which included transportation to and from markets as one of its features, and for the further reason that their labor supply consisted of negroes fairly capable in the existing routine, but inert for any remodeling of systems.

In the matter of social relations, a characteristic item was the stimulating of the penchant among the well-to-do for making visits to kindred and friends. Not only did everybody who was anybody have scores of cousins scattered throughout their own and neighboring states, but with the aid of railroads thousands of these cousins of one generation after another were able to become personally acquainted with and bound to one another. The old Southern custom of visits extending often for weeks or months became still more common, especially among the youths and maidens; and this of course promoted a greater social solidarity in a state or section.

As to the negroes, the coming of the railroads made them more easily mobilizable by their masters, but otherwise affected them very little in slavery times.

As a precaution against unwittingly helping fugitive slaves to escape, many railroad companies established rules forbidding their agents to sell transportation to colored persons except upon the exhibition of passes from their owners or guardians giving express authority for them to travel. The excursion habit was of course not then developed among the negroes, and they were permitted none of the aimless shifting of habitation to which in later days they are so prone. Nowadays the penetration by a railroad into a black belt district where none has operated before changes at once the labor situation; for very many negroes, formerly steady and contented as peasants of the locality, slip from their moorings and seek novelty of experience and freedom from responsibility. Before the war, this roving habit was unknown and impossible. The railroads aided the slave-traders and the migrating planters in their constant transit with their slave squads toward the Southwest; but aside from this with the negroes it was as if the trains did not run.

As to their effect upon political policy, the railroads promoted the spread of news and opinions and in particular emphasized the uniqueness, the difficulty, and the dangers of the position and problems of the South. They therefore tended on the whole to solidify the South in a sectional policy.

In the stress of war, while the water courses proved to be lines of weakness to the Confederacy, the railroads did very much to provide the sinews of war, and were in practically all cases lines of strength.

In *post-bellum* times, after the waste of several decades in a chaotic transition, the railroads furnish a large part of the equipment by which, as a result of the freeing of capital from its bondage to the slavery system, the cotton belt is developing widely diversified industry and is beginning to enjoy a prosperity unexampled in its past.

BIBLIOGRAPHICAL NOTE

In addition to the pamphlet, newspaper, manuscript, and other local material mentioned in the text and the footnotes, the following books contain some descriptive data for the periods of their publication: —

[George Armroyd,] Connected View of the Whole Navigation of the United States, natural and artificial, present and prospective. Phila., 1826. Enlarged and corrected edition, Phila., 1830.

Guillaume-Tell Poussin, Travaux d'Améliorations Interieures, projétés ou exécutés par le Gouvernement Général des Etats Unis d'Amérique, de 1824 à 1831. Paris, 1834, 1 vol. and atlas. Second edition, 1836.

Mitchell's Compendium of the Internal Improvements of the United States. Phila., 1835.

Henry S. Tanner, A Description of the Canals and Rail Roads of the United States. . . . N.Y., 1840.

Michel Chevalier, Histoire et Déscription des Voies de Communication aux Etats Unis. . . . 2 vols. and atlas. Paris, 1840–1841.

F. A. von Gerstner, Die Innern Communicationen von Nordamerica. 2 vols., Vienna, 1842–1843. (Specially full in data upon roadbeds, track, equipment, etc.)

Phelp's Traveller's Guide through the United States. . . . N.Y., 1847.

J. Calvin Smith, A New Guide for Travellers through the United States. . . . N.Y., 1848.

American Railroad Guide and Pocket Companion. N.Y., 1851.

Mitchell's New Traveller's Guide through the United States. . . . Phila., 1853.

George W. Edwards, The American Railway and Steam Navigation Guide for the United States and Canada. N.Y., [1860].

The *ante-bellum* work of H. V. Poor (Henry Varnum Poor, History of Railroads and Canals of the United States of America, exhibiting their progress, cost, revenues, expenditures, and present condition. Vol. 1, N.Y., 1860) was, regrettably, never carried beyond volume one, which confines its scope to the Northern states.

INDEX